The Nuer Conquest

The Nuer Conquest

The Structure and Development of an Expansionist System

RAYMOND C. KELLY

Ann Arbor   The University of Michigan Press

For my parents,
Helen J. Kelly and Rowland L. Kelly

Copyright © by The University of Michigan 1985
All rights reserved
Published in the United States of America by
The University of Michigan Press and simultaneously
in Rexdale, Canada, by John Wiley & Sons Canada, Limited
Manufactured in the United States of America

1988   1987   1986   1985   4   3   2   1

Library of Congress Cataloging in Publication Data

Kelly, Raymond C. (Raymond Case), 1942–
  The Nuer conquest.

  Bibliography: p.
  Includes index.
  1. Nuer (African people)—History.   2. Nuer (African
people)—Social life and customs.   3. Dinka (African
people)—History.   4. Dinka (African people)—Social life
and customs.   I. Title.
DT155.2.N85K45   1985   306'.08996   85-1409
ISBN 0-472-10064-5
ISBN 0-472-08056-3 (pbk.)

Acknowledgments

A preliminary formulation of the general interpretation developed in this book was originally presented in a series of six departmental lectures at the University of Michigan in 1978. The questions, comments, and suggestions of students and colleagues contributed to the development of these ideas through subsequent archival and library research and analysis of the material collected. Archival research in England and the Sudan during the spring and summer of 1979 was supported by a Faculty Research Grant from the University of Michigan Horace H. Rackham School of Graduate Studies. Dr. P. P. Howell provided valuable assistance both through his comments on a preliminary paper on Nuer expansion and in directing me to relevant archival collections in England. The staff at the Public Records Office and the Science Library of the British Museum were most helpful. Elizabeth Cory, archivist of the University of Durham School of Oriental Studies Sudan Archives was very generous with her time in helping me to locate pertinent materials.

I was fortunate to have an opportunity to meet and talk with Dr. Abdel Ghaffar M. Ahmed of the Department of Anthropology and Sociology at the University of Khartoum when he visited the University of Michigan in 1978. When I later traveled to Khartoum he provided generous assistance in facilitating my access to the university library and to government archives, and in directing me to individuals and government agencies involved in research concerning the Jonglei Development Project. W. J. A. Payne, senior consultant to the United Nations Development Program, was especially helpful in discussing my research and in providing me with copies of some very useful government reports concerning the potential impact of the Jonglei canal on the Nuer and Dinka economies.

I received support that was instrumental in writing this book from the National Endowment for the Humanities (NEH, Fellowship for Independent Study and Research, 1979–80), the John Simon Guggenheim Memorial Foundation (fellowship, 1982–83) and the Center for Advanced Study in the Behavioral Sciences (fellowship, 1982–83). The National Science Foundation (Grant No. BNS8206304), and the John D. and Catherine T. MacArthur Foundation provided funding to the Center for Advanced Study in the Behavioral Sciences for support of center fellowships (1982–83). The University of Michigan and NEH provided essential support during the early phases of this study while the Guggenheim Foundation and Center jointly funded the fellowship year that enabled me to bring it to completion. I am pleased to acknowledge the fellowship support received from all these sources.

Hugh Gilmore, Doug Jacobs, and Susan Nelson provided research assistance during the initial stages of this project. Derwin Bell prepared the map. The secretaries in the Anthropology Department at the University of Michigan typed many drafts of the manuscript. The permanent staff of the Center provided final typing, secretarial, and library services. Lisa Headington helped with the proofreading. I would like to take this opportunity to express my appreciation to all these individuals for their helpful assistance.

During the preparation of this study I have benefited from discussions with many friends and colleagues at the University of Michigan and the Center for Advanced Study in the Behavioral Sciences. Abdel Ahmed, Jim Fernandes, Kent Flannery, Robert Hefner, P. P. Howell, David Kertzer, Bruce Knauft, Sherry Ortner, Michael Peletz, Roy Rappaport, Marshall Sahlins, and Aram Yengoyan have read earlier or later drafts of all or part of the book and offered many valuable comments and suggestions. Sherry Ortner deserves to be singled out for her useful critical and editorial comments on all successive drafts of the manuscript. I appreciate the encouragement I have received from the late Meyer Fortes and from Roy Rappaport and Marshall Sahlins. I have given many course lectures based on materials drawn from this study and have also been encouraged by the interest expressed by many graduate and undergraduate students.

Contents

Introduction

In the early 1800s the Nuer occupied a territory of about eight thousand seven hundred square miles located in the west central portion of the Upper Nile Basin and entirely encompassed by a Dinka domain more than ten times this size. By about 1890, the Nuer had expanded to the eastern edge of the Upper Nile Basin, cutting a hundred-mile-wide swath through the center of Dinka territory and appropriating a substantial portion of Anuak country that lay to the east of the latter. In all, the Nuer increased their territorial domain four-fold, to a total of thirty-five thousand square miles, during the period from about 1818 to 1890. Exogenous factors subsequently brought Nuer expansion to an abrupt halt.

Nuer displacement of the Dinka (and Anuak) represents one of the most prominent instances of tribal imperialism contained in the ethnographic record. Both the Nuer and Dinka sociocultural systems are particularly well-described ethnographically and historical data are ample to document the main features and phases of the Nuer conquest. The method of controlled comparison can be employed under nearly ideal conditions. The case thus provides an excellent opportunity to examine a number of important theoretical issues pertaining to the causes and means of territorial expansion, the interplay and relative significance of social and ecological factors in accounting for the latter, the formal properties of an expansionist system (that is considered a striking example of evolutionary success), the general applicability of analytic models based on the concept of self-regulation, and the nature of structural change. The relevance of the Nuer/Dinka case to these issues is developed in the following pages.

The Nuer and Dinka are derived from a common stock, speak closely related languages, formerly occupied a common ecological zone, share a common transhumant system of economic production, and display many other cultural similarities (as well as a few notable differences). The dominance of the Nuer and the rapidity and extent of their conquest are puzzling in light of these commonalities. Howell (1954a:7) has remarked that

> it remains a mystery why the Nuer should have emerged as a separate people with comparative suddenness about the beginning of the nineteenth century, driven the Dinka out of much of their country, seized so many of their women and cattle, and absorbed whole sections of Dinka into their own society.

The primary objective of this study is to resolve this mystery and to provide answers to the four central questions posed by the Nuer conquest. These questions concern: (1) the proximate and underlying causes of Nuer territorial appropriation; (2) the means by which this was accomplished, and particularly the nature of the decisive Nuer advantage that enabled them to so readily displace neighboring groups; (3) the developmental process of divergence from a common stock that eventuated in Nuer hegemony (and entailed significant structural changes); and (4) the factors that account for Nuer, rather than Dinka, development of both the impetus to territorial acquisition and the capacity to bring this about. The relevance of these specific questions to several of the theoretical issues listed earlier is readily apparent.

A number of scholars have been intrigued by one or more of these questions, and there is an extensive series of publications in which they have been addressed that spans the last four decades. The ongoing debate, which is one of the most protracted in the anthropological literature, dates from Evans-Pritchard's publication of the first Nuer monograph in 1940 and includes important contributions by Howell (1954a, 1954b), Lienhardt (1958), Sahlins (1961), Gough (1971), Newcomer (1972), Glickman (1972), Southall (1976), Sacks (1979), and Johnson (1980, 1981, 1982). The publications that specifically address the causes and means of Nuer territorial expansion are discussed as a group in chapter 2, and it is in this context that the issue of the relative significance of social and ecological factors comes to the fore. It arises in relation to each of the four central questions noted above. A review of this literature thus provides a capsule treatment of the history of anthropological approaches to a specific theoretical issue that has been of enduring concern. (The Nuer case is, of course, important in many other respects and has perhaps been more discussed and reinterpreted than any other. A recent article by Karp and Maynard [1983] provides a useful review of this literature.)

The insatiable character of Nuer territorial expansion and the striking absence of negative feedback mechanisms this suggests provides the basis for consideration of other important theoretical issues. The Nuer had succeeded in doubling their initial territorial domain by the 1850s and yet proceeded to quadruple it during the following decades. Any postulated shortage of material components (such as water resources, grazing areas, agricultural land, etc.) which may have existed before the inception of Nuer expansion (in about 1818) must have been more than amply satisfied by the doubling of Nuer territory, since the Nuer population could not have subsisted on a material base that represented less than half their minimal requirements prior to 1818. Why, then, did the Nuer continue to expand and to redouble the size of their territory? Why didn't the system achieve homeostasis at some early point (or, indeed, at any point)? The historical evidence indicates an absence of internal regulatory processes conducive to the cessation of territorial expansion and other data bear out this conclusion.

This raises two interrelated theoretical issues. The first of these concerns the general applicability of analytic models based on the core concept of a self-regulating system. Such models have been widely employed in ecological anthropology. Moreover, the concept of self-regulation is taken to be intrinsic to adaptation and therefore applicable, in principle, to every ethnographic case (Rappaport, 1979:147). Given the presumed relationship between adaptiveness and evolutionary success, the Nuer case represents a particularly significant test of these concepts. The second issue concerns specification of the formal properties of an intrinsically expansionist system (in the systems theory sense of the term). Although archaeology and historical linguistics attest to the spread of particular cultures over vast regions in prehistoric times, little effort has been made to delineate the formal properties and distinctive features of expansionist systems in the relatively few ethnographic cases in which the phenomenon of cultural displacement is accessible to a comprehensive analysis.

A number of the theoretical issues mentioned in the preceding pages represent aspects of a more fundamental issue, namely the nature of the system of relations in which material components are embedded and the manner in which this system governs the selective realization of material causality. This issue is central to the social theory of Marx and Weber and lies at the heart of many current anthropological debates. (See Sahlins, 1976; in the conclusion to his critical assessment of the literature, Sahlins [ibid.:206] presents the core issue in much the same terms as it is formulated above.) The distribution of environmental features, the prominence of material components such as land and cattle in Nuer expansion, and the potential for a comprehensive controlled comparison of the Nuer and Dinka provide an unusual opportunity to address this issue. The larger goal of the present study is to make a contribution to this important area of anthropological inquiry.

The richness of the available data should be noted here. Although the ethnographic studies of Evans-Pritchard and Lienhardt are well known, there is little awareness that the ecology of the Upper Nile Basin and the economy of the Nuer and Dinka have been the subject of very detailed and comprehensive study. This work was carried out in the early 1950s by the Jonglei Investigation Team and its successor, the Southern Development Investigation Team, to serve as the basis for the formulation of economic policy. Topography, climate, hydrology, geology, soils, vegetation, and the distribution of ecotypes were extensively studied by specialists in each of these respective fields, as were agriculture, animal husbandry, fishing, diet, nutritional status, and the health and demographic characteristics of the population. The results of this research are published in five lengthy volumes (Howell, 1954*b*, 1954*c*, 1954*d*, 1954*e*, 1955).[1] Subsequent research by Payne and El Amin (1977) augments and updates this corpus. The data contained in these reports is much more copious than the most diligent anthropological field-worker could collect and it provides the basis for a thorough consideration of material components and interrelations. When brought into relationship with an equally rich ethnographic corpus, these data also provide fertile ground for examination of the nature of the system of relations in which material components are embedded in two eminently comparable cases. The inquiry can thus be conducted within the framework of a controlled comparison that provides clearer and more definitive conclusions than are typically available from a single case study.

Controlled comparison is employed in this study to elucidate questions of process, change, and development. That it is particularly suited to such objectives has been widely noted (Eggan, 1954). However, this method has contributed to the analysis in other ways that are less readily apparent and that have heretofore gone unnoticed in methodological discussion. It will be useful to make these contributions explicit, since they have played an important role in shaping the analysis that follows. Moreover, they are germane to current debates concerning the appropriateness of various categories and modes of analysis.

At the most basic level, controlled comparison is grounded in the proposition that the differences between two cases being compared cannot be explained with reference to the features common to both. It follows that the distinctive features of each case (respectively) are themselves interconnected causally, developmentally, or by mutual entailment. Thus if the Nuer and Dinka differ in their bridewealth systems, in certain details of their economic organization, and in segmentary organization, an interconnection among these is posited and becomes the object of investigation. Although controlled comparison has conventionally entailed an effort to elucidate such interconnections through the specification of independent and dependent variables, this is not an intrinsic or inseparable feature of the method. It may be that there are reticulate, mutual-causal relations between the "variables" or that, like arms and legs, they simply constitute aspects of a coherent whole. In any case, one of the central advantages of controlled comparison is the identification of relational clusters. Moreover, the distribution of similarities and differences between the two cases being compared also specifies points of disarticulation within each sociocultural system. Common features are not only incapable of accounting for the development of differences, but must also be loosely interconnected to the distinctive features of each sociocultural system. In other words, a controlled comparison of historically related sociocultural systems that are structurally distinctive necessarily isolates the relational cluster that provides the dynamic of structural transformation in each case.[2] This not only informs the analysis, but also contains an implicit crystallization of the structure that informs theoretical conceptions of the latter.

Inasmuch as controlled comparison specifies both relational clusters and points of disjunction, it also defines the boundaries of the analytic domains that are appropriate to elucidation of the sociocultural systems under consideration. These may be quite different from those associated with extant theory. Features that are assumed to be integrally interrelated may not co-vary and others that are normally treated separately may be brought into association within a common analytic framework. In the present case, the bridewealth system and segmentary system emerge as components of a single relational cluster. This calls into question the conventional wisdom of regarding bridewealth as part of the domestic domain, analytically distinct from that of politico-jural relations (and often, as in Evans-Pritchard's work, treated in a separate monograph). On the contrary, the bridewealth system specifies the relations between kin relations; the structure it thereby encodes is central to the organization of local groups and the wider tribal polity. In this and other respects, the bridewealth system is focal to the analysis presented in the following chapters. The main point to be noted here is that this focality is not an artifact of the application of any existing paradigm, but rather follows from the application of the method of controlled comparison.

Evans-Pritchard's categorical distinction between domestic and political domains also severs key interrelations between economic and political organization. Evans-Pritchard makes the very important observation that economic relations are embedded in kin relations, but then proceeds to consign both to the domestic domain and set them aside.

> I may sum up by repeating that economic relations are part of general social relations and that these relationships, being mainly of a domestic or kinship order, lie outside the scope of this book. (1940a:92)

The relational cluster isolated by controlled comparison encompasses what Evans-Pritchard here excludes from analysis.[3] The bridewealth system is the connecting link inasmuch as it not only orders kin relations that entail economic obligations but also effectively organizes economic production. Although the Nuer and Dinka share a common transhumant system of production, they differ with respect to the relationship between the cattle herding and agricultural components that comprise such a system. The distinctive characteristics of the Nuer and Dinka variants of transhumance are directly attributable to differences between these two cultural groups in the magnitude and composition of their respective bridewealth payments. These relatively minor differences in economic organization also have a very significant impact on both segmentary organization and the dimensions of political units, since they largely determine the size, spatial distribution, and range of associations of local groups. These interrelationships will be elucidated in due course. The principal objective here is to delineate the general conformation of the analysis and the relational cluster that is central to it.

A reanalysis of the Nuer that is grounded in comparative methodology represents a somewhat ironic turn of events. In his essay on social anthropology, Evans-Pritchard (1951*b*:90) criticizes prior forms of the comparative method as unduly time-consuming and seldom productive of answers to the questions posed. He proposes, as an alternative, an "experimental method" entailing the testing of hypotheses through the study of individual cases and the refinement, reformulation, and retesting of them through additional case studies. He also notes, quite prophetically, that this methodological program "can be continued indefinitely" (ibid.). What he did not foresee was that extant theory not only proposes testable hypotheses but also stipulates the analytic categories through which such tests are conducted. The limitations of a categorical distinction between the domestic and politico-jural domains consequently persist through innumerable successive applications of the experimental method. Controlled comparison thus has an important role to play in the reconceptualization of the analytic apparatus through its capacity to isolate relational clusters appropriate to the cases at hand.[4] Comparative and experimental methods are thus complementary; the former contributes to the efficacy of the latter.

The reanalysis of the Nuer presented in the following chapters does not controvert the key features of Evans-Pritchard's analysis but rather recontextualizes them and elaborates upon them. However, it is the consideration of relationships Evans-Pritchard set aside that provides the basis for this recontextualization, and thus lays the groundwork for further elucidation of the Nuer sociocultural system. Inasmuch as structure is grounded in relationships, the rearrangement of these essentially constitutes a reconceptualization of Nuer social structure. The bridewealth system emerges as a central component of this structure. The distribution of bridewealth cattle among specified matrilateral and patrilateral kin stipulates the relations between kin relations that govern the constitution of local groups and their interrelations. Moreover, the bridewealth system is the primary context in which kinship valuations are encoded and experienced. In short, the bridewealth system is a key symbol (Ortner, 1973).[5] It plays an important role in stipulating the values upon which the political structure is grounded, and through which it is actualized. (The role of values, in these respects, is noted by Evans-Pritchard, 1940*a*:263.) However, the bridewealth system is also something more than a key symbol inasmuch as it also organizes economic production and indirectly determines the size and distribution of the local groups that constitute the basic units of the political system. An early divergence in the bridewealth systems of the proto-Nuer and proto-Dinka thus physically reshaped the proto-Nuer political system as well as serving as a basis for social actors' reconceptualization of unit definition and interrelationship. This, in very brief, is the core of the argument developed in a later chapter concerning the organizational differentiation of the Nuer and Dinka and the structural transformation that eventuated in Nuer hegemony.

A brief chapter summary will provide a guide to what follows. The first chapter is principally devoted to presenting what is historically known or can be deduced concerning Nuer territorial expansion and displacement of the central Dinka and western Anuak. It covers the prehistory of the Nuer and Dinka, early migrations (circa 1500 to 1800), the dates and phases of nineteenth-century Nuer expansion and the movements of each Nuer and Dinka tribal population during this period. (In the ethnography of the region, the term *tribe* designates a political unit that constitutes the maximal group that unites in warfare.) The character of Nuer raids, their effects on the Dinka population under attack, and the ultimate fate of the very substantial population displaced by the Nuer are considered in some detail.

In all, the data presented in chapter 1 delineate the phenomena to be explained and provide a basis for assessing earlier arguments pertaining to the causes and means of Nuer expansion. This body of literature is critically evaluated in chapter 2, with a view to more precisely defining those areas where further explication is required. Most of the previous attempts to explain the impetus to Nuer territorial expansion rely implicitly or explicitly on notions of "population pressure" as the principal causal factor. A detailed examination of the relevant variables leads to the conclusion that population pressure could not have provided a sustained impetus to Nuer expansion and, at the same time, lays the groundwork for the development of a more satisfactory explanation.

The underlying causes of Nuer expansion are considered in chapter 3. The explanation presented here largely focuses on the manner in which the Nuer bridewealth system establishes social requirements for cattle. The latter effectively determine the size, composition, and growth characteristics of Nuer herds, thereby defining the extent of Nuer grazing requirements. Recurrent shortages of dry season pasture (that are ultimately attributable to bridewealth requirements) provide the immediate impetus to successive rounds of territorial appropriation. Much of the chapter is devoted to a comprehensive comparative analysis of the Nuer and Dinka bridewealth systems. This not only establishes important sociological differences but also provides a basis for delineating the distinctive Nuer and Dinka variants of transhumance. Difference between the Nuer and Dinka in the allocation of land between competing agricultural and grazing utilizations follows from dissimilar grazing requirements that are in turn attributable to differences in the magnitude and composition of their respective bridewealth payments.

Chapter 4 focuses on the organizational basis of the Nuer military advantage that enabled them to carry out devastating large-scale raids against the Dinka and regularly turn back infrequent Dinka raids with staggering losses. The chapter provides a detailed comparative analysis of Nuer and Dinka segmentary organization and documents the relationship between segmentary organization and tribal size. The relationship between the bridewealth system and segmentary system is also developed in the concluding section.

The processes of cultural divergence and organizational differentiation that resulted in Nuer hegemony are examined in chapter 5. The complex interrelationships among bridewealth requirements, economic organization, segmentary structure, and tribal size analyzed in earlier chapters are here presented in the form of a coevolutionary developmental sequence. As noted earlier, the core of the argument concerns the multiple, interactive effects of an early divergence in bridewealth systems on the proto-Nuer and proto-Dinka. This provided an initial advantage in tribal size that enabled the proto-Nuer to expand within the "homeland" region (west of the Nile) in the centuries prior to 1800. This early expansion produced de facto changes in both the composition of local groups and the nature of the interrelationships among them. The bridewealth system, which was itself recontextualized by these changes, provided a basis for reconceptualization of the segmentary order. This engendered a structural transformation of the Nuer political system that entailed a threefold advantage over the Dinka in tribal size, setting the stage for the rapid and extensive Nuer territorial expansion of the nineteenth century.

In the final chapter, the Nuer case is examined as an instance of an expansionist system, characterized by an unremitting constitutional predisposition to territorial appropriation. It is, in this respect, a nonequilibrium system. The distinctive formal properties of this system (*qua* system) are analyzed with a view to specifying the characteristics that are instrumental to Nuer expansionism and to the constitution of intrinsically expansionist systems more generally. This raises important theoretical issues concerning the general applicability of the concept of self-regulating systems and the role of self-regulation in adaptive structures that evidence marked evolutionary success. Rappaport's (1979) comprehensive formulation of these concepts is critically evaluated in relation to the Nuer case. This rounds out consideration of what was earlier identified as the fundamental issue that motivated this study: the nature of the system of relations in which material components are embedded and the manner in which this system governs the selective realization of material causality.

CHAPTER 1

The History of
Nuer Expansion

The principal aim of this chapter is simply to present what is known, or can be inferred, concerning Nuer territorial expansion, and to do so in a context that is distinct from any particular interpretation of it. The extent to which published interpretations account for the available data is taken up in the following chapter.

The presentation begins with the consideration of linguistic evidence, pertaining to the divergence of the Nuer and Dinka from a common stock, and archaeological evidence, concerning the antiquity of the transhumant economy shared by these two cultural groups. We then proceed to a chronological account of Nuer and Dinka migrations (and territorial expansion) during the period from about A.D. 1500 to 1800. This material is important in establishing that the subsequent nineteenth-century Nuer expansion was not a unique or unprecedented event. We then turn to the latter period, which is the principal focus of this study. A description of the initial locations and subsequent movements of Nuer, Dinka, and Anuak tribal groups provides a general picture of Nuer territorial expansion and displacement of the Central Dinka and Western Anuak during the nineteenth century. The remainder of the chapter is concerned with a more detailed examination of the character of Nuer raids and their effects on the Dinka population under attack.

Colonial records archived in England and the Sudan contain information on twenty-six Nuer (and three Dinka) raids that took place between 1905 and 1928. Although the reports of particular raids are each somewhat incomplete, this material can be pieced together to establish a composite picture of the timing, scope, duration, and scale of Nuer forays into Dinka territory. The broad outlines of Nuer military organization and tactics can be ascertained. In at least some instances these records also provide specific information concerning the number of Dinka villages attacked, the number of people killed and captured, and the number of cattle stolen. These data, together with information provided by Evans-Pritchard (1940a), document the widespread devastation produced by large-scale Nuer raids and clarify the role that these played in Nuer territorial expansion. Nuer expansion was largely accomplished through the occupation of areas from which the Dinka had withdrawn as a consequence of recurrent Nuer raids.

The vast area conquered by the Nuer during the nineteenth century was previously occupied by a Dinka and Anuak population estimated to have numbered at least 186,000 persons. The ultimate fate of this population is one of the most interesting questions pertaining to Nuer expansion. It is also of considerable theoretical significance because the extent of Nuer assimilation of the Dinka has a direct bearing on various arguments that have been put forward to account for Nuer expansion. Simply put, the central issue here is whether Nuer population growth was a principal cause of territorial appropriation or merely a consequence of the process of expansion itself. The final portion of the chapter is thus directed to determining what happened to the Dinka population displaced by the Nuer, and thereby also determining the extent to which the Nuer population was augmented through Dinka accretions.

THE NUER AND DINKA BEFORE 1800

The Nuer and Dinka speak genetically related Western Nilotic languages that are derived from a common proto-language.[1] Recent studies (McLaughlin, 1967:13–27; Johnson, 1980:84, 575–76) are consistent with the long-standing view that the Nuer and Dinka languages are more closely related to each other than either is to any third Nilotic language. This suggests that Nuer and Dinka differentiated from each other after the common language from which they are mutually derived began to diverge from other Nilotic languages. This continues to be the simplest explanation of available lexico-statistical data, although it is not the only explanation.[2] The percentage of shared cognates in the basic core vocabulary of the Nuer, Dinka, Shilluk, and Anuak languages reported by McLaughlin and Johnson are reproduced below. Although Johnson's figures are consistently higher than McLaughlin's, both confirm the point that the closest relationship obtains between Nuer and Dinka.

McLaughlin	*Percent*
Eastern Nuer and Bor Dinka	42–44
Eastern Nuer and Anuak	37–40
Bor Dinka and Anuak	33–37
Johnson	
Western Nuer and Western Dinka	58
Western Nuer and Northern Dinka	56
Eastern Nuer and Western Dinka	57.5
Eastern Nuer and Northern Dinka	55.5
All Nuer and Shilluk	50
All Nuer and Anuak	50
Western Dinka and Shilluk	42.5
Northern Dinka and Shilluk	41.5
Western Dinka and Anuak	41.5
Northern Dinka and Anuak	41.5

McLaughlin applies the dating technique of glottochronology to his lexico-statistical data and arrives at the following conclusion:

> It seems most reasonable to suppose that the language group of which Anuak was a member began to separate from the Nuer-Dinka language group around 335 B.C., and that Nuer and Dinka began to separate some 420 years later, around A.D. 85. (McLaughlin, 1967:27)

The much higher percentage of shared cognates reported by Johnson would, of course, produce a much later date for the beginning of Nuer-Dinka divergence. Moreover, glottochronology is not credited with a high degree of accuracy. Given these uncertainties, it seems appropriate to employ a very broad time range and to restrict our conclusions to the observation that the Nuer and Dinka languages probably began to diverge from a common proto-language sometime between two thousand and fourteen hundred years ago. If one assumes that Nuer and Dinka would have ceased to be mutually intelligible dialects of the same language approximately seven hundred years after they began to diverge, this would have occurred between A.D. 700 and 1300. No great weight should be attached to these dates. However, the linguistic evidence does suggest that a significant degree of linguistic (and cultural) divergence had taken place prior to A.D. 1500, when the combined Nuer-Dinka population began an accelerated expansion toward the outer margins of the Upper Nile Basin.

Although little archaeological investigation has been carried out in the Upper Nile Basin, excavations at the Kadero and Zakieb sites (on the Nile about four hundred miles north of the basin) indicate the presence of an economic system virtually identical to that of the Nuer and Dinka at the early date of 3372 B.C. (or 5350 B.P.) (Haaland, 1978:31–34). Kadero has been interpreted as an elevated wet season site devoted to agriculture and animal husbandry. More than 88 percent of the mammalian skeletal remains are those of domestic animals, with cattle remains predominating over those of sheep by a ratio of three to one (Krzyzaniak, 1976:41). The cattle bones are reported to be quite similar to those of a modern Nuer ox obtained for comparative purposes (Krzyzaniak, 1977:46). The cultivation of two varieties of sorghum and four varieties of millet is indicated by a type of pottery decorated with impressions of these domesticated cereals, and by the presence of numerous grindstones (Klichowska, 1978:43; Haaland, 1978:31).

The contemporary companion site at Zakieb has been interpreted as a dry season herding and fishing camp for the proximate Kadero population. The mammal bones found here are predominantly those of cattle and the pottery is of the same type as that found at Kadero, although potter's tools are absent (Haaland, 1978:31–33). Fish bones and fishhooks are prevalent. Grindstones are very scarce, suggesting that cultivation was confined to Kadero. In all, these sites suggest a transhumant economic system based on cattle herding, fishing, and wet season cereal cultivation that is virtually indistinguishable from that of the Nuer and Dinka in the ethnographic present. Moreover, human skeletal remains from a burial ground at Kadero are said to have affinities with Negroid populations to the south (Krzyzaniak, 1976:41).

An economic system based on the same cereals and domesticated animals is also reported for the Ethiopian highlands at a projected date of three to four thousand years ago (Sutton, 1968:86). This complex had spread southward to the Kenya highlands by 1000 B.C., and may reasonably be assumed to have spread into other environmentally suitable areas by the same date.

The principal staples of the Nuer and Dinka economic system could thus have been derived either from the Ethiopian highlands, directly to the east of the Upper Nile Basin, or from the Kadero area, which is only four hundred miles to the north (and located directly on the Nile). The establishment of a cattle- and grain-based economy in the basin itself cannot be precisely dated through archaeological evidence at this time. However, the spread of proto-Nilotic-speaking populations during the second millenium B.C. is generally interpreted as a consequence of this economic transformation (see Johnson, 1980:55), and it is widely assumed that it also predates the processes of linguistic differentiation among the Western Nilotics discussed earlier. In other words, it is highly probable that the transhumant economic system of the Nuer and Dinka was in place sometime before the beginning of their divergence from a common proto-language. As noted earlier, this divergence probably began sometime between two thousand and fourteen hundred years ago. The earlier date is more than three thousand years after the earliest evidence for the presence of this transhumant economic system at the Kadero and Zakieb sites.

Expansion toward the Outer Margins of the Upper Nile Basin

Nuer and Dinka oral traditions indicate a very substantial enlargement of the area occupied by these two cultural groups during the period from about A.D. 1500 to 1800. A doubling of the combined territory inhabited by the Nuer and Dinka conveys the approximate order of magnitude of this expansion (which cannot be precisely measured). Three broad population movements can be discerned, and these appear to represent interrelated developments. First, the Atwot separated from the main body of the Nuer and migrated southward to their present location on the border between the Dinka, Jur, and Mandari (see map 1). Second, the Western Dinka, who previously occupied only a relatively narrow strip of land on the west side of the Bahr el Jebel, expanded throughout the extensive area of the Bahr el Ghazal province that they currently inhabit. Third, some elements of the Central Dinka migrated into the area north of the Sobat River and east of the White Nile. Each of these population movements will be discussed in turn, and an effort will then be made to assess the interrelationships among them. However, the broad outlines of this general territorial expansion may be noted at the outset. Nuer-speaking peoples progressively appropriated territory in the south central portion of the Upper Nile Basin and Dinka-speaking peoples progressively expanded to the northeastern and western margins of this ecological zone.

The following discussion will entail reference to a number of Nuer and Dinka groupings and it may be useful to provide a lexicon before we begin. The Nuer, Dinka, Shilluk, and Anuak will be labeled "cultural groups." The Dinka are subdivided into (1) the Western Dinka, who reside west of the Bahr el Jebel; (2) the Northern or White Nile Dinka, who live north of the Sobat River; and (3) the Southern Dinka, who occupy the area south of the Nuer and east of the Bahr el Jebel. These three clumps of territory are readily apparent on map 1. In addition, I will use the term "Central Dinka" to refer to the Dinka population that inhabited the area between the Bahr el Jebel and the Sobat River before nineteenth-century Nuer expansion.

The Dinka are further subdivided into "tribal groups" consisting of a number of politically autonomous tribes that share a common regional identity and a common history of migration. Thus, the Rek Dinka tribal group includes twenty-seven independent tribes, the Malwal six, the Bor two, and so forth. Most of the named Dinka groups shown on map 1 are tribal groups. Exceptions are the Rut, Thoi, Eastern Luaich, Eastern Ngok, Ghol, and Nyarraweng, which are single tribes. (A tribe is defined as a group that regularly unites in warfare. Other criteria that enter into the definition need not concern us here.)

In contrast to the Dinka, most of the named Nuer groups shown on map 1 are single tribes, rather than tribal groups. The exceptions here are the Jagei, Eastern Jikany, and Western Jikany, which include four, three, and two tribes, respectively. The Nuer are conventionally divided into three regional groups: (1) The Western or "Homeland" Nuer, residing west of the Bahr el Jebel; (2) the Central or Zeraf Valley Nuer, which includes the Lak, Thiang, and Gaawar; and (3) the Eastern Nuer, which includes the Lou and Eastern Jikany. The Atwot are historically part of the Homeland Nuer but are currently moving toward the status of a separate cultural group. The Atwot migration that brought about this separation constitutes the first of the three main population movements to be discussed.

The Atwot Migration

The Atwot (Atuot) were formerly a component tribe (or tribal section) of the Nuer, occupying an area near the present border between the Jagei and Dok Nuer (Evans-Pritchard, 1940a:260; Burton, 1978a:31). Both Atwot and

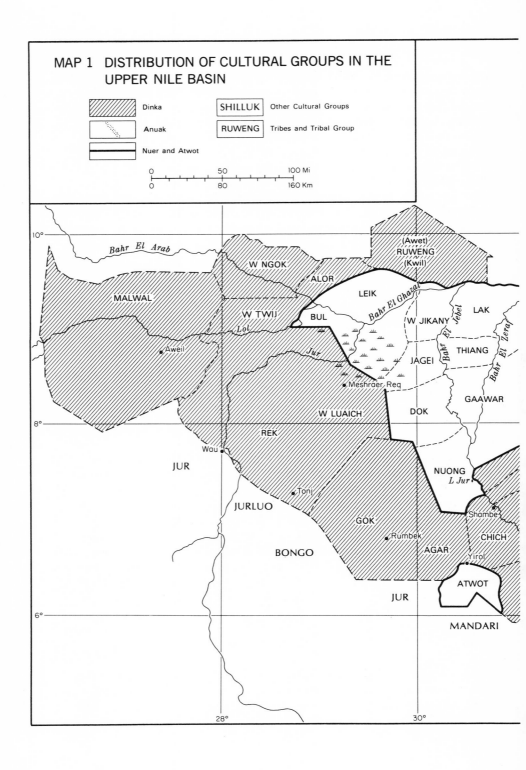

MAP 1   DISTRIBUTION OF CULTURAL GROUPS IN THE
        UPPER NILE BASIN

Dinka

Anuak

Nuer and Atwot

SHILLUK   Other Cultural Groups

RUWENG   Tribes and Tribal Group

0   50   100 Mi
0   80   160 Km

10°

Bahr El Arab

W NGOK

(Awet)
RUWENG
(Kwil)

ALOR

MALWAL

LEIK

Bahr El Ghazal

LAK

W TWIJ

BUL

W JIKANY

Lol

Aweil

Jur

THIANG

JAGEI

Bahr El Jebel

Bahr El Zeraf

Meshraer Req

GAAWAR

8°

W LUAICH

DOK

REK

Wau

NUONG

L Jur

JUR

Toni

Shambe

JURLUO

GOK

CHICH

Rumbek

BONGO

AGAR

Yirol

ATWOT

JUR

6°

MANDARI

28°   30°

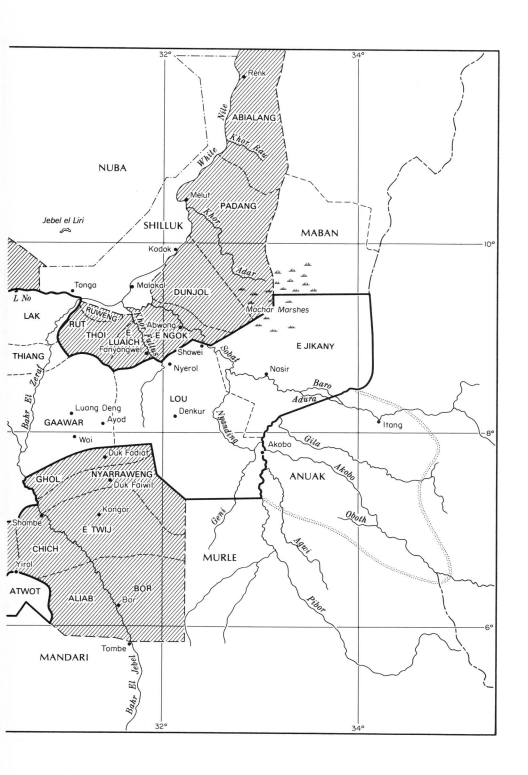

Western Nuer oral traditions hold that the Atwot migrated southward as a result of conflict with other Nuer groups. Burton (1978*a*:32) suggests:

> It is likely that when they began to migrate south, Atuot moved with their herds along the inland *toic* of the river Payii . . . and upon entering their present country, found it inhabited by hunters and trappers (*adep*), fishermen (*atuoc*) and iron workers (*ajuong*). The Dinka who now live around Atuotland are said to have already been there.

The Atwot migration, which covered about 130 miles, thus entailed a movement through territory held by the Dinka. However, the area in which the Atwot originally settled was occupied by the Jur, whom the Atwot fought and successfully displaced (Burton, 1978*a*:11; Santandrea, 1967:111–12, cited in Burton, 1978*a*:59). The Atwot maintain that hostile relations prevailed between them and their Dinka neighbors, and that they never married these "evil-eyed people" before the colonial period (Burton, 1978*a*:59). However, portions of the indigenous Jur population were assimilated through intermarriage (ibid.: 49). Some additional migration from Nuerland also appears to have added to the Atwot population. It is likely that the area originally settled was subsequently expanded somewhat at Dinka expense.

Burton (1978*a*:29) reports that the Atwot left Nuerland at a time beyond the twelve generations included in the typical Atwot genealogy. If one allows 30 years per generation, this suggests that the Atwot migration began more than 360 years ago (i.e., before 1620). On the other hand, the similarity of the Atwot dialect to the language spoken by the Nuer indicates a relatively short period of linguistic divergence and hence of Nuer-Atwot separation. Burton (1978*a*:19) notes that the Nuer could understand him when he spoke to them in the Atwot dialect, and that he could likewise comprehend their replies in Nuer. Given the spatial segregation of the Nuer and Atwot, this degree of mutual intelligibility suggests that they probably have not been separated for more than four or five hundred years (Eckert, personal communication). This narrows down the most plausible time of the Atwot migration to sometime between about 1500 and 1620.

The same logic suggests that the main thrusts of Dinka expansion to the west and northeast took place no earlier than the time of the Atwot migration. Although the Northern and Western Dinka are widely separated, they nevertheless speak mutually intelligible dialects of the Dinka language. Moreover, Johnson's lexico-statistical comparisons indicate very little difference between these Dinka groups in basic vocabulary. The Northern Dinka and Western Dinka each share 41.5 percent basic vocabulary with the Anuak and differ by only 1 percent (42.5 to 41.5) in a similar comparison of these respective linguistic groups with Shilluk. These data suggest a date of separation for the Northern and Western Dinka that is somewhat more recent than that of the Nuer and Atwot. More generally, the linguistic evidence confirms Nuer and Dinka oral traditions concerning the recency of their expansion throughout the Upper Nile Basin. Although the Nuer and Dinka occupy an area of about 113,000 square miles, the differences among Dinka dialects, and among Nuer dialects (including Atwot), are not great.

The Atwot migration closely parallels the later migration of the Jikany that initiated Nuer eastward expansion in the early 1800s. In both cases a Nuer group migrated over a hundred miles to an area on the periphery of Dinka territory, and in both cases this movement is said to have been prompted by conflict with other Nuer groups. This parallel is significant in establishing that the Jikany migration was not a unique event. By the same token, the similarity between these two instances has important implications for our understanding of the earlier Atwot migration. We know that the Jikany exodus was merely one element of a larger process of Nuer territorial expansion generated by factors affecting the Nuer as a whole. This suggests that the Atwot migration may likewise have been one component of a more general Nuer expansion within the ''homeland'' region (i.e., the area west of the Nile occupied by the Nuer in 1800, and representing the base from which they expanded in the period from 1800 to 1890). This interpretation is consistent with the limited data available concerning Nuer and Dinka population movements prior to 1800 (as will be explained in due course). More importantly, it suggests that these population movements were, at least to some extent, interrelated. In other words, Dinka expansion toward the periphery of the area defined by the flood plain of the Upper Nile Basin becomes more readily intelligible in relation to a Nuer expansion at the center of the same area, during the same time period. (The flood region is depicted on map 2.)

Western Dinka Expansion

The oral traditions of the principal Western Dinka tribal groups generally contain references to a westward migration from the vicinity of the Bahr el Jebel. In most instances, these migrations are said to have originated from the region between the border of the Nuer homeland (which was then further north) and the Atwot enclave. We will briefly consider the migration history of each of these tribal groups, beginning with the Malwal Dinka who are furthest west (see map 1). This will lay the groundwork for suggesting some general features of Western Dinka expansion.

The Malwal are reportedly derived from a branch of the Rek (Raik) who in turn originated from the Agar Dinka (Stubbs and Morrison, 1938:351). The Agar are the western neighbors of the Atwot. The antecedents of the Malwal are said to have reached the River Jur in about 1638 and to have gradually pushed further west in the following centuries (ibid.). No date has been

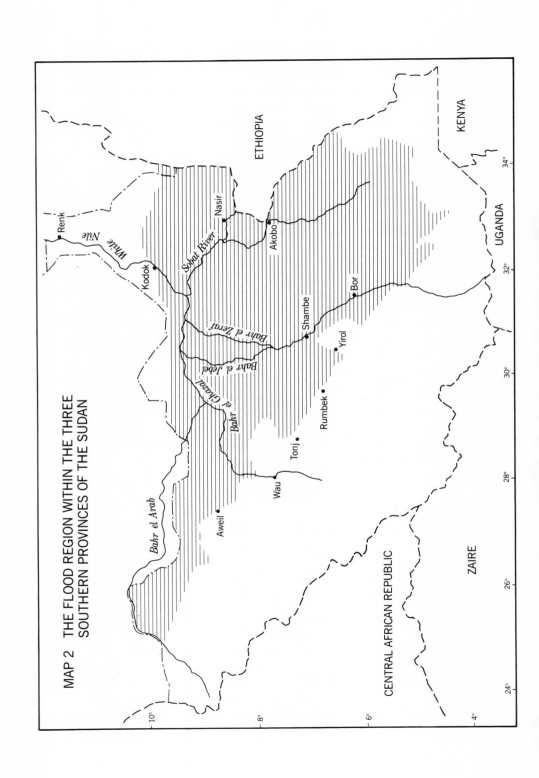

MAP 2   THE FLOOD REGION WITHIN THE THREE
SOUTHERN PROVINCES OF THE SUDAN

proposed for the beginning of the initial movement, from the Agar area to the River Jur. However, it is not implausible that this coincided with the migration of the Atwot into this area sometime between 1500 and 1620. The fact that only slight dialect differences obtain between the Malwal and other Dinka groups suggests that their migration probably did not begin earlier than this.

Before they were expelled by the Nuer in the early 1800s, the Eastern Luaich occupied the southern half of Zeraf Island (the triangle enclosed by the Bahr el Jebel, Bahr el Zeraf, and White Nile; see map 1) (Howell, 1961:98). The Western Luaich currently reside in a territory due west of the southern half of Zeraf Island, but separated from it by Dok Nuer territory. This clearly suggests that the Luaich were split into two separate groups by the southward expansion of the Nuer during the centuries prior to 1800. We know that the Nuer territorial domain encompassed this area in the 1800s (Fergusson, 1921:154), and that the westward displacement of the Western Luaich occurred before that date.

As with the Luaich, the Twij are split into two widely separated groups. The Western Twij trace their origin to the area presently inhabited by the Eastern Twij (see map 1). Oral traditions hold that a segment of the Twij crossed to the west bank of the Bahr el Jebel at Shambe and resided for some time among the Chich Dinka (Lienhardt, 1961:186). Conflict between these two groups precipitated the westward migration of this branch of the Twij. This migration entailed movement into the territory of an unrelated (i.e., non-Dinka) people whom the Twij fought and ultimately displaced (ibid.). Some Rek Dinka clans possess very similar myths that include an ultimate origin east of the Bahr el Jebel, a passage through Chich and Agar territory, and finally the displacement of a non-Dinka population (referred to as the Lwel) that held the region beyond the borders of the Chich and Agar (Lienhardt, 1961:177).

Little is known concerning these former inhabitants of the Bahr el Ghazal province and their probable linguistic and cultural affinities need not concern us here (see Santandrea, 1967, for an extended discussion of this issue). However, they are described in Dinka oral traditions as a people who built (and lived on) large flat-topped mounds, and the distribution of the latter attests to the fact that they previously occupied much of what is currently Western Dinka territory (west of a line from Tonj to Meshra er Req). The recent excavation of one of these mounds (at 9° 0'N, 28° 21'E) indicates that the earlier inhabitants differed from the Dinka in burial customs, in the absence of the practice of dental evulsion, and in the utilization of a humpless variety of cattle (David et al., 1979:53–54). The central part of this mound contains a sequence of burials, culminating in

the mass disposal of at least fourteen adults, who although wearing ornaments were only roughly laid out and covered with a little clay and earth. Burials then ceased in this part of the site which, from the homogenization of the deposits, would appear to have been thereafter used as a cattle pen. (Ibid.:54)

This intriguing burial may mark the transition from Lwel to Dinka occupation of this site (although further excavation will probably be necessary to establish this). However, the preliminary archaeological evidence confirms that the Western Dinka presently occupy an area formerly inhabited by a culturally dissimilar population, and thus substantiates Dinka oral traditions in this respect.

The preceding discussion suggests that the westward expansion of the Dinka may have been related, at least in part, to the southward expansion of the Nuer. The Western Luaich appear to have been pushed west by the Nuer, and the Malwal, Western Twij, and Rek all moved west after residing for some period of time in the area between the Atwot enclave and the Nuer homeland. It is not unreasonable to suppose that Dinka populations in this area were compressed between these two points where Nuer expansion was taking place. In any event, it is clear that the Nuer (and Atwot) came to occupy a larger portion of the central and southern region of the Upper Nile Basin while the Dinka expanded to its western margins.

Dinka Expansion to the North

There was a general flow of Dinka population to the north as well as the west during the period under consideration. However, most of this movement probably occurred in the eighteenth century. The Ruweng (Kwil, Awet, and Alor) Dinka reportedly migrated to their present territory north of the Bahr el Ghazal between 1730 and 1780 (Johnson, 1980:29; Howell, 1954b:116). It is not clear where they resided immediately prior to this. However, they claim their ancestors were ultimately derived from the Bor and Twij Dinka. The Abialang, who migrated northeast at the same time, also claim the same antecedents. These two northern segments of the Dinka population may thus represent subdivisions of a common migrant population (from the Bor/Twij area) that occupied the area adjacent to the White Nile between the Zeraf and Sobat rivers in the early 1700s and moved to the northeast and northwest during the eighteenth century. No other Dinka tribes or tribal groups are reported to have occupied this particular region before 1700 and it thus constitutes the most probable staging area for Ruweng and Abialang migration.[3] The Thoi Dinka moved north into the portion of this area between the Zeraf and the Khor Fullus before the end of the eighteenth century (Howell, 1945:321; Johnson, 1980:79) and this probably coincided with the exodus of the Ruweng and Abialang.

Although the initial penetration of the area north of the Sobat may date to circa 1635 (Johnson, 1980:79), the bulk of the early settlement occurred between 1730 and 1780 (ibid.; Gleichen, 1905:129; Beavan, 1931:2; Bedri, 1948:40). The antecedents of the Abialang established themselves in the region during this period. Elements of the Dunjol moved north of the Sobat between 1800 and 1826 (see the Appendix) and many Dinka tribesmen displaced by Nuer expansion took refuge there between about 1826 and 1860.

The area into which the Abialang (and later the Padang and Dunjol) migrated was dominated by the Funj kingdom of Sennar until the mid-eighteenth century, and the northward expansion of the Dinka coincided with, and was facilitated by, a contraction of the Funj domain. This was a product of rebellion and intertribal wars in the north that increasingly occupied the Funj army after 1758 and culminated in the effective political dissipation of the kingdom in 1786 (Gleichen, 1905:229). In about 1775, the Dinka successfully expelled the Arab population of Funj subjects from what is currently Abialang territory (Johnson, 1980:76; Gleichen, 1905:129).

The Funj (Fung) kingdom consisted of a substantial urban center, located at Sennar, that exercised political domination over a large peripheral region that extended far to the south (James, 1977). A standing army that included more than fifteen thousand men in 1772 provided at least part of the basis for this domination. Although the administrative structure of the kingdom is not well known, it is evident that tribute was exacted from the peripheral region. This took the form of gold from the Blue Nile Valley and slaves from the "southern hills" adjacent to the area currently occupied by the Northern Dinka. Sennar was connected by caravan routes to the regional trade networks of the Middle East, and gold and slaves appear to have been its principal exports. Early descriptions of Sennar date from 1522. (See James, 1977, for a discussion of historical sources.) It is likely that the Funj constituted an impediment to Dinka occupation of the area north of the Sobat from at least 1600 to 1758. The Funj are probably also responsible for the fact that the powerful Shilluk Kingdom is confined to the west side of the Nile.

It is important to note that Dinka expansion to the west and north coincided with a series of internal migrations and relocations. A number of these emanated from the west bank of the Bahr el Jebel and may have been precipitated by the southward expansion of the Nuer, on one hand, and the establishment of the Atwot enclave on the other. The Chich (Cic) Dinka were formerly much further north and were pushed south to Lake Jur sometime before 1800 (Johnson, 1980:768; Fergusson, 1921:154) and still further south to their present location in the latter half of the nineteenth century. The Angai originally occupied the area around Lake Jur and migrated east across the Bahr el Jebel sometime before 1800 (Wyld, 1930). It would appear that they were displaced by the Chich who were pushed south by the Nuer. Similarly, the Leit section of the Twij Dinka is said to be a "foreign element" that migrated across the Bahr el Jebel from a territory on the west bank near Shambe, about twenty miles south of Lake Jur (ibid.). Ghol oral traditions recount that they were formerly southern neighbors of the Aliab and migrated some distance northeast to the vicinity of their present territory (ibid.). Ghol territory would thus have abutted that of the Atwot, and it is likely that their migration was related to Atwot occupation of the area (or subsequent Atwot expansion). The area into which the Ghol moved was adjacent to Thoi territory (Johnson, 1980:768; Howell, 1945:321). It has already been noted that the Thoi migrated north to the Zeraf hills and that this may have been related to Ruweng and Abialang migration to the northwest and northeast, respectively.

We do not know the precise temporal sequence of the various migrations described here and no firm conclusions are warranted. However, available evidence suggests that Nuer expansion within the homeland region may have played a role in Dinka expansion toward the periphery of the area delineated by the flood plain of the Upper Nile Basin. It is evident that Nuer (and Atwot) expansion did take place during the same general time period (i.e., 1500 to 1800). A coincident expansion of both center and periphery can thus be documented, but a causal relation between them cannot be firmly established. However, after 1800 it is clear that Nuer expansion and displacement of the Dinka provided the impetus to Dinka migration toward the margins of this ecological zone, and this may have been true of the period from 1500 to 1800 as well.

It is worth emphasizing the most obvious conclusion that emerges from the preceding discussion, namely that nineteenth-century Nuer expansion was hardly a unique event. It was, rather, the culmination of an extended process whose main features are quite clear. Nuer-speaking peoples progressively appropriated territory in the center of the Upper Nile Basin and Dinka-speaking peoples progressively expanded to the northern and western margins of this ecological zone (of some 160,000 square miles).[4] We shall see that the Nuer assimilated an extraordinary number of Dinka and it is likely that the Dinka likewise assimilated most of the former inhabitants of the periphery. The most prominent feature of this remarkable transformation is thus the replacement of one set of cultural systems by another, i.e., an "ecological succession" of cultural forms.

Nuer and Dinka expansion during the period from 1500 to 1800 is too far removed from the historical period (and the ethnographic present) to be susceptible to any detailed explication. The data are not sufficient to provide plausible answers to any of the intriguing questions it raises. However, the Nuer expansion of 1800 to 1880 poses much the same questions and is sufficiently well known to make it possible to answer them. A detailed analysis of this final phase of Nuer expansion can thus enhance our understanding of the larger process of which it was a part.

NUER EXPANSION AND DINKA DISPLACEMENT DURING THE NINETEENTH CENTURY

At the beginning of the nineteenth century the Nuer were confined to the area presently occupied by the Bul, Leik, Western Jikany, Jagei, and Dok tribes, west of the Bahr el Jebel and north of 7°52′north latitude. By the end of that century the Nuer had pushed eastward to the Ethiopian escarpment and south to about 7°21′ north latitude, cutting a hundred-mile-wide swath through the center of Dinka territory and expelling all but a few pockets of Anuak from the Sobat River area. In all, the Nuer increased their territorial domain four-fold, from about eight thousand seven hundred to thirty-five thousand square miles. The bulk of these enormous territorial gains were secured in the short span of sixty years, during the period from about 1820 to 1880. (See the Appendix regarding the dating of the main events and phases of Nuer expansion.)

In broad outline, nineteenth-century Nuer expansion may be described in terms of two principal movements. The first of these was the Jikany migration that eventuated in the establishment of an enclave on the Sobat River more than one hundred miles from the Nuer homeland. This was followed by the second wave of Nuer expansion, spearheaded by the Lou and Gaawar, that proceeded almost due east through the heart of Central Dinka territory to the border of the Jikany enclave. These two movements were independent and did not constitute elements of some coordinated strategy. On the other hand, it is evident that the Central Dinka were, in effect, flanked by the Jikany and caught between the two main thrusts of Nuer expansion. This undoubtedly played a role in the rapidity of the Nuer conquest.

As we have already noted, the Jikany migration paralleled that of the Atwot several centuries earlier. In both cases a Nuer group passed through (or around) adjacent Dinka tribes and established an enclave on the periphery of Dinka territory more than one hundred miles from the Nuer homeland. More-over, in both instances there was a subsequent expansion of the Homeland Nuer toward this enclave. At a general level, nineteenth-century Nuer expansion thus conformed to the pattern of the preceding era. The principal difference pertains to the second phase of this sequence. The Nuer were much more successful in appropriating the territory of neighboring Dinka tribes after 1800 than they had been during prior centuries. This indicates a shift in the relative military (or raiding) capabilities of the Nuer and Dinka (a shift that will be elucidated in subsequent chapters). In short, nineteenth-century Nuer territorial expansion may be seen as a more effective version of an earlier pattern of expansion.

In considering the context of nineteenth-century Nuer expansion, it is important to recall that Dinka population movements during the preceding centuries altered the conditions along Nuer borders in the north and west. The Western Twij replaced the Lwel opposite the Bul Nuer and a substantial population of Ruweng Dinka occupied the entire northern rim of Nuer territory between 1730 and 1780. By the end of the eighteenth century all potential avenues of expansion in these areas were blocked by the Dinka, who now surrounded the Nuer on all sides. The Jikany migration of the early 1800s thus took place in the context of this recently completed envelopment.

The fact that the Jikany Nuer migrated, rather than expanding at the expense of the neighboring Ruweng Dinka, appears to have been a product of the particular relationship between these two groups. Johnson (1980:95–96) reports that there was substantial intermarriage between adjacent Jikany and Kwil Ruweng sections and that the Jikany supported the latter in their conflicts with other Ruweng. It may be argued that extensive ties of kinship and affinity inhibited the development of the preconditions for territorial appropriation. Nuer expansion against neighboring Dinka tribes typically followed a protracted period of intensive raiding in which the burning of settlements, destruction of crops, and theft of cattle eventually precipitated a Dinka withdrawal. Such sustained and intensive conflict was unlikely to develop between closely intermarried groups. Although oral traditions record that the Jikany migration was preceded by conflict between Jikany sections, and between the Jikany and Bul Nuer (Johnson, 1980:96), the externalization of this conflict through segmentary processes[5] was inhibited by intermarriage with the neighboring Dinka tribe. This interpretation accounts for a seemingly paradoxical feature of Jikany history, namely, the fact that they did not appropriate neighboring Ruweng territory yet expanded readily against Dinka (and Anuak) groups once they reached the Sobat.

The beginning of the Jikany migration cannot be dated to a specific year. Available evidence indicates that it probably commenced sometime between 1817 and 1826 (see Appendix). Oral traditions pertaining to the migration have been recorded by a number of different authors and these are largely consistent with respect to the main features of the route (see Stigand, 1919:226; Bacon, 1922:115; Jackson, 1923:78; Johnson, 1980:97–98). The Jikany first proceeded north to Jebel el Liri on the edge of Nuba territory and thence along the border area between the Nuba and the Shilluk. They then cut across Shilluk territory in the vicinity of Melut and crossed the Nile into Northern Dinka country (see map 1). After fighting the Dinka and reportedly capturing many of their cattle, the Jikany turned south and proceeded to the lower Sobat River, settling temporarily in the area between Abwong and the border of Shilluk territory near the Nile. From here they pushed upstream along both sides of the Sobat to the vicinity of their present territory.[6]

Shilluk oral traditions are consistent with the Nuer account presented above concerning the northern route taken by the Jikany, their crossing through Shilluk territory near Melut, and their temporary settlement on the lower Sobat bordering Shilluk country (Johnson, 1980:97). However, the two cultural groups differ in their accounts of various conflicts between them. The Shilluk hold that the *reth* Awin recruited the Jikany to aid in subduing a rebellion in the southern part of Shilluk territory. When the Nuer subsequently extended their raids to loyal subjects, Awin rallied his forces and defeated them (Riad, 1959:161; Johnson, 1980:98, 686). The Shilluk also take credit for dislodging the Jikany from the lower Sobat and precipitating their movement upstream. The Jikany, on the other hand, maintain that they defeated Awin's forces and drove the latter from Fashoda (Jackson, 1923:78). In Jikany oral traditions there is no mention of having been defeated in battle by the Shilluk or pushed upstream by Shilluk raids. There are no grounds for adjudicating the differences between these two cultural accounts. However, we may safely conclude that there was a period of conflict between the Jikany and Shilluk before the former moved up the Sobat to their present territory.

Consideration of environmental and economic factors suggests that the movement from the Jikany homeland to the Sobat was accomplished relatively quickly. The Nuer could only have crossed the Nile at Melut during the dry season. Jikany oral traditions recorded by Stigand (1919:226) state that the Nile was unusually low, indicating that the migration also took place during a particularly dry year. However, the area to the north of Shilluk territory through which the Jikany passed would be unsuitable for cattle under these conditions and the Nuer must consequently have traversed it rapidly.

The limited food resources available to the Jikany during the course of their migration would impose similar constraints. In the ethnographic present, grain provides more than two-thirds of the calories in the Nuer diet (Howell, 1954e: fig. E12). The Jikany could not have carried much more grain than they would need for seed purposes and would not be able to harvest their first crop until about four months after they settled at a new location. In the meantime, it would be necessary to subsist largely on cattle products, supplemented by fish and collectible wild foods. One may conclude that the Jikany must have possessed very substantial herds. It is also likely that they sought to quickly establish themselves at a location where they could resume the agricultural component of their transhumant economy and reduce their reliance on cattle products. This suggests a rapid migration.

The Jikany migration encompassed not only fighting men, but also women, children, and large numbers of cattle. Such a group would have been vulnerable to attack and this may explain the roundabout route taken by the Nuer. The distance along a direct route from the Jikany homeland to the mouth of the Sobat is only about a third of the distance actually covered by the migrants. However, the longer route had the advantage of taking the Nuer through an area north of the Shilluk that would have been unoccupied during the dry season. The fact that the Jikany elected this route suggests that they sought to avoid conflict during the course of the migration itself.

The area along the lower Sobat where the Jikany first settled was appropriated from the Dunjol Dinka, who reported to an early missionary that they were pushed northward by the Nuer (see the Appendix; Beltrame, 1975[1861]:130). Jikany occupation of this area appears to have been brief. It is unlikely that the Jikany migration began before 1817 and we can be relatively certain that they had already moved up the Sobat beyond Abwong by 1826. The period of their stay on the lower Sobat thus could not have exceeded ten years and was probably considerably less. In sum, the Jikany probably covered the distance from their homeland to the lower Sobat during a single dry season and remained in the latter area for only a few years before proceeding upstream. Historical sources indicate that the Jikany were securely established throughout an extensive area approximating their present territory by the late 1850s (see Appendix).

The Northern Dinka area through which the Jikany passed, and in which they briefly settled, was invaded by the Egyptian Army in 1821 and 1827. Although this does not appear to have had any bearing on the Jikany migration, the possible significance of this external intrusion nevertheless requires discussion. In 1820, the northern Sudan was conquered by the invading army of Muhammed 'Ali, the ruler of Egypt (which was then a province of the Ottoman Empire) (Gray, 1961:2–3). In one of the campaigns of the following year, Muhammed 'Ali's forces reached Northern Dinka territory. They fought the Abialang Dinka at Renk with mixed results. Gleichen (1905:129) reports that the Abialang prevailed in some battles but were ultimately forced to withdraw. They retreated south to the upper reaches of the Khor Rau, where they were "completely routed" by the invaders, who "seized and carried off their cattle" (ibid.). Nevertheless, it was the Egyptian Army that withdrew at this juncture and Johnson (1980:82) argues that they were forced to retreat. Casualties on both sides appear to have been substantial.

In 1827, the Egyptian Army again invaded Northern Dinka territory and on this occasion they penetrated as far south as the Sobat River. Although Muhammed 'Ali's forces succeeded in capturing a number of Dinka (for enslavement in the north), this campaign also was met by substantial Dinka resistance and was quite costly in terms of casualties (ibid.). The Egyptians again withdrew quickly and no other major campaigns were carried out in the area until 1863 (Gleichen, 1905:129). The return of the Egyptians at that time was provoked by Dinka raids that penetrated as far as Karkoj, 110 miles northeast of Renk (ibid.). Between 1827 and 1863 the Abialang had only to contend with raids by the Arab tribes they had pushed out of the area in 1775, and with whom they had long been in conflict. Although the Arabs were often aided by contingents of Egyptian forces, the pattern of raid and counterraid differed little from that which preceded the arrival of the Egyptians. The Abialang continued to hold the area they had appropriated in the eighteenth century and to carry out raids far to the north.

Jikany oral traditions lack any reference to the Egyptian incursions. This indicates that the Jikany had already migrated upstream from the lower Sobat River area before the Egyptian campaign of 1827 (which penetrated as far south as the Sobat). The Jikany enclave was established to the southwest, in an area unaffected by external intrusions. It is also important to recall that the Jikany migration from their homeland to the lower Sobat may have taken place during any year between 1817 and 1826. It may therefore have occurred before the Egyptian campaign of 1821. The latter would also have had no significant effect on the migration, even if this occurred after 1821. The point at which the Jikany entered Northern Dinka territory was fifty miles south of Khor Rau—where the Abialang fought the Egyptians in 1821—and in an area inhabited by other Dinka groups. The Jikany did not attempt to settle in this area (near Melut) but proceeded south to the Sobat. Inasmuch as the area through which they passed was well outside the zone of conflict between the Dinka and Egyptians, it is difficult to see how this conflict could have affected the Jikany migration. There is no reason to believe that the capacity of the Dunjol Dinka to resist Nuer settlement on the Sobat was in any way altered by events in Abialang territory far to the north. (The general question of the potential effect of external influences on nineteenth-century Nuer expansion is more fully examined in the Appendix. The conclusions reached there will be introduced into the discussion when appropriate.)

Jikany expansion in the eastern region was rapid and extensive. The Jikany began to move up the Sobat by 1826 and by 1860 occupied an area that extended from the high ground in the north central part of what is presently Lou Nuer territory in the west to the foothills of the Ethiopian escarpment in the east (see Appendix; Johnson, 1980:101; Bacon, 1922:115). The Jikany dominated this region, although it continued to contain pockets of Dinka and Anuak settlement that were not assimilated until well into the present century. While the initial Jikany conquest was less than complete in this respect, the extent of the territorial gains secured within a period of about thirty-five years is nevertheless remarkable. The Jikany domain in 1860 was about the same size as the entire Nuer homeland in 1800.

The Jikany enclave was established at the expense of both the Anuak and the Dinka. The former occupied the land adjacent to the Sobat and its major tributaries while the latter held the inland territory on both sides of the river system. The full extent of Anuak territorial losses during the nineteenth century are described in detail by Evans-Pritchard (1940c:8).

The traditions of both Anuak and Nuer and the reports of travellers suggest that a century ago Anuak occupied parts of what is now Jikany Nuer country to the north of the Sobat, parts of what is now Jikany and Lou Nuer country to the south of that river, the banks of the Pibor to its junction with the Sobat, and the banks of the Sobat to within a few miles of Abwong. The Ballak people, who still occupy the right banks of the Sobat slightly to the east of Abwong recognize that they are partly of Anuak descent, though they all speak Dinka today, and pockets of Nuer who admit their Anuak origin are to be found at the mouth of the Nyanding and elsewhere on the Sobat.[7]

The bulk of the former Anuak inhabitants of the Sobat were pushed into the upland region to the southwest that they currently occupy (see map 1), while the remnants of the Anuak population that remained in the area were ultimately assimilated by the Nuer (as noted in the passage cited above). The Padang Dinka, who formerly occupied the inland area on both sides of the Sobat (Howell, 1961:98), were likewise displaced by the Nuer and migrated northward to their present territory on the White Nile. A substantial number of Padang Dinka were also assimilated by the Lou and Eastern Jikany (Evans-Pritchard, 1940a:221; Johnson, 1980:180). There may also have been other smaller Dinka tribes residing north of the Sobat that have disappeared as tribal entities through dispersion and assimilation. We know that more than half of the circa 1930 Lou and Eastern Jikany population of 124,000 persons was of Dinka extraction, and the rate of assimilation commensurate with this composition substantially reduced the population of Dinka tribes that had resided in areas appropriated by the Nuer.

Nuer appropriation of a particular area of Dinka territory was typically the culmination of intensive annual cattle raiding carried out over a period of years. A summary description of the main features of these raids will make the rapid expansion of the Jikany intelligible. Large-scale Nuer raids were carried out by a force of as many as fifteen hundred men organized into five columns that simultaneously attacked an equal number of Dinka settlements, coalesced to meet any counterattacks, and moved progressively deeper into Dinka territory. These large raiding parties commonly penetrated eighty miles into Dinka territory overrunning as many as thirty wet season settlements and capturing more than two thousand head of cattle. The force committed to an attack on any particular Dinka community typically outnumbered the defenders by better than three to one, rendering resistance futile. The Dinka consequently fled with as many cattle as they could salvage, leaving their settlements temporarily in the hands of the Nuer. Before departing with their captured cattle, the Nuer characteristically burned the habitations and destroyed the standing crops. Nuer raids often coincided with the main harvest season and the Dinka therefore suffered the loss of an entire year's supply of grain in addition to many of their cattle. Although they could return to their former settlements, they confronted not only the immediate hardship of famine but also the prospect of repeated Nuer raids in the following years. As a result, many Dinka settled elsewhere with kinsmen who could help them through a lean year. The ranks of those that remained were thus depleted, impairing their capacity to resist subsequent Nuer raids. This enabled the Nuer to progressively extend the scope and duration of their incursions year by year. Finally, the Nuer simply settled into the communities from which the Dinka had fled in the course of the latest of a sequence of annual raids, rather than returning to Nuer territory with their captured cattle.

Cattle raids were thus instrumental to both the enlargement of the Jikany enclave and the eastward expansion of the Lou and Gaawar. The data that support this conclusion, and document the preceding generalizations concerning the nature of these raids, will be presented later in the chapter. However, the significance accorded to cattle raids in Evans-Pritchard's (1940a:126–30) account of Nuer expansion should be noted here. This is evident in the following passage, which also fleshes out the general picture presented above.

> The raiders spent several weeks in Dinkaland and sometimes remained there throughout the dry season, living on the milk and flesh of captured cattle, on pillaged grain, and on fish. Using a captured kraal as a base, they extended their raids against distant camps. Nuer migrations seem to have been conducted on these lines, the raiders settling permanently in Dinka country and by systematic raiding compelling the inhabitants to withdraw farther and farther from the points of occupation. In the following season, a new series of raids was initiated and the process was repeated till the Dinka were compelled to seek refuge with their kinsfolk of another tribe and leave their country to its invaders. If settlement was not contemplated, however, the raiders returned home when they considered that they had sufficient booty. (Evans-Pritchard, 1940a:128)

The group that we have referred to as "the Jikany" included members of the aristocratic lineages of other Nuer tribes and was similar in composition to the tribal units described by Evans-Pritchard (1940a:203–11) in this respect. The Jikany migration thus encompassed some members of the Jinaca clan, whose lineages are the dominant or aristocratic lines within the Lou tribe (Evans-Pritchard, 1940a:211; Johnson, 1980:101). In the course of the Jikany expansion, these members of the Jinaca clan came to occupy the area to the west of the Sobat (Johnson, 1980:101). When the eastward expansion of the main body of Lou Nuer reached this area, these members of the Jinaca clan were redefined as aristocrats within the Lou tribe rather than "strangers" residing among the Jikany (and the territory they occupied become part of the Lou tribal domain). Lou oral traditions hold that the Mor primary section is derived from Jinaca lineages that accompanied the Jikany, while the Gun primary section stems from the Jinaca lineages that formed the leading edge of

Nuer eastward expansion through the heart of Central Dinka territory (Johnson, 1980:101).[8] At some point (probably during the 1850s) the Padang Dinka were thus caught in a vise between these two major components of the Lou Nuer. As noted earlier, many Padang were assimilated while others migrated north and relocated along the White Nile (where they presently reside). The reunion of the Lou thus connected the two main thrusts of Nuer eastward expansion.

The eastward movement of the Lou and Gaawar that initiated the second major thrust of Nuer territorial expansion began not long after the commencement of the Jikany migration (see the Appendix). The Gaawar, who formerly resided in the southern portion of Dok Nuer territory, crossed the Bahr el Jebel and settled on the edge of the swamp near the tip of Zeraf Island (Evans-Pritchard, 1940*a*:231; Howell, 1954b:208–9). The Lou, who originally occupied the southern part of Jagei territory,[9] crossed the Bahr el Jebel about fifty miles further north at about the same time (i.e., during the 1820s). These two footholds served as twin bases from which the Nuer extended their conquest, through raiding, in the manner described earlier. The Ngok (Ngork) Dinka, who held the northern half of Zeraf Island, withdrew under the pressure of Lou raids and migrated in two separate groups, westward to the Bahr el Arab and eastward to the area between the Khor Fullus and the Sobat (see map 1) (Howell, 1951:241). The Gaawar likewise pushed the Eastern Luaich (Luac) out of the southern half of Zeraf Island and the latter settled on the Khor Fullus opposite the Eastern Ngok. The expulsion of the Dinka from Zeraf Island was probably completed by the 1840s, since the Gaawar were already in possession of the high ground on the east bank of the Zeraf by the end of the following decade and had progressed as far as Luang Deng by 1865 (see Appendix; Johnson, 1980:95).

The northern portion of present-day Gaawar country east of the Zeraf was previously occupied by the Rut Dinka, who were pushed northward to the banks of the Nile (Howell, 1961:98). Both the Rut and Eastern Luaich appropriated sections of Thoi Dinka territory which had formerly extended from the Zeraf to the Khor Fullus (see map 1). Howell (1945:320–21) reports that the Thoi were "affected more by the influx of refugees than by the direct attacks of the Nuer, for the latter never occupied their country and have a contempt for it as cattle country." However, the Thoi were much reduced in both numbers and territory as a result of conflicts with the Rut and Luaich, who were "driven in upon them."

Conflict between Dinka refugees and the Dinka inhabitants of areas in which they sought refuge is also reported to have occurred in the Southern Dinka region (Wyld, 1930:5–6). However, this does not appear to have taken place in the northern area where the Padang and Eastern Ngok settled. It may be recalled that the decline of the Funj kingdom in the latter part of the eighteenth century markedly decreased resistance to Dinka expansion in the area north of the Sobat and east of the White Nile. As the Abialang pushed north displacing former Funj subjects, they seem to have left the area to the south of them thinly settled. This provided scope for accommodating the subsequent influx of Padang displaced by the Jikany. The Eastern Ngok settled on the lower Sobat, in the area from which the Jikany had formerly evicted the Dunjol (before moving upstream). This area was probably sparsely populated when the Ngok arrived. However, it was subject to Shilluk raids that may have played a role in dislodging the Jikany. Ngok settlement in this area may therefore have entailed conflict with the neighboring Shilluk rather than other Dinka (see Riad, 1959:241).

The eastward expansion of the Gaawar across the Bahr el Zeraf in the 1850s was paralleled by the eastward movement of the Lou further north. The Lak and Thiang Nuer crossed the Bahr el Jebel into the northern half of Zeraf Island, previously conquered by the Lou, and Howell (1961:98) suggests that the combined pressure exerted by these two tribes impelled the Lou further east. Upon crossing the Zeraf, the Lou confronted the Rut Dinka, who were also beset by Gaawar raids (further south) during this period. The Lou thus played a role in compressing the Rut into Thoi Dinka territory to the north. At least some of the Lou Nuer remained in what is presently the northern part of Gaawar territory until the early 1880s (Johnson, 1980:94). However, other elements of the Lou moved eastward at a much earlier date.

Although the progress of the Lou advance toward the borders of the Jikany enclave cannot be precisely dated, the maps and reports of early traders and explorers suggest that the Nuer occupied an area that extended from the Zeraf to the Sobat by the early 1860s (see Evans-Prtichard, 1940a:129; Johnson, 1980:101). However, the Duk ridge (which extends from forty kilometers north of Ayod through the latter to Duk Fadiat and Duk Faiwil) was still in the hands of the Dinka at this time (see Appendix). The corridor connecting Lou and Gaawar territory along the Zeraf with Lou and Jikany holdings along the Sobat was thus quite narrow at this point. In other words, the Lou bypassed the dense concentration of Central Dinka settlement along the Duk ridge and joined forces with the Lou (or Jinaca clan) elements who already held the area along the Sobat as far west as Nyerol on the Khor Fullus (Bacon, 1922:115).

Lou movement eastward along this path of least resistance had two important effects. First, the Padang Dinka were confronted with Nuer raids emanating from the northeast as well as the west. Second, the successful occupation of Padang territory by the Lou left the northern half of the Duk ridge surrounded on three sides by the Lou and Gaawar. The Ric Dinka who occupied this part of the ridge (Johnson, 1980:81) were consequently subject to raids by both of these powerful Nuer tribes in the 1870s (and eventually fell back upon the Nyarraweng Dinka to the south). The Dwor, who held a territory between the Padang and the Duk ridge (including part of the latter), were in a similar position and ultimately sought refuge north of the Sobat with the Padang (Howell, 1961:98; Johnson, 1980:81).

The irregular pattern of Nuer expansion tended to create pockets of Dinka settlement between areas appropriated by the Nuer. The Nuer seem to have made no effort to evict remnant groups but instead assimilated them over an extended period of time. Such assimilation was especially prevalent in the eastern region where the Padang and Dwor Dinka were caught between elements of the Lou Nuer and other Dinka and Anuak groups were similarly enveloped by the Lou and Jikany (Evans-Pritchard, 1940a:224).

After successfully completing the occupation of Padang Dinka territory by about 1870, the Lou directed their attention to the Nyarraweng Dinka in the south and the Anuak to the east. At this time Nyarraweng territory stretched from the Bahr el Jebel to the Khor Geni and included the portion of present-day Lou territory south of 8° N latitude (see map 1) (Wyld, 1930:5). By about 1880, the sparsely settled eastern half of Nyarraweng territory was largely controlled by the Lou.[10] The combined pressure of Lou and Jikany raids against the Anuak also induced the latter to progressively withdraw further up the tributaries of the Sobat to the upland region they currently occupy. Nuer expansion against the Anuak was completed sometime before the decade 1870 to 1880, the time period to which Evans-Pritchard dates the last Nuer attempt to occupy Anuak territory.

> Sixty to seventy years ago (the Nuer) advanced along the Akobo and Oboth and devastated the country, destroying most of the villages, including the populous village of Ukaadi, as far as the sacred rock "Abula," near Ubaa village, at the southeastern extremity of Anuakland. Here they are said to have eaten a tortoise which came out of the rock and to have died in large numbers. The Nuer, who seem to have been both Lou and Jikany, came with their wives and children intending to settle in the country and their hasty retreat along the Gila was probably due mainly to loss of stock from tsetse. The invasion badly broke up the Anuak. Many were killed and many died in the famine that resulted, though it was mitigated by the stores of millet they had hidden in deep holes in the ground before fleeing into the bush. Most of their cattle were stolen. This invasion was succeeded by raids on a large scale, but none penetrated as far eastward as the earliest intrusion and there was no attempt to settle in the main Anuak country. However, Nuer . . . frequently raided Anuak villages . . . Bottego and Michael refer to these raids. (Evans-Pritchard, 1940c:10)

In the eastern region, Nuer territory thus reached its maximum extent (and present boundaries) by no later than 1880. After this date the Lou and Jikany continued to raid the Dinka and Anuak for cattle but eschewed further territorial appropriations. With the exception of portions of the Duk ridge, Nuer territorial gains in the west and central regions were also completed by this date (see the Appendix).

While the Lou, Gaawar, and Eastern Jikany were expanding Nuer territory east of the Bahr el Jebel, the Nuong Nuer moved south along the west side of this river. In about 1845 the Nuong pushed the Chich (Shish) Dinka south from 7°52′ N latitude to 7°40′ and in 1876 further extended Nuong territory to approximately its present boundary at 7°20′ (Fergusson, 1921:154). The interval between these two phases of Nuong expansion is attributable to external influences. Merchants engaged in the slave and ivory trade established a trading station at Shambe in 1856, and their private armies aided the Chich Dinka in this vicinity in their conflicts with neighboring groups. This appears to have inhibited the southward movement of the Nuong for several decades. The resumption of Nuong expansion in 1876 followed shortly after the activities of the traders were curtailed in 1874, and at a time when the Chich were no longer able to enlist their armed support. (See the Appendix for further discussion of this point.)

The Homeland Nuer are not reported to have extended their territory in the north or west during the nineteenth century, and the final Nuong appropriation of 1876 thus marks the close of territorial expansion in the western region. The absence of westward expansion is not surprising given the fact that large areas of the Nuer homeland were vacated by the Lak, Thiang, Gaawar, Lou, Eastern Jikany, and Nuong.

The intervention of the merchants in local conflicts also had the effect of retarding Nuer expansion in the central region. In about 1865, several trading stations were established along the Zeraf, in Gaawar country, and inland at Ayod on the Duk ridge in Ric Dinka territory. An aspiring Gaawar leader (Nuar Mer) of the Radh primary section enlisted the support of these traders in a conflict with members of the Bar primary section who opposed his succession to the position of land priest. A protracted fued followed in which unusually large numbers of Gaawar were killed (and others enslaved). Nuar Mer also raided the Lak, Thiang, and Lou Nuer, as well as neighboring Dinka tribes to the south. His support among the Radh Gaawar became progressively more attenuated as a result of internal conflicts he generated, and his following increasingly came to be composed largely of Dinka (of the Thoi, Luaich, Rut, Ngok, and Dwor tribes). The withdrawal of the traders in 1874 left him vulnerable to his many enemies among the Gaawar, who were successfully united by Deng Lakka. In 1878, Deng Lakka led a raid on Nuar Mer's settlements in which the latter was killed and his followers dispersed with heavy losses. Shortly thereafter, the reunited Gaawar expelled the Ric Dinka from the northern half of the Duk ridge and forced the Ghol Dinka along their southern border to fall back on the Nyarraweng (as did the Ric). Gaawar expansion, which had been in abeyance during the nine years trading stations operated on the Zeraf, thus resumed shortly after the latter were disbanded in 1874. (The historical material presented here is largely drawn from Gray, 1961, and Johnson, 1980. See the Appendix for precise references and a more detailed discussion of this period.)

In the late 1870s and early 1880s, the Duk ridge Dinka were also subject to raids by the Lou Nuer, who had recently consolidated their position on the high ground about forty miles to the east. The Nyarraweng, who were densely settled in the vicinity of Duk Fadiat and Duk Faiwil, gradually succumbed to the combined pressure of Lou and Gaawar raids and withdrew to Faijing, about eight miles north of Kongor in Twij territory (*SIR* 177, 1909:16; Wyld, 1930:7). With the occupation of the southern half of the Duk ridge by the Lou sometime between 1885 and 1895, Nuer territory reached its maximum extent of approximately thirty-five thousand square miles. This part of the Duk ridge was restored to the Dinka by the British colonial administration in 1910, and the boundaries of Nuer territory depicted on map 1 were also established at that time. (These boundaries approximate the extent of Nuer territory in the early 1880s.)

The main phases of Nuer expansion may be briefly summarized here. The Jikany migration began sometime between 1817 and 1826 and the Lou and Gaawar invasion of Zeraf Island followed shortly thereafter. The appropriation of Zeraf Island was probably completed by the 1840s and the Nuong Nuer also extended their territory fifteen miles southward during this decade. By about 1860 the Gaawar held the high ground on the east bank of the Zeraf, the Lak and Thiang had moved into the northern half of Zeraf Island displacing the Lou, and the latter had reached the borders of the Jikany enclave (which extended from Nyerol to the Ethiopian escarpment). The relative positions of the Nuer tribes were thus established by this date (Evans-Pritchard, 1940a:130) and the Nuong, Gaawar, Lou, and Eastern Jikany were each entrenched in the northern portion of the territories they currently occupy. The general direction of Nuer expansion was primarily eastward until about 1860 and southward along a broad front thereafter. The northern area into which the Rut, Thoi, Eastern Luaich, and Eastern Ngok were compressed was regarded as inferior cattle country by the Nuer and the latter made no effort to appropriate it (Howell, 1945:320–21; Evans-Pritchard, 1940a:127).

The establishment of trading stations near Shambe in 1856, and along the Zeraf in 1865, had the effect of retarding Nuer territorial appropriation in these areas until the latter half of the 1870s. Nuong and Gaawar expansion resumed shortly after the Zeraf stations were disbanded, and the activities of the Shambe station curtailed, in 1874. However, the Lou and Eastern Jikany were unaffected by such external intrusions and continued to expand southward during the 1860s and early 1870s.

The final thrusts of Nuer territorial expansion commenced between 1870 and 1880 throughout Nuerland. The Nuong moved south to their present borders in 1876 and the Gaawar began a rapid occupation of the northern half of the Duk ridge in 1878. The Lou and Eastern Jikany launched a massive invasion of upland Anuak territory that penetrated to its extreme southeast border during the same decade. Although the Nuer had intended to settle in the areas along the Akobo and Oboth from which they evicted the Anuak, they withdrew rapidly after trypanosomiasis reduced their herds (Evans-Pritchard, 1940c:10). The Nuer made no further attempts to appropriate upland Anuak territory thereafter.

By 1880, Nuer territorial expansion was largely completed. Part of the Duk ridge was the only significant block of territory added after that date. The Gaawar made substantial gains in the occupation of the northern half of the ridge between 1878 and 1883 and the Lou completed the expulsion of the Dinka from the southern half sometime between 1885 and 1895 (see Appendix). Overall, the pace of Nuer expansion began to slow significantly in about 1880 (or the early 1880s) and had virtually ceased by the early 1890s. Although the Nuer continued to raid the Dinka and Anuak for cattle, they did not occupy all the areas from which the Dinka withdrew as a result of these raids. In the early 1900s, extensive uninhabited areas separated Nuer and Dinka settlements along the southern borders of both Nuong and Gaawar territory (*SIR* 177, 1909:16; *SIR* 323, 1921:12). In both cases, these were areas where the Nuer had been aggressively occupying former Dinka settlements several decades earlier. In general terms, the period from about 1880 to 1900 was characterized by cattle raiding and the assimilation of pockets of Dinka and Anuak settlement within areas already controlled by the Nuer, rather than the active occupation of new territory. The bulk of Nuer territorial expansion was accomplished during the relatively brief period from about 1820 to 1880.

The virtual cessation of Nuer territorial expansion in the early 1890s corresponds quite closely with the introduction of rinderpest, which can be dated to this same period (see the Appendix). The slowing of Nuer expansion in the early 1880s likewise corresponds to the introduction of other less serious epidemic cattle diseases. The earliest of these is difficult to date but probably entered the area sometime between 1872 and 1885 (see Appendix). Others followed between this period and 1890. Mortality rates among the cattle population thus increased from at least the early 1880s onward. Nuer herds first ceased to grow as rapidly as they are capable of growing and then, with the introduction of rinderpest in the early 1890s, began to decline rapidly in numbers. It will be argued in later chapters that these herd reductions resulting from rinderpest (and other introduced cattle diseases) initiated a chain of events that dissipated the forces behind Nuer territorial expansion. It is sufficient here simply to note the temporal correspondence between these two sets of events, and to point out that Nuer expansion ceased long before the Anglo-Egyptian colonial administration became a significant factor in Nuer-Dinka relations. The British suffered extensive reverses in the northern Sudan during the Madhia (1881–98), and their presence in the Upper Nile Basin was quite attenuated until after the reconquest of the Sudan was completed (see Appendix). The earliest efforts to control raiding and fix the boundaries between the Nuer and Dinka date to 1908–10 and were largely ineffective until 1917.

The preceding account has been largely concerned with the dates and phases of nineteenth-century Nuer expansion, and with successive changes in the disposition of tribal groups and territories during this period. We now turn to a more detailed consideration of the character of Nuer-Dinka conflict and to the fate of the very substantial Dinka population displaced by the Nuer.

NUER RAIDS AND THEIR EFFECTS ON THE DINKA

The vast area appropriated by the Nuer during the nineteenth century was formerly occupied by a Dinka and Anuak population that can be estimated to have numbered at least 186,000 persons.[11] The fate of this population is one of the most interesting questions pertaining to Nuer expansion. How many Dinka were killed by the Nuer? How many died of starvation? How many migrated to other areas? How many were assimilated? The answers to these questions are of considerable theoretical as well as intrinsic interest. Arguments that rely on population pressure as the critical causal factor in Nuer expansion logically presuppose the expulsion of the Dinka from areas seized by the Nuer. If overpopulation and land shortage prompted Nuer territorial acquisition, the extensive assimilation of the inhabitants of conquered territory would make little sense. In short, the fate of the former Dinka and Anuak inhabitants of areas appropriated by the Nuer is entwined with Nuer demographic history, and data pertaining to both are important to understanding the causes of Nuer expansion.

Although Nuer territorial appropriation had virtually ceased by the early 1890s, the Nuer continued to raid the Dinka for cattle until 1928. Government records contain information on twenty-six Nuer (and three Dinka) raids that took place between 1905 and 1928. Although the reports of particular forays are each incomplete, this material can be pieced together to establish a composite picture of the timing, scope, and duration of Nuer raids. The general outlines of Nuer military organization and tactics can be ascertained. In some instances these records also provide specific information concerning the number of Dinka settlements attacked, the number of people killed and captured, and the number of cattle stolen. These data elucidate the devastating consequences of Nuer raids and clarify the role that raiding played in Nuer expansion. In addition, the data on captives and casualties will provide a basis for assessing the effects of Nuer raids on the Dinka population under attack. By projecting this information back in time to the period of Nuer expansion (which had only recently ended), we can partially answer the questions posed above concerning the fate of the Dinka (and Anuak) inhabitants of areas appropriated by the Nuer.

Three large-scale Nuer raids against the Southern Dinka that took place in 1914, 1916, and 1928 are of particular interest. In each of these instances the Nuer penetrated eighty miles into Dinka territory and twice captured over three thousand head of cattle. These raids were, in many respects, comparable to the initial thrusts of the Nuer during their earlier period of territorial expansion, and document the scale of devastation wrought by Nuer aggression. In other respects they differed. The primary Nuer objective during this period was the acquisition of cattle rather than territory and the Nuer consequently withdrew quickly with their booty rather than extending their raids from bases established in captured Dinka villages. The efforts of the British colonial administration to suppress intertribal warfare also imposed constraints. A major offensive by the Anuak, who had recently acquired a large number of rifles, diverted Nuer attention from the Dinka. In order to understand the context of these Nuer raids, it will thus be necessary to examine the colonial conditions under which they took place, and to sketch the history of both Nuer-Dinka and Nuer-Anuak conflict during the early period of British administration (1900–1928).[12]

During the closing phase of Nuer expansion, the Gaawar and Lou Nuer pushed the Ric, Ghol, and Nyarraweng Dinka south as far as Faijing (at about 7°18′ N latitude) in present-day Twij country (*SIR* 177, 1909:16). In the first decade of the twentieth century the Nuer and Dinka continually raided each other for cattle along this border. These raids were intensified by severe rinderpest epidemics in 1905 (Johnston, 1934:26) and 1908 (*SIR* 165, 1908:3, 10) as each tribe sought to recoup its stock losses at the expense of the other.[13] The Nuer progressively gained the upper hand in these conflicts, and in 1906 launched a large-scale raid on the Faijing settlements that forced the Dinka to withdraw about eight miles further south to Kongor (*SIR* 177, 1909:16).[14] Cattle raids by both sides followed. Then in 1908 the Gaawar attacked the Dinka at Kongor, burning their crops and settlements and killing eleven men (ibid.).

In 1908–10, the British sought to end the fighting and establish control over the area. A new border between the Nuer and Dinka was established at Duk Fadiat, fifty miles north of Kongor, and the Ghol, Ric, and Nyarraweng were awarded about four thousand square miles of territory they had previously lost during Nuer expansion (ibid.). Although a substantial portion of this grant represented an uninhabited no-man's-land between the Nuer and the

Dinka, the Nuer were also required to relinquish territory under active occupation. They undoubtedly viewed the transfer as a government-sponsored
Dinka invasion. The Nuer were supposed to be content to receive the government's recognition of their right to retain the remainder of their earlier territorial gains. A minor case of cattle theft was settled in favor of the Nuer,
with restoration effected. The Nuer, on their part, were required to pay a
compensation of seventy head of cattle for the deaths inflicted by their most
recent raid. All other claims arising from incidents prior to June 1908 were set
aside. A police post was established at Duk Fadiat (in 1910) to maintain the
boundary and enforce the imposed settlement, and reports were filed touting
the prospects for the establishment of "law and order" (*SIR* 177, 1909:16–
17; *SIR* 189, 1910:4–5).[15]

In February, 1910, several months before the Duk Fadiat post was established, the Gaawar attacked a group of Ghol Dinka who had precipitously
reoccupied Faijing, killing nine individuals (*SIR* 187, 1910:5). In June, 1910,
the Nuer attacked the newly established government post itself. In April of the
following year a government patrol of 140 soldiers was dispatched to arrest
the "ringleaders" responsible. This was accomplished after a brief skirmish
in which eight Nuer were killed attempting to escape from a surrounded
settlement (*SIR* 201, 1911:5).

No further Nuer raids are reported along this border for several years.
However, this inactivity appears to have been due largely to the fact that the
Nuer were contending with a major Anuak offensive that penetrated to within
thirty miles of the Bahr el Zeraf. The sequence of Nuer-Dinka conflict will be
set aside briefly to take up this Nuer-Anuak clash, as it forms the backdrop for
the only successful large-scale Southern Dinka raid on the Nuer reported in
colonial records from this period.

Toward the close of the nineteenth century and during the first decade of
the twentieth, the Anuak acquired a large number of rifles from various
Ethiopian sources in exchange for ivory. By using these guns to hunt ele-
phants and procure additional ivory, they added to their armory. In 1911, they
were estimated to possess twenty-five thousand rifles as against one thousand
held by the Eastern Jikany, who had more limited contact with some of the
same sources (*SIR* 202, 1911:4). Possession of firearms enabled Anuak nobles
to enlarge the number of villages over which they exercised political control,
and this increased the fighting force they were able to mobilize against the
Nuer (Evans-Pritchard, 1940*c*:11). Having long been the victims of Nuer
raids, the Anuak then took the offensive. Twice during this period armed
expeditions were sent against the Jikany, but both were defeated. However,
the Anuak advantage in weapons increased significantly when they acquired
breech-loading (as opposed to muzzle-loading) rifles, and in 1911 they commenced a devastating series of raids (ibid.).

In June an Anuak party attacked several Lou Nuer settlements, capturing "a number" of women and cattle (*SIR* 203, 1911:3). The Nuer mobilized a large force and succeeded in recovering these losses, but thirty-five Nuer were killed in the initial Anuak raid and Nuer counterattack that followed (*SIR* 204, 1911:3). A second Anuak raid on another Lou community followed shortly. Thirty Nuer were killed, all the women and children captured, and 240 head of cattle stolen (*SIR* 205, 1911:4). In August, the Lou lost an additional five persons killed, an "unknown number" of women and children, and 150 head of cattle. In a September raid, twenty Nuer were killed and additional captives and cattle (150) taken (*SIR* 207, 1911:5). By October, the Anuak were reported to have established a base in Lou country (reduplicating the pattern of Nuer incursions). From this base they extended their raids as far as Awoi in the middle of Gaawar territory, killing a "considerable number" of Nuer and capturing "many" women and cattle. The Anuak force, led by Akwei-wa-cam, was reported to consist of four hundred well-armed men (*SIR* 207, 1911:2).[16]

At this point a gunboat was dispatched up the Sobat and Pibor rivers (ibid.). Anuak settlements on the Pibor were shelled, causing "considerable loss of life," and all accessible villages on the lower Akobo River were burned (Evans-Pritchard, 1940*c*:13–14). In March of the following year (1912), a punitive expedition was carried out against the Anuak noble (Akwei-wa-cam) and those of his followers who were actually responsible for the earlier raids on the Nuer. (Akwei-wa-cam's district was located on the upper Akobo, well beyond the limits of navigation that had circumscribed and defined the earlier gunboat expedition). Ninety Anuak were reported killed and a number of villages burned by the British-led Sudanese army column (*SIR* 214, 1912:3; Evans-Pritchard, 1940*c*:14). However, the government force of 439 men also suffered heavy casualties, losing 47 killed and 12 wounded (*SIR* 211, 1912:4; *SIR* 212, 1912:3).

During this same year (1912), the Jikany and Lou Nuer undertook their own reprisal against the Anuak.[17] The Nuer raid was directed against the Anuak villages on the north bank of the Baro River from the Ethiopian border to Itang, a distance of about fifty miles. Later reports indicated "All the villages in this formerly prosperous neighborhood have been devastated and their cultivations destroyed" (*SIR* 218, 1912:2–3).

This extended raid illustrates the Nuer capacity to mount a large-scale counteroffensive after experiencing a series of defeats. The key to Nuer effectiveness in this respect was their ability to comprise internal differences and unite in the face of external aggression. Government reports note that several Lou Nuer sections set aside long-standing feuds in order to combine against the Anuak (*SIR* 203, 1911:3). This documents one of the principal features of Nuer segmentary lineage organization described by Evans-Pritchard (1940*a*) and discussed more fully in a later chapter.

Nuer-Anuak raiding tapered off in 1913 and 1914 and virtually ceased after 1915. During this period there were five reported engagements, four of which were quite minor (*SIR* 235, 1914:3–4; *SIR* 237, 1914:5). Evans-Pritchard (1940*c*:14) attributes the cessation of raiding to a strong government presence at the Akobo post, first established only in 1911 as part of the punitive action against the Anuak. This interpretation seems accurate with respect to deterring the Anuak, and an absence of Anuak raids obviated the need for either retaliatory or preemptive strikes by the Nuer.[18] The Nuer then turned their attentions elsewhere. The most plausible interpretation for their lack of further interest in the Anuak would seem to be that cattle were more readily pillaged from other less well armed peoples who possessed them in greater numbers. Although the government presence at Akobo and other smaller posts undoubtedly had some effect, it is difficult to believe that this constituted a sufficient deterrent inasmuch as the Nuer showed no reluctance to carry out raids in close proximity to government posts elsewhere, and even to attack such posts directly, in the years that followed.

The Lou Nuer thus renewed their raids on the Dinka, while the Eastern Jikany attacked the Burun to the northeast. The latter were as yet outside the sphere of British administrative attention and could be raided without interference. The intensity of Jikany raids on the Burun later became apparent when colonial administration began to be extended into this area and reporting improved. There were seven Nuer raids in 1919 and four in 1920 before "systematic bombing and gunning" of Jikany settlements by the Royal Air Force (R.A.F.) ended the Jikany offensive (*SIR* 311, 1920:14).[19] However the manner in which the benefits of "law and order" were brought to the Jikany and other Nuer tribes in the 1920s comes much later in our continuing chronological account of Nuer raiding during the colonial period. Hence we return to the Southern Dinka region in 1912, the year following the major Anuak raids on the Nuer.

Sometime during the summer of 1912, Dinka tribesmen from the recently reoccupied Duk Fadiat area carried out a highly successful raid against the Lou Nuer, capturing "several thousand" head of cattle. No further details are reported (*SIR* 224, 1913:3). This raid evidently took place during the period between March and September when the Lou and Jikany were engaged in laying waste to a fifty-mile-long strip of Anuak settlements along the Baro River. The large number of cattle taken is thus partly attributable to the fact that Lou fighting strength was attenuated at the time. Although the Southern Dinka are said to have raided the Nuer before 1907, this is the only Dinka offensive that occurred after that date. In contrast, there were ten reported Nuer raids on the Southern Dinka between 1907 and 1918. The timing of this isolated Dinka raid thus seems to have been a product of their perception of a temporary advantage over the Nuer.

The Dinka near Duk Fadiat were raided by the Nuer (probably Lou) in

September, 1913. One Dinka was killed and "some" cattle stolen (*SIR* 230, 1913:3). The following month the Gaawar Nuer attacked the Dinka near Awoi, capturing a large number of cattle (*SIR* 231, 1913:3). In light of the "truculent attitude" displayed by the Gaawar in raiding the Dinka, "refusing to pay tribute," and firing on telegraph line workers, an army patrol was dispatched that ultimately confiscated eleven hundred cattle (*SIR* 233, 1913:3–4; *SIR* 234, 1914:4). However, it is unclear whether this number represents Dinka losses exclusively or also includes the unpaid tribute.[20]

This patrol was attacked by "about a thousand" Gaawar Nuer shortly after they were landed on the east bank of the Zeraf River. The Nuer were driven off and fifteen hundred head of cattle seized. However, the Nuer succeeded in stampeding and recapturing more than half of them during the following night (*SIR* 233, 1913:4). The patrol then moved eastward through Gaawar country, seeking to arrest the Nuer leader (Machar Diu) believed to be responsible for the raid on the Dinka. Three subsequent engagements between the Nuer and government forces resulted in the capture of twenty-two prisoners and an additional four hundred cattle. One soldier and a dozen Nuer were killed. However, Machar Diu escaped (*SIR* 234, 1914:4–5).

In early June of the following year (1914), Machar Diu led a raid on the Dinka a few hours' walk from Duk Fadiat. An unspecified number of cattle were captured, but Machar Diu and two other Gaawar Nuer were killed in the course of the raid (*SIR* 239, 1914:4).

Less than five days later, a large party of Lou Nuer crossed the government-delineated border and overran the Ghol Dinka area near Duk Fadiat, capturing three thousand head of cattle and inflicting "severe losses" on the Dinka populace (*SIR* 239, 1914:6). The police post was also attacked, but the Nuer were repulsed, losing twenty-six men while killing six policemen and wounding two in the engagement (Collins, 1971:199). The Nuer raiding party pressed south to within a few hours' walk of the government station at Bor, ninety miles deep into Dinka territory. In the course of these raids they captured "large numbers" of cattle, women, and children (in addition to the three thousand cattle noted above). In the area under attack, the Bor Dinka "suffered very severely, every family having lost all their cattle and many of their relatives" (ibid.). After a span of less than three weeks the Nuer successfully withdrew with their spoils. Two separate army detachments sent out on June 21 and 22 reached the area under attack after the Nuer had returned to home territory of their own accord (*SIR* 239, 1914:6; *SIR* 240, 1914:4–5).

Elements of the Ghol Dinka who fled the Nuer advance were reportedly harried by the Twij Dinka, who "stole all the women and cattle they could lay hands on" (*SIR* 240, 1914:5). Two other large groups of Dinka refugees moved north into Nuer territory in an attempt to evade the Lou onslaught and one of these was subsequently raided by the Zeraf tribes and relieved of all their cattle (*SIR* 240, 1914:3). There was a degree of intermarriage between the Nuer and Dinka along this border (Johnson, 1982:194) and these Dinka probably sought refuge with Nuer kin or affines. However, it is evident that kin ties with one Nuer tribal section did not invariably provide security against attacks by others.

In August, 1914, the Nuer again attacked the Duk Fadiat post but were "driven off." It is unclear whether this occurred in conjunction with a raid on the neighboring Dinka (*SIR* 242, 1914:4). The Southern Dinka were raided by elements of the Lak, Thiang, and Gaawar in October, but no details are reported (*SIR* 244, 1915:4). In December, the Gaawar were said to be "ruthlessly killing women and children of the Twi and Gol [Ghol] Dinkas" (*SIR* 245, 1914:3). Impending attacks on government posts were repeatedly reported to be imminent in the last quarter of 1914 and throughout 1915, although none materialized (*SIR* 244, 1914:4; *SIR* 245, 1914:3; *SIR* 247, 1915:5; *SIR* 252, 1915:5). However, this expectation kept government forces pinned down within their posts in late 1914 and none of the above-mentioned Nuer raids on the Dinka were investigated. The district administration clearly lacked confidence in their ability to protect the Dinka from Nuer raids during this period, inasmuch as rifles and ammunition were issued to the Dinka for their self-protection on two occasions (*SIR* 242, 1914:4; *SIR* 258, 1916:3). At this time the Lak, Thiang, and Gaawar reportedly had few rifles and no ammunition (*SIR* 248, 1915:4).

During the latter part of the 1914 rainy season (August through October), the Lak and Thiang each carried out separate raids on the Northern Dinka (Rut, Thoi, and Eastern Luaich). The Dinka were reported to be "very much scattered" by these raids and to have lost many of their cattle to the Nuer. The Rueng [Ruweng] Dinka "to whom they came for refuge, seized most of the rest" (*SIR* 246, 1915:4).

In May, 1916, the Nuer again struck deep into Dinka territory, penetrating to within sixteen miles of the Bor post (Johnston, 1934:12). At this point, a contingent of 300 Nuer tribesmen was spotted by Dinka scouts sent out to reconnoiter, and a large number of Dinka accompanied by a Sudanese army officer and six soldiers moved out to intercept them. After initial contact was made, the Nuer retreated with the soldiers and Dinka in pursuit. Employing a stratagem they were to use on other occasions, the Nuer thus drew their antagonists into an ambush. Suddenly, the Nuer were heavily reinforced and attacked in strength, scattering the Dinka and wiping out the army detachment. In this engagement and the Nuer raid that preceded it, 165 Dinka were killed while the Nuer lost only 30 men (Johnston, 1934:3; *SIR* 265, 1916).[21]

Not long after this decisive Nuer victory a native officer led forty riflemen and a large party of Dinka against the Nuer. Eighty-three Nuer and forty-two Dinka were killed in this encounter and over 1,000 cattle successfully recaptured (Johnston, 1934:3; *SIR* 263, 1916). However, the Nuer withdrew to home territory with 3,006 head of Dinka cattle and forty-six young women and children captured in the course of this extended raid (ibid.; *SIR* 265, 1916). The Nuer force that took part was largely composed of Lou and Gaawar tribesmen, but also included elements of the Eastern Jikany (*SIR* 265, 1916).

The following year (1917) the British launched a major punitive expedition against the Lou Nuer, resulting in the capture of 108 male prisoners, 4,496 cattle, 3,000 sheep and goats, and a "large quantity" of millet (Stack, 1917:9). Heavy casualties were said to have been inflicted on the Nuer in a number of engagements, but no precise figures are available.

In April, 1918, the Gaawar attacked the Southern Dinka along their common border, killing six individuals and capturing eighty cattle (*SIR* 286, 1918:3). From this date until August, 1925 (for which monthly reports are available), no further Nuer raids on the Southern Dinka are reported.[22] Some minor raids took place in 1926 and the Lou Nuer were thought to be planning a major offensive in 1927 (Coriat, 1939:230–33). This prompted a series of government patrols that sought unsuccessfully to arrest the prophet Gwek, believed to be the source of Lou "unrest." Government action included R.A.F. bombing of the pyramid of Dengkur, which was both a religious shrine and Gwek's home base (*SIR* 401, 1927:9).

In August, 1928, the Gaawar and elements of the Lou launched a large-scale raid that penetrated deep into Southern Dinka territory, following the now familiar pattern established in 1914 and 1916. Thirty villages were burned and the crops destroyed, eighty-seven Dinka were killed, one hundred women and children captured, and seven hundred cattle taken (Wyld, 1930:II–8). A Nuer raiding party with an estimated strength of fifteen hundred warriors (with one hundred rifles) also attacked the government post at Duk Faiwil in the course of this raid. The Nuer succeeded in driving off fifty head of government cattle but suffered heavy casualties: forty-eight men killed and eighty wounded (*SIR* 409, 1928:8).

The colonial administration responded with the "Nuer Settlement" of 1928–29. All the Lou Nuer were ordered to gather in two designated settlement areas during the dry season in an effort to separate Gwek and other recalcitrants from the elements more amenable to colonial administration. All those who failed to move to the designated areas were, in theory, subject to arrest and, in practice, fair game for marauding army patrols that sought to draw them into battle (Coriat, 1939:235).[23] This tactic succeeded and Gwek and a number of his followers died in battle at the Dengkur pyramid (ibid.). There were few Nuer raids during the remainder of the colonial period (to 1956), although Collins (1971:191) mentions five hundred cattle being taken from the Western Dinka as late as 1943.

The Nuer Settlement brings us to the ethnographic present. The battle at Dengkur took place in February, 1929, and Evans-Pritchard commenced his fieldwork among the Nuer in early 1930 at the behest of the government of the Anglo-Egyptian Sudan (Evans-Pritchard, 1940a:7–8).

The preceding account focuses on Nuer-Dinka conflict (and administrative attempts to suppress it) in the central region between the Bahr el Jebel and Sobat rivers. With a few exceptions, reported Nuer raids were confined to the Southern Dinka. The southern border between the Nuer and Dinka to the west of the Bahr el Jebel experienced analogous levels of conflict. The pattern of raiding in this area is quite similar to that already described and a complete chronological account would add little to the general picture that has emerged thus far. However, selected data that extend and supplement this picture may be briefly mentioned.

Government reports include information on nine Nuer raids on the Western Dinka and one Dinka raid on the Nuer between 1914 and 1922.[24] (The groups involved were the Nuong and Dok Nuer and the Chich, Western Luaich, and Agar Dinka.) The single Dinka offensive entailed an attack by at least two separate contingents that ended in a disastrous defeat in which one party lost three hundred men killed and another bolted with unspecified losses (*SIR* 253, 1915:3).[25] Dinka casualties from Nuer raids are differentiated by sex in two instances: nine men and seven women were killed in one attack and seven men and five women in another (*SIR* 299, 1919:4; *SIR* 336, 1922:6). One hundred women and children were captured in the former raid and "some" were reported taken in three others. The Nuer stole eight hundred cattle in one raid (*SIR* 333, 1922:8) and unspecified numbers in the other eight. Two additional large-scale raids that took place between 1923 and 1926 are noted by Digerness (1978:81).[26] In the first of these the Nuer seized forty captives and two thousand cattle and in the second over one thousand cattle. Twenty Dinka were killed in the former instance.

One of the important points that emerges from consideration of early-twentieth-century Nuer raids is the extent to which Dinka disunity undercut their resistance to Nuer incursions. The preceding account includes several instances in which Dinka refugees from Nuer raids were beset by members of neighboring Dinka tribes (into whose territory they had fled) and deprived of many of their remaining cattle. Wyld (1930:5–6) reports that this occurred regularly in the southern region.

> Being further removed from early incursions of the Nuer, the Twi, like the Bor, have suffered far less from yearly raids and have fattened upon their brother Dinka's misfortunes. There is no doubt that they (the Twi) regarded the yearly flight for refuge into their country by the Nyarraweng and Ric as a chance for profit and were in the habit of annexing a large percentage of the herds of these tribes when the latter retired disorganized upon them for support.

These thefts of Nyarraweng refugees' cattle by the Bor and Twij had further repercussions. A substantial number of Nyarraweng tribesmen displaced by Gaawar Nuer raids took refuge with the Rumjok segment of the Lou Nuer, with whom they had previously intermarried, and encouraged the latter to raid the Bor and Twij Dinka (Johnson, 1982: 191–92). The residence of this element of the Nyarraweng with the Lou Nuer provided them with a measure of security from Gaawar (as well as Lou) raids but, at the same time, depleted the fighting strength of the remaining Nyarraweng and left the latter even more vulnerable to the Gaawar. Both this internal division of the Nyarraweng and the depredations they suffered at the hands of the Bor and Twij undercut their capacity to defend their home territory against Gaawar incursions.

The case of the Nyarraweng provides insights into the processes by which the Nuer appropriated Dinka territory and assimilated a portion of its former inhabitants. Dinka disunity clearly facilitated this, and the two aspects of this disunity (within and between tribes) evident in the Nyarraweng instance were widespread. Johnson (1982:196–97) reports that "Some Twij were raided by the Lou while others joined the Lou in raids against the Bor." Rut and Angac [Angai] Dinka living among the Gaawar (who had appropriated their territory) likewise joined in raids on the Ghol, Nyarraweng, and Twij Dinka (ibid.:190, 199). Other Angac who resided among the Twij continued to be subject to Gaawar raids (ibid.:196). The Rut Dinka who were previously compressed into the territory north of the Gaawar were on good terms with the latter in the early 1890s, but were raided by the Lak and Thiang Nuer, and lost many of their remaining cattle to the Ruweng Dinka into whose territory they fled (Johnson, 1981:190; *SIR* 246, 1915:4).

This pattern of debilitating conflict between Dinka tribes confronted with external aggression was equally evident in earlier periods. Lienhardt (1958:108) reports that the Western Dinka tribes also failed to unite in confronting the depredations of slave traders in the latter half of the nineteenth century, but rather "harried each other in temporary alliances with the invaders until they began to understand the scale of subjugation which they were all inviting."

Dinka alliances with the Nuer had analogous effects. The alliance of a Dinka tribal section with a segment of one Nuer tribe provided security against raids by other Nuer only for that particular Dinka section, and only if the latter lived among their Nuer kin and affines. Moreover, the presence of such Dinka elements within a Nuer tribe did not deter them from raiding other Dinka (including, in some instances, other sections of the same Dinka tribe). Since Dinka refugees were often deprived of their cattle by members of other Dinka tribes, they were not reluctant to urge their Nuer hosts to raid the latter.[27]

A general characterization of large-scale Nuer raids, and their effects on the Dinka, can be developed from the material contained in government reports and the information provided by Evans-Pritchard.

> The favorite season for raiding Dinka was at the end of the rains, though they were also invaded at their commencement. Leek tribesmen told me that when they raided Dinka to the southwest they used to sleep the first night near the villages of the Wot tribe and the second night in the brush. They took no food with them and ate only what fish they might hastily spear on the way, travelling with all speed throughout the day and part of the night. On the third day they attacked the Dinka villages or camps at dawn. The Dinka seldom put up any resistance, but loosened their cattle and tried to drive them away. No one seized cattle till the enemy had been dispersed. Then each took what prizes he could, often not troubling to tether his captures but slashing their rumps in sign of ownership. Afterwards the beasts were tied up in the enemy's krall, the oxen being mainly slaughtered for food. If the Dinka gathered reinforcements and returned to fight they were met in full battle formation. Nuer fight in three divisions with two or three hundred yards between each, and if one division is engaged the others advance and retreat parallel to it according to the fortunes of war. A party of scouts are in advance of the central division and they charge up to the enemy, hurl their spears at them, and fall back on the main body. (Evans-Pritchard, 1940a:127–28)

This description provides a clear picture of the sequence of events in a typical Nuer raid. By drawing on available information concerning more than twenty-five reported Nuer raids on the Dinka during the early colonial period, we can both expand on and analyze Evans-Pritchard's observations regarding the seasonal nature of Nuer raids, the organization of raiding parties, the absence of any concerted Dinka resistance to an initial attack, the possibility of subsequent counterattack, etc. An assessment of the extent of Dinka losses in casualties, captives, and pilfered cattle will also provide a basis for addressing the questions posed earlier concerning the fate of the Central Dinka and Anuak population displaced by the Nuer.

Evans-Pritchard's generalization concerning the seasonal characteristics of Nuer raids on the Dinka is largely borne out by colonial records. Ten of twenty-three datable raids[28] were initiated in the period from August through November, during the last three months of the rainy season and the first month of the dry season. Eight raids took place in May and June, at the beginning of the rains, and the five remaining instances are scattered evenly among the other six months of the year. It is perhaps most accurate to say that raids might occur at any time, but infrequently took place at the height of the rainy season (in July) or during the bulk of the dry season (December through April). The savannah is generally inundated with several inches of water from about mid-June until the beginning of September (Evans-Pritchard, 1940a:54) and August raids coincide with reports of an unusually early break in the rains.

However, the favored periods for raiding the Dinka are not simply a function of the ease of movement across the savannah, which is greatest during the dry season (especially in December, when the burned-over grasslands have just regrown and the streams are still flowing). Nuer raids were timed so as to coincide with periods of planting and harvest, when Dinka herds were pastured close to their elevated wet season communities and agricultural sites. Attacks at these times had devastating effects on Dinka grain supplies, as well as their herds, and harvest-period raids offered prospects for capturing large stocks of stored grain.

More importantly, rainy season raids maximized the Nuer organizational advantage over the Dinka. During this period the Dinka were grouped into small clusters of communities isolated from their neighbors by long stretches of open savannah, in a seasonal mode of population distribution dictated by their economic adaptation to the environment. Although the Nuer conformed to the same requirements, their segmentary lineage organization enabled them to transcend environmentally determined disaggregation. In other words, Nuer social organization enabled men from a wide range of communities to unite in large-scale raids at a time when seasonal economic exigencies dictated a dispersed distribution among these scattered settlements. At the height of the dry season both the Nuer and Dinka would coalesce into multicommunity groupings and superior Nuer organizational capacities would be partially neutralized.

Large-scale Nuer raids undertaken at the close of the rainy season had markedly different effects on Dinka food supplies than those initiated during the early rains. The prospects for extending raids from established bases in Dinka territory also differed with respect to seasonal timing. In order to elucidate these two interrelated points it will be necessary to sketch the Dinka agricultural cycle and concomitant seasonal variations in reliance on different food resources.

Monthly variations in the contribution of different types of foods to the total diet are depicted in figure 1. These data are applicable to the "flood region" as a whole, which includes the Nuer homeland, the Central Dinka region conquered by the Nuer, and the Southern Dinka area subject to intense Nuer raids in the first quarter of the twentieth century.[29] Although the Dinka rely more heavily on agricultural products than the Nuer,[30] this general outline of seasonal food utilization is sufficient to bring out the differential effects of raids conducted at the beginning and end of the rains.

The Nyarraweng and Ghol Dinka plant a catch crop of maize, legumes, cucurbits, and quick-maturing sorghum (millet) near their homesteads as early as the commencement of the rains permits (in the April–May period). Under favorable circumstances this will produce a small harvest of the sorghum staple in June (Howell, 1954*b*:366–67). The main sorghum crop, which is

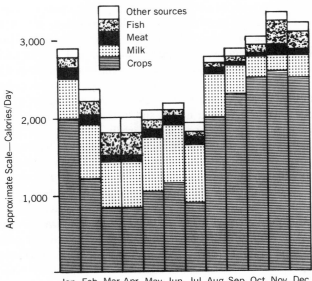

FIG. 1. Nutrition Levels in the Flood Region (*Source:* Barbour, 1961:247, fig. 96. Reprinted by permission.)

slower maturing but provides better yields, is planted a few weeks later and harvested in four to five months (i.e., August–September). Another late variety is planted in June and yields in five to six months (October–November).[31] A final crop of the quick-maturing sorghum is planted in September–October for a late harvest in November–December (ibid.).

Sorghum is stored in granaries at the wet season agricultural settlements and is accessible during the early dry season when cattle herds (and people) have not moved too far afield. By the late dry season (January–February) grain provisions run low and the population has moved to grazing areas along major water courses, too distant from the granaries to readily replenish their supplies (Howell, 1954b:245–46). The bulk of the remaining grain is consumed in March–April when the population returns (in stages) to the wet season settlements. Supplies then begin to run out and the months from May to the beginning of the main harvest in August generally constitute a "hungry period," partially alleviated in June by the catch crop (which is not always reliable). Unseasonable drought or flooding frequently impairs one or more of the four plantings and grain shortages are quite common (Howell, 1954b:367). Under these circumstances grain supplies are exhausted early and the "hungry period" is exacerbated.

Nuer raids during the most-favored period from August through November coincided exactly with the main harvest season. A year's supply of sorghum would be ripening in the fields and/or stored in the granaries. This enabled Nuer raiding parties to remain in Dinka territory for an extended period of time, subsisting on captured grain and cattle and extending their raids from bases established in captured Dinka villages. Even when the Nuer did not remain long in Dinka territory, they characteristically burned the settlement and destroyed whatever stored grain and standing crops they were unable to consume or carry off.[32] Since the main preoccupation of a Dinka community under attack was to escape with as many cattle as possible, the complete loss of community grain supplies was the typical outcome of all but the most minor Nuer raids. In the large-scale raid of August, 1928, thirty villages were put to the torch and the crops destroyed. This raid deprived an estimated nine thousand Dinka of a year's grain supply. Since grain provides the bulk of Dinka caloric intake (see fig. 1), there can be little doubt that raids of this scale produced severe and widespread famine conditions.

The Dinka had limited possibilities for responding to the famine conditions resulting from harvest-period raids. Unoccupied wet season agricultural sites (where exhausted soil was recovering fertility during the fallow period) could serve as temporary camps until the normal migration to dry season pastures commenced in November. Displaced Dinka would thus encounter no initial difficulty in finding adequate pasturage and dry footings for their remaining cattle. If the Nuer raid had come before October, there might still be time to plant a quick-maturing sorghum crop at this new location, provided that seed grain could be obtained. Wild fruits, roots, and seeds ripen at about the same time as agricultural crops and these "famine foods" could partially replace lost grain through the early dry season (Evans-Pritchard, 1940a: 72–75). In the later dry season game animals gather at limited pools and rivers where they can be readily taken by hunters (ibid.). Fish are normally an important part of the diet at this time and would continue to be available. Despite the utilization of these alternative food resources, displaced Dinka would confront a dire predicament. Grain normally provides 2,000 to 2,500 calories a day during the months from August through January (fig. 1) and the complete loss of the normal crop would create a deficit too large to be fully replaced by alternative sources of food.

However, the real crunch would come during the period from February to first harvest in June, when game and wild foods are unavailable and cattle products are normally utilized to the fullest extent. With reduced herds, no grain, little fish, and "famine foods" unobtainable, the Dinka confronted severe famine conditions during these months, when food resources are constricted even under normal circumstances. Labor requirements are also maximal at planting time and would be further increased by the necessity of

rebuilding dwellings and cattle shelters destroyed by the Nuer. The gap between caloric requirements and food intake would thus reach critical proportions. Although cattle might be slaughtered for meat, the slaughter of cows
(representing about 90 percent of the adult animals in Dinka herds) would
reduce milk supplies that constitute the only remaining major contribution to
the diet. When one considers that a large-scale Nuer raid resulted in the
capture of over three thousand head of cattle (representing the total per capita
holdings of about 1,850 Dinka),[33] and that the herds of displaced Dinka
tribesmen were further depleted by the depredations of their neighbors, it
becomes clear that famine was an inevitable outcome of large-scale Nuer
incursions. This was the principal factor that prompted the Dinka to withdraw
from border areas subject to recurrent Nuer raids and to seek refuge among
kin and affines residing elsewhere. Some of these impoverished Dinka also
joined the Nuer. Evans-Pritchard (1933:53) reports that

> many Dinka families came into Lou country to escape hunger and the other
> attendant miseries to which they had been reduced by constant Nuer raiding that
> left them cattleless.

Nuer raids undertaken at the beginning (rather than end) of the rains had
markedly different effects. Dinka villages would contain no recent harvests or
standing crops and the reduced supplies of grain on hand could probably be
carried by Dinka attempting to evade Nuer raiding parties known to have
entered the area. Lacking a supply of captured grain, the Nuer would not be
encouraged to operate from established bases in Dinka territory. The impending seasonal flooding of the savannah would also dictate early withdrawal
with whatever cattle they had acquired. The Dinka could consequently dis-
perse temporarily and still return to their villages by the time the June and/or
September millet crops were normally planted. Earlier crops that had been
destroyed could be replanted in quick-maturing varieties and future food
shortages could thus be minimized.

As noted earlier, the Nuer typically attacked a Dinka village at dawn
when the cattle were lodged in shelters or tethered near the homesteads. The
Dinka seldom offered any concerted resistance but rather sought to escape
with as many cattle as possible (Evans-Pritchard, 1940a:127). Later a counterattack might be undertaken with the aid of reinforcements from other
communities. This strategy of initial withdrawal conceded the destruction of
the settlement and, in harvest season raids, the loss of grain supplies. However, the failure of the Dinka to defend their communities is readily intelligible
when one considers the size of Nuer raiding parties. A single Dinka community was hopelessly outnumbered and physically isolated from allies that might
otherwise come to their aid. To refuse to give ground would have meant total
annihilation.

Fifteen hundred warriors participated in the Nuer raid of 1928 (*SIR* 409, 1928:8) and this probably represents the maximum size of Nuer raiding parties. However, the Nuer were capable of mobilizing even larger groups in defense of home territory. In direct confrontations with government punitive expeditions, the Nuer are twice reported to have fielded two thousand men (*SIR* 307, 1920:3, *SIR* 367, 1925:4). Titherington (1927:198) notes that a large Nuer raiding party was typically organized into five columns (or contingents) that simultaneously attacked a number of Dinka communities at separate locations. Given a total force of fifteen hundred, each of these contingents would consist of three hundred men, a figure consistent with the reported size of the component units involved in the large-scale raid of 1916 (Johnston, 1934:12). Minor raids on the Dinka were carried out by single groups composed of as few as two hundred Nuer (*SIR* 245, 1914:4). Available data thus indicate that Nuer raiding parties consisted of anywhere from two hundred to fifteen hundred men, with the larger forces subdivided into multiple contingents. A Dinka community under attack was thus typically confronted by a contingent of about three hundred Nuer.

A Nuer force of this size would outnumber the seventy-five fighting men of an average Dinka community of three hundred persons by four to one.[34] Aided by the element of surprise, the Nuer could readily overwhelm and annihilate the defenders before men of neighboring villages would have time to come to their aid. A Dinka community under attack thus had no effective recourse except to retreat salvaging as many cattle as possible.

The Dinka also employed several columns of about the same size in their raids on the Nuer, but there are no reported instances in which a Dinka raiding party exceeded six hundred warriors. The largest Dinka raid for which figures are available took place in 1915 when one contingent of three hundred Western Luaich Dinka was completely wiped out and another routed by the Dok Nuer in separate (but roughly simultaneous) engagements (*SIR* 253, 1915:3). Titherington (1927:188–89) also notes that the Raik (Rek) Dinka were incapable of mobilizing a five-column force comparable to that of the Nuer and were unable to successfully turn back Nuer incursions. In his view,

> had the Nuer ever wished to occupy the whole of Raik country systematically, it seems unlikely that the Raik could have stopped them.

The failure of the Dinka to unite on a large scale and the resultant numerical superiority of Nuer forces is a recurrent theme in the literature (cf. Lienhardt, 1958:198).

Five Nuer contingents of three hundred men each could simultaneously attack as many communities and later regroup at one or two captured villages with their stolen cattle to await any counterattack that might be launched.

Should the Dinka return with reinforcements, they would then confront the full force of fifteen hundred men. However, the mobilization of an equivalent number of Dinka warriors would require the full participation of all the fighting men of about twenty villages with a total population of six thousand. Political unity on this scale was rarely achieved by the Dinka and the Nuer were thus free to extend their raids deep into Dinka territory. (The average size of Nuer and Dinka tribes will be examined in chap. 4.)

The record of the early colonial period reveals that the Dinka counterattacked Nuer raiding parties only when the latter were quite small or when government troops spearheaded the counteroffensive. Only twice did the Dinka succeed in repulsing the Nuer and recovering all or part of their stolen cattle without government assistance, and in one of these instances the Nuer force numbered only two hundred (*SIR* 245, 1914:4; *SIR* 338, 1922:3). On two occasions when the Dinka joined government forces in operations against large-scale Nuer raiding parties they suffered devastating defeats. A 1922 debacle described by Titherington (1927:198) closely parallels the disastrous 1916 counterattack discussed earlier. The Nuer pursued the same strategy in both cases. A single column which encountered resistance from a combined force of Dinka and government troops withdrew in apparent disarray with the Dinka in hot pursuit. While some of the Nuer feigned disorderly retreat, the majority ambushed the Dinka from two sides inflicting heavy casualties (ibid.; Johnston, 1934:3).[35] There are no recorded instances in which the Dinka succeeded in countering a large-scale Nuer offensive without government assistance, despite the fact that they were issued guns and ammunition by the administration and held a strong advantage in this respect. In two of the three instances when the Dinka joined government forces against large-scale Nuer raiding parties they were defeated with severe losses. The Dinka prevailed only once, when they accompanied a government party of forty riflemen (*SIR* 263, 1916).[36] Available evidence from the colonial period therefore suggests that the Dinka would not have been capable of resisting large-scale Nuer incursions prior to the arrival of European arms and assistance.

Evidence from the colonial period also indicates that the Dinka rarely carried out raids on the Nuer. Available sources contain reports of only three Dinka raids as against twenty-six conducted by the Nuer during the period from 1906 to 1928.[37] Although early colonial officials reported that the Dinka engaged in a number of successful minor raids (or cattle-rustling forays) prior to the first administrative attempts to control intertribal fighting in 1908 (*SIR* 177, 1909:16), the paucity of Dinka offensives after that date suggests that the indigenous level of Dinka aggression may have been inflated. In other words, early colonial officials may have taken credit for bringing about the virtual cessation of Dinka raids which were, in actuality, an infrequent occurrence. Of the three reported raids which took place after 1908, only one was successful (resulting in the capture of several thousand cattle) while the other two culminated in crushing Dinka defeats. In a 1915 Western Luaich raid (discussed earlier), the Dinka lost more than half of the six hundred warriors who took part. In about 1912,

> a large [Raik Dinka] raiding party surprised a Nuer village and, Dinka-like, sat down to a happy day of wrangling over the spoils. It was their last, for meanwhile the Nuer surrounded them, and in the ensuing panic slaughtered them to the last man. (Titherington, 1927:199)

Available evidence thus indicates that Dinka raids on the Nuer occurred infrequently, were carried out by comparatively small groups, and were rarely successful. Dinka oral traditions celebrate comparatively few victories (see Fergusson, 1921) while historical sources document several disastrous defeats. The Dinka were evidently incapable of mounting an effective counteroffensive that would have tied down Nuer forces in defense of home territory and were likewise unable to recoup their steady losses in cattle and land. The Nuer were thus free to leave their villages undefended while they engaged in extended raids, operating from bases established in conquered Dinka villages. Although a Dinka counteroffensive against undermanned Nuer communities undoubtedly would have curtailed extended Nuer raids and offered highly favorable prospects for capturing large numbers of cattle, there is no evidence that the Dinka ever adopted this strategy. Moreover, the Dinka were unable to mobilize a defensive force equivalent in size to the fifteen hundred men who comprised a large Nuer raiding party and were consequently unable to contain their advance. (Under the prevailing conditions of primitive warfare fought with spears and clubs, a much larger force with a strong numerical advantage would have been required to dislodge the Nuer.) Lacking the capacity to mount an effective counterattack, the Dinka had no recourse other than withdrawal. Under these circumstances, the rapid Nuer conquest of the vast Central Dinka region is not difficult to understand.

It is also quite clear that Nuer military domination of the Dinka was grounded in their capacity to field a numerically superior fighting force, and in the organizational features through which mobilization on a large scale was effected. Other aspects of the Nuer advantage were secondary and derivative. Nuer tactics were relatively simple and straightforward. It is difficult to imagine that they were unknown to the Dinka. Moreover, a multiple column force and the potential for strategic maneuvers this engendered both depended on, and capitalized upon, numerical superiority.

The fact that the Nuer employed this tactical configuration on large-scale raids probably enhanced the effectiveness of small, single-contingent forays. When a Dinka community was alerted to a Nuer raid on their neighbors, they were forced to consider the possibility that they themselves were also in danger of imminent attack. Coming to the aid of their neighbors entailed the risk of leaving their own herds and homesteads unguarded. The threat of a multiple column raid thus effectively undercut mutual defense among neighboring Dinka communities and promoted a lack of unity in countering Nuer aggression. Moreover, the expectation that aid would not be forthcoming undoubtedly contributed to the Dinka inclination to withdraw from an area under attack. Though simple, Nuer tactics were thus highly effective.

The Nuer also held an advantage in experience. Annual raids produced seasoned warriors, well practiced in both the arts of war and in coordinating their efforts in combat. This enabled the Nuer to execute simple strategies effectively and to maintain a disciplined state of readiness during raids. This point is well illustrated by the contrast between Nuer and Dinka procedures for dividing up the spoils of a successful raid. When the Nuer attacked a Dinka community, the taking of cattle was deferred until the populace was dispersed. In addition, the cattle captured by individuals over the course of an extended raid were subsequently redistributed among all participants in the following manner:

> The prophet whose revelations sanctioned the raid first made a round of the camp and selected from each household a cow for the divine spirit of whom he was the mouthpiece. By this time a household possessed some fifty head, so that it was no hardship to be asked to give one to the spirit. Then there took place a general scramble and everyone rushed amid the herd to earmark beasts for himself. A man who could first seize an animal, tether it, and cut its ear had an absolute claim to it. The man who originally captured a cow had the advantage that it was tethered near his windscreen, but if he and members of his household had an undue share of the booty they could not earmark all the beasts before they were seized by others. As might be supposed, men frequently sustained injury in these scrambles, for if two men seized the same cow they fought with clubs for possession of it. One must not use the spear on these occasions. Men of neighboring camps took part in one another's redistributions and there must have been great confusion. Captives, women of marriageable age, boys, and girls were not redistributed but belonged to their original captor. (Evans-Pritchard, 1940a:128)

These procedures precluded "wrangling over the spoils" during the course of a raid and thus avoided the inattention to the enemy at hand that allowed a Dinka raiding party to be overcome and annihilated by a Nuer counterattack (as described earlier). The absence of such conventions on the part of the Dinka is consistent with a low frequency of raids on the Nuer and a concomitant lack of battlefield experience in offensive situations.

The discipline of Nuer forces is also demonstrated by a remarkable capacity to continue to press an assault while sustaining very heavy casualties. When the Eastern Jikany were attacked early in 1912 by a heavily armed

Ethiopian force of Galla and Amhara intent on taking slaves, the Nuer lost 100 men in the course of overrunning the invaders' machine gun emplacement. The Ethiopians were successfully routed losing 250 killed and 30 missing (*SIR* 215, 1912:3). The Nuer also made a number of concerted attacks on fortified government posts (described earlier). In one instance in which a Nuer raiding party was intercepted by a government patrol, the Nuer lost 84 men in the initial engagement but nevertheless counterattacked the same night and again the following day before withdrawing to home territory (*SIR* 336, 1922:6).

Systematic Nuer cattle raids, conducted on an annual basis, created a periphery of debilitated Dinka communities that yielded readily to Nuer territorial appropriation. Seasoned Nuer raiding parties were pitted against famine-ridden Dinka groups struggling to survive through periods of scarcity resulting from previous raids. Under the circumstances it is not surprising that the Dinka were unable to mount any effective resistance to continuing Nuer territorial expansion. As this expansion proceeded, displaced Dinka groups were pushed into adjacent areas where they came into conflict with the existing population whose land and grazing rights they infringed. These conflicts undoubtedly contributed to a lack of unity in meeting subsequent Nuer attacks. Successful Nuer cattle raids thus engendered conditions favorable to territorial expansion, and the continuation of this expansion was further facilitated by the aftermath of prior Dinka defeat. The expansion process fed on the conditions it created. The impressive fighting force which the Nuer possessed in the early nineteen hundreds may likewise be seen as the product of a century of military success. However, a strong case can be made that the Nuer possessed an initial advantage in their capacity to mobilize and field numerically superior offensive forces, and that this set in motion the self-fulfilling processes outline above. This argument will be taken up in a later chapter.

Casualties, Captives, and Cattle

The fact that the Dinka typically withdrew from villages under attack without offering any concerted resistance tended to minimize the casualties resulting from Nuer raids. The number of Dinka killed in the large-scale Nuer raids during the twentieth century was surprisingly small. In 1928, only 87 Dinka lost their lives in the course of Nuer attacks on thirty villages. This averages to only about three deaths per community of approximately 300 Dinka. In 1916, 165 Dinka were killed in Nuer raids on an unknown number of villages. However, the Nuer penetrated about eighty miles into Dinka territory in both instances and the area under attack was comparable. Assuming thirty villages of 300 persons each were also raided in 1916, the number of Dinka killed would represent 1.83 percent of the population in the area under attack. The comparable figure for 1928 is 0.97 percent and the average for both incursions is 1.4 percent. The higher casualties in 1916 are probably attributable to the abortive counterattack (discussed earlier) in which the Sudanese army detachment was annihilated. A substantial (but unspecified) number of Dinka warriors were also killed and these losses are included in the total (165) cited in government reports. Direct engagements resulting from Dinka counterattacks would necessarily increase casualties on both sides. Since counterattacks were encouraged by the government forces that spearheaded them during the colonial period, the lower casualty figure (87) is probably more representative of large-scale Nuer raids during the period of territorial expansion.

In other, generally smaller Nuer raids for which figures are available, the number of Dinka killed was none, one, six, nine, eleven, twelve, sixteen, and twenty in respective cases. These raids generally involved attacks on "several" communities; the precise number is not specified in the reports.[38]

Mortality from Nuer raids was not restricted exclusively to Dinka warriors. Evans-Pritchard (1940a:128–29) reports that "older women and babies were clubbed and . . . their bodies thrown on the flaming byres and huts" when a Dinka community was overrun. Dinka casualties are differentiated by sex in only two government reports. In one instance nine men and seven women were killed, and in another seven men and five women (*SIR* 299, 1919:4; *SIR* 336, 1922:6). Although the number of cases is small, they suggest that nearly half (i.e., 43 percent) of the total casualties were female. Available data concerning three small Beir (or Murle) raids on the Dinka, conducted in much the same manner as Nuer raids, tend to corroborate these conclusions. Five Dinka men and one woman were killed in one instance, eight men, eight women, and two girls in the second, and two men and three women in the third, yielding a total of 48.3 percent female casualties (*SIR* 177, 1909:4; *SIR* 185, 1909:6; *SIR* 187, 1910:5). Since girls and women of marriageable age were the objects of capture, older women probably account for the majority of female casualties, as Evans-Pritchard suggests. No girls were killed in the two above mentioned Nuer raids on the Dinka, while girls represent only 14 percent of the women killed by the Beir.

Nuer raids also resulted in the capture of substantial numbers of women and children. Forty-six captives were taken in the 1916 raid on the Southern Dinka and 100 in the 1928 incursion. A 1919 Nuer raid on the Western Luaich also resulted in the capture of 100 women and children, although only 16 Dinka were reportedly killed by the Nuer (*SIR* 299, 1919:4). The number of captives taken also outnumbers casualties inflicted by 40 to 20 in one of the mid-1920s raids on the Western Dinka mentioned by Digerness (1978:81). Similarly, 2 children were captured in a small Nuer raid in which 6 individuals were wounded, but none killed (*SIR* 304, 1919:5). In these five instances, representing all cases for which both sets of data are available, the total number of Dinka captured precisely equals the total number killed (288). If the heavy losses the Dinka suffered in the disastrous government-led counterattack of 1916 could be segregated from total casualties, captives taken would exceed the latter by a significant margin. This is a remarkable finding, although it is entirely consistent with the previously described Dinka pattern of rapid withdrawal from a settlement under Nuer attack, and with the unexpectedly high proportion of female casualties (43 percent) noted earlier. While Dinka warriors attempted to salvage as many cattle as possible, women and children were evidently left to make their escape as best they could. Elderly women and young children under about age eight undoubtedly fared poorly under these circumstances. This accounts for both the large number of (mostly older) women killed and the high ratio of captives relative to total casualties.

Captives taken by the Nuer included boys, girls, and young women of marriageable age (Evans-Pritchard, 1940a:128), but the number of each is not specified in government reports concerning the above-mentioned raids. However, it seems likely that the preponderant majority were females who would generate bridewealth cattle for their captors when subsequently given in marriage to other Nuer men (Evans-Pritchard, 1940a:222). With Nuer bridewealth entailing a payment of 40 to 60 head of cattle during the period of territorial expansion (Evans-Pritchard, 1940a:19–20), female captives were, in this respect, equivalent to very substantial numbers of cattle taken in raids. Moreover, captives, unlike cattle, were not subject to redistribution among coparticipants in a raid. Boys, who were generally adopted into the family and lineage of their captors (Evans-Pritchard, 1940a:221), lacked the potential to bring in bridewealth payments (and indeed would later need to have such payments made on their behalf). One would consequently expect that few male captives were taken. If one Beir raid on the Dinka (for which figures are available) can be taken as a guide, young female captives outnumbered boys by a ratio of about three to one. In this instance, 11 young women, 14 girls, and 9 boys were captured (*SIR* 185, 1909:6, *SIR* 187, 1910:5).[39] The percentage of the total represented by each category are 32.4, 41.2, and 26.5 respectively. The proportion of women to children captured on this raid is comparable to that of several Eastern Jikany raids on the Burun in 1918, during which 80 young women and 168 children were taken (along with 2,000 sheep and 640 head of cattle) (Digerness, 1978:57). In this case, young women constituted 29.4 percent of all captives. Unfortunately, the sex distribution of the children is not given.

One of the most significant points that emerges from consideration of Nuer-Dinka conflict during the early colonial period is the extent to which the female segment of the Dinka population was affected by Nuer raids. Although pertinent data are limited, they suggest that females accounted for 43 percent of the casualties incurred and about 75 percent of the captives taken. This finding is of considerable importance in explaining the ultimate fate of the Dinka population displaced by Nuer expansion.

The number of cattle captured by the Nuer in large-scale raids on the Dinka is surprisingly large, especially given the fact that the Dinka strategy of withdrawal was predicated on minimizing cattle losses. In 1914, 3,000 cattle were stolen from the Ghol and Nyarraweng alone while a number of Bor Dinka villages further south lost all their stock. Since an average Dinka village in this area possessed an estimated 486 head of cattle,[40] the total acquired by the Nuer on this occasion must have been on the order of 5,000 head. The Nuer captured more than 4,000 cattle in 1916 (of which 1,000 were subsequently recaptured by a large government force and accompanying Dinka) and 700 in 1928. The three most productive Nuer raids on the Western Dinka likewise netted 800, 1,000, and 2,000 cattle respectively. The average Dinka loss from these six large-scale incursions was 2,250 head.

Several thousand cattle represent the subsistence base of a substantial number of Dinka tribesmen. At 1950s rates of 1.62 cattle per capita for the Bor District (inhabited by the Ghol, Nyarraweng, Twi, and Bor Dinka), 2,250 cattle would constitute the total holdings of 1,389 people (Howell, 1954*b*:230). The total of 9,000 cattle taken by the Nuer in the 1914 and 1916 raids combined would have supported 5,556 Dinka. If we assume that these losses were sustained by thirty villages with a total population of 9,000 Dinka and 14,580 cattle,[41] the closely spaced raids of 1914 and 1916 would have reduced the cattle holdings of the affected Dinka by 34.3 and 27.4 percent respectively. A large-scale raid yielding the average of 2,250 cattle would engender a 15.4 percent herd reduction. These figures amplify the point that large-scale Nuer raids had devastating effects on Dinka food supplies.

THE DEMOGRAPHIC CONSEQUENCES OF NUER EXPANSION

The fate of the former Dinka and Anuak inhabitants of areas appropriated by the Nuer remains to be considered. It is evident from the data presented thus far that migration, assimilation, and mortality resulting from Nuer raids are the relevant categories of analysis, but the relative significance of each has yet to be examined. This can be assessed in general terms but cannot be precisely determined. The results of such an assessment are nevertheless of considerable theoretical interest because the demographic history of the Dinka and Anuak is closely intertwined with that of the Nuer and assumptions concerning Nuer demography are central to most of the extant explanations of Nuer expansion. As noted earlier, the central issue here is whether Nuer population growth was a cause or consequence of territorial expansion. The data presented in this section will thus lay the groundwork for an evaluation of "population pressure" arguments considered in the next chapter.

Available data indicate that direct mortality from Nuer raids had a negligible effect on the Central Dinka (and Anuak) population over the long term while the taking of captives had a very significant effect. This is a consequence of the distinctive age and sex distribution of casualties and captives, respectively. Most of the individuals killed in Nuer raids were men and older women while most of those captured were young women and girls. The loss of males and postreproductive females would not significantly affect the birth rate, as the latter would already have produced their demographic replacements while the wives of the former would continue to bear children after their remarriage to other men. The population would thus be reduced only by the difference between the average age and normal life expectancy of those killed, multiplied by the annual casualty rate. In contrast, the loss of a female of childbearing age (or younger) through capture removes two individuals from the population in the next generation, representing the demographic replacements of both the female and her spouse. The demographic replacements of these absent offspring are also lost to the following generation. If grandchildren are normally born before their grandparents die, then two generations of direct descendants of a woman will be alive at any given time. The capture of a single Dinka woman or girl thus reduces the Dinka population by four individuals several generations later, and adds a like increment to the Nuer population. Allowing for a somewhat shorter life expectancy, such that grandparents die some years before their grandchildren are born, the loss of a single reproductive female through capture is estimated to eventually reduce her natal population by 3.4 individuals. (The derivation of this figure will be explained in due course.) The key point here is that the capture of young women and girls had cumulative effects and the demographic consequences of the high rate of capture characteristic of Nuer raids were thus quite substantial.

It will be useful to illustrate the comparative demographic effects of these two consequences of Nuer raids over time by presenting a numerical model. This will also provide some indication of the order of magnitude of these effects. Although the resultant figures are largely a product of the assumptions employed, they are nevertheless instructive.

The relevant assumptions concern the frequency of Nuer raids, the age and sex distribution of those individuals killed and captured, and the demographic characteristics of the Central Dinka and Anuak population affected. This population may be estimated to have numbered at least 177,000 persons at the inception of Nuer expansion (this being equivalent to the Nuer population of former Anuak and Central Dinka territory east of the Bahr el Jebel in

circa 1930 censuses).[42] We will assume that the Central Dinka and Anuak
were subject to one large-scale raid and one or two smaller raids every year,
resulting in an annual loss of 100 captives and 100 persons killed. Seventy-
five percent of the captives and 43 percent of the casualties are assumed to be
females. The casualty rate from large-scale raids, the equivalence between
casualties and captives, and the female component of these two categories are
drawn from the historical data pertaining to twentieth-century Nuer raids discussed earlier.

The proposed frequency of Nuer raids during the expansion period is a
rough estimate. We know that Nuer expansion was accomplished through
raiding and the intensity of the latter is presumed to have approximated the
higher levels attained during the early colonial period. It may be recalled that
there were nine Nuer raids on the Southern Dinka in 1913–14 and eleven raids
on the Burun in 1919–20. The Southwest Dinka were subject to nine raids
during the eight-year period from 1914 to 1922. The Central Dinka and
Anuak were initially subject to raids by the Lou and Gaawar in the west and
the Jikany in the east, with the Lak and Thiang becoming involved somewhat
later in the expansion process. The proposed annual frequency of Nuer raids
encompass all these tribes. Data that will be introduced subsequently concerning the number of captives and immigrants residing among the Nuer in the
early 1930s suggest that this estimate may be too low. However, this assumed
frequency of Nuer raids will serve our present purpose of illustrating the
comparative demographic effects of an equivalence between the number of
casualties sustained and the number of captives lost to the Dinka in Nuer
raids. It also provides a rough index of the magnitude of these effects.

If we assume that the average age of males killed by the Nuer was
twenty-five years, and their life expectancy fifty years, then each male casualty would represent a loss to the population for twenty-five years. At a
constant rate of fifty-seven male deaths annually, the combined Central Dinka
and Anuak population would be decreased by 1,425 persons. This represents
the number of men who would have been alive (at any given time) in the
absence of mortality from Nuer raids. If we likewise assume that the average
age of female fatalities was forty years, and their life expectancy fifty years,
the population would be reduced by an additional 430 persons for a total of
1,844. This represents only slightly more than 1 percent of the estimated
Central Dinka and Anuak population of 177,000 persons that formerly inhabited the areas appropriated by the Nuer. In other words, this numerical model
indicates that direct mortality from Nuer raids would have reduced the Dinka
and Anuak population by only about 1 percent.

The preceding illustration assumes that no women of childbearing age
(or younger) were killed in Nuer raids. The death of even a small number of
reproductive females would significantly alter the results. If such women

constituted one-tenth of total casualties (or one of every 4.3 female casualties) incurred in annual raids from 1818 to 1905,[43] the Central Dinka and Anuak population would be reduced by 2,958 additional individuals. (Subsequent discussion of the effects of taking captives will clarify the basis of this calculation.) The reduction of the Central Dinka and Anuak population attributable to mortality from Nuer raids would then increase to a total of 2.7 percent. However, the figure remains small and both of the calculations presented here are conducive to the same general conclusion: direct mortality resulting from Nuer raids carried out in the course of territorial expansion probably had only a negligible effect on the population displaced by the Nuer. However, it should also be noted that famine conditions resulting from Nuer raids might have added substantially to the mortality rate of the population under attack. This possibility will be considered later in this section.

A calculation of the demographic consequences of the capture of reproductive females requires additional assumptions. For these purposes we will assume that female captives are, on average, acquired at the age of fifteen, marry at twenty, reproduce between the ages of twenty and forty, and die at age fifty. The two children born to a woman are assumed to be equally distributed throughout her reproductive period so that a woman is, on average, separated from her children by a generational span of thirty years. A woman's grandchildren would then be born ten years after her death, producing a 70 percent overlap between generations. On average, then, 3.4 descendants of a woman would be alive at any given time. The loss of a single reproductive female is thus estimated to reduce her natal population by 3.4 individuals several generations later, and to add a like increment to the population she joins. The capture of 75 young women and girls a year during the period from 1818 to 1905 would remove 6,525 reproductive females from the Central Dinka and Anuak population and thus eventually decrease that population by 22,183 individuals.

The capture of 25 boys a year over the same period would decrease the Central Dinka and Anuak population by an additional 1,050 persons. (This figure is based on the assumption that male captives are, on average, eight years of age and thus lost to their natal population for the remaining forty-two years of their assumed life expectancy of fifty.) In sum, the proposed rate of capture would effectively transfer 23,235 persons from the Central Dinka and Anuak population to that of the Nuer. This represents 13 percent of the total estimated population of these groups prior to Nuer expansion.

One of the most significant points that emerges from an examination of twentieth-century Nuer raids is that the number of captives taken was equivalent to the number of casualties. The preceding calculations are intended to illustrate the comparative demographic consequences of this distribution (given the assumptions outlined earlier). These calculations indicate that the demographic impact of the loss of one hundred captives per year is nearly five times as great as an equal number of casualties. Moreover, it is evident that the annual capture of a modest number of reproductive females would, over the long term, effectively transfer a substantial portion of the reproductive potential of the Central Dinka and Anuak population to the Nuer. This is of considerable importance because it suggests that the same raids that were instrumental to Nuer expansion also resulted in substantial additions to the Nuer population.

It has already been established that a number of Dinka tribes (or portions thereof) migrated to other areas under pressure of Nuer raids, and that elements of the Anuak likewise withdrew to the southwest. The remaining and much more difficult question concerns the proportion of the original Central Dinka and Anuak population that might be accounted for by such migration. A comparison of the displaced Dinka and Anuak population with that of the Nuer tribes that replaced them indicates that the former population is only a fraction of the latter, and these data will enable us to suggest an answer to this question.

The population of both the Nuer tribes that expanded eastward across the Bahr el Jebel and the Central Dinka tribes they pushed into adjacent areas are listed below. The figures are derived from an administrative census carried out in the early 1950s (Howell, 1955:77–80).[44] It is important to note that the Dinka groups listed here include not only those tribes that migrated, but also those that reportedly incorporated large numbers of refugees (i.e., the Dunjol, Thoi, and Nyarraweng). In other words, the Dinka total represents a maximum estimate of the population that could be derived from nineteenth-century Dinka migrants. The only Dinka tribes east of the Bahr el Jebel that are excluded are the Abialang in the extreme north and the Twij and Bor far to the south (see map 1). The unfriendly reception that the Twij and Bor accorded to Central Dinka refugees was noted in earlier discussion of twentieth-century Nuer raids.

Dinka Tribes		*Nuer Tribes*	
Padang	14,560	Lak	42,550
Dunjol	9,990	Thiang	14,200
Eastern Ngok	17,820	Gaawar	47,135
Western Ngok	25,000	Lou	74,750
Nyarraweng and Ghol	22,900	Eastern Jikany	96,945
Rut, Thoi, Eastern Luaich,			275,580
and Ruweng (Paweng)	16,975		
	107,245		

The Anuak who withdrew to the southwest under pressure of nineteenth-century Nuer raids are not distinguishable from those who previously resided within the borders of what is presently Anuak territory. However, the total Anuak population was estimated to be only 35,000 persons in the latter part of the 1940s (Evans-Pritchard, 1947:64). The maximum number of Anuak that could be derived from nineteenth-century migrants thus cannot exceed 35,000. Adding this maximum estimate to the corresponding figure for the Dinka yields a total of 142,245 persons. However, this is only a little more than half (51.6 percent) of the Nuer population of the conquered territory east of the Bahr el Jebel at the same date. In other words, even if we assume nearly all of the Dinka and Anuak population east of the Bahr el Jebel is derived from migrants, and allow for no indigenous (pre–1820) population of the territory they currently occupy, the total still falls far short of the Nuer population that occupies former Dinka and Anuak domains.

Available census materials from circa 1930 indicate that the displaced Dinka tribes grew much more rapidly between this date and the early 1950s than did the Nuer, and that the disparity between the total population of the two aggregate groups compared here was even greater at that time. The 1930 census omits some of the relevant Dinka tribes, but more limited comparisons can be drawn and these are instructive. In 1930, the Nyarraweng and Ghol, together with the remnants of the Angai, Ric, and Luaich residing among them, numbered only 6,234 (Wyld, 1930: Appendix 2). By the early 1950s the population of the same groups (and territory) had increased to 22,900. Similarly, the Rut, Thoi, Eastern Luaich, and Eastern Ngok in the north numbered only 7,916 in 1930 (Alban, 1930:2–3; Upper Nile Province Handbook, Zeraf Valley section, 1930:2A). These Dinka tribes, plus the small Ruweng Paweng group omitted in the 1930 enumeration, had a combined population of 34,795 in the early 1950s. In contrast, the Nuer east of the Bahr el Jebel only increased from 177,000 to 275,540 during the same period.[45]

The very substantial increase in the population of these displaced Dinka tribes is quite significant because it indicates that they did not decline in numbers as a consequence of being compressed into unfavorable environmental areas incapable of supporting them. If such population decline can be ruled out, then the number of Dinka that migrated into adjacent areas as a consequence of Nuer expansion cannot exceed the census population of these areas. The very small 1930 population of the Rut, Thoi, Eastern Luaich, Eastern Ngok, Nyarraweng, Ghol, Angai, and Ric thus suggests that only a relatively small proportion of the original (pre–1820) Dinka population of territory appropriated by the Nuer migrated to other areas. Although 1930 census materials are not sufficiently complete to estimate this proportion, an extrapolation from the data presented above indicates that it would necessarily be less than 50 percent. In short, one may conservatively conclude that less than 50 percent of the former Dinka and Anuak inhabitants of the territory east of the Bahr el Jebel appropriated by the Nuer took refuge in adjacent areas to the north and south.

Evans-Pritchard (1933:33) has suggested that the Nuer absorbed "a very large element" of the original Dinka population of the conquered territory east of the Bahr el Jebel. A portion of the Anuak population was likewise absorbed (Evans-Pritchard, 1940c:8). Assimilation of the Dinka and Anuak on the massive scale proposed by Evans-Pritchard is particularly significant because it would not only account for the fate of these peoples, but would also suggest that Nuer population growth was largely a consequence of expansion. It is thus important to assess the magnitude of Nuer assimilation and to attempt to determine the approximate size of the population involved.

The proposition that the Nuer increased in numbers largely as a consequence of assimilation of the Dinka during the course of territorial expansion is substantially confirmed by an enormous disparity between the population of the Homeland Nuer tribes and the population of the expanding tribes. The Nuer homeland carried a total population of only 61,000 in 1930 when it was inhabited by the Dok, four Jagei tribes, two Western Jikany tribes, the Leik, and the Bul (Evans-Pritchard, 1940a:117). In contrast, the Nuong, Lak, Thiang, Gaawar, Lou, and the three Eastern Jikany tribes that inhabited conquered territory numbered 186,000 at the same date. The average size of the nine homeland tribes is only 6,778 persons while the average size of the eight expanding tribes is 23,250 persons. These striking differences in both total population and average tribal size cannot be attributed to differential population growth stemming from an expansion of the resource base because such expansion was equally applicable to both sets of tribes. While the expanding tribes acquired territory by conquest, the resource base of the Homeland Nuer was likewise vastly increased by the exodus of nearly half the tribes that had resided there before 1818. The availability of pasture and agricultural sites increased in both cases and this constant factor cannot account for the very substantial differences in both total population and average tribal size. However, a difference in the rate of assimilation of captured and displaced Dinka can easily account for the divergent outcomes. The same Nuer raids that were instrumental to territorial acquisition entailed the capture of substantial numbers of reproductive females and also engendered famine conditions that prompted Dinka families to seek refuge among the Nuer. Population growth was thus a concomitant of territorial expansion and this accounts for the differential growth rates of the Homeland Nuer tribes and those tribes that participated directly in Nuer expansion.

Nuer assimilation of large numbers of Dinka is well supported by other data. Evans-Pritchard (1940a:221) has estimated that

> persons of Dinka descent form probably at least half the population of most [Nuer] tribes. These Dinka are either children of captives or immigrants who have been brought up as Nuer, or are themselves captives and immigrants who

are residing permanently among Nuer. They are *"Jaang-Nath,"* "Dinka-Nuer," and, it is said, *"caa Nath,"* "they have become Nuer."

The tribes to which Evans-Pritchard refers are those that participated in Nuer territorial expansion. In numerical terms, his estimate thus translates into at least 93,000 captives, immigrants, and their children within a total (circa 1930) population of 186,000 persons for these tribes. This social composition would require the incorporation of at least 31,000 Dinka in the last two generations, i.e., between about 1875 and 1930. (A single captive or immigrant who marries and has two surviving children would add three "Dinka-Nuer" to the population, and 31,000 such individuals would thus provide 93,000 individuals in this category.)[46] However, this period from 1875 to 1930 includes only the last fifteen years of Nuer expansion and was also marked, in the last decade, by colonial efforts to enforce a boundary between the Nuer and Dinka and to repatriate Dinka living among the Nuer (Johnson, 1982:200). The number of captives and immigrants absorbed by the Nuer during the preceding fifty-five-year period from 1820 to 1875, which encompasses the most active phase of Nuer expansion, would presumably have been much greater. While a similar rate of assimilation during this earlier period would have added another 31,000 Dinka to the population of the expanding Nuer tribes, a substantially larger figure would be more plausible given the greater intensity of Nuer raids (that both prompted immigration and garnered captives). In short, the social composition, in 1930, of the Nuer tribes that participated in territorial expansion suggests a rate of assimilation that would entail the incorporation of a *minimum* of 62,000 Dinka captives and immigrants. The assimilation of more than 80,000 captives and immigrants during the course of Nuer expansion is probably a more accurate estimate.[47]

It is important to note that Evans-Pritchard (1940a:221–24) emphasizes the effectiveness of the assimilation process in social and cultural terms, and the consequent difficulty of distinguishing the second-generation descendants of captives and immigrants from other Nuer. Most importantly, the key features of Nuer social and economic organization that were instrumental to territorial expansion remained unaltered by the massive assimilation of Dinka and Anuak tribesmen (as discussed in later chapters).

Dinka accretions to the Nuer population were not limited to captives and immigrants.

> There must also have been pockets of the original Dinka occupants of country overrun by the Nuer who submitted and gave up their language and habits in favor of those of the Nuer. At any rate, there are today in all tribes many small Dinka lineages, and villages are often named after them. (Evans-Pritchard, 1940a:224)

The irregular pattern of Nuer expansion tended to create pockets of Dinka and Anuak settlement between areas appropriated by the Nuer. This was particularly true of the eastern region (Evans-Pritchard, 1940a:224). Many small Anuak enclaves along the Sobat that were noted by explorers in the late 1880s were no longer distinguishable from the surrounding Nuer by the 1930s. Johnson (1980:180) notes that

> the Padang occupied much of the territory the Lou later settled in, and most of them were assimilated into Lou lineages. The Maiker section of the Gun Lou . . . was composed almost entirely of Padang. . . . .

Johnson (1982:194) also estimates that ''nearly half'' the Nyarraweng sought refuge among the Lou Nuer in the early 1900s, while groups of Angac (Angai) and Rut lived among the Gaawar. Both refugee groups and enclaved Dinka and Anuak communities were eventually assimilated into the Nuer lineage (and territorial) system through intermarriage and the subsequent tracing of genealogical connection through a Nuer female forebear (Evans-Pritchard, 1940a:227).

The number of Dinka and Anuak absorbed in this way is difficult to estimate, but something on the order of 20,000 to 30,000 persons appears quite plausible. This would bring the total number of Dinka and Anuak assimilated during the course of Nuer territorial expansion to approximately 100,000 to 112,000 persons.[48] Both the high proportion of ''Dinka-Nuer'' and the prevalence of Dinka lineages within the Nuer tribes that participated in territorial expansion indicate a figure of this order of magnitude.

The extent to which this massive assimilation added to the Nuer population and reduced that of the Dinka and Anuak over the long term would depend upon the proportion of reproductive females among those individuals who joined the Nuer. Most captives were girls and young women of marriageable age and females would be expected to comprise half the members of families that sought refuge among the Nuer either individually or in groups. Young men who migrated to Nuerland often came to join a captured sister (Evans-Pritchard, 1940a:223) and consequently would not outnumber the females acquired by capture. In short, there is no reason to believe that females were underrepresented within the total number of Dinka and Anuak assimilated during the course of Nuer expansion. The estimated 100,000 to 112,000 persons assimilated thus represents a like addition to the Nuer population.

The proposition that Dinka and Anuak accretions added about 100,000 to 112,000 persons to the population of the expanding Nuer tribes would account for the enormous disparity between these tribes and the Homeland Nuer in both total population and average tribal size. A like reduction in the Dinka and

Anuak population that formerly inhabited present-day Nuer territory would also account for the fate of the bulk of these displaced peoples. If less than half of the original Central Dinka and Anuak population migrated to adjacent areas and the long-term effects of mortality from Nuer raids were negligible, then the whereabouts of more than half of this original population remains to be explained. Their assimilation by the Nuer provides an explanation, and one that is fully consistent with the social composition of the expanding Nuer tribes in 1930.

The possibility that famine conditions engendered by Nuer raids added substantially to the mortality rate of the Central Dinka and Anuak population remains to be considered. The effects of large-scale Nuer raids on Dinka food supplies make it clear that severe shortages resulted. Under famine conditions, inadequate nutrition increases susceptibility to a wide range of diseases resulting in an increased mortality rate. Infants, children under the age of five, and the elderly are typically the most heavily affected segments of a population. The death of potential reproductive females in the youngest age groups can produce a significant population decline in the following generation. It is difficult to determine whether this occurred, or to what extent. Evans-Pritchard (1940c:10) reports that "many" Anuak died during a famine resulting from the major Nuer invasion of upland Anuak territory that took place in the 1870s. However, there are no comparable reports of extraordinary famine-related mortality among the Dinka. This may be due to the fact that the Dinka possessed substantially more livestock than the upland Anuak, and that the slaughter of cattle, sheep, and goats sustained them during periods of food shortage. It is also important to note that the Nuer are reported to have readily accepted Dinka families and individuals that migrated to Nuerland to escape hunger (Evans-Pritchard, 1933:53). We have also seen that the Lou Nuer took in nearly half the Nyarraweng Dinka in the early 1900s. Many Dinka also sought refuge with their kin of other Dinka tribes and sections. The availability of these recourses points to the conclusion that famine-related mortality was not great. It is unlikely that the original Central Dinka and Anuak population was substantially reduced by this factor.

We are now in a position to summarize the material presented in this section, and to draw some general conclusions concerning the fate of the former Dinka and Anuak inhabitants of areas appropriated by the Nuer, and the demographic history of the latter. The displaced Dinka and Anuak population is estimated to have been at least as large as the Nuer population of the conquered territory in 1930, i.e., 186,000 persons (including the population of Nuong territory as well as Nuer territory east of the Bahr el Jebel). However, this displaced population may have been considerably larger. The official government census of 1955–56 indicates the area in question is capable of supporting more than 300,000 persons. It may be assumed that the original

Dinka and Anuak population of the conquered territory fell between these two extremes. Evans-Pritchard's statements concerning the social composition of the Nuer in the early 1930s and Johnson's recent historical research suggest that Dinka and Anuak accretions added approximately 100,000 to 112,000 persons to the Nuer population (and reduced the Dinka and Anuak population by a like amount). Consideration of both the comparatively small size of the Dinka and Anuak population east of the Bahr el Jebel in 1950, and of demographic trends between 1930 and 1950, suggests that no more than 88,500 persons migrated to adjacent areas to the north and south as a consequence of Nuer raids. A comparable rate of migration in the area of Nuong Nuer expansion would increase this figure to 93,000. Finally, it was shown that Nuer raids resulting in 100 fatalities annually would (given certain assumptions about the age and sex distribution of those killed) eventually reduce the Dinka and Anuak population by about 4,800 persons. However, the number of captives and immigrants (and their offspring) residing among the Nuer in the early 1930s suggests that the assumed frequency of Nuer raids employed in this calculation may be too low. Doubling this frequency would produce a high estimate of 9,600 persons (i.e., a population reduction of 9,600 due to direct mortality from Nuer raids). Famine-related mortality stemming from Nuer raids may have reduced the Dinka and Anuak population by a like amount.

The sum of the higher estimates presented here is about 225,000 persons, a figure that represents a plausible initial (pre–1820) Dinka and Anuak population of the territory conquered by the Nuer. Although none of these estimates are presumed to be precise, I would argue that they are of the correct order of magnitude and that they provide a plausible approximation of the demographic consequences of Nuer territorial expansion. They are consistent with, and interrelate, a substantial body of data. It will be argued in the following chapter that "population pressure" arguments implicitly propose an alternative model of demographic processes that is both internally contradictory and inconsistent with available data. The difficulties emerge when one attempts to translate the underlying assumptions into any plausible set of numbers, and it is partly for this reason that numerical values have been introduced into the discussion in this chapter. It should also be noted that the proposed Nuer assimilation of something on the order of 100,000 to 112,000 Dinka and Anuak (and a commensurate increase in Nuer population) provides a basis for both estimating Nuer population density at the inception of nineteenth-century Nuer territorial expansion and reconstructing the social demography of the Nuer at that time. Nuer demographic history is particularly germane to the earlier explanations of Nuer territorial expansion to which we now turn.

CHAPTER 2

A Review of
Earlier Explanations

Nuer territorial expansion and their displacement of the Central Dinka (and Western Anuak) represents one of the most prominent cases of "evolutionary success" contained in the ethnographic record. Although we know from archaeological and linguistic evidence that many cultural systems have spread over vast areas, physically displacing and/or transforming the neighboring cultures that lay in their path, there are very few instances in which this relatively common phenomenon of the prehistoric past can be studied ethnographically in terms of extant cultures. The Nuer-Dinka case thus provides a rare opportunity to enhance our understanding of the causes, processes, and mechanisms by which one cultural system replaces another within a particular region.

Given the theoretical significance of the case, it is not surprising that it has attracted considerable scholarly attention. There are a number of published articles that have attempted to elucidate the causes and means of Nuer expansion and their displacement of the Dinka. This chapter is principally devoted to a review of this literature. This will serve as a basis for clearly formulating the central questions that remain to be answered and hence lay the groundwork for a comprehensive account of Nuer territorial expansion developed in subsequent chapters. Although all previous interpretations have made important contributions to the subject, none have addressed or accounted for the full range of available data. It may also be noted in advance that all previous attempts to explain the impetus to Nuer expansion rely implicitly or explicitly on notions of "population pressure" as the principal causal factor. A substantial portion of the chapter is thus devoted to evaluating this explanation. Material presented in the preceding chapter is particularly relevant to this question. We have seen that the Nuer assimilated very large numbers of Dinka and that the Nuer population increased very substantially as a result. This strongly suggests that population growth was primarily a consequence of Nuer expansion rather than a cause, and thus casts doubt on extant explanations that invoke or depend upon "population pressure."

Earlier explanations of Nuer territorial expansion are also significant in another respect: they constitute a historical sequence of anthropological approaches to a specific issue that has been of enduring concern. These successive explanations are grounded in theoretical positions that have been prominent in the history of anthropological theory over the last half-century and thus present a selective slice of that history. Although the present study is primarily concerned with elucidating the issues pertaining to Nuer expansion, rather than the history of anthropological theory, the following review of the literature on this subject necessarily constitutes a commentary on the contributions and lacunae of the various theoretical perspectives that inform the explanations put forward. I have consequently made an effort to maintain the integrity of each author's formulation by noting the principal issues addressed and the relation of the issue of Nuer expansion to these. Specific arguments are extracted from the broader context in which they were originally presented only after this context has been noted. Each explanation is also considered in historical sequence and in relation to those that preceded it. This mode of presentation is not as economical as some of the alternatives, but it is the most appropriate for consideration of a series of formulations that are of interest in terms of both the history of theory and the elucidation of specific theoretical issues.

EVANS-PRITCHARD

Evans-Pritchard's books and articles on the Nuer constitute the single most important body of material pertaining to Nuer territorial expansion, and his ethnographic contributions have been mined by all subsequent authors who have attempted to explain it. It is consequently important to examine Evans-Pritchard's perspective on questions relevant to this subject. However, it should be kept in mind that developing an explanation of Nuer expansion was not a principal objective of any of Evans-Pritchard's publications, and that detailed comparative materials on the Dinka essential to the enterprise were largely unavailable at the time of his writing. In general terms, Evans-Pritchard's perspective in his central work on the Nuer (1940*a*) reflects his primary concern with the principles of operation of a segmentary structural system.

In Evans-Pritchard's interpretation, the general nature of the relationship between the Nuer and the Dinka is predicated on their inclusion within a single structural system: "Contiguous Dinka and Nuer tribes are segments within a common structure as much as are segments of the same Nuer tribe. Their social relation is one of hostility and its expression is in warfare" (Evans-Pritchard, 1940*a*:125). Evans-Pritchard emphasizes the point that this warfare is a manifestation or expression of a structural relationship of segmentary opposition, not merely a contest for cattle and land (1940*a*:50, 131).

However, this raises questions concerning the source of this structural relationship. Evans-Pritchard addresses these questions by arguing that the structural relationship itself is largely determined by the marked *cultural similarity* between the two tribes—a similarity attributed partly to common habitat and mode of livelihood and partly to historical circumstances of linguistic and cultural divergence from a common stock (1940a:131). In other words, the Nuer are said to most readily enter into relations of hostility with those neighboring tribes that most nearly resemble them in culture. Although these cultural similarities most notably include the possession of extensive grazing land and large numbers of cattle (which the Nuer seize in raids), Evans-Pritchard clearly seeks to avoid reducing the question of intercultural relations to these terms.

> An explanation of warfare between Nuer and Dinka by reference to cattle and pastures alone is too simple a reduction. Hostility is expressed in terms of cattle, and desire for cattle accounts for some peculiarities of the struggle and some characteristics of the political organizations involved in it, but the struggle itself can only be fully understood as a structural process. (Evans-Pritchard, 1940a:50)

Evans-Pritchard's position is supported by the fact that all major Nuer tribes share a border with the Dinka (see map 1), an arrangement of territories which is remarkable given the extensive migrations of these autonomous units during the nineteenth century. Although this is consistent with the view that segmentary opposition played a role in Nuer-Dinka warfare, this structural relationship does not explain Nuer territorial expansion. In other words, it is relevant to the occurrence of fighting between these two cultural groups but does not account for the fact that territory changed hands.

Nonstructural factors are not excluded from Evans-Pritchard's formulation but are generally regarded as secondary or subsidiary. Herd reductions brought about by rinderpest are thus said to have intensified Nuer cattle raiding, since the Nuer traditionally recouped their stock losses at Dinka expense. However, rinderpest was first introduced into the area in the early 1890s, while Nuer raids are known to have been most extensive during the earlier period of territorial expansion. The economic dislocation that resulted from these herd reductions therefore cannot be regarded as a causal factor in the development of Nuer-Dinka hostilities, or in the territorial expansion of the Nuer (already completed by that time).

The Nuer expansion itself is attributed, in part, to the skill and courage of the Nuer in military engagements that were brought about by the structural relation between these two cultural groups; segmentary opposition was expressed in warfare and the Nuer consistently prevailed, attaining a "moral ascendancy" over the Dinka (Evans-Pritchard, 1940a:126–27). However,

Evans-Pritchard also notes (1940a:111, 131) that the Nuer appropriation of Dinka territory was precipitated by overpopulation and facilitated by the absence of any ecological impediments to Nuer utilization of these lands.

That the Nuer and Dinka occupied a common ecological zone is highly significant in the context of the evolutionary (or adaptive) approach later adopted by Sahlins (1961), inasmuch as this datum makes the Nuer expansion amenable to explanation through application of principles derived from ecology and evolutionary biology. (This interpretation is discussed more fully in a subsequent section.) In contrast, this ecological factor fits awkwardly into Evans-Pritchard's analytic framework, and he therefore fails to appreciate the full significance of it. He regards the common habitat shared by the Nuer and Dinka as a cause of the cultural similarity that engenders the structural relationship which finds its expression in warfare.

The argument that Nuer expansion was a consequence of overpopulation is a recurrent theme in the literature concerning Nuer-Dinka warfare and one which requires careful scrutiny. Evans-Pritchard (1940a:111) reports that the Nuer themselves invoke population pressures as the cause of their eastward expansion, and he concurs in this interpretation. Evans-Pritchard estimates the average population density of Nuerland as 5 to 6 persons per square mile and argues (1940a:111) that "it may be doubted whether it [Nuer territory] could support a much larger population than it does." This has clearly been disproved by history inasmuch as Nuer population increased from 247,000 in the circa 1930 census to 460,000 in 1955 (Sudan Government Census, 1955). Both the extent of Nuer territory and the transhumant subsistence economy remained essentially unchanged throughout this period. Population density thus increased from 7.9 to 14.7 persons per square mile. The former figure represents a correction of Evans-Pritchard's estimate based on a more accurate determination of the Nuer territorial domain provided by Howell (1954a:239), and a Nuer population (circa 1930) of 247,000. The total of 247,000 represents the sum of the Nuer tribal populations enumerated by Evans-Pritchard (1940a:117), although he employs a Nuer population of only 200,000 in calculating Nuer density (ibid.:111). This error in calculation is immaterial; the main point here is simply that Nuer population densities at the time of Evans-Pritchard's fieldwork did not approach the environmental limits of Nuer territory as he suggests. The Nuer did not experience population pressure in the early 1930s and there is consequently no evidence that it provided the impetus to Nuer territorial expansion.

There are a number of additional reasons for rejecting this supposition. If the Nuer were induced to invade Dinka territory in order to achieve a reduction of excessively high population density (by distributing their population over a more extensive area), then the complete expulsion of the Dinka would logically be their prime objective. However, we have already seen that the

Nuer assimilated captives, migrants, and entire communities on a massive scale during the period of territorial expansion. Such extensive assimilation of Dinka tribesmen is clearly inconsistent with any attempt on the part of the Nuer to reduce population densities through territorial expansion. Moreover, each successive stage of Nuer conquest significantly reduced Nuer densities and thus would have obviated the need for further territorial appropriation prompted by population pressure. Such pressure therefore could not have provided a sustained impetus to Nuer expansion unless the Nuer population was increasing at a rapid rate. However, the assumption of a rate of internal population growth necessary to sustain population pressure throughout the expansion period entails a Nuer population so small in 1800 that both pressure and the capacity to expand would be inconceivable. This self-falsifying feature of the population pressure argument will be more fully explained later in the chapter, in the context of a more detailed examination of the issue. It is sufficient to note here that it can be demonstrated that Nuer population density declined very substantially between 1800 and 1890, despite the assimilation of more than 100,000 Dinka, and that population pressure therefore cannot have provided a sustained impetus to Nuer territorial expansion. It may also be noted, in anticipation of subsequent discussion, that a consideration of cultural factors affecting the ratio of cattle to grazing land (rather than human population density) does illuminate the central features of Nuer appropriation of Dinka lands.

SAHLINS

Sahlins (1961) addresses the question of Nuer expansion from an evolutionary perspective within the context of a more general argument concerning the succession of evolutionary forms. His principal objectives are to explain the emergence and distribution of segmentary lineage systems as a specific type of organization or, more precisely, as a "specific adaptive variety" within the tribal level of general evolutionary progress (Sahlins, 1961:322–24). The Nuer and Tiv are the two representatives of this adaptive variety insofar as they alone possess full-fledged segmentary lineage organization (defined by the presence and co-occurrence of six formal characteristics: lineality, segmentation, local-genealogical segmentation, segmentary sociability, complementary opposition, and structural relativity).

Sahlins views segmentary lineage systems as an adaptive response to identifiable selective pressures. In general terms, his argument thus entails a specification of the selective circumstances that give rise to this form of organization and a delineation of the central adaptive functions served by it. His case rests on the convergence represented by the Tiv and Nuer instances: closely comparable selective pressures engender identical organizational forms (in terms of the six characteristics noted above). In the present context, we are concerned only with his analysis of the Nuer case as it pertains to the central question of Nuer expansion. In brief, Sahlins proposes that segmentary lineage organization is an adaptation to a social environment characterized by the selective pressures of intercultural competition between tribes that occupy the same ecological zone. Nuer-Dinka warfare is a manifestation of this competition and the Nuer segmentary lineage system serves the adaptive function of supplying a numerical advantage in these hostilities (through the mobilization of superior numbers of Nuer tribesmen). The events of Nuer expansion stand as testimony to both competition and adaptive advantage.

Sahlins argues (1961:339) that "Nuer expansion represents the successful conquest of a particular ecological niche: the true savannah of the Sudan." The dimensions and boundaries of this niche are defined in terms of environmental features and also by the suitability of a given area to the Nuer "mode of production." The territory of the (eastern) Ngok Dinka and the Shilluk are located in areas of poor pasture that are said to be marginal to the Nuer mode of production, while the Anuak have been pushed into tsetse-fly-infested forests inimical to the maintenance of large cattle populations. The Western Dinka are likewise seen as having been expelled from the true savannah and pushed into a savannah-forest ecological zone (a region of grassy areas interspersed among tracts of forest). This region presents no serious handicaps to the Nuer mode of production (although largely outside the true savannah as environmentally defined), and the Dinka are consequently the most frequent victims of Nuer predation (Sahlins, 1961:339).

It is not entirely clear whether Sahlins intends to delineate the boundaries of a niche by environmental features (such as savannah versus savannah-forest) or by suitability to a particular mode of production. The Western Dinka region is outside the Nuer niche by the former criterion but included within it by the latter. However, this point is not critical to Sahlins's argument at this juncture. A "mode of production" definition of the relevant ecological niche would only mean that the Nuer conquest of it was incomplete at the time territorial expansion ceased.[1] By either definition the Nuer and the Dinka would be co-occupants of a single niche at the inception of Nuer territorial expansion. This is the principal ground for adducing the selective pressure of intercultural competition that is central to Sahlins's formulation. The adequacy of these grounds will be considered after additional elements of Sahlins's argument have been introduced.

Having argued that the Nuer conquered an ecological niche, Sahlins (1961:339) goes on to suggest that

> Nuer expansion is perhaps an outstanding instance of the Law of Cultural Dominance, the principle that the cultural system most effective in a particular en-

vironment will spread there at the expense of thermodynamically less effective systems. (Kaplan, 1960)

However, no evidence is presented that would indicate that the Nuer are more thermodynamically effective than the Dinka, i.e., more effective in terms of energy capture. This would presuppose some significant difference in economic organization, while Sahlins (ibid.) emphasizes the differences between the Nuer and Dinka in lineage organization, noting that they are culturally similar in other respects. It is the Nuer organizational advantage that enabled them to unite on a larger scale than the Dinka and consequently expel the latter. (Sahlins cites Lienhardt [1958:108] to document this point.)

Further difficulties arise with respect to measurement of thermodynamic effectiveness. Kaplan (1960:76), who formulated this law, notes that "it offers no measure of a cultural system's thermodynamic effectiveness independently of the fact that it does indeed prevail and tend to spread at the expense of rival systems in a particular environment." Kaplan recognizes this as a shortcoming that should be clarified through further research. In subsequent discussion of a specific case, Kaplan (1960:79) proposes that "population density figures may serve as an approximate measure of the relative amounts of energy captured by these cultural systems in their respective environments." In other words, a comparatively higher density is indicative of greater thermodynamic effectiveness. However, the application of this metric to the case at hand leads to the conclusion that the Dinka are more thermodynamically effective than the Nuer. Dinka population densities are consistently 4 to 6 persons per square mile higher than those of the Nuer when any two adjacent districts are compared. Howell (1955:76) provides the following figures based on administrative census materials collected in the early 1950s.[2]

Dinka Districts		*Nuer Districts*	
Lakes	16.2	Western Nuer	13.9
Jur River	20.2	Lou and Zeraf Valley	11.0
Aweil	18.5	Eastern Nuer	13.6
Bor	15.0		
average	17.7	average	12.5

The Western Nuer (at 13.9 persons per square mile) are neighbors of the Jur River Dinka (at 20.2) and the Lou and Zeraf Valley Nuer (at 11.0) are neighbors of the Bor District Dinka (at 15.0). The latter comparison is particularly significant due to the environmental similarities between these respective Nuer and Dinka districts. Both are within the true savannah and there is no environmental discontinuity along the border between them. Moreover, it is important to recall that four thousand square miles of Lou and Zeraf Valley Nuer territory was ceded to the Bor District Dinka (i.e., the Southern Dinka) by the colonial administration in 1910. This increased Central Nuer population density while at the same time decreasing that of the Bor District Dinka by nearly doubling their domain. Yet Dinka density was still more than a third higher than that of the neighboring Nuer in the early 1950s. (This consistent difference between the Nuer and Dinka in population density will be explained in a later chapter.)

Measuring thermodynamic effectiveness by population density therefore leads irrevocably to the conclusion that the Dinka are more effective in this respect than the Nuer. The Law of Cultural Dominance would then dictate that the Dinka should spread at Nuer expense rather than the converse. Nuer expansion thus stands as a prominent exception to Kaplan's Law and is clearly not elucidated by Sahlins's citation of it.

The selective pressure of competition between two cultural groups that jointly occupied a single ecological niche would logically apply equally to both. Why, then, did the Nuer rather than the Dinka adapt to this selective pressure by developing a segmentary lineage organization that enabled them to expand at Dinka expense? Sahlins answers this question by proposing that the Nuer and Dinka were confronted with different selective circumstances associated with the sequence of occupation of the region.

> The Dinka appear to have spread without great opposition. *They were first.* They naturally grew by segmentation, and fissioning units could, in the absence of external threat, afford to organize as small, virtually self-contained entities. . . .
>
> The Nuer, by contrast, were invaders. They spread through an already occupied niche, one held by the Dinka, and the very large Nuer population, over 200,000, is testimony to their success. The Nuer had different adaptive problems than the Dinka, precisely because *the Dinka were already there.* This selective circumstance placed a premium on the ability to fuse as well as to segment, on complementary opposition. Nuer segmentary lineage organization was the adaptive response. The Dinka, whose development in an open environment had favored segmentation but minimized fusion, then found themselves socially ill-equipped to cope with Nuer predation. (Sahlins, 1961:340)

This does not entirely answer the question posed above, since the Dinka would be confronted with the same adaptive problem as the Nuer once the latter arrived on the scene (i.e., at the same time that the Nuer were confronted with the Dinka). However, it is implicit in Sahlins's argument that the Dinka adaptive response to the presence of the Nuer was limited and constrained by a prior adaptation. This position would also be consistent with the well-documented Law of Evolutionary Potential developed by Service (in Sahlins and Service, 1960:97).

The more specialized and adapted a form in a given evolutionary stage, the smaller is its potential for passing to the next stage.

However, this raises further questions concerning the prior adaptive commitments of the Nuer, who appear somewhat magically after the Dinka are already established in this ecological niche. Where were the Nuer when the Dinka first spread throughout this region and what selective circumstances confronted the Nuer at that time? Why did their prior adaptation to those circumstances impose a lesser degree of constraint on the later development of a segmentary lineage organization than the prior adaptation of the Dinka? A similar point concerning the whereabouts of the Nuer is taken up by Newcomer (1972) in an article discussed later in the chapter.

It is evident here (as elsewhere) that competition between the joint occupants of a common ecological niche constitutes the critical selective pressure in Sahlins's formulation. The Nuer segmentary lineage system represents both an adaptation to this selective pressure and the adaptive advantage that enabled the Nuer to expand at Dinka expense. The absence of comparable competition at an earlier stage of Dinka development produced a comparatively disadvantageous adaptation that constrained further evolutionary advance. Moreover, Nuer territorial expansion itself is a consequence of the same competition to which they adapted. While competition is thus central to the entire argument, the causes of this competition are not clearly established or adequately explained. On what grounds are the Nuer and Dinka taken to be in competition with each other and what, in the final analysis, are they competing for? The answer to the second question would appear to be that they are competing for the sole possession of an ecological niche. The answer to the first question is implicit in the presentation of Sahlins's argument: joint occupancy of a single ecological niche provides the grounds for adducing the selective pressure of competition. Competition is thus operative when the Nuer and Dinka both occupy the true savannah, but not before this.

The key question, then, becomes one of the legitimacy of adducing competition from joint occupancy of a particular ecological niche. Consideration of the principle of competitive exclusion, developed by evolutionary biology, provides a means of answering this question, since the principle contains a precise specification of the conditions under which competition constitutes a selective mechanism. Competitive exclusion is explained by Smith (1966:419) as follows:

> Essentially this principle means that if two noninterbreeding populations occupy exactly the same ecological niche, if they occupy the same geographic territory, and if population *A* multiplies even the least bit faster than population *B*, then *A* eventually will occupy the area completely and *B* will become extinct.

The differential growth rates of populations *A* and *B* may be due to a number of complex factors. However, it is frequently the case that such populations share the same food resources and that each is food limited. In this case, the food consumed by one population is unavailable to the other. The population that consumes more and translates this consumption into a higher reproductive rate then prevails. The critical point here is that a shared food resource must be in short supply so that the two populations press against the capacity of their common environment. Similar species *can* in fact coexist when shared resources are adequate (Smith, 1966:419). This would occur when populations are maintained below capacity by other factors, such as disease.

This clearly indicates that intercultural competition between the Nuer and Dinka is not inevitable simply because they occupy the same ecological niche. As a minimal condition for adducing such competition it would be necessary to establish that some strategic resource was in short supply and that the two cultural populations jointly pressed against the capacity of the niche with respect to that resource. In other words, competition is not inherent in the Nuer-Dinka context but contingent on a general condition of "population pressure." However, it has already been noted that the Nuer were not compelled to appropriate Dinka territory by population pressure (measured in terms of human population density). The causes of the intercultural competition that supplies the selective pressure in Sahlins's argument therefore remain unexplained.

Sahlins raises the issue of population pressure but does not invoke it as a principal cause of Nuer (and Tiv) expansion. He notes Evans-Pritchard's position (discussed earlier) and goes on to suggest (1961:341)

> Perhaps population pressure in critical central locations gives impetus to both Tiv and Nuer predation. Yet it seems to us that a certain relativity is required in assessing land hunger among societies competing for occupation of a specific habitat. Because the success of one contestant is necessarily to the detriment of the other, neither has *enough* land until the other has been eliminated. The need for "living space" is built in: it becomes a cultural attitude and theory, particularly in that society which has the decisive competitive advantage. Among the invaders a natural increase of population beyond the carrying capacity of present resources will be taken for granted and at least for them land hunger exists—the idea is adaptively advantageous—even if, by objective standards, there is enough land to support the present population.

In Sahlins's view, the cultural perception of land shortage thus provides the motivating force behind Nuer expansion. However, this perception is seen to follow from an *objective* condition of competition between societies that occupy a common niche. It has already been pointed out that joint occupancy of a niche is an insufficient ground for adducing competition. The Nuer may well exhibit the cultural attitudes that Sahlins attributes to them, but it is as yet unclear why they must necessarily hold these views.

It is important to point out that most of the criticisms of Sahlins's formulation presented here focus on the incompleteness of certain arguments. The difficulty is not that competition could not constitute a selective mechanism, but that Sahlins fails to demonstrate that it is applicable to the case at hand. Similarly, cultural perceptions may play a significant role in providing the impetus to Nuer expansion as Sahlins argues. The difficulty is that he does not adequately account for these perceptions, linking them to a scientific principle of competition rather than the specific conditions of Nuer cultural life. Both of these points pertain to sins of omission rather than commission. However, noting these lacunae is fully consistent with the principal objectives of our critical review of the literature concerning Nuer territorial expansion. We seek to specify the questions that remain to be answered so that they can be addressed in subsequent chapters. This is not intended to diminish the very significant contributions to the subject made by earlier authors. The interpretation presented in later chapters builds directly on these advances, as will be readily apparent.

NEWCOMER

Newcomer's general objective is to outline a unidirectional and cumulative process of sociocultural development that would ''account for the emergence of socio-cultural entities as such'' (Newcomer, 1972:5). He employs the Nuer-Dinka case as an illustration of the general features of this process.

Newcomer opens his inquiry into Nuer origins by considering a null hypothesis, viz., that the Nuer are to be regarded as an intrusive group. He presents Evans-Pritchard's (1940a:5) map and notes that this could be interpreted as suggesting a Nuer invasion that has cut a wide swath through Dinka territory, separating the Eastern and Western Dinka by 150 to 200 miles. However, he rejects this interpretation on the following grounds. Cultural and linguistic similarities, together with the size of the two populations, suggest a long period of contact between Nuer and Dinka. Thus the Nuer are not recent migrants to the area. However, ''if we grant long contact, competition, and consistent victimization of Dinka, why are any Dinka left at all?'' (Newcomer, 1972:6). Newcomer therefore concludes that it is more reasonable to assume that the Nuer were formerly Dinka, having emerged through internal processes of sociocultural differentiation.

This conclusion is essentially correct, although it would be more accurate to say that the Nuer and Dinka share a common origin than that the Nuer are derived from the Dinka. It is well established that the Nuer and Dinka languages are derived from a common linguistic stock. This point was made by Evans-Pritchard (1940a:3) and has been more recently confirmed by McLaughlin's (1967:13–27) and Johnson's (1980:575) lexico-statistical data (presented in chap. 1). Similarly, more accurate maps than the one Newcomer presents indicate that Dinka territory surrounds that of the Nuer on the north as well as the west (see map 1). Thus there is no open corridor on the northwest border of Nuerland and the present geographical distribution of the Nuer and Dinka does not lend itself to any interpretation of past events entailing a Nuer invasion launched from a point outside present-day Nuer territory. It is also well established that the Nuer expanded to the east and south from Nuer homeland located on the west bank of the White Nile (as discussed in chap. 1).

It is evident that this initial question Newcomer raises concerning the possible external origin of the Nuer arises in relation to Sahlins's formulation, although Newcomer never makes this explicit. Sahlins (1961:340) maintains that the Nuer were "invaders" who appeared after the Dinka were already established in the region.[3] This provides the differential selective circumstances that account for the development of segmentary lineage organization by the Nuer, but not the Dinka. If the Nuer are in fact derived from the Dinka, then the nature of the difference in selective circumstances would not be readily apparent and would require further explication (as noted earlier). Although Newcomer's initial point is thus quite significant with respect to Sahlins's argument, he neglects to point this out.

Having established the plausibility of the hypothesis that the Nuer originated within the confines of Dinka territory, Newcomer (1972:7) proposes the following sequence of events to account for their emergence as a distinct sociocultural entity.

> Imagine Dinka- and Nuer-land, perhaps 400 years ago, as occupied by one culture/people/society resembling present-day Dinka in social structure. As time passes, population pressure upon land leads to expansion to ecological boundaries (for this type of society, the limits of unoccupied cattle country). Continued population pressure leads to raiding and wars. Over time, groups become differentiated and intergroup competition tends toward a war of all against all. Each group raids others in statistically random fashion.
>
> Now postulate a group of these "Dinka" who develop a social mutation which works like Sahlins' conception of the segmentary lineage (Sahlins 1961), that is, as an adaptation for predatory expansion.

Sahlins's point concerning the organizational advantage of the Nuer segmentary lineage system in mobilization for warfare is then adduced to account for the spread of this "social mutation." Warring continues and the proto-Nuer prevail, incorporating additional territory and assimilating captured or defeated Dinka. The "mutant group" thus expands outward to the east, west, and south (from an area depicted on Newcomer's map [1972:9] as centered along the White Nile or Bahr el Jebel, somewhat south of the Nile–Bahr el Ghazal confluence).

The successful territorial expansion of the Nuer attests to a decisive advantage in intertribal warfare. In assessing the factors responsible for this, Newcomer emphasizes the capacity of the Nuer to combine on a larger scale than the Dinka (a point noted earlier by Lienhardt [1958:108] and emphasized by Sahlins). While this capacity is primarily attributed to Nuer segmentary lineage organization (following Sahlins), Newcomer (1972:8) also suggests that environmental factors may have played a significant role in the development of organizational differences between the Nuer and Dinka. The distribution of wet and dry season pastures in the savannah-forest ecological zone occupied by the Dinka allows them to maintain their herds comparatively close to their villages throughout the year. The Dinka engage in less wide-ranging migrations to seasonal pastures than the Nuer, and this reduces the degree of interaction among Dinka communities, contributing to the autonomy of local groups. When fission occurs, the resultant groups are not subsequently brought into association by seasonal migrations and hence tend to operate as independent entities. Dinka territorial segments consequently combine less readily for offensive and defensive warfare than do those of the Nuer, and this conferred a decisive advantage on the latter.[4]

Newcomer's formulation differs from Sahlins's in proposing an ecological basis for the dissimilar organizational capacities that characterize the Nuer and Dinka social systems. Although both authors focus on differences concerning the maintenance of post-fission relationships, Sahlins attributes these differences to selective circumstances associated with the sequence of occupation. The Nuer entered an already occupied niche and thus were confronted with a situation in which the maintenance of post-fission relationships offered a definite adaptive advantage; the Dinka had previously expanded within a largely uncontested or "open" environment in the absence of these selective pressures.

Newcomer discounts the argument that the Nuer were intrusive and proposes a sequence of events that does not entail two distinctive phases of occupation. The Dinka proper and the Dinka (or proto-Nuer) "social mutation" therefore were not confronted with dissimilar selective circumstances on that account. Newcomer's formulation consequently requires an alternative explanation of the fact that the Nuer possess a highly developed segmentary lineage system while the Dinka do not, and he tentatively suggests that this organizational difference is traceable to ecological co-variants (as discussed above). However, Newcomer does not develop this potentially promising alternative explanation; indeed his major point is undercut by his insistence that social systems are *not* dependent variables with respect to environmental factors (Newcomer, 1972:5). In concluding, he argues (1972:10),

> It has not been "the environment," or "technology," or "culture contact" which has brought men up through their history, but rather the process by which the possibilities, logic, and contradictions within each social system produces the successor to that social system. It is this set of possibilities, this logic of development, and these contradictions which must provide the raw materials for the study of society.

Despite this rather intriguing statement, Newcomer nowhere discusses contradictions within the Dinka social system. The preeminent causal factors he does adduce are population pressure, intergroup competition, and environmental differences (all of which are external to the social system per se). Population pressure is a critical factor in his argument insofar as it is a necessary prerequisite for both intergroup competition and the proto-Nuer territorial expansion. The argument that population pressure provided the impetus to Nuer expansion has already been called into question on several grounds and will be considered in more detail later in the chapter.

In summary, Newcomer makes two important contributions to our understanding of Nuer territorial expansion. He focuses attention on the fact that the Nuer developed through cultural differentiation from the Dinka. This implicitly undercuts Sahlins's argument that Nuer segmentary lineage organization (and their resultant capacity to unite on a larger scale than the Dinka) can be accounted for in terms of differences in the sequence of occupation. Newcomer then goes on to tentatively propose an alternative explanation of organizational differences between the Nuer and Dinka that relates these to the effects of environmental differences on seasonal patterns of aggregation.

GLICKMAN

Glickman (1972) addresses the issue of the development of the Nuer social system in direct response to Newcomer's article. Although he agrees that there is no factual basis for assuming that the Nuer are intrusive rather than autochthonous, Glickman criticizes Newcomer's utilization of the notion of "social mutation" to account for Nuer origins. He points out (quite justifiably) that it is based on an inappropriate analogy drawn from evolutionary biology, that it invokes processes which are not elucidated, and that the term consequently conveys little more than "social change" and does not add to our understanding. In addition, Glickman (1972:586) faults Newcomer for attenuating "the significance of the environment in explaining differences in the Nuer and Dinka social systems" and proposes to rectify this shortcoming by developing an ecological explanation to account for these differences.

Glickman's formulation draws on Newcomer's earlier insights concerning the differential distribution of Nuer and Dinka seasonal pastures and the effects of this on patterns of dry season migration and intercommunity interaction—insights that are inconsistent with Newcomer's programmatic statement and are consequently deemphasized and incompletely developed.

Glickman (1972:586–87) notes that the Nuer differ from the Dinka in lineage organization and also manifest a marked superiority in cattle raiding. These differences are prominent against a background of basic similarities and, as a result, "a causal connection between fighting power and segmentary lineage structure has tended to be stressed at the expense of underlying ecological factors." In contrast, he argues that an analysis of ecological relations and economic resources accounts for both of these distinctive differences between the two groups. He develops this analysis by first specifying the organizational differences between the Nuer and Dinka and then linking these to co-varying ecological conditions.

In comparing Nuer and Dinka social organization, Glickman points out that the maximal Dinka group that regularly combines for offensive and defensive purposes is numerically smaller than its Nuer counterpart. (Such units are designated as "tribes" by both Evans-Pritchard and Lienhardt.) Moreover, Dinka tribes possess at least one less level of superordinate organization and also evidence a tendency toward temporary, unstable military alliances. Glickman (1972:587) summarizes what he feels to be the critical differences in alignment and hence mobilization as follows[5]:

> When a [Dinka] village joins a high order alliance its unity with its low order partner is often too weak to carry that partner along with it. To use Leinhardt's terminology, which differs from that of Evans-Pritchard, two sublineages may form part of the same main lineage, but they may belong to different sub-clans, or alternatively, one of the sublineages may not belong to a sub-clan at all. The neat Chinese box order of segments among the Nuer is lacking among the Dinka . . . [and] higher order political bodies frequently cut across lower order ones.

Insofar as Glickman's ecological analysis focuses on variations in seasonal patterns of migration (and their effect on the autonomy of local groups) it will be useful to review the basic features of the Nuer seasonal cycle before presenting this analysis. (The following account is drawn from Evans-Pritchard, 1940*a*:51–98.) At the height of the dry season (i.e., January to April), the Nuer gather in large camps along the major rivers and graze their cattle in the adjacent (partly drained) marshes. In April or early May, just before the rains commence in earnest, the older (married) individuals move from these cattle camps to the permanent village sites (located on higher ground, away from the rivers) to prepare the soil for the initial maize gardens.

Toward the end of May, the younger members of the community drive the herds from the dry season camps to these permanent settlements. After the community is reunited, the clearing and hoeing of the more extensive millet gardens is undertaken. The first millet crop is sown in late May or early June, and a second is planted in September. Ceremonies are generally held after the first harvest (in late September) when millet is available for making beer and porridge.

During the early part of the rainy season the extensive plains surrounding the permanent settlements provide lush pastures of new growth stimulated by the renewed precipitation. As the rains intensify, these grazing areas are progressively diminished by flooding conditions until pasturage is ultimately restricted to the limited areas of high ground where the permanent settlements are located. These sites become isolated islands from mid-June to the beginning of September, and intervillage communication and interaction are consequently attenuated.

As the rains begin to diminish (in late September), the rate of regrowth in the heavily grazed ridgetop pastures also diminishes, and the herds are gradually moved to the previously flooded plains as the water recedes. However, the plains rapidly become overgrown with mature perennial grasses that provide poor grazing and also impede the movements of the herd. The Nuer consequently burn off these areas as soon as this becomes feasible in order to stimulate a regrowth of easily accessible tender shoots. This provides extensive areas of good pasture toward the end of November and the younger members of the community move the cattle out from the area adjoining the ridgetop settlements to temporary camps near water pools on the burned-over plain. Meanwhile, the older people remain in the villages to harvest the second millet crop. After this is completed (in early January), the cattle are briefly returned to the settlement to graze on millet stalks in the harvested gardens. Old and young members of the community then join together in small temporary cattle camps, widely scattered across the plain near the remaining sources of standing water. Progressive drying of these intermediate pastures and water holes prompts a gradual migration toward the marshes, permanent water supply, and extensive fishing grounds available along the major watercourses. In January, the dispersed camp groups of the community coalesce at these dry season pastures where they remain until April or May when the older individuals again return to the permanent settlements to initiate the wet season gardens.

Interaction between wider social groups generally takes place during the height of the dry season when several communities or tribal sections may gather at adjacent cattle camps along the larger rivers. However, Evans-Pritchard points out that there are variations within Nuerland in the size of these gatherings, and these variations provide the ground for Glickman's hypothesis. Evans-Pritchard (1940*b*:275–76) argues that environmental differences between the regions of Nuerland located east and west of the White Nile account for co-varying differences in tribal size (see also Evans-Pritchard, 1940*a*:117–19). Eastern Nuerland is characterized by a comparative scarcity of water and pasture during the dry season, and this necessitates both more far-ranging migrations and larger concentrations of people at the limited dry season camps along major rivers. Widely distributed groups are consequently brought into close contact at this time of the year. In addition, there are wide stretches of elevated land in the eastern region, and this permits larger local concentrations of population to aggregate during the rainy season as well. In contrast, western Nuerland is characterized by narrower, more restricted areas of elevated ground (suitable for wet season occupation) and by more plentiful dry season pastures located in close proximity to permanent settlements. Environmental conditions therefore impose a comparatively greater degree of isolation and autonomy upon Western Nuer local groupings in the rainy season and, moreover, permit the maintenance of this local autonomy in the dry season as well. In Evans-Pritchard's view, the comparatively smaller size of Western Nuer tribes is explicable in these terms.

Glickman (1972:588) cites Evans-Pritchard's argument and goes on to suggest that Dinkaland presents the same environmental features as the Western Nuer region in a more accentuated form.

> There is a wider distribution of water during the dry season (Lienhardt, 1958:115) than for Nuer groups. These ecological factors, as well as the consequent proximity of each group's wet and dry season pastures (1958:132) make for a comparatively frequent fragmentation of communities with little "rule of law" (1958:133) between them. By contrast, the character of Nuer intercommunity ties is of major importance for speedy and effective mobilization.

Glickman concludes that these ecological differences provide a *sufficient* explanation for the previously described differences between the Nuer and Dinka in both social organization and fighting ability. In other words, both Nuer organizational characteristics and Nuer superiority in cattle raiding can be accounted for with reference to the underlying ecological factors which "give rise to" permanent associational ties among Nuer communities (as compared with the relative autonomy of Dinka local groups). As Glickman (1972:590) puts it, "I would argue that groups are able collectively to raid their neighbors because they have come together in the past for mutual cattle herding and milking (Evans-Pritchard, 1940*a*:115–16) and other purposes."

Although Glickman's hypothesis appears quite plausible, it presupposes a sequence of events which is totally at variance with the historical facts of the Nuer expansion. The area east of the Nile that is held to be ecologically favorable to the development of superiority in raiding and large-scale political consolidation was in the hands of the Dinka prior to 1800. If the ecological conditions of this area do, indeed, "give rise to" segmentary lineage organization and superior fighting power, then the Dinka should logically have possessed these characteristics. Under those circumstances, it would be difficult to understand how the Nuer might have successfully dislodged the Dinka, especially insofar as the Nuer were located west of the Nile prior to 1800, i.e., within the region deemed to be conducive to the development of local autonomy and comparatively slight military capabilities. The ecological factors that Glickman adduces therefore do not account for the Nuer's decisive advantage in warfare, the organizational differences between the two cultural groups, or the impetus to Nuer expansion. However, it should be noted here that Glickman does not explicitly attempt to account for the eastward expansion of the Nuer; indeed, he expresses a degree of doubt that any deliberate, large-scale invasion took place (1972:588) and argues against interpretations which utilize a "conquest theory" to account for features of Nuer and Dinka organization (1972:591).

Newcomer also proposes that environmental differences between Nuer and Dinka territory contributed to the Nuer capacity to combine on a larger scale than the Dinka, and his argument is consequently susceptible to the same criticisms, stemming from the intractable fact that the Nuer are where the Dinka were.

SOUTHALL

In a more recent article, Southall (1976:463–91) reviews the interpretations advanced by Sahlins, Newcomer, and Glickman, redefines the central question as one of cultural divergence, and proceeds to offer an explanation of the processes by which two somewhat different linguistic and cultural groups emerged from a common stock. In Southall's view,

> the burning question is how did a speech community whose members called themselves Naath [i.e., the Nuer], with a degree of common culture which we cannot precisely specify, emerge as distinct from another "congeries of peoples" (as they are evasively called) perceiving themselves as Jieng [i.e., the Dinka] and referred to by the Naath as Jaang? (Southall, 1976:466)

It should be noted that Southall's objectives overlap only partially with the central concerns of this book (i.e., the causes and means of Nuer territorial expansion) and discussion of his article will thus focus primarily on points relevant to these concerns.

Southall begins by inquiring into the reality that underlies the labels "Nuer" and "Dinka." In brief, he sees the Naath (Nuer) and Jieng (Dinka) as ethnic identifications associated with "some perceptible shifts of emphasis in various social institutions and cultural features'' (Southall, 1976:464).[6] He endorses Newcomer's point that the Nuer emerged from the Dinka (or more properly the proto-Dinka) and hence defines the central question as one of accounting for the "shifts" noted above. In other words, he is concerned to explain the development of two partial transformations of a common protoculture. In general, he takes the view that Nuer expansion itself accounts for the principal differences between the Nuer and Dinka (or Naath and Jieng as he prefers to call them). He endorses Gough's (1971) argument that Nuer political organization is largely a product rather than a cause of Nuer territorial expansion and proceeds to develop the logical complement of this position, viz., that Dinka political organization is likewise a product of centuries of defeat and displacement at the hands of the Nuer.[7] He thus concludes:

> The more the Naath attacked the more the Jieng withdrew and the more their group alignments were disturbed, the more they turned to the Masters of the Fishing Spear as the focus of mystical unity which they could not achieve politically and a working coordination which they were unable to maintain by permanent descent based structures. (Southall, 1976:488)

The central point that Nuer territorial expansion played a role in shaping certain features of both Nuer and Dinka social and political organization is well taken and a coevolutionary perspective that encompasses this point is adopted in a later chapter. However, it should be noted that this makes the questions of the causes and means of Nuer expansion all the more pressing. If Nuer segmentary lineage organization—and their attendant capacity to unite on a larger scale than the Dinka—were largely products of territorial expansion, then what made this expansion itself possible?

In addressing this question, Southall makes many of the same points noted earlier in discussion of Sahlins's and Glickman's formulations. He rejects Sahlins's argument that the sequence of occupation accounts for the Nuer advantage on the grounds that neither the Naath nor the Jieng are newcomers to the area and concludes that only differences in ecology could conceivably account for the Nuer capacity to expand at Dinka expense (Southall, 1976:468). However, he also rejects Glickman's ecological argument on the grounds that the Dinka occupied the areas said to be most conducive to the development of military superiority before nineteenth-century Nuer expansion took place (ibid.:473). The basis of the Nuer advantage must consequently be linked to the ecology of the Nuer homeland. Although Southall argues that this area is the most flooded part of the savannah in the rainy season, he fails to establish any connection between this environmental feature and the Nuer capacity to expand and dislodge the Dinka. Instead he simply asserts,

We must assume that the population of this corner of the country grew, reached optimum point and passed it, prompting efforts to expand. (Southall, 1976:474)

He further proposes that it is

quite plausible that this should have been the first niche in the whole region to reach overcapacity and hence also larger population groupings and organization. (Ibid.)

In assessing this argument it is useful to recall that the average size of Nuer communities in the homeland region is only 194 persons while the average size of their Zeraf Valley counterparts is 292 persons (Kerreri, 1931:3–8; Upper Nile Province Handbook, Zeraf Valley Section, 1930:2A). This documents Evans-Pritchard's (1940a:117–18) observation that the homeland region contains less extensive stretches of high ground than areas further east, and supports his suggestion that this factor partially accounts for the comparatively smaller average size of the homeland tribes. These data pose considerable difficulties for Southall's argument. Even if one grants Southall's assumption that the homeland region was the first locale to experience population pressure, this would not support Southall's deduction that the Homeland Nuer possessed a numerical advantage over the Dinka residing in Zeraf Island. On the contrary, Homeland Nuer communities would reach overcapacity at a size considerably smaller than Zeraf Island communities that were well below attainable population limits, since the latter are more than 50 percent larger, on average.

These data make it quite clear that the Nuer advantage must have been grounded in organizational features rather than simple demographic factors. If the Nuer were capable of uniting on a larger scale than the Dinka they expelled, this can only have been the consequence of a Nuer tribal organization that encompassed a larger number of local groups than that of the Dinka. Moreover, there is no necessary relation between larger population groupings and larger organizations as Southall argues. A large population aggregate can readily split into two small, autonomous tribes. Only organizational features pertaining to the maintenance of relations between major segments can prevent this. However, Southall regards organizational differences between the Nuer and Dinka as largely a product of Nuer territorial expansion, rather than a source of the Nuer capacity to expand at Dinka expense. His assertion that only the demographic correlates of ecological differences can conceivably account for the Nuer advantage (Southall, 1976:468) is disconfirmed by the relevant data. This not only leaves the means of Nuer expansion unexplained but also casts doubt on the proposition that organizational differences between the Nuer and Dinka were a product of it, rather than a cause.

In Southall's formulation, population growth culminating in population pressure becomes the prime mover par excellence, insofar as it supplies both the impetus to Nuer expansion and the basis of the Nuer advantage. This represents maximal reliance on an argument that is pervasive in the literature but not at all persuasive. Although contrary data and logical inconsistencies in this argument have already been extensively noted, these do not exhaust the negative evidence that can be adduced. Additional problems with the population pressure argument will be noted later in the chapter.

Thus far, explanations proposed by various authors have been examined with respect to their internal logical consistency and the degree to which they are consistent with, and account for, available data. An attempt has been made to maintain the integrity of each author's formulation by not extracting specific arguments from their broader context.[8] As a result, various viewpoints have not been exhaustively compared to bring out the critical points at which they differ, and no attempt has as yet been made to finally resolve these differences. To accomplish this, it will be necessary to briefly review the preceding explanations and the main features of the Nuer territorial expansion they address. These features include: (1) the impetus or motivating force that impelled the Nuer to appropriate Dinka lands (and to continue these appropriations over an extended period); (2) the critical characteristics that differentiate these two cultural groups with respect to their military capabilities, i.e., the characteristics that conferred a decisive advantage on the Nuer and thus provided the effective mechanism facilitating successful Nuer incursions; and (3) the causal factors adduced to account for these critical cultural differences (and hence the Nuer advantage).

Both Sahlins and Newcomer designate Nuer segmentary lineage organization as the principal source of the Nuer's decisive advantage in warfare; the attendant Nuer capacity to mobilize and field a larger fighting force than the Dinka follows from the formal characteristics and structural principles governing the operation of segmentary lineage systems. Glickman also specifies essential differences in organizational capacity that he regards as critical to Nuer superiority in cattle raiding. However, he attributes these organizational differences to dissimilarities in the range of intercommunity association and cooperation (established through divergent patterns of seasonal migration) rather than structural features inherent in specific types of lineage systems. Southall delineates organizational differences, but regards these as a result rather than a cause of Nuer expansion. He attributes the Nuer advantage to "larger organization" resulting from population growth. In other words, Nuer tribes encompassed more personnel within an organizational framework that did not differ significantly from that of the Dinka.

One can readily concur in Sahlins's and Newcomer's assessment of the significance of Nuer segmentary lineage organization in facilitating nine-

teenth-century Nuer territorial expansion. Glickman's contrasting emphasis
on established patterns of intercommunity cooperation is not convincing. He
does not explain why local groups that come together seasonally to milk and
herd their cattle (at closely contiguous locations) would necessarily join together in cattle raids as well. Aggregation at restricted dry season pastures
might well engender conflict and divisiveness rather than cooperation and
unity. Indeed Howell (1954a:187–88) reports that boundaries between the
traditional marshland pastures of local groups and tribal sections are closely
guarded in lean years and that violation of another group's dry season grazing
rights "almost invariably led to hostilities" in these unfavorable years. In
contrast, the principles of structural relativity and complementary opposition
that govern the operation of the Nuer segmentary lineage system provide an
explanatory framework that makes intercommunity conflicts of this order
intelligible and, at the same time, accounts for the Nuer capacity to comprise
internal divisiveness and unite on a tribal scale when engaged in hostilities
with the Dinka. It is also important to recall the quite remarkable fact that
every Nuer tribe shares a border with the Dinka despite the extensive migrations and territorial rearrangements of the nineteenth century. This geographical arrangement confirms the important role played by complementary
opposition.

     In Glickman's formulation ecological factors co-vary with, and account
for, the critical differences between the Nuer and Dinka. The Eastern Nuer
territory is characterized by both wide stretches of high ground (capable of
supporting a large rainy season population) and a limited number of locations
suitable for dry season cattle camps (leading to the aggregation of many local
groups at these sites). Western Nuer territory is less favored in these respects,
and Dinka territory manifests characteristics that are located near the opposite
end of the scale. As a result, the Nuer developed a pattern of extensive
cooperation between local communities in cattle raiding, a characteristic absent or attenuated in the case of the Dinka.

     Newcomer presents a quite similar argument to account for the develop-
ment of Nuer segmentary lineage organization (rather than patterns of cooperation per se); post-fission relationships are maintained in the Nuer case (but
not the Dinka) as a consequence of continued association and interaction at
dry season cattle camps. Both Newcomer and Glickman explain the distinctive differences between these two cultural groups by adducing the same
environmental factors.

     In contrast, Sahlins argues that segmentary lineage systems develop as
an adaptation to a social environment characterized by intercultural competition between groups which occupy a common ecological zone (initially, the
true savannah). A common ecological zone is defined by an absence of
significant environmental variation (internally), and Sahlins's formulation

therefore does not envision any attempt to account for the organizational differences between the Nuer and Dinka in terms of co-varying ecological differences. On the contrary, Sahlins relies on the sequence of occupation; competition is effectively joined when the Nuer appear on the scene (subsequent to prior Dinka occupation of the true savannah), and post-fission relationships are maintained by the Nuer as an adaptive response to the selective pressures of intercultural competition (absent in the case of the Dinka, who arrived first).

Although Sahlins's formulation is open to criticism on the grounds that it raises several questions which he does not resolve, his explanation nevertheless avoids the self-falsification that characterizes the ecological hypotheses proposed by Newcomer and Glickman. The latter are definitively refuted by the implacable fact that the environmental features deemed to be most conducive to the development of military superiority are located precisely in the area occupied by the Dinka prior to nineteenth-century Nuer expansion, while the Nuer then resided in an environmental zone conducive to inferior mobilization. Thus the Dinka should logically have possessed the military capability to expand at Nuer expense, rather than the reverse.

It should be noted that formidable obstacles confront any hypothesis that attempts to account for critical differences between the Nuer and Dinka in terms of co-varying environmental factors. The elevated wet season agricultural sites located in the Nuer homeland *are* generally smaller in size than comparable sites located in Nuer territory east of the Bahr el Jebel, as Evans-Pritchard (1940a:118) noted. Moreover, it is clear that this environmental characteristic does, in fact, co-vary with differences in the size of local groups. The average size of Homeland Nuer communities is only 194 persons while the comparable figure for the Zeraf Valley settlements (i.e., those of the Lak, Thiang, and Gaawar Nuer) is 292 persons.[9] The Dinka who formerly occupied the Zeraf Valley would thus have held a considerable advantage over the invading Nuer in this respect. If Nuer and Dinka tribes encompassed equivalent numbers of local groups, the Dinka tribes would be 50 percent larger. Moreover, Evans-Pritchard was also correct in pointing out that the largest dry season aggregations—conducive to the incorporation of a large number of local groups within the framework of single tribal polity—are also characteristic of the eastern region. These large dry season aggregations are attributed to environmental differences as well. Homeland Nuer communities are able to find adequate dry season pasture and water not far from their respective wet season settlements while their Eastern Nuer counterparts are compelled to migrate to major watercourses at the height of the dry season, and large numbers of local groups are thus brought into association at these locations (Evans-Pritchard, 1940a:118).

Both of the critical environmental factors favoring the development of

large tribes are therefore most accentuated in the region east of the Bahr el
Jebel, formerly inhabited by the Dinka. Moreover, the Nuer tribes that now
occupy this region are, indeed, considerably larger than their Homeland Nuer
counterparts. The figures provided by Evans-Pritchard (1940a:117) are presented below.

Homeland Nuer		*Zeraf Valley Nuer*		*Eastern Nuer*	
Bul	17,000	Lak	24,000	Lou	33,000
Leik	11,000	Thiang	9,000	Gaajak	42,000
2 Western Jikany tribes	11,000	Gaawar	20,000	Gaagwang	7,000
4 Jagei tribes	10,000	TOTAL	53,000	Gaajok	42,000
Dok	12,000			TOTAL	124,000
Nuong	9,000				
TOTAL	70,000				

The average size of the ten Homeland Nuer tribes is 7,000 persons while the
comparable figures for the Zeraf Valley Nuer and Eastern Nuer are 17,667
and 31,000 persons, respectively. Inasmuch as the four Jagei tribes frequently
combined in raids on the Dinka and the two Western Jikany tribes likewise
operated as a single military unit, the number of such units in the homeland
region may be counted as six (rather than ten), increasing the average size of
each to 11,666 persons. However, even this more generous assessment of the
scale of military units in the homeland region does not alter the fact that the
latter are considerably smaller than their Zeraf Valley and Eastern Nuer
counterparts. [10]

   The central point here is that any explanation that attempts to link Nuer
numerical superiority and Dinka inferiority to the demographic correlates of
co-varying environmental factors must take the above data into account. Yet
these data clearly point to only one conclusion: environmental factors definitely favored the Dinka rather than the Nuer. Thus while Southall realizes that an
environmental explanation of the Nuer advantage in mobilization must focus
on the ecological features of the homeland region (contra Glickman), he is
unable to provide a cogent explanation of how these features could have
conferred a numerical advantage on the Nuer. Southall proposes that we
"assume" that the demographic limits of the homeland were exceeded while
the Zeraf Valley remained below these limits. However, even if one were to
entertain Southall's assumption, it would not support the conclusion that the
Nuer held a numerical advantage for two reasons. First, the population of
Zeraf Valley settlements would have to be at only two-thirds of environmental
capacity to make them equivalent in size to fully occupied Homeland Nuer
settlements. However, this would merely establish a demographic parity and

would confer no advantage upon the Nuer. Second, differences in tribal size can only be satisfactorily explained in terms of the level at which fission takes place. There is no necessary relation between population growth and tribal size inasmuch as such growth may simply result in fission that engenders two small tribal polities. It should also be noted that Southall's assumption is inconsistent with available comparative data concerning Nuer and Dinka population densities. These data indicate that the population density of Dinka administrative districts is consistently higher than that of adjacent Nuer districts. Southall proposes that we assume the opposite.

The preceding discussion suggests that the events of Nuer territorial expansion are unlikely to be illuminated by a simple environmental explanation. The basis of the Nuer advantage cannot successfully be reduced to a dependent variable with respect to invariant environmental factors such as landforms and pasture distributions. However, the inadequacy of this particular approach does not imply that ecological relations are completely extraneous to the development of the distinctive differences between these two cultural groups. In subsequent chapters a comprehensive analysis of critical interrelationships between sociocultural and ecological variables will be employed to elucidate both the development of a Nuer advantage and the sustained impetus to Nuer territorial expansion. However, extant explanations of the latter must first be considered.

Evans-Pritchard, Newcomer, and Southall argue that population pressures prompted the Nuer (or proto-Nuer) appropriation of Dinka territory. Glickman seeks to explain Nuer superiority in cattle raiding, rather than territorial encroachment, and consequently does not concern himself with the causes of the latter. Sahlins suggests that a cultural perception of land shortage (where none objectively exists) is an expectable concomitant of intercultural competition between tribes occupying the same ecological zone, and this perception supplies the only motivation behind Nuer expansion that is proposed in his formulation. Although actual (rather than perceived) population pressure is not explicitly adduced, such pressure is nevertheless an implicit condition of Sahlins's argument. Joint occupancy of a common niche does not, in itself, constitute a sufficient ground for analytically establishing a state of competition. Competition is additionally contingent upon an objective shortage of some strategic resource, with "shortage" being defined relative to the size (or density) of the populations inhabiting the circumscribed niche. In other words, some form of "population pressure" is a precondition for the state of competition that supplies the critical "selective circumstances" in Sahlins's formulations. Any cultural perceptions of shortage that emerged as a consequence of such competition would thus represent quite accurate assessments of the situation.

A Critical Evaluation of the "Population Pressure" Assumption

Although all extant explanations of the impetus to Nuer expansion rely implicitly or explicitly on notions of "population pressure," the precise nature of this variable has not been carefully examined. Both Newcomer (1972:7) and Southall (1976:474) simply assume that the Nuer experienced such pressure without offering any justification for this position. Although negative evidence suggesting that this is an untenable assumption has already been presented, the question has not been systematically treated. A thorough examination of the relevant variables will make it clear that population pressure could not have provided a sustained impetus to Nuer territorial expansion and will, at the same time, lay the groundwork for providing a more satisfactory explanation.

Evans-Pritchard's (1940*a*:110–11) observations represent the original source of the view that population pressure stimulated Nuer territorial expansion. He suggests that the hydrological conditions of Nuerland impose an upper limit on human population density that is approached at five to six persons per square mile. Although he does not specify the precise nature of the limiting factors in the context of this discussion of overpopulation, they may be inferred from his general description of the Nuer economy. Evans-Pritchard (1940*a*:82) notes that the Nuer food supply is unreliable, and starvation is not infrequent in bad years; the older age sets are not expected to survive the co-occurrence of crop failure and stock reductions caused by rinderpest. The general tenor of Evans-Pritchard's discussion suggests that the Nuer population is regarded as food-limited, and that overpopulation refers to an imbalance in the relation between human population density and the food resources that can be derived from a delimited territorial domain. This is a highly questionable proposition and one which must be evaluated in the light of a careful examination of all available data. The presentation and analysis of these data will, at the same time, involve material important to the development of an alternative hypothesis, to be presented subsequently.

The proposition that the Nuer population is food-limited can be tested against available data concerning the nutritional status of the Nuer. Howell (1954*b*:246–52, 1954*e*: fig. E12) provides detailed information concerning the proportional contributions of various foods to the total diet and both seasonal and annual variations in the supply of each. These data are based on studies conducted in the early 1950s. In considering them, it is important to recall that the Nuer population increased from 247,000 in the circa 1930 census to 460,000 in the 1955–56 census. If the Nuer are food-limited, this 86 percent increase in the population should have severely restricted food supplies. In other words, nutritional data from the 1950s are particularly suitable for evaluating the hypothesis at hand. Indeed, it will be argued later in the chapter that the population density of the Nuer homeland in 1800 was less than the population of the same region in 1955–56.

Figure 1 (presented in chap. 1) specifies monthly variations in the consumption of milk, meat, fish, and crops in terms of caloric values. These data pertain to the flood region as a whole and thus present a composite picture of Nuer, Dinka, and Shilluk nutrition. Although there are differences among these groups in the proportional contributions of the major foods to the total diet, Howell (1954b:246) points out that there is little variation in the total number of calories consumed annually. This is also suggested by the fact that the average body weight of adult males varies only slightly among the three populations. Howell (1954b:249) provides the following figures: Dinka, 59.6 kg; Shilluk, 59.7 kg; Nuer, 62.1 kg. The Nuer, who weigh about five and one-half pounds more than the Dinka and Shilluk, thus consume somewhat more calories than are represented in the composite data (fig. 1) and the other two groups consume a few less.

The Nuer are also somewhat better off than the composite data indicate in terms of the quality of the diet. The Shilluk have considerably fewer cattle than the Nuer (and Dinka) and rely more heavily on grain and fish (Howell, 1954b:245–47). Grain also constitutes a somewhat larger proportion of the Dinka diet in comparison with that of the Nuer (as is discussed in a later chapter). In general, then, it should be kept in mind that the Nuer consume more milk and meat, and somewhat less grain than is represented in figure 1, as well as a larger number of total calories.

In evaluating the Nilotic diet, Howell (1954b:247–48) makes the following points:

(i) The general level of nutrition varies considerably throughout the season.

(ii) These variations are mainly governed by the migratory mode of life of the people and the availability of grain at different times of the year. The general level of nutrition is more dependent on grain than any other food.

(iii) The fall in grain consumption at certain times of the year is at least partly compensated for by the increased consumption of animal products (milk, fish, game animals) and the products of indigenous vegetation. As a result, the lowering of calorie intake usually coincides with an improvement in the quality of the diet.

(iv) The seasonal level of nutrition is in balance with the activities of the people. It is at its lowest in the middle of the dry season, when comparatively little work is done; it rises at the beginning of the rains when preparation of the fields and sowing of crops demand hard work; it falls again in late June and early July, when the hardest preparation work is completed. It begins to rise rapidly at the end of July, when the preparation of the ground, weeding, and sowing of the main and late crops reach a climax. Finally, it reaches its peak at the end of the rains and early part of the dry season when the harvest, some initial preparation of the cultivations for the following season, and the maintenance of the homesteads require the maximum effort.

In sum, the Nilotic diet is particularly well adapted to seasonal variations in caloric requirements. The quality of the diet, in terms of the proportional representation of different types of food, is quite good. Protein intake is quite high by world standards and the diet as a whole is more than adequate in terms of fulfilling nutritional requirements. Moreover, the Nuer are somewhat better off than other Nilotic populations in all these respects. These data clearly do not support the hypothesis that the Nuer population is food-limited. This conclusion is equally applicable to the Dinka, despite the fact that their territorial domain was vastly reduced by Nuer expansion.

Nuer stature provides another index of a highly favorable nutritional status. It is well established that adult stature is strongly affected by the general level of nutrition throughout the growth period. The fact that the Nuer are quite tall, with the average height of adult males being 179 centimeters (or 5 ft. 10 in.), therefore attests to the quality of the Nuer diet.[11] Moreover, the tall stature of the Nuer is noted in the earliest reports dating from 1840. Many of the adult men observed at that time would have attained adult stature prior to the Lou and Gaawar Nuer invasion of Zeraf Island in the 1820s, indicating a favorable nutritional status before the period of territorial expansion. This further undercuts the proposition that the Nuer population is (and was) food-limited.

Evidence of nutritional deficiencies also provides an index of food-limited status. Food-limited populations are typically characterized by clinical signs of nutritional deficiencies that are chronic in average years and become critical when the food supply is minimal. Such deficiencies constitute one of the primary mechanisms by which food supply limitations are translated into rates of mortality that effectively limit population density and are consequently a key indicator of food-limited status. In discussing the nutritional status of the Nilotics generally, Bloss (1955) reports no protein deficiency diseases or clinical signs of such deficiencies. Vitamin deficiency diseases are also uncommon, although there are clinical signs of B and C deficiencies among some individuals during the period from garden preparation to first harvest (Bloss, 1955:160). However, these temporary seasonal vitamin deficiencies would not be significant with respect to mortality rates. In short the Nuer population of 1955 did not manifest any clinical signs of nutritional deficiencies commensurate with food-limited status, despite the fact that this population had increased 86 percent in the prior twenty-five years.

The question of famine remains to be considered. The Nuer population could conceivably be food-limited—despite its generally favorable nutritional status—if it were subject to drastic and unpredictable shortages of critical items in the diet, and if the population also lacked alternative sources of food that could be substituted for those in short supply. A review of the year-to-year dependability of the principal items in the diet will show that grain shortages are indeed a common occurrence, but also one for which the Nuer are well prepared.

The major components of the Nuer diet, in order of their caloric contribution, are grain, milk, fish, and meat (see fig. 1). It is noteworthy that more fish than meat is consumed. Fish are also the most dependable component of the diet, and are most plentiful during two of the leanest months (March and April). Moreover, the fact that fish provide an assured source of protein throughout most of the year reduces the impact of shortages of other foods on the nutritional status of the population (Evans-Pritchard, 1940a:83).

Grain provides about two-thirds of the Nuer caloric intake over the course of a year (see fig. 1) and is the most important single item in the diet in this respect. However, the size of the millet harvest is quite variable from year to year and grain is thus also the least dependable component of the diet. Data provided by Howell (1954b:369) for the Central Nuer District, which is the area most subject to grain shortages, amply documents this point.[12] These data are reproduced below.

Tribal Domain	Total Number of Years Reported	Number of Years with Grain:			Number of Years when Cause of Shortage Was:	
		Surplus	*Sufficiency*	*Shortage*	*Flood*	*Drought*
Lak	21	6	7	8	6	2
Thiang	21	5	9	7	6	1
Gaawar	21	3	7	11	8	2
Lou	5	1	—	4	4	—

The occurrence of inadequate harvests ranges from one year in three (for the Thiang) to four years out of five (for the Lou). Variations in rainfall are the principal cause of the shortfall (Howell, 1954b:368). The first millet crop is planted as early as the onset of the rains permits, and the newly sprouted seedlings may be killed by brief periods of drought or, alternatively, washed out by unusually heavy rains (Evans-Pritchard, 1940a:77–78). Yields of the main crop, planted somewhat later, may be reduced by flooding in years of high water (Howell, 1954b:210). The late crop, which is planted in lower areas after the water level begins to recede, is subject to drought. Parasites, insects, and the depredations of birds and other animals may also reduce the harvest. However, losses even in a poor year are only partial, and the success of one of the three crops may partially compensate for the reduced yields derived from another (Howell, 1954*b*:210).

Although grain shortages are common, it is important to note that the size of the shortfall is quite small on a per capita basis. Howell (1955:179) reports that the Lou Nuer need to import three hundred metric tons of grain in an average year, and a maximum of six hundred tons under the worst conditions. Given a population of 103,638 (based on the Sudan Government Census of the same year), this works out to a supplement of only 2.9 kilograms of grain per person per year, on average, and a maximum of twice this figure. From a nutritional standpoint, a shortfall of this magnitude is insignificant and would have no effect on the mortality rates of the population. In short, these data do not support the view that the Nuer population was food-limited at the historically high population densities that obtained in 1955.

The Nuer have a number of means of coping with grain shortages. Crop failures are characteristically localized[13] and additional supplies can be obtained from kinsmen whose crops have fared better, or by trading cattle for grain with unrelated neighboring peoples including the Dinka (Howell, 1954*a*:188; Howell, 1954*b*:210, 369; Howell, 1955:179). Alternatively, sheep, goats, oxen, and infertile cows may be slaughtered to compensate for reduced grain consumption. Wild fruits, seeds, and roots, which normally comprise only a small portion of the diet, are also more fully utilized when grain is in short supply (Evans-Pritchard, 1940*a*:45). Water lily roots, in particular, are an important source of food during periods of hunger (Howell, 1954*b*:246–47). Game is also plentiful and the casual hunting normally practiced by the Nuer can be significantly expanded in lean years (Evans-Pritchard, 1940*a*:72–74). A shortfall in the grain harvest can thus be made up through trade or reliance on alternative sources of food, precluding serious nutritional deficiencies.

Cattle products are, in many respects, the most critical components of the Nuer diet. They provide nearly all the milk and meat[14] that constitutes the principal source of protein and the second most important source of calories in the total diet (see fig. 1). In July, when caloric intake reaches its minimum, the caloric contribution of milk and meat approximates that of grain. Moreover, the Nuer rely on these cattle products, and on grain secured in exchange for cattle, to carry them through the leanest years. Cattle thus represent the Nuer's main security against starvation (Howell, 1954*b*:210). It is notable in this connection that Evans-Pritchard (1940*a*:82) explicitly links the occurrence of famine to the general depletion of Nuer herds. Crop failures alone did not produce famine conditions; the latter occurred only when these were combined with severe herd reductions brought about by the introduction of rinderpest.

Although millet is the most important single item in the diet in caloric terms, it is the availability of cattle products that ultimately imposes an upper limit on human population density (but a limit that, we will argue, has not been reached). The importance of cattle products in this respect is primarily due to the fact that the cattle population constitutes a reserve that can carry the population through a year of crop failure until the following year's harvest. Grain can be acquired, in quantity, in exchange for cattle, and meat from slaughtered animals can be directly substituted for millet in order to maintain adequate nutritional levels. Moreover, there are a number of wild foods that can be collected to compensate for grain shortages. These include water lilies, wild yams, and the seeds of wild sorghum and other grasses that ripen at the same time as domesticated grains (Evans-Pritchard, 1940*a*:72–75). In contrast, there are no commensurate substitutes for cattle products. Fish are a dependable source of protein, but the catch cannot readily be expanded. The quantity of game taken can be expanded, but favorable opportunities for hunting are seasonally limited. Moreover, very substantial amounts of meat would be required to replace the milk normally consumed by the Nuer. Cattle can be obtained in exchange for grain, but not in quantity nor on nutritionally advantageous terms. It takes a number of years for a depleted cattle population to breed up to former levels and the available substitutes are not adequate to compensate for a severe and protracted shortage of cattle products. The maximum attainable Nuer population density is thus limited by the size of the cattle population and by its stability over time.

It should be noted that Nuer reliance on cattle products is due as much to cultural preferences as to inherent environmental limitations affecting agriculture. There are a number of ways in which grain production could be increased, thereby reducing Nuer dependence on their cattle to carry them through periods of grain shortage. The feasibility of these measures is indicated by the fact that many of them are practiced by the Dinka. For example, yields could be increased by the application of readily available cattle manure, a technique practiced by the Western Dinka (Stubbs and Morrison, 1938) but abjured by the Nuer (Evans-Pritchard, 1940*a*:79; Howell, 1954*a*:185). Planting schedules could be elaborated—as they are among the neighboring Southern Dinka—to include four separate crops instead of three and thereby spread the risk of partial crop loss due to untimely rain or drought. The amount of land in production might also be expanded inasmuch as it is widely reported that garden land is plentiful (Jackson, 1923:99; Evans-Pritchard, 1937:44; Tothill, 1948:169; Howell, 1954*b*:328).[15] The Nuer are also described as casual cultivators who devote little effort to protecting their gardens from the depredations of birds and wild animals (Evans-Pritchard, 1940*a*:78). Intensification, expansion of the quantity of land cultivated, and better protection of standing crops all represent potential means of enhancing the possibility of adequate millet harvests. However, the Nuer fail to employ these procedures and instead concentrate their efforts on maintaining and expanding the cattle herds they rely on to sustain them in years of grain shortage. Evans-Pritchard (1940a:80–81) emphasizes the Nuer's disdain for agricultural pursuits and their tendency to reduce the size of their cultivations to the extent permitted by the growth of family herds. Howell (1954b:326) likewise reports that Nuer agriculture is directed to the objective of producing only the minimum quantity of grain necessary for subsistence. In short, the Nuer transhumant economy displays a specific mix of herding and horticultural components that represents one of several equally viable possibilities. This point will be elaborated in subsequent chapters by showing that the Nuer and Dinka economic systems vary in this (and other) respects. The conclusion we wish to draw here is that the Nuer economic variant of transhumance—and the ultimate reliance on cattle it entails—represent a cultural preference rather than an adaptive necessity imposed by environmental conditions. This is significant in the present context because the limiting factors under discussion pertain to the specific Nuer economic variant of transhumance.

The Nuer's ultimate reliance on cattle products specifies the principal criteria for addressing the question of food-limited status. To the degree that the Nuer population is indeed food-limited, these limits will be determined by the size and density of the cattle population. The question then turns on a specification of the factors pertaining to the latter.

The maximum upper limit of cattle density is determined by the availability of wet and dry season pastures, respectively. In general, the effective limits pertain to dry season pasture rather than wet. In nearly all (if not all) areas of Nuerland the cattle population is limited by circumscribed dry season grazing areas of restricted distribution. These pastures are fully utilized and grazing shortages occur regularly. In contrast, wet season pasturage is generally adequate. However, severe rainy season grazing shortages that produce significant herd reductions may occur at intervals of about forty years. At these times the cattle population is reduced to a level below that supportable by dry season pastures. However, the cattle population then recovers, in relatively few years, to the point where dry season pasture is the limiting factor.

This general picture can most readily be fleshed out by considering the seasonal plane of nutrition of the cattle population. The most favorable period is the early rainy season when the most nutritive grasses begin their regrowth and fresh water is also plentiful (Howell, 1954b:281). As the rains intensify, the rising water level floods the savannah and available pasture contracts. By early to mid-August, high water, mud, and rank vegetation restrict the cattle population to the elevated wet season pastures. This marks the beginning of a period of hardship for the livestock population, since both the quantity and quality of available grazing progressively declines over the remainder of the rainy season (ibid.). The condition of the cattle thus declines until late September when the receding flood waters and vegetational changes make the surrounding area amenable to grazing once again.[16] The tall grasses are burned off in early November (or as soon thereafter as conditions permit) and the regrowth provides "a tonic to livestock which have been merely surviving under difficult conditions and on poor pasture for the previous four months" (Howell, 1954b:280).

Although this is a difficult period for the cattle, and results in a decline in their condition, this decline proceeds from the highest point in their annual plane of nutrition and is partially alleviated in late September when previously flooded areas become accessible to grazing. A reduction in the size of the cattle population does take place at this time, but this is restricted to the culling of older and weaker animals. Sacrifices coincide with the harvest period, beginning in August (Evans-Pritchard, 1940a:82, 97), and thus also coincide with the period of hardship for the cattle population. Howell (1954b:247) points out that failing animals are prime candidates for slaughter. The net result is a culturally managed herd reduction that leaves the reproductive (and milk producing) potential of the cattle population undiminished. In other words, this period of seasonal grazing shortage did not produce the kind or degree of mortality that would limit the cattle population at the densities that prevailed in 1954. Wet season grazing shortages impose a potential limit, but one that had not yet been reached.

In the early dry season pasturage is plentiful throughout Nuerland. However, grazing shortages may occur at the height of the dry season when the herds are moved to restricted areas of marshland along major watercourses. These shortages are a consequence of fluctuations in the river level. In years of low water the cattle can penetrate further into the marsh and graze extensively on the most desirable grasses (Howell, 1954b:281). Ease of movement and ample pasturage provide very favorable conditions. Conversely, in years of high water the herds are restricted to the margins of the marsh and grazing shortages typically occur. This prompts efforts to seek alternative grazing at other locations. However, these also tend to be overstocked in such years and available pasture may prove insufficient to carry the cattle population through the dry season (Howell, 1954b:211). Conflict between Nuer tribal sections and between the Nuer and Dinka frequently occurs under these circumstances (Howell, 1954b:237).

The dry season grazing shortages that occur in high-water years are aggravated by the difficulties of distributing the cattle population evenly over scarce resources. Although there are local variations in the severity of the shortages, an effective redistribution of the cattle population is hampered by the fact that grazing rights restrict access to pastures that are capable of supporting additional cattle. Traditional boundaries are closely guarded in lean years and Howell (1954a:118) reports that conflicts resulting from the infringement of grazing rights frequently resulted in bloodshed.

The decline in the condition of the cattle that occurs during dry season grazing shortages produces a different distribution of mortality than that associated with the wet season decline. The cattle population is concentrated in herds that include as many as five thousand animals (Howell, 1954b:211), providing ideal conditions for the transmission of contagious diseases, internal parasites, and diseases transmitted by insects.[17] Mortality from these diseases increases under prevailing conditions of nutritional stress. The losses include cows and cow-calves, as well as other animals, and this consequently reduces not only the size but also the reproductive potential of the cattle population. Dry season grazing shortages thus impose an effective limit on the cattle population.

High-water years that engender dry season grazing shortages occur quite frequently. Howell (1954b:239) provides detailed data on water levels in the Aliab Valley (in Dinka territory) between 1905 and 1952. High minima occurred in thirteen of forty-eight years and conflict over restricted dry season pasture also took place during most of these years. The frequency of conflict between the Nuer and Dinka is even greater. In six of eleven years between 1942 and 1952, dry season grazing shortages prompted Nuong Nuer encroachment on the pastures of their Southern Dinka neighbors (Howell, 1954b:237–38). These data clearly indicate that the Nuong Nuer cattle population had exceeded the limits of the dry season pasture available within its own territorial domain during this period.

The limits imposed by infrequent years of deep and protracted wet season flooding remain to be considered. However, it should be noted at the outset that pertinent data are quite limited. Evans-Pritchard (1937:55) reports that cattle may starve in years of very high flood, particularly in the least favored areas of Nuerland. Howell (1954b:279) likewise notes that heavy flooding constricts wet season pasture, producing overgrazing and "perhaps even death of livestock from starvation, though there may be grass ten feet tall surrounding them." This is not implausible given the annual decline in the condition of the cattle during the wet season. The proposition that significant herd reductions occurred in years of deep and protracted flooding will thus be accepted, on logical grounds, although it is not well documented by available data.

The worst floods occurred in 1917–18. Jackson (1923:65–66) reports that government posts were isolated by high water in 1918 and that a canoe was employed to travel a distance of eighty miles normally traversed on foot. At the height of the dry season of the same year, the Nile carried two and one-half times its average volume of water (Howell, 1954*b*:239).[18] These extreme conditions presumably had the capacity to reduce the cattle population to a level below that imposed by the limits of dry season grazing (although the actual extent of the herd reductions that occurred cannot be established).[19] However, such conditions occurred very infrequently. Nothing remotely comparable to the 1917–18 flood is recorded for the period from 1905 to 1952. Unusually heavy flooding is noted for the years 1878 (Howell, 1954*b*:253) and 1961–64 (Elsammani and El Amin, 1977:13), but the severity of conditions and their effects on Nuer (or Dinka) herds is unreported. These data suggest that heavy flooding occurred at intervals of about forty years. In the prerinderpest era it is probable that some reduction in the cattle population resulted from this. However, the cattle population would recover from these losses in relatively few years and thus increase to the point where dry season grazing once again constituted the effective limit. For extended periods of time the limits imposed by available dry season pasture restricted the cattle population to a level that could be accommodated during the wet season.

The preceding discussion documents several points that are of considerable importance in explicating Nuer territorial expansion. The Nuer variant of transhumance entails an ultimate reliance on cattle as the principal security against starvation. The Nuer do not endeavor to increase millet production, but rather concentrate their efforts on expanding the cattle population that they rely on to sustain them in years of grain shortage. As a result, the cattle population regularly presses against the ecological limits of Nuer territory, and dry season grazing shortages are a common occurrence. These invariably lead to conflict between Nuer and Dinka tribes that utilize neighboring pastures (and share a common border). Nuer raids, which take place at the beginning or end of the rains, are directed against the same Dinka tribes that the Nuer come into conflict with at the height of the dry season. The evident significance of persistent dry season grazing shortages for Nuer territorial expansion will be more fully explored in due course. We must first conclude the present evaluation of the "population pressure" argument, an argument that has been couched in terms of the human population rather than the cattle population.

The fact that Nuer cattle regularly experienced nutritional stress in both the wet and dry season (during the 1950s) constitutes clear evidence that the cattle population had increased to the maximum size that could be accommodated within the ecological limits of Nuer territory. The presence of recurrent nutritional stress also indicates that the cattle population was predominantly food-limited, rather than disease-limited. In other words, mortality from disease did not restrict the cattle population to a level below the maximum that could be supported by available pasture, but only operated to produce herd reductions when the cattle population had attained maximum proportions and was consequently weakened by a decline in condition resulting from grazing shortages.

The conclusion that the Nuer cattle population is food-limited is not only applicable to the 1950s, when rinderpest had been largely brought under control, but also to the period of Nuer territorial expansion, before this (and other) diseases had been introduced. Although cattle are subject to several major diseases that were present prior to the introduction of rinderpest (principally contagious bovine pleuropneumonia and trypanosomiasis) these did not effectively limit the pre–1880 cattle population for a number of reasons. First, these diseases are endemic rather than epidemic in character and would consequently produce a constant but relatively low rate of mortality in the cattle population. Second, the calving rate of Nilotic cattle is quite high, and it has been estimated that the cattle population has the capacity to increase at a rate of 3.5 percent per annum (Payne and El Amin, 1977:11, 84).[20] The third and most important factor is the traditional Nuer practice of recouping their stock losses by raiding the Dinka herds (Evans-Pritchard, 1940a:20, 69). This effectively countered any disease-induced stock reductions and enabled the Nuer to maintain their herds at levels that periodically exceeded the grazing capacity of their territory.

Although the food-limited status of the cattle population can be established, available data suggest that the human population was not food-limited prior to the extensive stock losses that resulted from the introduction of rinderpest and other epidemic cattle diseases. The extent of these losses is documented by early colonial records. A survey of fourteen Gaawar settlements conducted in 1908, during the course of an epidemic, revealed that the corpses of dead cattle represented 30 to 40 percent of the total herd (*SIR* 165, 1980:3). Herd reductions of this magnitude would clearly reduce milk and meat supplies quite drastically for a number of years. This, in turn, would render the Nuer vulnerable to the grain shortages that are an inevitable occurrence in many parts of Nuerland, producing the conditions of famine and starvation mentioned by Evans-Pritchard (1940a:82). It is important to recall that Evans-Pritchard specifically linked starvation to the effects of rinderpest and this strongly suggests that the Nuer population was *not* subject to famine conditions prior to the introduction of this disease.

The Nuer reliance on cattle to sustain them through periods of grain shortage effectively precluded famine as long as the cattle population was not susceptible to drastic reductions. None of the sources of cattle mortality that prevailed during the prerinderpest era appear to have been capable of producing cattle losses comparable to those resulting from epidemic diseases. It has been noted that endemic cattle diseases (such as contagious bovine pleuropneumonia) produce a relatively constant low rate of mortality in the cattle population. It is also unlikely that extreme wet season flooding would engender a 40 percent herd reduction. Moreover, the Nuer would be able to govern a herd reduction necessitated by wet season grazing shortages so as to insure both the reproductive and milk-producing potential of their herds. Data that will be presented in a later chapter will document the point that wet season grazing requirements could be reduced by 40 percent simply by culling oxen and bullocks. The Nuer capacity to recoup their cattle losses by raiding the Dinka would also mitigate (or obviate) protracted depletion of their herds. Given all these factors, it is improbable that the prerinderpest Nuer population was subject to famine conditions of sufficient severity to produce significant increases in mortality. Even the extreme conditions engendered by rinderpest epidemics did not result in the type of mortality that limits a population. Evans-Pritchard (1940a:82) reports that the Nuer expect the older age sets to be "wiped out" when there is a co-occurrence of crop failures and rinderpest, and one may presume that this expectation is based on past experience. However, the premature death of members of the older age sets would have no significant effect on the Nuer population inasmuch as the number of reproductive females would be totally unaffected. In addition, the older age sets would contain those age cohorts that comprise the smallest percentage of the total population. In a relatively short time, any local population experiencing this misfortune would thus increase to former levels.

In sum, a thorough examination of available data indicates that the Nuer human population was not food-limited prior to the introduction of epidemic cattle diseases in the late 1800s, or at the historically high human densities that prevailed in 1955. There is simply no evidence to support the position that the Nuer were food-limited during the period of territorial expansion, and consequently no grounds for adducing "population pressure."

The absence of any evidence that would support a deduction of food-limited status suggests that mortality stemming from diseases prevalent in the area[21] effectively limited the nineteenth-century Nuer population to a level below that dictated by the food supply alone. This interpretation squares nicely with the recent demographic history of the Nuer. The 86 percent increase in the Nuer population that took place between the early 1930s and 1955 was clearly due to a reduction in mortality that is directly attributable to a government medical services program initiated in the 1920s.[22] The population growth that resulted from an improvement in health care testifies to the role of disease as a limiting factor. Alternatively, if one were to argue that the population was food-limited, it would be necessary to postulate a massive increase in food supplies during this period. However, a capacity to so readily expand food supplies is hardly consistent with food-limited status. A food-limited population is rarely capable of achieving dramatic growth without a significant increase in the intensity of land use, or in the quantity of land effectively available for cultivation. However, a disease-limited population that does not fully utilize existing resources can readily achieve such growth without a change in these factors. No such changes took place in the Nuer case.

All available data suggest that the population density of the Nuer homeland in 1800 was actually less than the density of this same region in 1955. Since the latter figure clearly represents a density that the Nuer could readily accommodate, "population pressure" cannot have played a role in triggering Nuer territorial expansion. The Nuer population in 1800 can be estimated by subtracting the 100,000 to 112,000 Dinka and Anuak assimilated in the course of Nuer expansion[23] from the 247,000 enumerated in the circa 1930 census. The resultant figures (135,000 to 147,000) should also be reduced by 10 percent to correct for the population growth that took place between 1920 and 1930 due to the introduction of improved medical care. This yields an initial population of 121,500 to 132,300. Given a Nuer homeland of eight thousand seven hundred square miles, Nuer population density would have been 14.0 to 15.2 persons per square mile in 1800. In 1955 this same area carried a population of 137,945 yielding a density of 15.9 persons per square mile.[24] This not only represents a density the Nuer could accommodate, but one they could accommodate without experiencing food shortages that increased mortality. Bloss's studies, conducted at about the same date, failed to reveal clinical signs of serious nutritional deficiencies that would increase mortality rates. In short, there is no evidence that the Nuer homeland experienced population pressure on food resources at a density of 15.9 persons per square mile.

It is important to note that the above estimate of Nuer numbers in 1800 presumes that the Nuer did not increase—except through the assimilation of Dinka tribesmen—from 1800 to 1920. This estimate thus incorporates the assumptions that the Nuer population was disease-limited (rather than food-limited) and in equilibrium with respect to the balance of birth and mortality rates. A food-limited population would have grown at a very rapid rate as territorial expansion (and evacuation of the Nuer homeland) increased the resource base. Even a modest intrinsic growth rate of 0.6 percent would have doubled the initial Nuer population between 1800 and 1920. If such a growth rate were assumed, the estimated population of the Nuer homeland in 1800 would have to be reduced by half, yielding an initial density of only 7.0 to 7.6 persons per square mile. However, the Nuer clearly could not have experienced food shortages at densities less than half as great as those that prevailed in 1955. The average size of Nuer tribes in 1800 would also be cut in half, and it would be difficult to comprehend how these small tribes successfully expelled the more densely settled Dinka.

The notion of "population pressure" implicitly assumes food shortages experienced by a food-limited population. The assumption of a food-limited population presupposes growth at densities below the limiting level, while such growth in turn presupposes a smaller population in earlier times. In other words, the population pressure argument contains an implicit reconstruction of Nuer demography from 1800 to 1930. However, this reconstruction invalidates the population pressure argument by making it clear that the Nuer could not have experienced such pressure in 1800. The alternative hypothesis that the Nuer population was disease-limited (before 1920), characterized by an internal balance between birth and mortality rates, and grew predominantly through assimilation of Dinka tribesmen, also proposes a reconstruction of Nuer demography over time. This alternative model is both internally consistent and compatible with the available data.

The proposition that the Nuer population was disease-limited (before 1920) and consequently increased predominantly through Dinka accretions is strongly supported by the marked difference, in 1930, between the average size of the Homeland Nuer tribes (6,779 persons) and the average size of those Nuer tribes that participated in territorial expansion (23,250 persons).[25] Although the resource base of both groups of tribes was greatly expanded—through outmigration and territorial gains, respectively—only the conquering tribes increased dramatically in numbers. As noted in chapter 1, this growth was a direct consequence of Nuer assimilation of the Dinka (and Anuak) that occurred in conjunction with the process of expansion. Thus the Homeland Nuer numbered only 61,000 in 1930 while the conquering tribes numbered 186,000. The difference is attributable to the fact that the latter assimilated an estimated 100,000 to 112,000 Dinka and Anuak.

The population density of the Nuer as a whole fell dramatically from the early 1800s to 1890 as the Nuer proceeded to quadruple their tribal domain to thirty-five thousand square miles through territorial expansion. Although large numbers of Dinka (and Anuak) were added to the population through capture, migration, and the incorporation of Dinka lineages, the rate of population increase lagged far behind the rate of territorial gains. This general characteristic was further accentuated by the fact that captured reproductive females played a very important role in Nuer population growth over the long term, although their full contribution to that growth was not realized until several generations after their capture. This delayed effect, plus the population growth that took place between 1920 and 1930, suggests that the Nuer would have been much less numerous in 1890 than they were in 1930. It is estimated that the Nuer numbered less than 200,000 when their territory reached its maximum extent in 1890. Given a total territorial domain of thirty-five thousand square miles, a population of 200,000 represents an overall density of only 5.7 persons per square mile. The estimates presented here thus entail a decline in Nuer population density from 14 or 15 persons per square mile in 1800 to 5.7 persons per square mile in 1890. Nuer population density then increased to 7.9 persons per square mile in 1930 as the population increased (to 247,000) and Nuer territory was reduced (to 31,270 square miles) by the restoration of a large tract of conquered territory to its former Dinka owners in 1908–10. By 1955, Nuer population had increased to 460,000 persons and an overall density of 14.7 persons per square mile (approximating the homeland density in 1800).

It is of particular interest that the major Nuer invasion of Anuak territory was launched during the 1870s when Nuer territory had already been increased nearly fourfold and population densities had fallen dramatically. Although "population pressure" could hardly have prompted this incursion, the Nuer advanced 140 miles into Anuak country and they "came with their wives and children intending to settle" (Evans-Pritchard, 1940c:10). This invasion stands as stark testimony to the unquenchable Nuer thirst for territorial acquisition. The fact that no measure of territorial gain, however great, brought an end to Nuer expansion during the period from 1800 to 1880 clearly betokens an absence of negative feedback and an inability to achieve stability or homeostasis. It is the root causes of this fundamental and intrinsic instability of the Nuer socioecological system that we ultimately seek to explain.

The extended critical evaluation of the "population pressure" assumption presented in the preceding pages is important not only in revealing the flaws in this proposition, but also—and much more importantly—in laying the groundwork for a more satisfactory explanation of the impetus to Nuer territorial expansion. The data and interpretation presented here are central to the argument that follows. Two points are of particular importance in this respect. First, mortality attributable to disease restricted the Nuer to population densities below the maximum that could be supported by the food resources derivable from the Nuer territorial domain, particularly the cattle products that represented the critical elements in the food supply. Second, a food-limited cattle population attained levels that fully utilized, and indeed regularly exceeded, the ecological limits represented by the availability of dry season pasture. Persistent shortages of dry season grazing produced a corresponding incidence of Nuer encroachment on Dinka pastures, and Nuer rainy season raids were directed at the same Dinka groups with whom they came into conflict in the dry season.[26] One may quite reasonably conclude that dry season grazing shortages provided the immediate impetus to Nuer territorial expansion. However, the two central points noted above logically entail an additional conclusion—that the Nuer possessed many more cattle than they required for subsistence purposes. While the cattle population regularly exceeded ecological limits, the human population was considerably less than this same cattle population was capable of supporting. Moreover, Nuer human density progressively declined throughout the expansion period as territorial gains outstripped population growth (including that resulting from assimilation). At the same time, the food-limited cattle population continually increased as its food supply was expanded (realizing its potential for 3.5 percent annual growth). The magnitude of this paradoxical disparity thus progressively increased. The question, then, is why the Nuer continually expanded in order to accommodate a cattle population that exceeded subsistence requirements by an ever-widening margin. Why didn't the Nuer simply slaughter sufficient cattle to maintain the cattle population at a level below ecological limits on grazing resources? This simple expedient would have obviated the recurrent grazing shortages that prompted round after round of territorial expansion. These questions will be addressed shortly.

It is evident from the preceding discussion that the question of ''population pressure'' is quite complex, and these complexities were not considered by earlier authors who invoked the concept. Evans-Pritchard discusses over-population in terms of human densities and fails to clearly distinguish the critical intervening relations of human population to cattle population and cattle population to grazing land. These relations are susceptible to independent variation such that the cattle population may experience shortages of grazing land at low human densities when the ratio of cattle to human population is high. Similarly, the human population may increase (as the Nuer population did between 1930 and 1955) while the ratio of cattle to grazing land remains unaffected (and cattle per capita declines). Distinguishing these relations thus provides a means of resolving the paradoxes that beset earlier explanations of the impetus to Nuer expansion—the subsequent increase of a Nuer population presumed to be experiencing ''population pressure,'' the massive assimilation of Dinka tribesmen, and the fact that Dinka population density is higher than that of the Nuer. In addition, the missing source of the intercultural competition adduced by Sahlins can be elucidated. A state of competition over a scarce resource (i.e., dry season grazing) may obtain despite the absence of ''population pressure'' defined with respect to human populations. Sahlins is also correct in emphasizing the importance of cultural perceptions, as it will be demonstrated that cultural definitions of appropriate bridewealth payments played a major role in Nuer territorial expansion.

Thus far, I have largely been concerned with a critical evaluation of previous accounts of the Nuer expansion and with the questions raised by them. The negative points made in the course of this review are a product of the objective of precisely defining those areas where further explication is required and are not intended to detract from the efforts of my predecessors. All previous writers have made very significant positive contributions to the subject, and these contributions have provided a foundation upon which further explanations can be constructed.

CHAPTER 3

The Impetus to Nuer Territorial Expansion

A full understanding of the remarkable Nuer territorial expansion of 1800 to 1880 requires that we provide answers to three central questions. The first of these questions concerns the impetus or motivating force that impelled the Nuer to appropriate Dinka and Anuak lands, and to continue these piecemeal appropriations over an extended period of time. The second question concerns the basic mechanisms that made this expansion possible, i.e., the source (or sources) of the decisive Nuer advantage that enabled them to continually defeat and dislodge the Dinka. The third question focuses on the causal factors that account for the development of the features or characteristics that conferred this decisive advantage on the Nuer. Given the fact that both the Nuer and Dinka sociocultural systems are derived from a common stock, what developmental processes would account for a cultural divergence that eventuated in the complete dominance of one of these cultural groups over the other? This raises a further question that is implicit in all the others: why did the Nuer, rather than the Dinka, develop both the impetus to territorial acquisition and the capacity to bring this about? These are the questions we seek to answer.

The present chapter, and the two that follow it, address each of these three central questions in turn. We begin, then, with a detailed examination of the factors that provided a sustained impetus to Nuer territorial expansion. An understanding of these factors, and of the more comprehensive system of relations in which they are embedded, will also establish the groundwork for subsequent examination of the development of the decisive Nuer advantage over the Dinka, including the development of differences in segmentary organization. In other words, the same set of interrelationships that informs an explanation of the impetus to Nuer expansion is also central to an understanding of the organizational differentiation that eventuated in a decisive Nuer advantage in warfare.

Fundamental relations between the Nuer population, the cattle population, and the quantity of grazing land are presented in diagrammatic form in

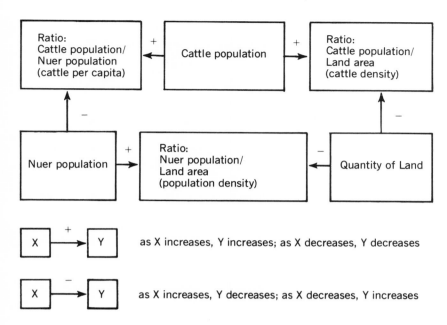

FIG. 2. The Effects of Changes in Key Variables upon Cattle per Capita, Cattle Density, and Human Density

figure 2. The diagram is a hueristic and analytic device that can be employed to consider the way in which these interrelated variables have been affected by a variety of factors that have played a role in Nuer territorial expansion.

As previously noted, the availability of dry season pasture areas imposes an upper limit on the cattle population. However, the cattle population regularly exceeded these limits in unfavorable years, and the resultant shortages of pasture characteristically led to violations of grazing rights that engendered armed conflict both among the Nuer and between the Nuer and Dinka. In the nineteenth century, large-scale Nuer raids periodically resulted in the expulsion or withdrawal of the Dinka followed by a Nuer appropriation of Dinka territory. This increase in the quantity of grazing land would reduce the density of the cattle population to viable levels (and, at the same time, also reduce Nuer human population density). At this point there would be no shortages, no conflicts resulting from them, and hence no further impetus to Nuer expansion. However, this sequence of events would recur if (and when) the cattle population increased to levels that once again exceeded the dry season grazing limitations of the expanded Nuer territorial domain. In other

words, the causal factors capable of providing a sustained impetus to Nuer
territorial expansion are those that affect the growth and demographic dynamics of the cattle population.

The cattle population would increase to the extent that births exceeded
mortality. Insofar as the cattle population was ecologically limited by food
supply rather than cattle diseases (before the introduction of rinderpest), an
expansion of grazing land would lead to a commensurate increase in the cattle
population. However, the realization of this ecologically determined outcome
would be contingent on the herd management practices employed by the
Nuer. By slaughtering cattle for meat consumption, the Nuer could potentially
maintain the cattle population at a constant density below ecologically defined
limits. This would obviate shortages of grazing land and the impetus to
expansion they represented. However, the Nuer did not elect this course of
action, and the reasons for their failure to do so constitute an important area of
investigation. It may be noted, in anticipation of future discussion, that Nuer
herd management practices are explicable in light of the fact that cattle have
social as well as subsistence value, and that they are required for bridewealth
and other social payments. In brief, the bridewealth system largely dictates
herd management practices.

It is important to emphasize the main points noted here insofar as they
frame the organization of the material presented in this chapter. Nuer herd
management practices are of particular importance, since herd reductions
effected by slaughter were capable of maintaining the Nuer cattle population
at levels compatible with fixed grazing requirements and thereby preventing
the shortages of dry season grazing that prompted Nuer territorial expansion.
Since the grazing shortages that provided the immediate impetus to Nuer
expansion could easily have been avoided by this simple expedient, the key
question becomes one of elucidating the factors that govern herd management
practices. To a very considerable extent, the latter are a product of social
requirements for cattle that are embedded in cultural conceptions of bridewealth. The bulk of this chapter thus focuses on a comparative analysis of
Nuer and Dinka bridewealth payments. It can be demonstrated that Nuer
bridewealth requirements are roughly twice as large as those of the Dinka, and
that ideal bridewealth conceptions directly affect not only the size but also the
composition of Nuer and Dinka herds. A comparison of Nuer and Dinka herd
structure clearly reveals that the Dinka cull many more animals for meat
consumption than do the Nuer, i.e., that there are significant differences in
herd management practices. Moreover, differences in ideal bridewealth requirements are closely correlated with differences in herd structure, indicating
that family herds are managed with a view toward precisely mirroring the
proportions of different types of animals required to meet an ideal bridewealth
payment. Both the larger size and particular composition of Nuer herds im-

poses significantly greater grazing requirements on Nuer local populations than on those of the Dinka, and this has important effects on economic organization in each case. In short, it can be demonstrated that the Nuer and Dinka possess distinctive economic variants of a shared transhumant system of production that can be directly linked to different herd management practices associated with their respective bridewealth systems. In a subsequent chapter it will be shown that these economic variants are conducive to differences in political organization. Although the political ramifications of differences between the Nuer and Dinka in economic organization will be taken up much later, they are briefly mentioned here in order to emphasize the central importance of the detailed comparison of the Nuer and Dinka bridewealth systems that forms the body of this chapter. With this in mind, we return to the consideration of herd management practices.

Nuer animal husbandry practices were directed to the objective of increasing their cattle herds, and the latter were managed for milk rather than meat production. (In contrast, the sheep and goats maintained by the Nuer were primarily utilized as meat animals.) Although oxen and infertile cows were slaughtered in sacrifice to ghosts and spirits (and consumed in the course of these ceremonies), a fertile animal was sacrificed only on the comparatively infrequent and specifically delimited occasion of mortuary rites (Evans-Pritchard, 1940a:26). This imposed no effective constraints on the size or growth of the breeding population, insuring a continual increase of the cattle population as a whole.

The size and density of the cattle population within a given local area was also materially affected by the transfer of cattle between communities in social transactions such as bridewealth payments and, to a lesser extent, homicide compensation. Indeed, it is clear from Evans-Pritchard's account that bridewealth payments (rather than slaughter) represented the principal means of effecting herd reduction locally.

> Cattle are everywhere evenly distributed. Hardly anyone is entirely without them, and no one is very rich. Although cattle are a form of wealth that can be accumulated, a man never possesses many more beasts than his byre will hold, because as soon as his herd is large enough he, or one of his family, marries. The herd is thereby reduced to two or three beasts and the next few years are spent in repairing its losses. Every household goes through these alternating periods of poverty and comparative wealth. Marriages and epidemics prevent accumulation of cattle and no disparity in wealth offends the democratic sentiments of the people. (Evans-Pritchard, 1940a:20)

Epidemics were not a major factor prior to the introduction of rinderpest and are not, in any event, subject to human control. The transfer of cattle in bridewealth was consequently the primary method of reducing the cattle population within local areas and also the most important factor affecting the distribution of cattle between them. Nuer marriage prohibitions are conducive to local exogamy (Evans-Pritchard, 1951a:35) and marriage therefore entails the transfer of cattle between communities. Although one might expect the number of cattle given and received to be approximately equivalent, the timing of male and female marriages provided scope for deviations from an otherwise expectable parity. Families (and kin groups) with comparatively few cattle deferred the marriages of sons while temporarily retaining the cattle received upon the marriage of daughters in order to augment their breeding stock. The family herd was thus enlarged by the natural increase of a daughter's bridewealth cattle even though the latter were ultimately given away on the occasion of a son's marriage. In contrast, families (and kin groups) with more ample herds would not defer male marriages and would thus effectively transfer not only the bridewealth cattle themselves but also the increment to their herds that would have resulted had they retained them for a longer period of time. The ideal Lou Nuer bridewealth payment includes seventeen cows, three heifers, eleven calves, and nine oxen (Evans-Pritchard, 1951a:75–76), and the offspring produced by this number of cows in one breeding season would be substantial. A bridewealth payment of this scale would also significantly reduce both the cattle population and breeding stock of the community (or communities) from which they were drawn. An average Lou Nuer community of 250 persons (Bacon, 1917) with 2.26 cattle per capita (Howell, 1954b:231) would possess a total herd of 565 animals. A single ideal bridewealth payment of forty head of cattle thus had the capacity to reduce the community herd by 7.6 percent.

The Nuer customs of polygyny and ghost marriage[1] also established conditions that made it possible for the number of marriages contracted by resident males to exceed the number contracted with resident females, within a given local area. More cattle might then be given in bridewealth transactions than were received during particular time periods, thereby reducing local cattle densities. The cattle exported in this way would be transferred to local areas of both high and low cattle density, with their destination depending solely on the natal community of the bride (a factor unrelated to cattle densities). Nevertheless, cattle would tend to be retained for longer periods of time by communities with lower cattle densities, and the offspring of cattle involved in a series of bridewealth transactions would thus be differentially distributed between high and low density areas. Over extended periods of time, this would be conducive to the maintenance of a relatively even distribution of cattle throughout Nuerland (relative to grazing resources). This interpretation accounts for the distributional characteristics reported by Evans-Pritchard (cited above), and also explains how these could be brought about by the marriages (and accompanying bridewealth payments) that he cites as a principal causal factor.

The transfer of cattle in homicide compensation played an analogous role in redistributing cattle from higher to lower density areas, since the bulk of the compensation payment was ultimately employed to marry a wife to the name of the homicide victim (see Howell, 1954*b*:39–41). Although homicide compensation was paid much less frequently than bridewealth, it may have operated as a more direct redistributive mechanism. This would be true to the extent that fatalities stemming from internal conflicts were more frequent in areas of high cattle density (as explained below).

Armed conflicts between Nuer local lineages and tertiary segments have been a common occurrence throughout Nuer history, including the late colonial period. Indeed, fighting was regarded by colonial officers as the "national pastime" of the Nuer (Howell, 1954*a*:39). Although injuries were frequent, fatalities were comparatively rare. When one or more deaths occurred, compensation and ritual were necessary to achieve a settlement restoring peaceful relations between the groups involved. The principle of compensation was based on the view that a wife must be married to the name of the deceased in order that her children would socially replace him (ibid.:41). Hence, compensation should be equivalent to the ideal bridewealth payment, i.e., forty head of cattle. Moreover, homicide compensation eventuated in herd reductions comparable to those following from a standard marriage (described above). There is, however, one significant difference between the two payments with regard to their operation as redistributive mechanisms. We know that disputes over grazing rights were a common source of conflict (Howell, 1954*a*:187–88) and it is certainly likely that such disputes were more frequent in areas of high cattle density. When fatalities occurred, the cattle paid in homicide compensation would ultimately be exported outside the area of conflict in the form of bridewealth. This would effectively remove cattle from high-density areas. Cattle densities would likewise be reduced somewhat by the sacrifice of three bull calves and a barren cow in the course of rituals connected with the settlement (ibid.:47). Homicide compensation thus functioned as a more direct readjustive and redistributive mechanism than bridewealth transactions. However, bridewealth transactions were so much more frequent than homicide compensation that the latter was ultimately far less significant than the former in these respects. It should also be noted that the bridewealth payment derived from homicide compensation reduced the local herd by ten times as much as the sacrifice connected with the settlement. This confirms the point made earlier that bridewealth rather than ritual slaughter was the principal means of effecting herd reductions.

Cattle transferred from one Nuer community to another in bridewealth or homicide compensation reduced local cattle densities but did not affect the overall density within Nuer territory as a whole. Such redistributive mechanisms would provide a temporary reprieve from local shortages of pasture but would not prevent a growing cattle population from eventually exceeding dry season grazing resources over wide areas of Nuerland. In the present context, the most significant aspect of bridewealth transfers is the fact that they represented the principal method of effecting a reduction in family herds and thus constituted a very important component of Nuer herd management practices. The export of cattle in the form of bridewealth and the slaughter of cattle for meat consumption represented alternative means of disposing of excess cattle—alternatives having very different effects on the mortality rate, growth rate, and overall density of the cattle population. The Nuer clearly favored the former alternative over the latter, and this virtually insured the continued growth of the cattle population, as opposed to the establishment of an equilibrium condition in which the cattle population was maintained at densities below ecological limits.

The growth of the Nuer cattle population was also insured by the Nuer practice of raiding the Dinka for cattle and by their consistent success in carrying out such raids. We have seen that the average large-scale Nuer raid on the Dinka netted 2,250 head of cattle. Although a persistent desire to augment family herds provided a perpetual source of motivation for raids, there were also several specific stimuli that are particularly significant. Evans-Pritchard (1940a:20, 69) notes that the Nuer systematically passed their stock losses on to the Dinka by raiding to replace cattle lost as a result of disease. This effectively countered natural sources of mortality that might otherwise have limited the Nuer cattle population. Raids were also carried out in order to accumulate cattle for bridewealth payments. According to Howell (1954a:98), a prospective bridegroom often acquired a portion of his bridewealth cattle by raiding Dinka herds (in the period before the establishment of administrative control over the area). This practice undoubtedly provided a strong inducement to raids by unmarried young men and also by married men desiring additional wives.

After one phase of Nuer territorial expansion was completed, Nuer cattle herds would increase to the point where they once again exceeded the limits of available dry season pasture, thus establishing the preconditions for a new phase of territorial expansion. The continual growth of the cattle population was ensured by the absence of any effective natural or cultural restraints on the birth and mortality rates of the breeding population and by Nuer success in acquiring additional cattle by raiding Dinka herds. The absence of effective cultural constraints on the growth of the cattle population was a product of Nuer herd management practices, and the latter were largely governed by cultural requirements that necessitated an accumulation of cattle for social purposes, principally bridewealth transactions. These same cultural requirements also provided a major stimulus to cattle raids.

The utilization of cattle in bridewealth payments and other social transactions played a major role in engendering the conditions that stimulated Nuer territorial expansion by creating cultural requirements for cattle far in excess of subsistence requirements. While subsistence needs dictated a minimum number of cattle per capita, social requirements necessitated the accumulation of additional livestock that could be given away without reducing family herds to levels below the subsistence minimum. Every effort was made to increase family herds in anticipation of the forthcoming marriages of sons and in order to meet obligations to contribute to the bridewealth payments of kinsmen. The obligation to provide a wife for the spirit of a brother or close male kinsman who died without male issue further increased these social requirements for cattle. According to Howell (1954a:74–75), "This is one of the strongest mutual obligations of kinship," and ghost marriage is nearly as frequent, statistically, as other types of unions. (Howell attributes this to high rates of mortality for males.) The desirability of acquiring a second wife provided a further stimulus to the augmentation of family herds. Although the cattle received on the marriage of daughters and close female kinsmen would supply a significant proportion of the cattle required for a son's bridewealth, the desirability of polygyny and the obligation to provide a wife for the spirit of a deceased kinsman lacking male issue established cultural needs for cattle beyond those an individual might expect to acquire from bridewealth distributions. Thus, while subsistence needs were fixed, cultural requirements for cattle were not correspondingly limited, and the latter provided a sustained impetus to the enlargement of family herds through breeding and raiding the Dinka. This, in turn, was conducive to a continual growth of the Nuer cattle population, a concomitant increase in the ratio of cattle to grazing land, and, in due course, the shortages of dry season pasture that prompted territorial expansion.

Other things being equal, the ratio of cattle population to human population (i.e., cattle per capita) would co-vary with social requirements for cattle and consequently with the magnitude of Nuer bridewealth. The higher the bridewealth payment is, the greater the number of cattle in excess of subsistence requirements that must be accumulated in family herds before a bridewealth transaction takes place, effecting a herd reduction. Insofar as cattle taken from the Dinka in raids often supplied a portion of the bridewealth payment, elevated bridewealth requirements would be expected to require a correspondingly high frequency of such raids resulting in large numbers of cattle being imported by the Nuer. This also would contribute to high cattle per capita holdings.

Culturally determined cattle per capita requirements would also indirectly determine the upper limits of human population density that could be attained before the cattle population exceeded available grazing land. With high cattle per capita requirements, shortages of grazing land would occur at relatively low human densities, far below the maximum human densities that could be supported if the ratio of cattle population to human population were dictated by subsistence needs alone. This accounts for the previously established fact that Nuer territorial expansion continued as population densities fell well below the initial homeland density (and the maximum density attained historically).

It is important to emphasize that cattle per capita requirements were effectively determined by social rather than ecological considerations, while the maximum cattle density was environmentally limited by the extent of dry season grazing areas. Insofar as these two critical variables were subject to independent determination, the Nuer socioecological system possessed an inherent tendency toward disequilibrium. Indeed, it was entirely possible for the Nuer to find themselves in a situation in which some individuals lacked sufficient cattle to marry while, at the same time, the cattle population as a whole exceeded available dry season grazing resources. Cutting back the size of family and community herds by increased slaughter of cattle for meat consumption would potentially resolve grazing shortages, but at the same time aggravate the shortage of bridewealth cattle—unless the size of bridewealth payments were correspondingly reduced. However, the size of bridewealth payments was dictated by factors other than the availability of dry season grazing resources, and there were consequently no mechanisms for effecting a reduction in the scale of payments under these circumstances. An expansion of the Nuer territorial domain by appropriation of Dinka lands represented the only solution that would alleviate shortages of dry season grazing resources without aggravating shortages of bridewealth cattle. However, this "solution" only temporarily resolved a situation that was the direct product of destabilizing interrelationships inherent in the Nuer socioecological system, leaving the system itself unaltered. A recurrence of the same dilemma was thus insured by the structure of the socioecological system that generated it, and the fundamental causes of Nuer territorial expansion are ultimately grounded in systemic structure. This point will be elaborated in the concluding chapter. At present, the critical importance of bridewealth payments has been established, and it is thus necessary to turn to a detailed examination of the nature of these payments.

This investigation begins with a general outline of the main features of Nuer bridewealth transactions and consideration of the factors governing the magnitude of bridewealth payments. We then proceed to a comparative analysis of the variations among Nuer tribes in bridewealth requirements, an analogous analysis of bridewealth variations among Dinka tribes, and a general comparison of the Nuer and Dinka bridewealth systems. This comparative analysis will proceed from consideration of sociological differences to examination of the distinctive herd management strategies these entail, and thus concludes with the delineation of Nuer and Dinka differences in economic organization.

<h2>THE GENERAL FRAMEWORK OF NUER BRIDEWEALTH TRANSACTIONS</h2>

The initiation of a marriage entails a number of different transactions in which cattle, sheep, goats, and other items are transferred from the groom's to the bride's family. Additional livestock are required to provide ceremonial feasts at various points in the proceedings. However, the major component of the transaction is the bridewealth cattle, a negotiated quantity of animals that are given to the bride's kin by the groom's before she takes up residence with the groom at his community. The present investigation concerns the size of these bridewealth payments, including the betrothal cattle given earlier in the proceedings.

The bridewealth payment is apportioned among the bride's family and certain designated close kinsmen in accordance with predetermined rules of division. These designated kin are "people of rights" (*ji cuongni*) who have definitive claims that are recognized in custom and voiced at the time the bridewealth is negotiated (Howell, 1954a:92; Evans-Pritchard, 1951a:76). For example, a cow and its calf, a calf, and an ox are specifically designated for the bride's father's elder brother (by the same mother as father himself), a cow and its calf and an ox for the bride's mother's brother (by a different mother), and so on. "In theory, the bridegroom must produce cattle to meet the claims of all these kinsmen of the bride" (Howell, 1954a:92). These kin-based allotments are also inherited and are consequently undiminished by deaths among the members of the bride's kindred. The customary size of bridewealth payments is thus largely determined by the number of recognized claimants and the number of animals allotted to each. These considerations define the general framework of the transaction.

However, there is scope for considerable variation within this framework. First, the specification of claimants and quantities is not uniform throughout Nuerland but varies from tribe to tribe. Second, each Nuer tribe delineates both "ideal" and "acceptable" customary rates, effectively defining a range of appropriate payments rather than a single, set value. Third, actual payments vary within this range in accordance with the availability of cattle to the groom's family and kin. Howell (1954a:99) points out that "it must be remembered that bridewealth varies not only from tribe to tribe but also within the tribe from year to year. A particularly heavy epidemic may carry off as much as 30 percent of the cattle population, and bridewealth must drop accordingly.'' The size of these payments is adjusted (within the acceptable to ideal range) to accommodate widespread stock losses due to rinderpest and trypanosomiasis so that a general poverty of stock does not preclude marriage. In earlier times, bridewealth payments likewise expanded in accordance with the growth of the Nuer cattle population. During the period of Nuer territorial expansion, when Nuer wealth in cattle reached its maximum, bridewealth payments substantially in excess of the ideal were made. However, the ideal itself remained unchanged. After the introduction of rinderpest, when Nuer herds declined to their lowest historical level, bridewealth payments fell to the minimum acceptable amount and frequently a portion of this was promised rather than paid at the time the union was celebrated. However, the minimum itself remained unchanged. These historical variations will be more fully examined in subsequent discussion. The point to be noted here is that the size of actual bridewealth payments is largely governed by the acceptable to ideal range of culturally defined values and that these values themselves are highly resistant to change. Although fluctuations in the size of Nuer herds engender variations in the magnitude of bridewealth payments that fall largely within this range, such fluctuations do not produce a redefinition of the acceptable and ideal payments that define it. These are very deeply embedded in kinship obligations. Although payments in excess of the ideal therefore pose no difficulty, a marriage cannot take place unless the minimum acceptable payment is pledged. However, the transfer of a portion of this may be deferred until a later date in order to facilitate marriage in times of severe cattle shortages. Under these circumstances the outstanding amount represents a lien on the family herd of the groom. In this respect, the culturally defined minimum acceptable bridewealth payment constitutes a fixed lower limit. The ideal, on the other hand, represents a goal that every family hopes to meet and perhaps even exceed. The difference between the two in this respect is more fully explained below.

Bridewealth negotiations are thus concerned with determination of the precise number and kind of cattle to be transferred, taking into account the customary claims and expectations of the bride's kin, on one hand, and the economic circumstances of the groom's kin on the other. When the dimensions of Nuer herds do not fluctuate greatly, the resultant figure varies from union to union within a tribally defined ''ideal'' to acceptable range.

The tribally defined ''ideal'' bridewealth possesses that quality largely because it fully satisfies the claims of the ''people of rights.'' Although this requires a definite (and quite substantial) number of cattle, the Nuer express the concept by listing the designated kinsmen of the bride and their appropriate allotments (Evans-Pritchard, 1951a:74–75; Howell, 1954a:99). A comparatively large bridewealth payment also has recognized social value. However, the value connected with size per se is a separable quality—one that pertains to the socioeconomic status of the parties to the transaction—and does not directly enter into the cultural definition of the ideal payment described by Howell and Evans-Pritchard.

The "ideal" bridewealth represents what is conventionally regarded as the reasonable demands of the bride's kin and imposes some limits upon the expectations of the parties entering into a bridewealth negotiation. The groom's party must meet these demands to the degree that they possess sufficient cattle to do so. In other words, negotiation of a lower payment is contingent upon a demonstrated inability to provide more. It should be noted in this connection that "the bridegroom's family are impoverished, sometimes to the point of privation, though their kinsmen and affines will help them if they reach this point; while in the bride's home the milk-gourds and butter-gourds are full" (Evans-Pritchard, 1951a:89). The bridegroom's family may thus be expected to retain no more than the bare minimum of cattle necessary for survival, with any surplus livestock over and above these minimum subsistence requirements being subject to the demands of the bride's kin. The Nuer conventional wisdom in such matters, expressed in a maxim reported by Howell (1954a:105), counsels "that a man must put his anger aside if his [prospective] wife's family are unreasonable in their demands."

The ideal bridewealth does not represent a maximum that cannot be exceeded, should the groom's family have more than the requisite number of cattle at their disposal. Evans-Pritchard (1951a:83) reports that "bridewealth cannot rise to more than the bridegroom and his people possess or are prepared to give, what they are prepared to give being mainly decided by what they possess." The availability of cattle is thus an important determinant of the size of bridewealth payments in and of itself; it exerts an influence which is independent of the ideal parameters of the transaction. However, the ideal represents a highly significant reference point in bridewealth negotiations: below this point, the bride's kin holds the initiative in pressing their demands; above it the initiative is transferred to the bridegroom's party. In the latter circumstance the groom's family and kin may, of their own volition, agree to give more than the ideal bridewealth. They are not required to provide available cattle beyond this amount, and a failure to do so would not jeopardize the successful arrangement of a union. This does not mean that the groom's party will refuse to give such additional cattle when they possess the means to do so; indeed, Evans-Pritchard's observations (cited above) clearly suggest quite the opposite. It means, rather, that such supernumerary cattle possess an entirely different significance and communicative value in the transaction. They are not given in satisfaction of the recognized claims of the bride's kin but as a tribute to the generosity and largesse of the groom's. They also bespeak the bridegroom's kinsmen's virtuosity in the valued arts of animal husbandry and cattle raiding. In sum, the ideal bridewealth is neither an upper limit nor an effective constraint. It is a benchmark of cultural value with reference to which the social standing of thĕ groom's kin may be expressed.

The acceptable bridewealth payment represents the minimum number of cattle required to bring about a union and the starting point for negotiations. "Whatever else the bride's family and kin get, they must get certain animals or the marriage cannot take place" (Evans-Pritchard, 1951a:80). As in the case of the ideal payment, these requirements are phrased in terms of the claims of the "people of rights," although the number of cattle allotted to each category of kin is markedly reduced (see table 1). These reduced requirements impose a fixed lower limit on bridewealth transactions that is not susceptible to further reduction irrespective of the livestock resources of the groom's family and kin. If the latter lack sufficient animals to meet these minimal claims a marriage may nevertheless be arranged, but only on the condition that the deficit will be supplied at a specified future date (e.g., following the marriage of the groom's sister).

The determination of bridewealth payments in actual instances involves an intricate interplay between culturally (or subculturally) defined conceptions of appropriate payments on one hand and the availability of cattle to the groom's family and kin on the other. The main features of this determination may usefully be summarized in light of the preceding discussion. The acceptable bridewealth payment is a rigidly defined minimum which represents the sine qua non of a socially recognized union. If the groom's party has less than this minimum quantity of cattle they may arrange a deferred transfer (but not a reduced payment). Within the ideal to acceptable range, the exact magnitude of individual bridewealth payments is strictly determined by the resources at the disposal of the groom's family and kin. They are obliged to provide whatever cattle they possess over and above their immediate subsistence requirements, and successful negotiations are contingent upon their willingness to do so. If the groom's party possesses more cattle than are required to meet the ideal payment, they may give more as an expression of their generosity and social standing but are under no formal obligation to do so. One would expect that they would not reduce their herds to subsistence levels under these circumstances. On the other hand, it should be noted that cattle in excess of comfortable subsistence requirements impose a burden on their owners. They require care, tending, and pasturage but return no economic benefits to an amply provisioned household. The prime value of such excess cattle is a social value which is most effectively realized when they are used to secure an additional wife or given as a contribution to a kinsman's bridewealth (or compensation) payment. Reciprocity may be expected should the donor need cattle at some future date and, in the meantime, the donor's labor and pasture requirements are conveniently reduced. This suggests that there is no effective upper limit on bridewealth payments, and that such payments would increase in direct proportion to increases in the availability of cattle beyond subsistence needs. This conclusion is supported by data Evans-Pritchard presents. Although the traditional ideal bridewealth payment of the Lou Nuer is forty cattle, Evans-Pritchard (1940a:19–20) reports that bridewealth payments were "forty, and sometimes fifty to sixty, head of cattle" prior to the general herd reductions brought about by the introduction of rinderpest in the early 1890s.

The preceding discussion documents the important point that the size of Nuer bridewealth payments increases as the number of cattle per capita increases. There are consequently no effective upper limits on social requirements for cattle. This is attributable to the expandability of bridewealth payments per union, on one hand, and to the cultural desirability of polygyny and ghost marriage on the other. These virtually unlimited social requirements for cattle provided a perpetual stimulus to the augmentation of family herds brought about by effective breeding, minimal slaughter of breeding stock, and cattle raids directed against the Dinka. The resultant growth of the cattle population (and of cattle per capita holdings) would lead to further increases in the magnitude of bridewealth payments and commensurate increases in social requirements for cattle. In other words, the expandability of bridewealth payments is the critical linkage in a positive feedback relationship between social requirements for cattle and the availability of cattle in per capita terms. This positive feedback relationship insured the growth of Nuer herds and engendered the periodic dilemma in which the cattle population exceeded existing dry season grazing resources, prompting Nuer appropriations of Dinka territory. At the same time, social requirements for cattle precluded a reduction of Nuer herds that could have brought them into adjustment with available pasture areas. Indeed, the less fortunate individuals who possessed comparatively fewer animals than their fellow tribesmen would experience "shortages" of cattle relative to both the tribally defined "ideal," and to prevailing expectations concerning the socially desirable size of bridewealth payments, at these times of pasture shortages.

Although an increase in cattle holdings (per capita) produced an increase in the size of actual bridewealth payments, a decline in cattle per capita in local areas did not immediately engender a corresponding decrease in bridewealth. On the contrary, the initial response was increased raiding of Dinka herds in order to replace animals lost through disease, or specifically to accumulate a bridewealth payment comparable to the ideal. In either case, there would be a tendency for cattle per capita to increase to previous levels while the size of bridewealth payments was maintained unchanged. Bridewealth payments declined toward minimum acceptable levels only in the event of decreases in the cattle population that were both widespread (rather than local) and also irreparable. These conditions occurred following the introduction of rinderpest in the early 1890s and bridewealth payments fell to the minimal acceptable level. Although the Nuer responded by intensifying their raids on Dinka stock (Evans-Pritchard, 1940a:69), this traditional recourse proved inadequate given the massiveness of the losses incurred and the fact that they depleted Dinka herds as well as those of the Nuer.

As was pointed out in chapter 1, no significant Nuer territorial expansion took place after the early 1890s, even though administrative efforts to prevent Nuer raids on the Dinka, and to establish fixed borders, were not implemented until 1910. The reduction in bridewealth payments, cattle per capita, and the ratio of cattle to grazing land brought about by the introduction of rinderpest effectively alleviated the impetus to Nuer expansion, and the fact that it came to a close under these circumstances provides strong confirmation for the proposed interpretation.

It is important to emphasize that perceived social requirements for cattle were influenced by the availability of cattle (in per capita terms) and were not directly responsive to changes in the availability of pasture. Thus as the cattle population increased (relative to the human population) social requirements would also increase while, at the same time, grazing resources would decrease (relative to the cattle population), ultimately reaching the level at which acute shortages occurred. If grazing resources were fixed, the cattle population would reach its food-limited maximum at this point and could not increase further. If the size and density of the cattle population were thus stabilized, social requirements for cattle would likewise stabilize and the socioecological system would attain an equilibrium condition. However, this equilibrium would obtain at maximum cattle densities, ensuring perpetual conflict over dry season grazing rights among the Nuer and, particularly, between the Nuer and the Dinka. The maintenance of equilibrium would then be contingent on the Dinka ability to hold their own in these hostilities and to successfully resist Nuer incursions. Dinka shortcomings in this respect are well documented historically, and the potential (but quite fragile) equilibrium outlined above was never attained prior to colonial intervention.

Thus far it has been demonstrated that the Nuer socioecological system was structured so as to provide a sustained impetus to Nuer territorial expansion. The mechanisms that facilitated that expansion, i.e., the sources of the Nuer military advantage over the Dinka at the critical junctures described above, have yet to be considered, together with the circumstances conducive to their development. The organizational differentiation of the Nuer and Dinka (that eventuated in a decisive Nuer military advantage) can be explained in terms of differences between these two cultural groups in the same three key variables central to an understanding of the impetus to Nuer expansion (i.e., cattle per capita, cattle density, and human population density; see fig. 2). The remainder of this chapter is thus devoted to establishing the marked differences between the Nuer and Dinka in these respects. This will provide further documentation of the preceding argument concerning the impetus to Nuer territorial expansion, on one hand, and lay the necessary groundwork for an explanation of organizational differentiation on the other. (The latter will then be directly addressed in a later chapter.)

A Comparison of the Nuer and Dinka Bridewealth Systems

We have seen that Nuer expansion was prompted by periodic shortages of dry season grazing land that resulted from the growth of the cattle population and a consequent increase in cattle density. However, the growth of the cattle population is a direct product of herd management practices, since Nuer herds could easily be maintained at a constant size and density (compatible with ecological limits on grazing resources) by the simple expedient of slaughtering cattle for meat consumption. Herd management practices are thus of central importance as they largely determine the growth or stability of the cattle population. They therefore largely determine cattle density (given fixed grazing resources) and strongly influence cattle per capita holdings. These herd management practices are in turn governed by social requirement for cattle, and especially social requirements for the deployment of large numbers of cattle in bridewealth transactions. Therefore, the differences between the Nuer and Dinka in cattle density and cattle per capita are closely linked to corresponding differences in their respective cultural definitions of ideal and acceptable bridewealth payments. These differences in cattle holdings likewise entail distinctive economic variants of the transhumant system of production shared by the Nuer and Dinka, with each variant conducive to a different organizational design.

It is thus of considerable importance to carefully document the differences between the Nuer and Dinka (and among the various Nuer and Dinka tribes, respectively) in the size of bridewealth payments, the composition of such payments in terms of breeding stock, and the social relationships emphasized in these transactions. These differences can be directly linked to significant variations in the respective economic systems of the Nuer and Dinka, on one hand, and to important differences in social organization on the other. Consideration of differences in the above respects between the Homeland Nuer and those Nuer tribes that formed the leading edge of territorial expansion will also make it possible to reconstruct the characteristics of the Nuer socioeconomic system prior to the inception of Nuer expansion (in the same way that a consideration of dialect variation makes it possible to reconstruct the original language from which a set of dialect differences developed). It is thus to this detailed comparison of bridewealth customs that we now turn.

Sociological Features of the Nuer Bridewealth System

The Lou Nuer delineation of both ideal and acceptable bridewealth payments is presented in table 1 (based on data from Evans-Pritchard, 1951a:74–82). There are three groups of kin that are significant to a comparative analysis of these transactions. The first of these is the bride's immediate family, including her father, mother, and brothers. The cattle received by these family members all join the father's herd, if he is alive, and will subsequently be deployed in the marriages of the bride's brothers, which take place in order of age seniority (Evans-Pritchard, 1951a:79). The two remaining groups are the bride's patrikin (father's brothers and one sister) and matrikin (mother's brothers and one sister). The distribution of cattle among these groups is shown below.[2]

Cattle received by:	Ideal Payment	Acceptable Payment
Bride's family	20	9
Patrikin	10	6
Matrikin	10	7
Total	40	22

In the ideal bridewealth payment, the bride's immediate family receives twenty cattle comprising half the total. In the acceptable payment only nine cattle are received, comprising 41 percent of the total. The bride's family thus receives proportionately less of the minimal payment while the scope of kindred participation and the collective nature of the transaction are maintained unchanged (see Howell, 1954a:110 and Evans-Pritchard, 1951a:83–87). In effect, the bride's father and other family members disproportionately relinquish their claims in favor of those of their kinsmen when bridewealth falls below the ideal quantity. However, the other side of this same coin is that the bride's father (and brothers) stand to gain the most from a large bridewealth transaction. The ideal bridewealth includes eighteen more animals than the minimum acceptable payment and eleven of these (or 61 percent) become part of the bride's father's herd. Four of the eighteen additional cattle go to the bride's patrikin and three to her matrikin. Thus, as bridewealth increases, there is a subtle but definite shift in the distribution of cattle that favors the bride's father, brothers, and paternal kin over her matrilateral relatives. The individuals that are disproportionately favored are all members of the bride's natal patrilineage.

An analogous pattern of co-variation between the size and distribution of

TABLE 1

Lou Nuer Bridewealth: Recognized Claims of the Bride's Kin

Ideal Payment (and Distribution)

Bride's Kin	Cattle	Total
Father	a cow & its calf, a cow & its calf, an ox, another ox, a cow & a calf	8
Brother by the same mother	an ox, another ox, a cow, another cow, a cow & its calf, another cow	7
Brother by a different mother	a cow & another cow	2
Father's elder brother by the same mother	a cow & its calf, a calf, & an ox	4
Father's brother by a different mother	a cow & its calf, & an ox	3
Father's younger brother by the same mother	a cow & an ox	2
Father's sister	a heifer	1
Mother	a cow & its calf & a heifer	3
Mother's elder brother by the same mother	a cow & its calf, another cow, & an ox	4
Mother's brother by a different mother	a cow & its calf, & an ox	3
Mother's younger brother by the same mother	a cow & its calf	2
Mother's sister	a heifer	1
Total		40

Acceptable Payment (and Distribution)

Bride's Kin	Cattle	Total
Father	a cow & its calf, a cow & an ox	4
Brother by the same mother	an ox	1
Brother by a different mother	an ox	1
Paternal grandparents (claims inherited equally by father's brothers of same & different mothers respectively)	a cow & another cow	2
Paternal uncles	a cow & its calf & an ox	3
Father's sister	a heifer	1
Mother	a cow & its calf & a cow	3
Maternal grandparents (claims inherited equally by mother's brothers of same & different mothers respectively)	a cow & another cow	2
Maternal uncles	a cow & its calf, an ox, & another ox	4
Mother's sister	a heifer	1
Total		18 to 22[a]

[a]See note 2 to chapter 3.

bridewealth payments is applicable to a comparison of Nuer and Dinka bridewealth requirements and will be more fully developed in that context. However, it may be noted here that the larger bridewealth payments of the Nuer
display a marked emphasis on patrilateral relationships in contrast to the more
heavily matrilateral emphasis of smaller Dinka bridewealth payments. These
differences also correspond to parallel differences between the Nuer and
Dinka in local and segmentary organization that are examined in a later
chapter in relation to the question of organizational differentiation. Although
the role of the bridewealth system in the coevolutionary divergence of the
Nuer and Dinka will be taken up much later, the topic is noted here in order to
emphasize the importance of a detailed comparative analysis of Nuer and
Dinka bridewealth systems.

   The relationship between the size and distribution of bridewealth payments noted above is largely a product of the fact that the matrikin's portion is
less variable, with respect to changes in the magnitude of bridewealth payments, than the portion allocated to the bride's family and patrikin. This
follows from the special status accorded to the matrikin's claims. The claims
of the bride's matrikin have a recognized priority over those of the bride's
family and patrikin because the cattle transferred are "regarded to some
extent as a deferred payment standing over from the marriage of the bride's
mother" (Evans-Pritchard, 1951a:82). Hence, the Nuer conclude the public
enumeration of the bridewealth cattle by stating, "and when the bride's
daughters are married more cattle will be paid to their mother's brothers"
(ibid.). The portion of a bridewealth payment allocated to the matrikin is thus
the least variable component of Nuer bridewealth transactions, since it largely
constitutes the final installment of the bride's mother's payment negotiated a
generation earlier. Given this relative invariance, the matrikin's allotment
tends to represent a large proportion of a small bridewealth payment and a
comparatively smaller proportion of an expanded payment. This largely accounts for the co-variation between the size and distribution of bridewealth
payments noted above.

   Other, less formalized arrangements for deferring payment of a portion
of the promised bridewealth cattle are a characteristic feature of Nuer transactions, as evidenced by the actual cases described by Howell (1954a:114–20).
Not infrequently, a few cattle are pledged to be delivered at a later date, when
the groom's family has had an opportunity to build up its herd or when a
younger sister marries. All these arrangements for deferring payment have the
effect of preventing bridewealth payments from falling below the established
minimum, irrespective of prevailing economic conditions. These outstanding
obligations represent a lien on the groom's father's herd that contributes to a
herd management strategy geared to growth.

   Conceptions of appropriate bridewealth payments are defined at the tribal level and vary among the various Nuer tribes, although they are uniformly expressed in terms of the claims of the "people of rights." Howell (1954a:100–110) describes the differences in kinship claims in some detail and gives the following variation in total payment: Bul, thirty-four; Leik, thirty-one; Dok, thirty; Western Jikany, thirty; Lak, thirty; and Thiang, thirty. In all instances, the number of cattle required is less than the Lou Nuer ideal of forty reported by Evans-Pritchard, an ideal that Evans-Pritchard appears to regard as generally applicable to the Nuer as a whole, give or take a cow or an ox (see Evans-Pritchard, 1951a:76). Howell (1954a:99, 102, 106) discusses a variety of possible reasons for this "disparity" between his and Evans-Pritchard's accounts. At one point he suggests that the Zeraf Nuer (i.e., Lak and Thiang) version he presents is "not an ideal, but is closer to reality and nearer to what is considered a minimum although not actually the minimum" (Howell, 1954a:106). However, the number of cattle given and promised in actual instances is less (and generally, substantially less) than the above figures in all reported cases (Howell, 1954a:114–21), and it is thus quite clear that these figures do not represent or even approximate the minimum and are not "closer to reality." My own reading of the data leads me to the conclusion that these differences represent authentic subcultural variations in conceptualization of the ideal payment and that the major disparity involves Evans-Pritchard's unwarranted generalization of the Lou Nuer (and Eastern Jikany) ideal to the Nuer as a whole. Howell clearly shows that there is significant variation among the Nuer tribes he considers, and further variation between these and the Lou Nuer is consequently expectable. However, there does appear to be one significant difference in reportage that should be taken into account. Evans-Pritchard includes the four head of cattle given as a betrothal payment as part of the sum total of forty while Howell excludes these from his total bridewealth figures, although they do constitute part of the total transaction among the subtribes he considers (see Howell, 1954a:102). Adding the four betrothal cattle to Howell's figures thus yields the following comparable total payments for the various Nuer tribes: Lou, forty; Eastern Jikany, forty; Bul, thirty-eight; Leik, thirty-five; Dok, thirty-four; Western Jikany, thirty-four; Lak, thirty-four; and Thiang, thirty-four.

The ideal bridewealth payments of these Nuer tribes vary in features other than sheer size. Some of these variations are quite minor and need not concern us here. However, there are three areas in which differences among Nuer tribes are relevant to a larger comparison of Nuer and Dinka bridewealth transactions. These internal variations concern the presence or absence of reciprocal payments, the kinsman encompassed by the transaction, and the proportion of the total payment allotted to the bride's family, patrikin, and matrikin (respectively).

The bridewealth transactions of the Dok, Aak, and Jagei Nuer incorpo-

rate a distinctive reciprocal payment (*thiuk*) that effectively reduces the net
number of cattle transferred. In these tribal versions,

> on final confirmation of the marriage two cows are paid to the bridegroom's
> family, one from the *kwi gwande* [paternal side] and one from the *kwi mande*
> [maternal side]. These are reckoned to be the right of the bride's future sons.
> (Howell, 1954a:113)

The effective loss of cattle to a Dok bridegroom's family and kin would thus
be thirty-two rather than thirty-four head. (No specific ideal bridewealth is
reported for the Aak and Jagei.) Considering this reduction, the total range of
reported variation in Nuer ideal bridewealth effectively transferred would thus
be thirty-two to forty head of cattle. It should be noted that all Dinka bridewealth transactions entail an analogous reciprocal payment, involving a much
larger number of cattle. As we shall see, this largely accounts for the differences between the Nuer and Dinka in the scale of bridewealth payments.

In examining the kin relationships that are encompassed by Nuer bridewealth distributions it is important to delineate the culturally relevant points of
reference. The two focal figures in this respect are the bride's father and her
senior mother's brother. Although ideal bridewealth payments are defined by
the claims of the "people of rights" and these claims provide a framework for
the distribution of cattle among the bride's kin, the composition of the bride's
kindred is unlikely to correspond precisely to that envisioned in the ideal and
adjustments are necessary. Thus,

> The bride's father must make his own terms about the distribution with his
> brothers and sisters, and the bride's senior maternal uncle with his brothers and
> sisters. (Evans-Pritchard, 1951a:79)

For certain purposes, the relationships that are recognized in the distribution
should thus be analyzed from the standpoint of these two male egos, although
analysis from the bride's perspective is also important in other respects (see
Evans-Pritchard, 1951a:77–78). Considering these two men as twin reference
points, it is clear that Lou Nuer bridewealth (described earlier) is distributed
entirely to siblings. The bride's father transfers a portion of the cattle received
to his full and half brothers and one sister (while cattle designated for himself,
his wife, and his sons become part of the family herd over which the father
exercises rights of disposal). The bride's senior mother's brother likewise
allocates cattle to his full and half brothers and one sister in a parallel fashion.
From this standpoint, the relationships that are emphasized are clearly those
between siblings, as Evans-Pritchard (1951a:77–79) notes.

As was pointed out earlier, the bridewealth cattle designated for the maternal side are seen by the Nuer as the final installment of the bride's mother's bridewealth payment. This aspect of the transaction may thus be viewed as a transfer of cattle from the bride's father to his wife's senior brother (the bride's mother's brother) in which this affinal relationship is affirmed. The second central aspect of the distribution emphasizes sibling relationships as noted above. However, the cattle allocated to father's sister and mother's sister (one heifer each) join these women's respective husband's herds, and the affinal relationship of the bride's father to his sister's husband, and of the senior mother's brother to his sister's husband, thus receive some recognition in the transaction. In sum the kin relationships that are affirmed in the Lou Nuer bridewealth distribution are those of siblingship and affinity (see Evans-Pritchard, 1951a:79–80).[3]

There are only relatively slight differences among the various Nuer tribes in the range of kinsmen encompassed by bridewealth transactions. However, these variations are of some interest in that they consistently indicate a more patrilineal emphasis among those Nuer tribes that spearheaded territorial expansion. The Lou and Eastern Jikany Nuer omit two matrilineal kinsmen included in the ideal bridewealth distributions of the Northern Zeraf Island and Western Nuer tribes (including the Lak, Thiang, Dok, Western Jikany, Leik, and Bul), i.e., the bride's father's mother's brother and the bride's senior mother's brother's mother's brother. The mother's brother of each of the two focal figures receives a cow-calf (Howell, 1954a:102–5). (In the event that these kinsmen are deceased, their rights pass to their sons.) In contrast, the Lou and Eastern Jikany recognize the claim of the bride's father's father's brother's son to a calf, if this request is included by the bride's kin (Evans-Pritchard, 1951a:85–86).[4] The two Nuer tribes that spearheaded the eastward expansion thus include a more distant patrilateral kinsmen in their bridewealth distributions, while the Homeland and Northern Zeraf Island tribes include a pair of analogously distant matrilateral kinsmen in their place. The Nuong and Gaawar Nuer tribes that were most active in expanding Nuer territory to the south likewise acknowledge this distant patrilateral claim (as do the Dok of the homeland region) (Howell, 1954a:105). This somewhat more patrilateral emphasis in the bridewealth payments of the expanding Nuer tribes is also evident in the proportions allocated to paternal and maternal sides (respectively), as will be documented shortly. Although the magnitude of these differences is not great, it is significant that the variations are consistently in the same direction. They may consequently constitute a series of common expressions of a more fundamental structural transformation.

The expanding Nuer tribes differ from the Homeland Nuer in a number of respects (noted throughout this study), and one of the most difficult questions concerning Nuer territorial expansion turns on the interpretation of these differences. Do these distinctive features of the expanding Nuer denote organizational differences that facilitated the expansion process or are they merely a consequence of that process, emerging after the fact? A comparative analysis of bridewealth payments suggests an answer to this question. Western Jikany bridewealth transactions are similar to those of other Homeland Nuer tribes in most respects, but differ somewhat with respect to the distant matrilateral kinsmen discussed above. A cow-calf is allocated to the bride's father's mother's brother on the marriage of the eldest daughter, and to the bride's mother's brother's mother's brother on the marriage of the second daughter (and so on in alternation) (Howell, 1954a:107). The claims of these matrikin are thus more attenuated in the Western Jikany case than among other Homeland Nuer tribes. In addition, the claims of the mother's brother on the patrilateral side are given temporal priority over those of his counterpart on the matrilateral side among the Western Jikany. It may be recalled that the Eastern Jikany, who initiated Nuer territorial expansion in the early 1800s, were derived from the Western Jikany of the Nuer homeland. It therefore stands to reason that the Eastern Jikany possessed the characteristics manifested by the Western Jikany before the former began their eastward migration and conquest, namely a tendency toward both the attenuation of distant matrilateral claims and toward a patrilateral priority among those claims. These tendencies, present at the onset, were then further elaborated during the course of Eastern Jikany expansion (such that these distant matrilateral claims were dropped altogether and an analogously distant patrilateral claim recognized in their place).

In general, then, the most probable answer to the question posed above is that the expanding Nuer tribes did differ from their homeland counterparts at the inception of Nuer expansion, and that these differences were further accentuated by the expansion process itself. The formation of new communities, lacking elders and consequently less encumbered by tradition, provided scope for the fuller expression of preexisting tendencies toward change. As would be expected, the expanding Nuer differ from the Homeland Nuer in the same general way that the latter differ from the Dinka, i.e., in terms of the organizational precedence of patrilateral relationships. The differences between the Nuer and Dinka are especially marked in the domain of community organization (discussed in a later chapter), but are also evident in the comparison of bridewealth payments considered here, particularly in the proportions of the bridewealth payment allocated to matrikin and patrikin (respectively). It is to a comparative analysis of such distributional variations among the Nuer tribes that we now turn.

Howell (1954a:109–10) provides information concerning the distribution of bridewealth cattle among the segments of the bride's kindred for a number of Nuer tribes. These data are summarized below.[5]

Cattle received by:	Dok	Lak	Thiang	Western Jikany	Leik	Bul	Lou	Eastern Jikany
Bride's family	13	13	13	14	14	16	20	20
Patrikin	10	11	11	10	12	11	10	10
Matrikin	9	10	10	10	9	11	10	10
Total	32	34	34	34	35	38	40	40

These figures illustrate several points made earlier with respect to the comparison of Lou Nuer ideal and acceptable bridewealth. As the size of bridewealth payments increases, the additional cattle generally tend to be allocated disproportionately to the bride's patrikin or immediate family. Although this general tendency does not apply to a comparison of the Dok (at thirty-two cattle) with the Lak, Thiang, and Western Jikany (at thirty-four), it is evident when the latter group is compared with the Leik (at thirty-five). Here the proportion has clearly shifted in favor of the patrikin over the matrikin. Among the Bul, Lou, and Eastern Jikany the additional cattle that figure in the bridewealth transaction (over and above that paid by other groups) are disproportionately allotted to the bride's immediate family. We shall see that Dinka bridewealth, which is considerably less than that of the Nuer, is consistent with this general relationship between size and distribution. Comparatively, the proportions favor the bride's matrikin.

Sociological Features of the Dinka Bridewealth System

Dinka bridewealth transactions differ substantially from those of the Nuer in the number of cattle required, the prevalence and scale of reciprocal payments, the absence of a minimum acceptable payment, and the composition of the bridewealth herd in terms of breeding stock. Although these two cultural groups do not differ significantly in the range of kinsmen encompassed by the transaction, the proportions allocated to the paternal and maternal ''sides'' diverge in opposite directions from a point of near overlap in terms of tribal (or subcultural group) variations in the delineation of ideal payments. Although the variations among Dinka tribes are not as fully documented in all respects as the differences among Nuer tribes described earlier, Stubbs's (1962) account of Malwal Dinka bridewealth and Howell's (1951) description of Ngok (Ngork) Dinka payments clearly elucidate the central features of the general Dinka pattern.

Among the Malwal (Aweil District) Dinka, bridewealth payments range from ''five cows and under'' to forty head of cattle (Stubbs, 1962:457). Available data (detailed more fully below) suggest that Dinka tribes characteristically lack a minimum bridewealth payment comparable to that of the Nuer. If a suitor has few cattle, a bridewealth payment commensurate with his

limited means can be arranged. Neither individual poverty of stock nor a
widespread decline in economic conditions makes it necessary to delay marriage, and deferred payments are not employed to prevent bridewealth from
falling below a relatively inflexible minimum as among the Nuer. Instead,
Dinka bridewealth simply decreases to whatever level is consistent with the
current availability of stock. Thus Lienhardt (1961:25) reports that the Dinka
were at one time reduced to marrying for sheep and goats, as a result of
rinderpest epidemics combined with intensified raids on the part of the Nuer to
repair their own epidemic stock losses. Gleichen (1905:145) likewise describes Bor District bridewealth payments as five cows or forty goats, with as
little as one cow being given in some instances. Even under the most adverse
circumstances, Nuer bridewealth payments never declined to comparable
levels.[6]

The Malwal Dinka bridewealth payment of forty cattle that Stubbs (ibid.)
employs to illustrate the principles of customary law represents an "ideal"
payment akin to those of the various Nuer tribes (discussed earlier). This
forty-cattle bridewealth thus represents the appropriate standard for comparison. Although the number of cattle included is equivalent to the largest
Nuer ideal (forty head), the Malwal Dinka transaction entails a reciprocal
payment (*aruweth*) of twenty cattle that effectively reduces this figure by half.
In other words, the bridegroom's kin give forty head of cattle to the bride's
kin but receive a reciprocal payment of twenty head that decreases their actual
outlay to only twenty animals. (The reciprocal payment generally follows
very shortly after the bridewealth is received.)[7] In effect, Malwal Dinka ideal
bridewealth is thus only half as large as that of the Lou Nuer, while the lower
range of five or less is far below the Lou minimum of eighteen to twenty-two
cattle.

Stubbs (1962:455–58) describes Malwal Dinka bridewealth in terms of
three sets of kinsmen on each side of the transaction: the bride's (or groom's)
father's family, her (his) father's *koc cuol tok* and her (his) mother's *koc cuol
tok*. The latter term designates members of the agnatic group within the range
of first cousins and first half cousins, e.g., the bride's father's siblings, his
father's brother's sons and his father's half brother's sons. The inclusion of
patrilateral parallel cousins gives these entities the same agnatic collateral
extension as the sets of kinsmen encompassed by Lou, Eastern Jikany, Dok,
Nuong, and Gaawar Nuer bridewealth transactions. Moreover, Dinka bridewealth payments can legitimately be analyzed in terms of the same three
categories employed with respect to the Nuer, i.e., the bride's immediate
family, her patrikin, and her matrikin.

The collection and redistribution of cattle in the Malwal Dinka ideal
payment is summarized in the following chart showing contributions to both
bridewealth and *aruweth* (reciprocal payment), and the net gains and losses to

each of the three sets of kinsmen on the bride's and groom's sides of the transaction (respectively).

	Among Groom's Kin			Among Bride's Kin		
Cattle given or received by:	*Contribution to Bridewealth*	*Aruweth share received*	*Net outlay*	*Contribution to Aruweth*	*Bridewealth portion received*	*Net gain*
Immediate family	10	3	7	5	6	1
Patrikin	20	8	12	10	16	6
Matrikin	10	9	1	5	18	13
Total	40	20	20	20	40	20

It is clear from these data that the proportions of bridewealth (less *aruweth* contributions) received by the bride's kin are distributed in a way that differs radically from that of the Nuer. The bulk of the cattle go to the bride's matrikin (i.e., thirteen head or 65 percent of the total net gain) while only one animal accrues to the bride's father's herd (representing 5 percent of the cattle acquired). Among the Nuer, the matrikin's portion ranges between 25 and 29 percent of the total bridewealth received, and 38 to 50 percent is allocated to the bride's immediate family (and joins the father's herd). However, there is little difference between the Malwal Dinka and the various Nuer tribes with respect to the patrikin's portion. This ranges from 25 to 34 percent of Nuer bridewealth and constitutes 30 percent of the Malwal Dinka bridewealth (in terms of net gains). Thus, the distinguishing feature of Malwal Dinka arrangements is that the bride's immediate family receives only a single cow at the time the union is celebrated. On the subsequent marriage of the bride's daughter, her father and brothers share in the substantial portion of the bridewealth payment that falls to the matrikin. In effect, the bulk of the bridewealth is a deferred payment standing over from the marriage of the bride's mother.

It should be noted that the matrikin's net contribution to a sister's son's bridewealth payment is not comparable to their net gain of thirteen cattle on a sister's daughter's marriage. The matrikin contribute ten cattle to a sister's son's bridewealth but receive nine from the reciprocal payment (of twenty) for a net loss of only a single animal. If one considers the marriages of a brother and sister as a pair of linked transactions, the results are a net gain of twelve cattle for this pair of siblings' matrikin and a net loss of six cattle each for their father's herd and their patrikin, respectively. From the standpoint of the family herd, the main flow of cattle in Malwal Dinka bridewealth transactions is thus outward on the marriage of sons (and brother's sons) and inward on the marriage of sister's daughters. This clearly structures Dinka kin relationships in a very different way from those of the Nuer. Among the latter, a man counts on the bridewealth derived from his daughter's marriage to provide the bulk of the cattle necessary to secure a wife for his son and hence perpetuate his line. The patrikin are obligated to contribute to a nephew's bridewealth but are not expected to provide as many cattle as they receive on the marriage of a niece. Matrikin are not formally obliged to contribute anything, although a mother's full brother may do so as a token of affection for his sister's son (Evans-Pritchard, 1951a:158–59, 163). The family herd is thus the principal source of bridewealth, and it is augmented by twenty cattle on the marriage of a daughter. Comparatively, the cattle derived from a sister's daughter's marriage add only two to four animals. In contrast, a Malwal Dinka man depends on his sister's daughter's marriage to provide the cattle necessary for the social reproduction of his line effected by his son's marriage. This centrality of the mother's brother–sister's daughter (and sister's husband–wife's brother) relationships in the flow of bridewealth cattle among the Dinka is fully consistent with the organization of local groups. Dinka wet season communities are conceptualized as being composed of a pair of agnatic segments linked by a matrilateral (mother's brother–sister's son) relationship, and they differ from Nuer communities in this respect. (These differences will be discussed in a later chapter.)

Dinka bridewealth transactions differ from those of the Nuer primarily in terms of the proportions allocated to the bride's immediate family, matrikin, and patrikin, rather than in terms of the range of kinsmen encompassed by the transaction. However, Dinka marriage customs include a special payment to the bride's elder sister's husband that is absent among the Nuer. This payment (termed *ariek*) is not required of a man who marries an eldest daughter, but is ideally included in the marriage payment made for a younger daughter. In these instances, the bride's elder sister's husband is entitled to five cattle on a forty-cattle bridewealth payment, four on a bridewealth of thirty, three on twenty, and one on ten (Stubbs, 1962:458). *Ariek* thus passes between men who have the same wife's brother (and wife's father) in common and whose children will have the same mother's brother. The recognition of such coaffinal relationships is appropriate to an organizational design in which marriage ties are seen as the focal links between the segments which make up a community.[8]

The ideal bridewealth payment of the Western Ngok [Ngork] Dinka is presented in table 2. These data are based on material recorded by Howell (1951:284–87) and are strictly comparable to Howell's data concerning Nuer bridewealth payments. The Ngok ideal is expressed in terms of the customary claims of the bride's paternal and maternal kin and is identical to Nuer ideal payments in this respect. The kinsmen encompassed by the distribution of bridewealth cattle are the bride's immediate family and the bride's father's and mother's sibling sets, the same kinsmen that are central to the bridewealth

TABLE 2

Ngok Dinka Bridewealth

Bride's Kin	Cattle	Total
Father	a cow, a cow-calf, & an ox	3
Brothers (uterine & patrilateral)	3 cows	3
Father's brother	a cow, & a cow-calf	2
Father's father (claim inherited by father's half brother by a different mother	a cow, a cow-calf, & an ox	3
Father's mother (claim inherited by father & father's full brothers)	a cow, & a cow-calf	2
Father's sister	a cow, & a cow-calf	2
Mother	a cow, a cow-calf, & an ox	3
Mother's brother	a cow, & a cow-calf	2
Mother's mother (claim inherited by mother's brother by the same mother)	a cow, & a cow-calf	2
Mother's father (claim inherited by mother's brother by a different mother)	a cow, a cow-calf, & a bull	3
Mother's sister	a cow, & a cow-calf	2
Total		27
	(less reciprocal payment of 9)	

distribution of all Nuer tribes. No more distant collateral relatives are included (although coaffines are incorporated when *ariek* forms part of the distribution). The main differences between the Ngok Dinka and the various Nuer tribes discussed earlier are thus in the custom of reciprocal payments, the quantity of cattle required, and the proportions allocated to the bride's immediate family, patrikin, and matrikin (respectively). (Ngok bridewealth also differs markedly from that of the Nuer in terms of the proportion of breeding stock. This comparison will be considered after the sociological variations have been discussed.)

The Ngok ideal bridewealth transaction entails a payment of twenty-seven cattle to the bride's kin and a reverse payment (*arweth*) of nine cattle given by the latter to the groom's kin. The net loss of stock is thus eighteen cattle or about half as much as the average Nuer ideal bridewealth. The same paternal and maternal kinsmen who receive portions of a bridewealth distribution also contribute to the accumulation of cattle for bridewealth payments (Howell, 1951:280), but the amount of their respective contributions is not noted.

Ngok bridewealth is distributed equally among the bride's immediate family, patrikin, and matrikin with each of these sets of kin receiving a third. However, this distribution does not take the *arweth* payment into account and the proportions would be significantly altered by differential contributions to it. Howell (1951:287) mentions that *arweth* is given "by the bride's family," and distributed among the groom's kin in the same proportions as bride-wealth. This suggests that the reciprocal payment is largely derived from the bride's father's herd. If this is the case, the proportional distribution of net gains in cattle would closely resemble that of the Malwal Dinka, i.e., nearly half of the eighteen cattle acquired would go to the bride's matrikin while the bride's immediate family would realize only token gains. Even if *arweth* contributions are disregarded (or equal contributions by the bride's immediate family, patrikin, and matrikin are assumed), the proportional distribution of Ngok bridewealth still falls outside of the range of variation reported for the Nuer. Among the Nuer, the matrikin's portion never exceeds 29 percent of the total bridewealth and the bride's immediate family's portion never falls below 38 percent. It is consequently clear that the Ngok bridewealth distribution tends toward that of the Malwal Dinka, and differs from the Nuer pattern, in the comparatively larger portion allocated to matrikin and the comparatively smaller portion allotted to the bride's family. It is only the extent of this tendency that cannot be precisely specified given available data. A dis-tinctively Dinka pattern of bridewealth distribution is thus evident, and this is confirmed by other sources.[9]

Although the bridewealth transactions of other Dinka tribes are not well documented, or described in any detail, there are some general statements and illustrative cases in the literature that provide additional information on the range of Dinka payments. Cummins (1904:150) reports a range of five to sixty cattle among the Western Dinka. Gleichen (1905:145, 160) notes a bride-wealth of five cattle or less in the Bor District (under adverse economic conditions) and a range of twenty-five to forty among the Western Dinka generally. O'Sullivan (1910:180) mentions two cases in which bridewealth consisted of eight cows and ten cows, respectively. In his account of the Raik (or Rek) Dinka, Titherington (1927:206) reports

> Twenty cows is an average price, but up to one hundred are asked and given if the man's family be rich. To give so many is more an act of ostentation than necessity; the women's position is thereby enhanced. The brideprice is generally completed before the wedding, and about a year later, if all goes well, the husband will receive back about one-tenth (up to one-quarter in some parts), of what he gave—not his own cattle returned, but others.

The one-tenth to one-fourth reciprocal payment would reduce the number of cattle effectively transferred in an average transaction to eighteen or fifteen head, respectively. Such reciprocal payments are a feature of bridewealth transactions among all Dinka tribes (Howell, 1951:287) and would reduce the effective size of bridewealth payments reported by the preceding authors as well.

In all, these scattered reports indicate a much wider range of Dinka bridewealth payments than that recorded for the Nuer. As noted earlier, there is no fixed minimum below which marriages cannot be negotiated and four different sources note Dinka payments of five cattle or less (i.e., Cummins, Gleichen, Stubbs, and Lienhardt, all cited earlier). At the other end of the scale, some extremely large bridewealth payments are also reported. Titherington (1927) mentions one hundred cattle, Deng (1971:262) reports the same figure (with a reciprocal payment of forty) and Howell (1951:280) states "a man may hand over as many as forty, fifty, or even a hundred head of cattle for the daughter of an important man," in order to effect an advantageous alliance with the latter. It is self-evident that extraordinary wealth in cattle is also required to make such a large payment, and these transactions thus appear to involve alliances among the most wealthy and influential families, including the families of "chiefs" in the colonial and postcolonial administrative system. This is supported by Seligman's (1932:173) statement that a well-endowed subchief personally contributed thirty cows and eight oxen to his eldest son's bridewealth.

Since the bridewealth required in a particular marriage arrangement varies with the economic circumstances of the groom's family and kin, the wider range of Dinka bridewealth payments (compared to the Nuer range) very probably indicates a more unequal distribution of cattle among Dinka households than among those of the Nuer. Given the fact that a bridewealth of one hundred cattle entails a reciprocal payment of forty, the effective Dinka range is from several cattle to sixty. The Nuer range is eighteen to forty cattle and neither Howell (1954a) nor Evans-Pritchard (1951a) report any bridewealth transactions involving more than forty cattle during the comparable time period (early 1900s onward). Although Nuer bridewealth payments of fifty or sixty cattle were sometimes made before rinderpest depleted Nuer herds, Evans-Pritchard (1940a:19–20) links these expanded payments to the fact that the Nuer as a whole were rich in cattle, rather than attributing it to the wealth of particular families. He also argues (ibid.) that cattle are generally quite evenly distributed among households. Such a distribution is consistent with the relatively narrow range of Nuer bridewealth payments. In contrast, recent studies indicate that cattle are rather unequally distributed among Dinka household heads. In a 1976 survey of 224 individuals (reported in Payne and El Amin, 1977:28), the upper 23.3 percent of household heads each own eleven to fifty cattle, representing 55.2 percent of the total cattle in the household sample. The lower 23.2 percent of household heads own one or two animals each, comprising only 4.8 percent of the total. The middle 53.5

percent of household heads own three to ten cattle each, representing 40 percent of the total. This uneven distribution is fully consistent with the wide range of Dinka bridewealth payments. Indeed, it is clear that poorer households would be hard-pressed to contribute anything to a bridewealth accumulation, while one or two wealthy households could contribute as many as forty head to a son's marriage.

It is also evident that a cattle distribution of this type would preclude the possibility of marriage among the sons of poorer households unless marriages could be contracted for a bridewealth of only several cattle. This is more readily apparent when the per capita holdings of the households in the sample are considered. The average household size among the Southern Dinka, among whom the above survey was conducted, is seven persons (Payne and El Amin, 1977:9). Although the average holdings of all individuals in the sample would thus be 1.14 cattle per capita, 76.7 percent of the households owning one to ten cattle (each) possess only 0.66 cattle per capita. At such levels few animals could be spared for contributions to bridewealth and the majority of marriages would entail payments toward the lower end of the range.

A Comparative Analysis of Nuer and Dinka Bridewealth Systems

It is clear from all the available data reviewed here that Nuer bridewealth payments are much higher than those of the Dinka in terms of the most significant standards of comparison, i.e., the ideal and minimum payments that determine social requirements for cattle among the general population. These social requirements influence herd management strategies that in turn determine the growth rate of the cattle population as a whole. Comparatively, the ideal payments of the Nuer tribes range from thirty-two to forty head of cattle while those of the Dinka entail a net outlay of eighteen to twenty head of cattle when reciprocal payments are considered. Among the Nuer, the ideal payment must be met to the degree that the groom's family and kin possess sufficient cattle to do so, and any livestock in excess of those required for subsistence are subject to the demands of the bride's kin in meeting the claims of the "people of rights." The higher level of Nuer ideal bridewealth payments—nearly double that of the Dinka—thus translates directly into higher social requirements for cattle.

The difference between these two cultural groups in minimum bridewealth payments is even greater than the difference in ideal payments. Among the Nuer, the bride's family and kin "must get certain animals or the marriage cannot take place" (Evans-Pritchard, 1951a:80). If there are no grandparental claims (due to the death of the latter before the bride's birth), this minimum is eighteen cattle. The Dinka possess no such minimum. Under adverse economic conditions marriages may be transacted for a payment of sheep and goats. More importantly, individual families who are poor in cattle may secure a bride for their son for a payment of only five animals (or less) even when general economic conditions are more favorable and the local cattle population as a whole is not depleted by disease or Nuer raids. The acceptability of these very small bridewealth payments appears to be an accommodation to a chronically unequal distribution of cattle among Dinka households. However, for present purposes the interpretation of these small payments is less important than the well-documented fact of their occurrence.

The absence of a fixed minimum payment among the Dinka has a very significant bearing on social requirements for cattle, on the herd management strategies dictated by these social requirements, and hence on the demographic characteristics of the cattle population (in terms of growth or stability). The capacity of a Dinka family to secure brides for their sons is not contingent on assembling a quite substantial minimum number of cattle, and the family herd need not be managed with a view to promoting the growth necessary to meet such a requirement. If few cattle beyond subsistence needs are available to the groom's family and kin, a small bridewealth payment consistent with this poverty of stock can be arranged. Social requirements for bridewealth cattle are not inflexible below a certain point as they are among the Nuer. Instead, the size of bridewealth payments can be adjusted downward in relation to the availability of cattle, and a decline in the latter produces a corresponding decline in the former. In other words, it is the size of the cattle population that determines the size of bridewealth payments in the actual transactions of a Dinka local population. The direction of this casual relationship is reversed among the Nuer. Bridewealth cannot be adjusted downward below the minimum payment of eighteen to twenty-two cattle and the accumulation of sufficient stock to meet this minimum stimulates raiding of the Dinka for cattle and herd management practices geared to the objective of growth. As a result, there is a predisposition of the cattle population as a whole toward sustained growth. Nuer bridewealth payments thus exert a strong positive influence on the size of the cattle population rather than merely being responsive to it, as are those of the Dinka. In the Nuer case, social requirements for cattle are not only much higher than those of the Dinka but are also impervious to reduction below a certain point. Indeed, that point, defined by minimum bridewealth payments, corresponds closely to the Dinka ideal payment of eighteen to twenty head of cattle. Thus, maximum Dinka social requirements for cattle are fulfilled at the point at which Nuer *minimum* requirements are fixed.

It is important to point out that the manner in which Dinka bridewealth payments are culturally delineated facilitates adjustments of the cattle population to the availability of dry season pasture. As the cattle population approaches the limits of dry season grazing, increased numbers of cattle can be slaughtered to maintain the cattle population below these limits. Flexible bridewealth payments are subject to decrease in relation to the decreased availability of cattle per capita and do not constitute an impediment to the herd reductions necessary to bring the cattle population into balance with existing grazing resources. Consequently, grazing resources need not be expanded. The Dinka socioecological system possesses a capacity to achieve homeostasis within a finite territorial domain, unlike that of the Nuer. The propensity of the Dinka to slaughter a larger proportion of their cattle than the Nuer can be documented by differences in the herd structure of these two cultural groups, and these differences are reflected in the composition of bridewealth payments. This point will be taken up later in the chapter after the comparison of the sociological features of Nuer and Dinka bridewealth is completed.

Although Nuer ideal bridewealth payments are roughly twice as large as those of the Dinka when reciprocal payments are considered, these reciprocal payments themselves account for the bulk of the disparity. There are no major differences between the Nuer and Dinka in the number of cattle presented to the bride's family and kin; the Dinka range of twenty-seven (Ngok) to forty (Malwal) largely overlaps the Nuer range of thirty-four to forty cattle. The two to one difference in the size of bridewealth payments emerges only after the reciprocal payment is made, but this return payment affects net outlay without reducing kin participation. As a result of this, the range of kinsmen encompassed by Nuer and Dinka transactions is largely unaffected by the disparity in the number of cattle lost to the groom's family and kin. Dinka reciprocal payments thus reduce the number of cattle actually required to achieve an ideal distribution among the bride's kin, while maintaining both the scope of kinship participation and the collective nature of the transaction. In this respect, Dinka reciprocal payments are an analogue of Nuer minimum bridewealth payments. The latter likewise maintain the same range of kinship participation as ideal payments, while reducing cattle requirements (Howell, 1954*a*:110); Evans-Pritchard, 1951*a*:83–87). The critical difference is that the Dinka reduction via reciprocal payments is institutionalized and built into every transaction, including ideal transactions, while the Nuer reduction represented by the minimum payment is contingent on the groom's poverty of stock. This indicates that Dinka bridewealth (compared to that of the Nuer) is permanently geared to the expectation that fewer cattle will be available for contribution to bridewealth, i.e., adjusted to an economic system entailing fewer cattle per capita. Additional data, to be presented later in the chapter, will document this difference between the Nuer and Dinka in cattle per capita holdings.

The size of Dinka reciprocal payments co-varies with the size of the bridewealth payment itself, but the former increases at a rate more than directly proportional to the latter. In other words, the larger the bridewealth payment, the higher the reciprocal payment as a *percentage* of the total number of cattle presented to the bride's kin. This general relationship is clear in Stubbs's (1962:457–58) report that no reciprocal payment is made on a bridewealth of five cattle, while a bridewealth of ten cattle requires a return of two (or 20 percent) and a bridewealth of forty cattle entails a reciprocal payment of twenty (or 50 percent). Likewise, Titherington (1927) notes a return of two to five cattle on a bridewealth of twenty (or 19 to 25 percent) and Howell (1954*a*) a reciprocal payment of nine on a bridewealth of twenty-seven head (or 33 percent).

This progressive increase in the magnitude of reciprocal payments would prevent a general increase in bridewealth payments from producing a corresponding increase in social requirements for cattle. This feature of Dinka bridewealth customs constitutes an impediment to the development of the kind of positive feedback relationship that obtains in the Nuer case between the availability of cattle and the size of bridewealth payments. Among the Nuer, all available cattle beyond the subsistence requirements of the groom's people are subject to the demands of the bride's kin and increased cattle per capita holdings translate directly into higher bridewealth payments. At the same time, the depletion of the family herds of the groom's father and kin, and the anticipation of future marriages, exerts pressure on the latter to augment their herds through breeding and raiding, increasing the cattle per capita holdings of the general population. In contrast, increased availability of cattle among the Dinka prompts higher bridewealth payments that are accompanied by progressively larger return payments. This ensures that the herds of the groom's people are not depleted to the minimum necessary for subsistence, thus attenuating pressures toward further expansion of the cattle population.

This contrast is yet another aspect of a general dissimilarity between the Nuer and the Dinka in the extent to which changes in social variables pertaining to cattle produce corresponding changes in economic variables pertaining to cattle and vice versa. Among the Nuer these two subsystems are tightly articulated and changes in one induce changes of the same magnitude in the other. Among the Dinka, interconnections between these two subsystems are buffered with respect to some variables (as in the above example) and disarticulated with respect to others. The fact that a poverty of stock (in the economic domain) does not preclude or delay the arrangement of a marriage (in the social domain) is one example of this disarticulation. The Nuer socioeconomic system is "hypercoherent," in Rappaport's (1979:162) terminology, and this structural characteristic is an important aspect of its instability. This point will be developed in the concluding chapter. Our present

concern is to delineate the sociological differences between the Nuer and
Dinka (in bridewealth customs) that will lay the groundwork for a subsequent
examination of variations in the articulation of social and economic variables.

Although there is little difference between the Nuer and Dinka in the
range of kinsmen encompassed by ideal bridewealth transactions, there are
significant variations between these two cultural groups in the distribution of
cattle among the bride's immediate family, patrikin, and matrikin. These
variations can be arranged on a continuum in which the Dinka occupy one
end, the Nuer tribes that formed the leading edge of Nuer expansion occupy
the other end, and the Homeland and Zeraf Nuer fill out the center. Among
the Malwal Dinka, the bride's immediate family receives only 5 percent of the
total bridewealth payment (in terms of net gains) and the matrikin garners 65
percent. Precise figures are unavailable for the Ngok, but the bride's family
acquires something between 11 and 33 percent of the total cattle gained, while
the matrikin are allotted 33 to 44 percent. Among the Homeland and Zeraf
Nuer the proportions span a range from 38 percent immediate family, 29
percent matrikin (Lak) to 40 percent family, 26 percent matrikin (Leik), to 42
percent family, 29 percent matrikin (Bul). The Lou and Eastern Jikany that
spearheaded Nuer territorial expansion both display proportions in which 50
percent of the bridewealth payment is allotted to the bride's immediate family
and 25 percent allocated to her matrikin. The pattern of differences is the
same as that noted earlier with respect to other variables, i.e., the Nuer tribes
that formed the leading edge of Nuer expansion differ from the Homeland and
Zeraf Nuer in the same way that the latter differ from the Dinka.

The clear trend along this continuum of variation is from a Malwal Dinka
distribution favoring the bride's matrikin at the expense of the bride's immediate family to a Lou and Eastern Jikany distribution that essentially inverts
these priorities. Moreover, there is a co-varying increase in the size of bridewealth payments along this same continuum: Dinka, eighteen to twenty cattle;
Homeland and Zeraf Nuer, thirty-two to thirty-eight cattle; Lou and Eastern
Jikany, forty cattle. This co-variation between the size and distribution of
bridewealth payments is consistent with the pattern noted earlier with respect
to the comparison of Lou Nuer minimum and ideal payments. When fewer
cattle are available, the bride's immediate family disproportionately relinquish their claims in favor of those of the bride's matrikin, whose comparatively inflexible allotment represents the final installment of the bride's
mother's bridewealth payment. In comparison with the ideal payment, the
Lou minimum is thus characterized by a shift in proportions that decreases the
bride's immediate family's share of the total bridewealth from 50 to 41
percent and increases the matrikin's share from 25 to 32 percent. Dinka
bridewealth thus conforms to the same principle of co-variation between the
size and distribution of bridewealth payments that obtains among the Nuer

(or, more accurately stated, the bridewealth payments of both cultural groups are governed by the same principles).

It is clear that the size of bridewealth payments is the independent variable in this co-variation, and distribution the dependent variable. Given the relatively invariant claims of the maternal side, the matrikin's allotment represents a large proportion of a smaller bridewealth and a comparatively smaller proportion of an expanded payment. Distributional changes thus follow from changes in the scale of bridewealth payments. Hence, the principal difference between the Nuer and Dinka is in the magnitude of their respective bridewealth payments and the distributional dissimilarities largely follow from this. This interpretation is supported by the fact that there is relatively little difference between these two cultural groups in the number of cattle allotted to the bride's matrikin in their respective ideal payments: nine to eleven head among the Nuer and nine to thirteen head among the Dinka. This component of bridewealth transactions has thus remained largely unchanged as the Nuer and Dinka have diverged in customs over time. What has changed during this divergence is the scale of payments and consequently their proportional distribution among the bride's family and kin.

It is also clear that the difference in the magnitude of Nuer and Dinka ideal bridewealth payments is largely attributable to the substantial reciprocal payment characteristic of Dinka transactions and absent or attenuated among the Nuer. As noted earlier, there is little difference between these two cultural groups in the number of cattle presented to the bride's people; the bulk of the disparity in net outlay arises only after the subsequent reciprocal payment of the Dinka is deducted. The cultural divergence of the Nuer and Dinka in bridewealth custom is thus traceable to a change concerning the reciprocal payment that effected a change in magnitude that, in turn, altered the distributional characteristics of the transaction.[10]

It is important to note that the Nuer reverse payment (*thiuk*), made by a few Homeland Nuer tribes (the Dok, Aak, and Jagei), is essentially different in character from the Malwal and Ngok Dinka reciprocal payment (*aruweth* or *arweth*). In the Nuer case, the two cows included in the payment are designated as belonging to the bride's future sons (Howell, 1954*a*:113). The newly formed domestic unit therefore holds exclusive rights of disposal (as distinct from the rights of disposal held by the groom's father over the family herd). The *thiuk* payment is consequently a dowry in the usual sense of the term (see Goody and Tambiah, 1973:20–21). In contrast, the Dinka reciprocal payment is not a dowry, since it is not assigned to the bride or the newly formed domestic group but rather distributed among the groom's kin and immediate family. This difference in the fundamental character of return payments suggests that the divergence of the Nuer and Dinka with respect to this custom is of long standing.

It is perhaps most plausible that both cultural groups once shared the custom of a small dowry payment, and that this was discontinued by almost all Nuer tribes while the Dinka expanded the payment and transformed its character. Linguistic evidence lends some support to this hypothesis. The Ruweng Dinka directly north of the Homeland Nuer and the Bor District Dinka to the south refer to their respective reciprocal payments as *athek* and *alok thok* (Howell, 1951:287).[11] These terms appear to bear some relationship to the Nuer term *thiuk*. However, the lack of close similarity also suggests that considerable time has elapsed since the Nuer and Dinka shared a common custom, designated by a common term. This is further supported by Atwot (Atuot) oral traditions. The Atwot, who separated from the main body of the Nuer about four to five hundred years ago, maintain that their traditional bridewealth transactions did not include a reciprocal payment. This distinguished them from their Dinka neighbors, who had (and still have) a reciprocal payment termed *arueth* (Burton, 1978a:59). Before the colonial period, the Atwot raided the neighboring Dinka tribes and did not intermarry with them. In recent times intermarriage has become common and the Atwot explain their current adoption of a reciprocal payment as a consequence of this (ibid.). The basic differences between Nuer and Dinka bridewealth that are connected with the Dinka custom of a substantial reciprocal payment thus appear to have been established before the time of the Atwot migration, four to five hundred years ago.

All available data suggest that Nuer bridewealth payments were considerably larger than those of the Dinka at the inception of Nuer expansion in the early 1800s (and, indeed, several centuries before this). The ideal and acceptable bridewealth payments recorded by Evans-Pritchard in the early 1930s (and by Howell somewhat later) are traditional formulations, not a product of current conditions. The massive reduction of Nuer herds due to the introduction of rinderpest reduced typical bridewealth payments far below the ideal from the early 1890s to the 1930s, yet the ideal was still firmly maintained at the latter date. This clearly indicates that conceptions of ideal bridewealth do not readily change to reflect economic circumstances, even when the latter have prevailed for extended periods of time. Indeed, the ideal to acceptable range of Nuer bridewealth is capable of encompassing a wide range of economic fluctuations without alteration. The same is true of the even more flexible Dinka range of bridewealth payments. Although the Dinka were reduced to contracting marriages for a bridewealth of sheep and goats in the early 1900s, traditional ideals of the nineteenth century were still maintained and reinstituted when economic conditions permitted. It is also noteworthy that the Malwal and Rek Dinka, who were far removed from the areas of Nuer expansion, have nearly the same ideal bridewealth (of eighteen to twenty cattle) as the Ngok who were displaced by the Nuer. The consistency of the basic Dinka pattern (including reciprocal payments) suggests that it has not been significantly altered by recent historical forces that have differentially affected various Dinka tribes.

In sum, we know that traditional Nuer and Dinka conceptions of ideal and acceptable bridewealth payments were applicable to the prerinderpest era of the late 1870s (based on the statements of informants alive at that time). We also know that these conceptions did not materially change despite massive reductions in the cattle population that persisted over the next forty years. The number of cattle transferred in actual transactions was depressed to minimum acceptable levels during the worst years of this period, but conceptions of the ideal (and acceptable) payment were nevertheless maintained unchanged. These conceptions are embedded in kinship obligations and are clearly highly resistant to economically induced change. Indeed, the acceptable to ideal range represents a mechanism for accommodating economic fluctuations without change. It is also remarkable that the same kinship obligations (to the same range of kinsmen) delineate Nuer and Dinka bridewealth after nearly two thousand years of linguistic and cultural divergence. Although Nuer and Dinka bridewealth customs have diverged (with respect to the reciprocal payment), these kinship obligations have been maintained unchanged. Given all these indications of a very slow rate of change, it is most plausible to assume that the basic differences between the Nuer and Dinka in the magnitude (and composition) of ideal and acceptable bridewealth payments evident in the ethnographic present were also evident well before the inception of Nuer territorial expansion in the period 1800 to 1820. Atwot oral traditions suggest that these basic differences were already established before the sixteenth century.

One would expect that the size of actual Nuer transactions would increase as a result of the wealth in cattle acquired in the course of raiding associated with territorial expansion. Such an increase is indicated by Evans-Pritchard's report that bridewealth rose to fifty or sixty head of cattle at the height of the expansion period. However, this increase in the scale of actual bridewealth payments did not engender a redefinition of the ideal payment as consisting of fifty to sixty cattle (just as the post-rinderpest reduction in the size of actual transactions did not alter the ideal). The fact that the Lou Nuer report that bridewealth payments exceeded the ideal (of forty cattle) during these years of prosperity presupposes that this ideal predates the growth of Nuer herds associated with territorial acquisition. This also supports the general point that the basic differences between the Nuer and Dinka in the scale and composition of bridewealth payments predate the expansion period.

There is, however, one body of data that may indicate some slight modification in Nuer and Dinka conceptions of ideal bridewealth associated with the expansion process itself. The forty-cattle ideal payment of the Lou and Eastern Jikany tribes that spearheaded Nuer territorial expansion is slightly higher than the high end of the range of variation among the Homeland Nuer (i.e., thirty-two to thirty-eight head of cattle). Similarly, the eighteen head of cattle included in the ideal payment of the Ngok Dinka, who were displaced by the Nuer, is slightly less than the twenty-cattle ideal payment of the Malwal Dinka, who were far removed from the areas where Nuer expansion took place. It is consequently conceivable that the Ngok ideal bridewealth payment has decreased by two head of cattle since 1800, while that of the Lou and Eastern Jikany has increased by a like amount. However, very significant differences in the scale of bridewealth payments would nevertheless have characterized the Lou Nuer and Ngok Dinka who contested Zeraf Island in the early phases of Nuer territorial expansion. In about 1820, the Lou Nuer crossed the Bahr el Jebel and dislodged the Ngok Dinka from Zeraf Island. Even if we assume that Lou Nuer ideal bridewealth was thirty-eight cattle (rather than forty) at this time, and the Ngok Dinka ideal twenty cattle (rather than eighteen), a major discontinuity in the scale of bridewealth payments would nevertheless be evident along the border where Nuer expansion took place.

ECONOMIC CORRELATES OF THE NUER AND DINKA BRIDEWEALTH SYSTEMS

As noted earlier, Nuer and Dinka ideal bridewealth payments differ not only in scale, but also in composition (in terms of the proportion of breeding and milk-producing stock included). These differences in the composition of bridewealth payments can be related to corresponding differences in the structure of Nuer and Dinka herds. In other words, a herd structure characterized by a high proportion of female animals co-varies with a bridewealth payment that requires a high proportion of female animals. Moreover, these differences between the Nuer and Dinka in herd structure are linked to, and constitute an aspect of, distinctive economic variants of a shared transhumant system of production. The Nuer and Dinka economic variants differ not only in herd structure but also in cattle per capita holdings, and these differences correlate perfectly with divergent social requirements for cattle dictated by differences in the scale of Nuer and Dinka bridewealth payments. In short, ideal bridewealth payments—through their very direct effects on herd management practices—shape the economic system. This section is concerned with documenting the key interrelationships that lead to this conclusion.

The proportions of different types of cattle included in the bridewealth payments of several Nuer and Dinka tribes are presented in table 3. In all, female animals representing actual or potential breeding and milk-producing stock constitute 89 percent of the Ngok Dinka ideal bridewealth but only 64

TABLE 3

Proportions of Different Types of Animals Included in Nuer and Dinka Bridewealth

Types of Animals	Lak and Thiang Nuer Ideal Bridewealth		Lou Nuer Ideal Bridewealth		Lou Nuer Acceptable Bridewealth		Ngok Dinka Ideal Bridewealth (less reciprocal payment)	
	Number	Percentage of Total	Number	Percentage of Total	Number	Percentage of Total	Number	Percentage of Total
Cows	15	44.1	17	42.5	10	45.5	9	50.0
Heifers	0	0	3	7.5	2	9.1	0	0
Cow-calves	9 or 10 (9.5)	27.9	5 or 6 (5.5)	13.7	2	9.1	7	38.9
Bull-calves	3 or 4 (3.5)	10.3	5 or 6 (5.5)	13.7	2	9.1	0	0
Oxen	6	17.6	11	22.5	6	27.3	1	5.5
Bulls	0	0	0	0	0	0	1	5.5
Total	34	99.9	40	99.9	22	100.1	18	99.9
Total potential breeding stock	24 or 25 (24.5)	72.0	25 or 26 (25.5)	63.7	14	63.6	16	88.9

Source: These data are based on information provided in Howell, 1954a:88, 102–4, Evans-Pritchard, 1951a:74–82, and Howell, 1951:284–87. Lou Nuer figures are based on the assumption that half the calves transferred under the designation "a cow and its calf" are females. Ngok Dinka figures are based on the assumption that the reciprocal payment includes the same proportions of breeding and nonbreeding stock as the bridewealth payment itself.

percent of both Lou Nuer ideal and acceptable bridewealth payments. The comparable figure for both the Lak and Thiang Nuer ideal payments is 72 percent. Although the larger Nuer ideal payments include a greater number of female cattle than the smaller Ngok bridewealth (in total), Nuer payments also incorporate substantial numbers of oxen and bull calves that are largely absent from the Dinka ideal. This is partly attributable to a difference in the specification of animals in kinship-based claims. Where Nuer bridewealth claims denote "a cow and its calf," Dinka claims specify "a cow and a cow-calf." Thus, only one-half of the calves included in a Nuer transaction would be female, while all those included in a Dinka payment represent potential breeding and milk-producing stock. In addition, Nuer payments include six to eleven oxen while the Ngok payment incorporates only one ox and one bull.

The differences among the Nuer tribes, and between the Nuer and Dinka, in the proportion of breeding stock included in ideal bridewealth payments conform to a familiar pattern. The Lou Nuer who formed the leading edge of Nuer expansion differ from the Zeraf Valley Nuer in the same way that the latter differ from the Dinka. As we move along a continuum from Ngok Dinka to Zeraf Nuer to Lou Nuer, the percentage of breeding stock declines from 89 to 72 to 64 percent. The difference between the Dinka and Zeraf Nuer is much greater than the difference between the latter and the Lou Nuer, but the tendency of the Lou to more fully express existing differences between the Nuer and Dinka (generally) is apparent. It is also evident that the scale of bridewealth payments co-varies with the proportion of breeding stock. As bridewealth increases (from eighteen cattle for the Ngok Dinka to thirty-four for the Zeraf Nuer to forty for the Lou Nuer), the proportion of breeding stock declines. The basis of this co-variation will become clear in due course.

The divergent percentages of female animals included in Nuer and Dinka bridewealth payments (respectively) parallel the percentages of female cattle in the adult population of Nuer and Dinka herds reported by Howell (1954b:309). Adult females (i.e., cows) represent 77 percent of a total of 67,541 adult animals in a large sample of Western Nuer herds and an identical 77 percent of a total of 86,344 adult animals in Lou Nuer herds. In contrast, cows constitute 86 percent of a Bor Dinka adult cattle population (of 123,684) and 91 percent of 20,504 adult animals in Aliab Dinka herds. These differences between the Nuer and Dinka in herd composition clearly indicate different herd management strategies. Moreover, the fact that parallel differences in herd composition are reflected in ideal bridewealth payments— payments that have been maintained unchanged despite dramatic fluctuations in the cattle population since 1880—indicates that these distinctive herd management strategies are of long standing and are deeply embedded in the respective economic adaptations of these two tribes.

The comparatively small proportion of adult male animals in Dinka herds is the end result of the systematic culling of young bulls for meat consumption. Given parity in the sex ratio at birth and equivalent natural mortality for both sexes, the preceding figures on herd composition indicate that 84 to 90 percent of the male animals born into Dinka herds are slaughtered when they reach maturity as opposed to 70 percent of those born into Nuer herds. This higher level of regular and dependable meat consumption among the Dinka would reduce their dependence on milk as a daily source of protein and allow the Dinka to satisfy nutritional requirements with fewer (living) cattle per capita. Cattle that have been slaughtered for food contribute to fulfilling subsistence needs but do not add to grazing area requirements. Thus, the Dinka herd management strategy would permit the Dinka to attain higher human densities than the Nuer at any given ratio of cattle to dry season grazing land. In contrast, the lower level of regular meat consumption among the Nuer would entail greater daily dependence on milk products and hence more female cattle per capita to provide this. Both these additional female cattle and the 14 to 20 percent more surviving male animals would increase the number of (living) cattle per capita necessary to fulfill subsistence needs under this Nuer herd management strategy and hence require significantly more grazing land than Dinka practices. Nuer grazing requirements are further augmented by the fact that bulls and oxen consume 50 percent more feed than milk cows.[12] A given unit of grazing land capable of supporting a fixed number of cattle would thus sustain fewer Nuer than Dinka, given the higher ratio of cattle per capita among the former.

Consideration of Nuer and Dinka herd compositions, and the distinctive herd management strategies these different compositions presuppose, thus suggests that Nuer human population density would necessarily be significantly less than that of the Dinka. The data on population density compiled by Howell (1955:76) square perfectly with this expectation. When any two adjacent Nuer and Dinka districts in similar ecological zones are compared, Dinka densities are 36.5 to 45.0 percent higher than those of the Nuer. Thus, the Bor District Dinka (with cows constituting 86 percent of adult animals in the herd) have a human population density of fifteen per square mile, while the Lou and Zeraf Valley Nuer (with 77 percent cows) have a density of eleven per square mile. The environment of these two areas is quite similar, with no ecological disjunction along the common border between the two cultural groups.

It is important to emphasize that Nuer and Dinka herd management strategies are not merely "subsistence strategies" that constitute "adaptations to the environment" but are rather geared to the fulfillment of a wide variety of cultural requirements. Evans-Pritchard (1940a:18–19) points out that the "Nuer tend to define all social processes and relationships in terms of cattle" and that cattle also play a central role in ritual. Cattle are dedicated to lineage spirits, sacrificed to ghosts, and contributed to bridewealth and homicide compensation. Herd management practices reflect these social and ritual needs as well as those pertaining to subsistence. An ideal bridewealth payment must contain "the ox of the uterine brother," "the cow of the mother's spirit," "the heifer of the paternal aunt," etc. (Howell, 1954a:107), and a man must manage the family herd in such a way as to be able to meet these social requirements for specific, symbolically appropriate kinds of animals. Cattle are not slaughtered in order to supply food, but are consumed when they are sacrificed on ritual occasions, each of which also requires a distinctive type of animal. Herd composition thus reflects both the frequency of various sacrificial rites and the cultural definition of the kind of animal symbolically appropriate for each. This is to say that the observed differences in the composition of Nuer and Dinka herds are the results of different culturally defined social requirements that govern the utilization of cattle in each case. In very brief, the Nuer require many oxen for inclusion in bridewealth payments and the Dinka require that a larger proportion of their young male animals be slaughtered as sacrificial offerings. The differences in herd management are not explicable in terms of subsistence needs, since the Nuer and Dinka do not differ in this respect, nor can they be explained by adaptation to the physical environment, as the Bor District Dinka and Zeraf Valley Nuer occupy closely similar environmental areas yet display dissimilar herd structures. While neither environment nor subsistence needs co-vary with the differences in herd composition, the social requirements for different types of animals encoded in Nuer and Dinka ideal bridewealth payments do co-vary quite closely with these distinctive herd structures. Moreover, Nuer bridewealth payments require a higher ratio of cattle per capita than those of the Dinka and Nuer herd composition likewise entails more cattle per capita. In short, the distinctive features of Nuer and Dinka economic organization are intelligible from a sociological perspective, and it is thus no accident that they have emerged from a comparison of bridewealth payments.

It should now be quite clear why the magnitude of bridewealth payments co-varies with the proportion of breeding and milk-producing stock, as noted in the earlier comparison of the Ngok Dinka, Zeraf Nuer, and Lou Nuer. A herd composition with proportionally fewer female animals necessitates higher cattle per capita holdings. The larger bridewealth payments of the Lou Nuer thus encode social requirements for both a comparatively high ratio of cattle per capita and a comparatively low proportion of breeding and milk-producing stock because these are intrinsically interrelated. The same interrelationship is equally manifest in Ngok Dinka and Zeraf Nuer ideal bridewealth payments. Indeed, the correlation between the scale of ideal bridewealth payments and the proportion of female animals included in them is nearly perfect. If a graph is constructed with the former quantity on one axis and the latter on the other, and a line is drawn from the Ngok Dinka at one extreme to

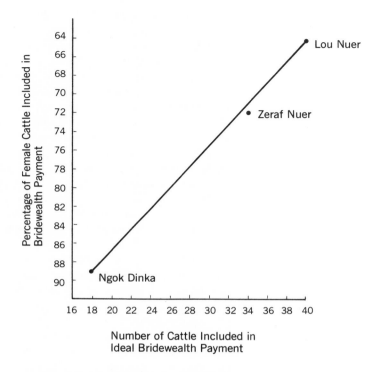

FIG. 3. Co-variation between the Magnitude and Composition of Bridewealth Payments

the Lou Nuer at the other, the Zeraf Nuer deviate from this line by only a very slight margin (see fig. 3).

Although both the Nuer and Dinka are characterized by a transhumant system of production, each of these cultural groups possesses a distinctive economic organization of systematically interrelated features. Social requirements for cattle delineate the herd management practices that differentiate Nuer herd composition from that of the Dinka. This herd structure, in turn, entails a higher ratio of cattle per capita that necessitates expanded grazing requirements. A given unit of grazing land capable of supporting a fixed number of cattle will thus support fewer Nuer than Dinka, and Nuer population density is correspondingly lower. The Nuer thus differ from the Dinka in two of the key variables identified in figure 2, i.e., cattle per capita and human population density. They likewise differ, for similar reasons, in the third, i.e., cattle density. We have seen that the magnitude of Nuer ideal bridewealth payments, and their inflexible minimum payment, dictate herd management practices geared toward growth. This continually pushes Nuer cattle densities toward ecological limits. At the same time, these social requirements for cattle preclude slaughter as a mechanism for achieving herd reductions when the cattle population approaches maximum density. In contrast, the Dinka evidence smaller ideal bridewealth payments, the absence of an inflexible minimum payment, and a progressive reciprocal payment that prevents the depletion of the groom's family's herd to subsistence levels (stimulating growth to achieve a margin of safety). Given this differential stimulus to the growth of family herds, Dinka cattle density tends to be lower than that of the Nuer. In addition, the Dinka possess a capacity to accommodate a decline in bridewealth payments commensurate with herd reductions, and more extensive social requirements for the sacrifice of young male animals that encourage and facilitate such reductions. The Dinka thus manifest not only a lesser impetus to the growth of their cattle population than the Nuer, but also the capacity for maintaining a constant cattle density compatible with ecological limits on grazing resources that is absent in the Nuer case.

These differences between the Nuer and Dinka economic systems in cattle per capita, human population density, and cattle density necessarily entail corresponding differences in the size of wet season communities, the scale of multicommunity aggregations in the dry season, and the relationship between the agricultural and herding components of the economy. Each wet season site, surrounded by inundated flood plain, possesses limited land area for grazing and agricultural utilization. Any given site is capable of supporting only a fixed number of cattle, and a higher ratio of cattle per capita therefore dictates a smaller human population. Nuer wet season communities are thus smaller than those of the Dinka. In addition, a smaller human population requires less agricultural land (and fewer dwellings), increasing the area available for grazing and hence the number of cattle that can be supported through the wet season. The density of the cattle population in wet season communities is consequently higher for the Nuer than the Dinka. The smaller human population and decreased agricultural acreage required per season also extends the number of years a given wet season site can be utilized before a decline in crop yields necessitates temporary abandonment of the site (to fallow) and movement to another location.[13] With a longer use period per site, more sites are available at any given time and a higher overall cattle density can be supported during the wet season, up to the limits imposed by the availability of dry season grazing. Maximum utilization of dry season grazing by the Nuer entails maximum aggregation of the human population along major watercourses at the height of the dry season. The Dinka, with a lower cattle density per wet season community and fewer potential wet season sites occupied at any given time (due to increased fallow requirements),[14] have a lower overall cattle density. This lower cattle density does not require maximum utilization of dry season grazing and the cattle population can be maintained at inland lakes and along the tributaries of major watercourses during the dry season. The Dinka human population thus remains more dispersed than that of the Nuer at the height of the dry season (although Dinka wet season communities are larger than those of the Nuer).

These differences in the scale of wet and dry season aggregations are central to an understanding of the development of organizational differentiation and the associated emergence of a decisive Nuer advantage in warfare. This will be elucidated in a later chapter (where additional evidence of these differences will be presented). The point to be noted here is that these systemically interrelated economic differences between the Nuer and Dinka all follow from differences in cattle per capita holdings that are engendered by different social requirements for cattle. Both the larger bridewealth of the Nuer and the requirement that Nuer bridewealth include a substantial proportion of male animals (necessitating a corresponding herd composition) dictate a higher ratio of cattle per capita. Thus while economic features have played a central role in the development of differences between the Nuer and Dinka in lineage organization, and military capability, these economic differences are themselves a product of divergent social requirements for cattle. Social evolution is thus a product of social (and cultural) forces engendering economic alterations that in turn modify social arrangements.

This also explains why the Nuer did not develop the economic (and organizational) characteristics of the Dinka once they had occupied the environmental areas from which they had expelled the latter. The distinctive features of Nuer economic organization (vis-à-vis that of the Dinka) are grounded in the Nuer sociocultural system and are not products of adaptation to the environment. The transhumant system of production shared by these two cultural groups does represent such an adaptation, but the Nuer and Dinka variants of this general system of production cannot be accounted for in adaptational terms. This is strikingly borne out by the comparisons drawn in this chapter. As the Nuer moved from west to east, they moved across an environmental gradient (discussed in chap. 2 in relation to Glickman's hypothesis). If environmental features were an important causal factor in shaping the distinctive characteristics of the Nuer system, one would expect the Eastern Nuer to become more like the Dinka who formerly occupied these areas. However, a range of comparisons consistently indicates that the Eastern Nuer differ from the Dinka to a greater extent than do their Homeland Nuer counterparts. Existing differences between the Nuer and Dinka were not attenuated by the Eastern Nuer occupancy of former Dinka environments, but were either maintained or accentuated in the course of this movement into new areas. Ideal bridewealth payments either became somewhat larger or were originally higher than those of other Nuer tribes and remained so.[15] The comparatively low proportion of potential breeding and milk-producing stock included in Homeland Nuer bridewealth payments (vis-à-vis those of the Dinka) likewise became even lower among the Eastern Nuer (or was original-ly lower and was maintained as such). These characteristics of the Eastern Nuer represent the fuller expression of pre-existing structural characteristics of the Nuer socioecological system, and a continuation of the direction of change evident in the prior cultural divergence of the Nuer and Dinka. The Eastern Nuer thus represent the florescence of the Nuer socioeological system and the fuller realization of its internal dynamic, not the adaptive modification of that system in response to the distinctive environmental features of a new area. The structure of the Nuer socioecological system consists of a distinctive, socially conditioned set of relations between the human population, cattle population, and agricultural and grazing resources that is expressed in charac-teristic ratios of cattle per capita, human density, and cattle density that are both interrelated and interdependent. It is these socially conditioned interde-pendent relationships that constitute the dynamic of the Nuer socioecological system to which I refer.

It should also be emphasized that the impetus to Nuer expansion is ultimately attributable to the structure of the interrelationships between the social and economic domains of the Nuer system. The same conditions that impelled the Nuer to cross the White Nile provided a continued impetus to territorial appropriation because these conditions were repeatedly generated by the unchanging structure of the Nuer socioecological system. Moreover, the same interrelationships that explain the impetus to Nuer expansion are also central to an understanding of the organizational differentiation of the Nuer and Dinka that eventuated in a decisive Nuer advantage in warfare. It is to consideration of these organizational differences that we now turn.

CHAPTER 4

The Basis of
Nuer Ascendancy

The structure of the Nuer socioecological system insured the continual growth of Nuer cattle herds and thus regularly brought the Nuer into conflict with the Dinka over limited dry season pasture. Historically we know that the Nuer consistently prevailed against the Dinka and expanded their territorial domain fourfold between 1800 and 1890. However, the factors responsible for Nuer ascendancy have not been fully considered. In other words, the historical facts of Nuer expansion have been established and the impetus or motivating force that prompted the Nuer to appropriate Dinka lands (and to continue these piecemeal appropriations over an extended period of time) has been elucidated. Two major questions remain: first, the critical characteristics that differentiate these two cultural groups with respect to their military capabilities, i.e., the characteristics that conferred a decisive advantage on the Nuer and enabled them to defeat and dislodge the Dinka, and second, the causal factors that account for the development of these critical cultural differences. The present chapter is devoted to the first of these interrelated questions and the next chapter to the second. Once the basis of Nuer ascendancy has been precisely specified, we can proceed to an investigation of the developmental processes through which it was established.

Nuer Dominance in Conducting Large-Scale Raids

Nuer appropriation of a given area of Dinka territory was typically the end product of systematic cattle raiding carried out over a period of years. The Dinka were debilitated by the aftermath of past defeats and reduced to famine conditions by the loss of grain supplies and large numbers of cattle. Nuer expansion was finally accomplished by the continued occupation of Dinka wet season communities from which the latter had been expelled in the course of the most recent of a series of raids. In short, Nuer cattle raids created the conditions that ultimately resulted in territorial appropriation. Accounts of Nuer (and Dinka) raids in the early 1900s clearly reveal the proximate causes

of Nuer dominance in this respect, and hence provide the basis for delineating
the features that made Nuer expansion possible.

It is evident that Nuer superiority in cattle raiding was grounded in an
organizational advantage that enabled them to mobilize both larger raiding
parties and larger defensive forces than the Dinka. Large-scale Nuer raids
were carried out by a force of fifteen hundred men organized into five columns
that simultaneously attacked a number of Dinka settlements and coalesced to
meet any counterattack that might be launched. There are no instances in
which the Dinka were able to mount an effective counterattack against a large-
scale Nuer raid without government assistance. Moreover, the Dinka were
routed with heavy casualties on two of the three occasions when they counterattacked large Nuer raiding parties with government assistance. On both
these occasions a single Nuer column under attack by a superior force retreated to a point where they were reinforced by other columns that ambushed and
defeated the pursuing Dinka and government riflemen. The fact that reinforcements turned the tide in these instances illustrates the importance of numerical
superiority and shows that the fifteen-hundred-man Nuer force exceeded
whatever the Dinka were capable of mustering in defense. The significance of
sheer numbers is also borne out by the fact that smaller Nuer raiding parties
were successfully repelled by the Dinka. In a rare instance in which the Nuer
were driven off by the Dinka (without any government assistance), the Nuer
raiding party numbered only two hundred warriors.

Inferior mobilization also limited the scale, frequency, and effectiveness
of Dinka raids on the Nuer. Available sources for the early 1900s report only
three Dinka cattle raids as opposed to twenty-six conducted by the Nuer.[1]
Although one Dinka raiding party successfully captured a large number of
Nuer cattle, the other two were cut to pieces. One raiding party was slaughtered to the last man. In the other instance, the Nuer totally annihilated one
three-hundred-man Dinka column and routed a second (of like size), inflicting
heavy casualties. This force of six hundred Dinka was much smaller than the
fifteen hundred men the Nuer were capable of fielding and this numerical
inferiority was undoubtedly the principal cause of their defeat. Although
Dinka raids were sometimes successful, the comparatively small size of Dinka raiding parties made them susceptible to annihilation. Moreover, losses of
the magnitude noted above would severely reduce the manpower of a Dinka
tribe in subsequent engagements, leaving them even more vulnerable to Nuer
raids and obviating the possibility of further offensives against the Nuer.

It is important to note that there were no significant qualitative differences between the Nuer and Dinka in weapons, military formations, or
tactics. The Dinka also employed a multiple-column force in some of their
(infrequent) raids on the Nuer and were clearly familiar with this formation
and its tactical deployment. However, the Dinka never succeeded in mobiliz-

ing a five-column force (of three hundred men per column) comparable in size to that fielded by the Nuer. The difference between the Nuer and Dinka in this respect was one of degree rather than kind. Moreover, the tactical advantages available to a five-column force were a direct product of the Nuer capacity to mobilize on this scale. Neither Nuer nor Dinka oral traditions record any major decisive battles in which some clever strategy determined the outcome and paved the way for subsequent Nuer expansion. Rather, the Dinka progressively lost territory as a consequence of hundreds of Nuer raids, carried out over a period of generations, in which the Dinka were regularly driven from their communities by numerically superior Nuer forces.

The Dinka not only failed to unite on a sufficient scale to successfully counter Nuer raids, but also systematically exploited the misfortune of neighboring groups that had been expelled from their home communities by the Nuer onslaught. Colonial records consistently report that refugees from one Dinka tribe were relieved of their remaining cattle by the members of another Dinka tribe in whose territory they sought refuge. In contrast, Nuer tribes sometimes combined forces in their raids on the Dinka (and Anuak). Although most of the twenty-six Nuer raids on the Dinka (for which data are available) were carried out by members of a single tribe, the Lak, Thiang, and Gaawar jointly participated in one raid and the Lou and Gaawar in two others. Evans-Pritchard (1940*a*:121) also reports that the Leek, Jagei, and Western Jikany combined in raids on the Western Dinka and the Lou and Eastern Jikany in raids on the Anuak. Nuer tribes also manifested a capacity to comprise internal differences and unite in the face of external aggression. Although feuds between the component sections of a tribe were quite common, these internal fights were discontinued when external enemies threatened. Thus colonial records report that actively feuding sections of the Lou Nuer broke off hostilities to join in a counterattack against the Anuak, when the latter penetrated deep into Nuer territory in 1911. This documents the central characteristic of Nuer segmentary organization described by Evans-Pritchard (1940*a*), and points to the importance of these organizational features in accounting for Nuer superiority in mobilization.

In summary, Nuer territorial expansion was primarily a consequence of Nuer success in conducting annual cattle raids against Dinka wet season communities that set the stage for eventual permanent occupation. Nuer superiority in carrying out such raids turned on their capacity to mobilize raiding parties that significantly outnumbered the defensive forces the Dinka were capable of mustering. This same numerical advantage enabled the Nuer to regularly turn back Dinka raids, often with devastating losses.[2] The Dinka not only failed to unite on a scale comparable to that of the Nuer but also failed to transcend their internal conflicts in the face of Nuer aggression. Rather than joining forces against this common enemy, Dinka tribes fell upon neighboring groups that had been weakened by Nuer raids and deprived them of their remaining cattle, undercutting their capacity to regroup and resist further Nuer incursions.

Nuer internal unity and their capacity to unite on a large scale are aspects of the same phenomena, grounded in Nuer segmentary organization. Dinka disunity and their inability to mobilize comparable forces are likewise traceable to a common organizational source. In short, the Nuer advantage in warfare is directly attributable to organizational differences between these two cultural groups (as Lienhardt [1958], Sahlins [1961], and Newcomer [1972] have all affirmed). In general terms, the Nuer segmentary system is characterized by more levels of superordinate organization than that of the Dinka, and the maximal group that regularly combines for offensive and defensive purposes (i.e., the "tribe")[3] is typically larger in the Nuer case. There are also important organizational differences between the Nuer and Dinka in the way in which relationships between segments are conceptualized, the circumstances under which they unite, and the lines of cleavage along which fission takes place. These differences in segmentary organization will be examined in some detail inasmuch as they played an important role in the differential military capabilities that enabled the Nuer to defeat and dislodge the Dinka. The discussion will proceed from the documentation of significant differences in tribal size to an examination of the formal differences in segmentary structure and finally to the conceptual basis of segmentary inclusiveness in each case.

Segmentary Organization and Tribal Size: A Comparison of the Nuer and Dinka

It is important to note that the named Dinka groups that appear on maps of the southern Sudan (including those reproduced in this volume) are generally not "tribes" in the organizational sense of the term, but rather groups of independent tribes that share only a common regional identity. The tribes that make up a named regional group are politically autonomous and do not unite in warfare or for any other purpose (Lienhardt, 1958:102). Thus the Rek Dinka includes twenty-seven independent tribes, the Malwal six, the Bor Dinka two, and the Twij two. The Rut, Thoi, Eastern Luaich, Eastern Ngok, Ghol, and Nyarraweng, which were reduced in numbers by Nuer territorial expansion, appear to have functioned as single tribes since about 1930, although they may not have been tribal entities in earlier times. In contrast, all the named Nuer groups depicted on maps are single tribes in the organizational sense, with the exception of the Jagei (which includes four small tribes), the Western Jikany (two tribes), and the Eastern Jikany (three tribes).[4] Moreover, both the Jagei tribes and the Western Jikany tribes generally functioned as tribal entities both in raiding the Dinka and in conflicts with other Nuer tribes (Evans-Pritchard, 1940a:143). The Jagei and Western Jikany are thus comparable to tribal entities in the respects significant to the questions at hand, although they may not meet all the criteria of Evans-Pritchard's definition (1940a:122).

Tribal Size

On average, Dinka tribes are much smaller than those of the Nuer. The total population of the twenty-seven tribes included in the Rek grouping is 156,000, yielding an average tribal size of 5,777 persons. The six Malwal tribes number 37,640 in all and average 5,773 persons each. The ten Abiem tribes, with a total population of 13,800, have an average membership of only 1,380 persons (Lienhardt, 1958:102). The nine Western Ngok tribes (discussed in more detail below) average 2,691 members (Howell, 1951:254). The median size of the nine Dinka tribes included in the Yirrol District is 5,325 (Upper Nile Province Handbook, Yirrol Section, 1930:18). The Rut, Thoi, Eastern Luaich, Eastern Ngok, Nyarraweng, and Ghol are all quite small (see chap. 1), although the figures are not indicative of the characteristic size of Dinka tribes since they represent the consequences of a century of intensive Nuer predation. The four tribes in the Bor and Twi groups that were further removed from Nuer raids (and perhaps augmented by refugees) are somewhat larger, averaging 8,644 members (Wyld, 1930: App. 2). In all, the average size of the sixty-five Dinka tribes enumerated above is 5,148 persons. Lienhardt (1958:102) reports that Dinka tribes range in size from less than 1,000 to 25,000 members. However, in the Yirrol and Bor districts, for which the size of individual tribes is reported, none exceeds 14,000 members. Available data suggest that the vast majority of Dinka tribes would be clustered around the average size of 5,148 persons, in a range extending from 1,000 to 9,000 members. There are a limited number of tribes in the 9,000 to 14,000 size range and only isolated cases of larger Dinka tribes.

By any measure, the average Nuer tribe is considerably larger than the average Dinka tribe. In the circa 1930 census, the seventeen Nuer tribes had a total population of 247,000, yielding an average tribal size of 14,529. If the four Jagei tribes that typically combined in warfare are counted as one military entity, and the two Western Jikany tribes are likewise counted as a single group, the number of units is reduced to thirteen and the average size of each increases to 19,000. If 1955 census figures for the Nuer population are employed, this average swells to 35,351 persons per tribe. However, all the preceding Nuer averages are considerably augmented by the inclusion of Nuer tribes that grew significantly in size as a consequence of the assimilation of large numbers of Dinka tribesmen during the course of Nuer expansion. It is consequently more appropriate to consider the estimated size of the Nuer tribes at the inception of Nuer territorial expansion in 1800. In chapter 2 it was estimated that the Nuer homeland carried a population of approximately 127,000 in 1800. At that time the homeland was inhabited by the Gaajok, Gaagwang, and Gaajak (from which the Eastern Jikany subsequently split), the four Jagei tribes (counted as one unit), the Bul, Leik, Dok, Nuong, Lak, Thiang, Gaawar, and Lou. The average population of these twelve tribal (or military) units would then be 10,583.

A comparable estimate of Dinka tribal size in 1800 would have to take into account the fact that tribal units were largely frozen by the colonial administration, inasmuch as they became units in the administrative system. Internal feuds that might otherwise have precipitated the fission of a large tribe into two distinct organizational entities were repressed. Thus any general increase in the Dinka population between about 1920 (when tribal units were recorded as elements of the administrative system) and the 1955 census would be distributed among a relatively fixed number of tribes, whose average size would consequently increase. (This is equally true of the Nuer, and accounts for the increase in average tribal size between the 1930 and 1955 census dates.) The Nuer population increased by 86.3 percent between 1930 and 1955 and is estimated to have grown by 10 percent between 1920 and 1930 (due to an excess of births over deaths and excluding assimilation). In other words, the Nuer population approximately doubled between 1920 and 1955. Assuming the same level of population increase among the Dinka (due to the same causes, connected with the introduction of inoculations, etc.), the population of Dinka tribes based on 1955 census materials should be reduced by half and the tribal population figures based on 1930 census materials should be reduced by 10 percent.[5] This yields an estimated 1920 population of 208,478 for the sixty-five Dinka tribes discussed earlier, producing an average of 3,207 persons per tribe. This represents a more reasonable estimate of the traditional characteristic size of Dinka tribes, applicable to the period of Nuer expansion and suitable for comparison with the estimated size of Nuer tribes in 1800. On average, Nuer tribes were thus more than three times as large as their Dinka counterparts at the inception of Nuer territorial expansion. This is consistent with the fact that Nuer tribes include one or two more levels of segmentary organization than those of the Dinka. Indeed, the disparity in average tribal size is largely a product of this difference in organization.

Among the Dinka, there is a definite relationship between tribal size and the degree of internal segmentation. The smaller Dinka tribes are composed of a number of constituent subtribes and contain only these two levels of segmentary organization. In the larger Dinka tribes, subtribal units are further segmented into several component sections, adding a third level of segmentary organization (Lienhardt, 1958:104, 134). Moreover, a comparison of the smaller (two-level) Dinka tribes reveals that the number of subtribal units per tribe increases along a gradient of tribal size. This is well illustrated by Howell's (1951:239–93) account of the Ngok (Ngork) Dinka. The Ngok are divided into nine independent tribes[6] ranging in size from 1,125 to 4,149 members each. The six smallest tribes, with 3,250 members or less, each contain two subtribes, while the next largest tribe (of 3,874 members) contains three subtribes, and the two largest tribes (of 3,988 and 4,149 members respectively) contain four subtribes apiece. Although Ngok subtribes vary in size from 563 to 1,602 members each, nineteen of the twenty-three subtribes fall in the narrower range of 800 to 1,300 members. (These figures represent average subtribal population, derived by dividing the total tribal population by the number of constituent subtribes. The population of individual subtribes is not reported.) The median subtribe contains 1,060 members, and the overall distribution is clustered around this.

Although Lienhardt (1958:103) notes that larger Dinka tribes evidence an additional level of segmentary organization, he does not indicate the size range at which this transition takes place. Available data from colonial records suggest that the third organizational level is characteristic of tribes with somewhat more than 5,000 members. The Chich Ajak, who number 5,180, are segmented into two subtribes, each of which is further segmented into sections (two in one case and three in the other). In contrast, the Adar tribe, with 5,060 members, contains seven coordinate subtribes and lacks the third level of segmentary organization (Upper Nile Province Handbook, Yirrol Section, 1930:4). The other tribes in the Yirrol District are consistent with this pattern, i.e., those with less than 5,060 members contain only two levels of organization while those with more than 5,180 members manifest three such levels.

It is important to note that sections in larger tribes are of the same size as subtribes in the smaller tribes, i.e., they include about 500 to 1,600 members. In the Yirrol District, the average size of sections in the four larger tribes ranges from 727 to 1,360 persons per section. (These figures are derived by dividing the reported tribal population by the reported number of sections; the population of individual sections is not given.) The minimal units of a Dinka tribe are thus of relatively constant average size, irrespective of the number of segmentary levels present.

The Apuk Patuan, with 22,000 to 25,000 members, illustrate the organization of one of the largest Dinka tribes. This tribe is composed of nine subtribes, eight of which contain either two or three sections. The ninth, consisting of a single section, is presently in the process of being assimilated into one of its coordinate groups (Lienhardt, 1958:121–25). It is of interest that the latter group has only 400 members, and falls outside the range of variation for minimal units in the Dinka segmentary system. The fact that it is currently being assimilated into a coordinate group is consistent with the maintenance of this range. The largest Apuk Patuan subtribe, with 3,000 members, is segmented into three sections with an average of 1,000 members each (Lienhardt, 1958:125). The average size of minimal segments in this unusually large Dinka tribe is thus consistent with the previously established range of variation.

The minimal segment of the Dinka segmentary system—be it a section or a subtribe—corresponds to the social group that shares a common wet season cattle camp (or *wut*) and is conceptualized in these terms (Lienhardt, 1958:110–11). Cattle from several agricultural settlements (*bai*) are jointly herded at wet season pastures that are generally adjacent to, but spatially segregated from, homesteads and cultivations. Several wet season agricultural settlements (*bai*) thus constitute the subgroups of a minimal segment, although the former are not conceptualized by the Dinka as particularly significant organizational entities (Lienhardt, 1958:129). However, for comparative purposes it is important to clearly specify the relationship between these local groups and minimal segments. Among the Nuer, minimal segments (tertiary sections) are also composed of a number of wet season agricultural communities. In this respect, Nuer and Dinka minimal segments represent equivalent units that can serve as a common point of departure for a comparative analysis of the formal properties of segmentary organization. However, it should also be kept in mind that the Nuer and Dinka differ in their conceptualization of these units. The Nuer do not conceive of tertiary sections as social groups that share a common wet season pasture (nor do the agricultural settlements that make up a tertiary section herd their cattle jointly during the rains). These differences between the Nuer and Dinka in the conceptualization of segments (and their interrelationships) will be considered after the formal properties of the two respective segmentary systems have been established.

In the Nuer political system a number of wet season agricultural settlements make up a tertiary section, two or three tertiary sections generally comprise a secondary section, two to five secondary sections constitute a primary tribal section, and two or three of the latter form a tribe (see Evans-Pritchard, 1940a:116, 139–41). These four progressively more inclusive orders of segmentation (above the level of the local group) are characteristic of all but the smallest Nuer tribes, i.e., the four Jagei tribes with a combined population of 10,000 persons (ibid.:139). The number of segmentary levels per tribe thus co-varies with tribal size among the Nuer as it does among the Dinka, and the size range at which the transition to an additional segmentary level takes place also appears to be roughly comparable for both cultural groups.[7] The central difference between them in segmentary organization is that small Nuer tribes contain three orders of segmentation (above the level of wet season agricultural settlements) while small Dinka tribes evidence only two. Similarly, large Nuer tribes possess four orders of segmentation as opposed to three for large Dinka tribes. These differences are compounded when a Dinka tribe of average size is compared with its Nuer counterpart. The average Dinka tribe (of approximately 3,200 members) is a "small" tribe with only two orders of segmentation, while the average Nuer tribe (of 10,500 members) is a "large" tribe and contains four orders of segmentation. These differences are illustrated in figure 4.

The Nuer also differ from the Dinka in that Nuer minimal segments (tertiary sections) may include a significantly greater population than their Dinka counterparts (sections of subtribes). Although the low end of the range of variation in minimal segment size appears to be comparable in both cases, the upper end (and the average) is definitely higher among the Nuer. The smallest and largest Nuer minimal segments are represented by the Thiang and Lou tribes respectively. The Thiang tribe, with 9,000 members, is segmented into two primary sections, each of which is subdivided into three secondary sections. One of these secondary sections is reported to be segmented into three tertiary sections, while the subdivisions of the five remaining secondary sections are not specified (see Evans-Pritchard, 1940a:141). However, inasmuch as secondary sections typically contain two or three tertiary sections each, it may reasonably be assumed that the Thiang possess thirteen to eighteen tertiary sections in all (i.e., two or three tertiary sections for each of the five unspecified secondary sections plus three for the one that is known). This yields an average of 500 to 692 persons per tertiary section, approximating the average size of the smallest Dinka minimal segments (i.e., 563 persons).

The Lou Nuer tribe (of 33,000 members) is divided into two primary sections that are further segmented into two and three secondary sections, respectively. One of these five secondary sections contains three tertiary sections, two others each contain two tertiary sections, and the subdivisions of the two remaining secondary sections are unspecified (Evans-Pritchard, 1940a:139). Assuming either two or three tertiary sections for the latter gives a total of eleven to thirteen such units for the Lou tribe as a whole, with an average of 2,538 to 3,000 persons per unit. This is considerably larger than the average size of the largest Dinka minimal segments (i.e., 1,602 members).

Available data concerning the Eastern Gaajak, Eastern Gaajok, Gaawar, and Lak (Evans-Pritchard, 1940a:140–41) indicate that they fall within the above range of approximately 500 to 3,000 persons per tertiary section. The low and high extremes for these four intermediate Nuer tribes (computed in the same way) are 1,052 to 2,677 persons per tertiary section. In three of these four tribes minimal segments exceed the largest reported among the Dinka.

It is evident that the Nuer segmentary system differs from that of the Dinka not only in manifesting an additional level of superordinate organiza-

An Average Dinka Tribe

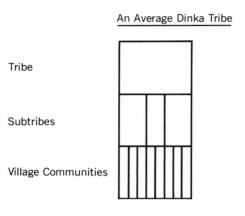

Tribe

Subtribes

Village Communities

An Average Nuer Tribe

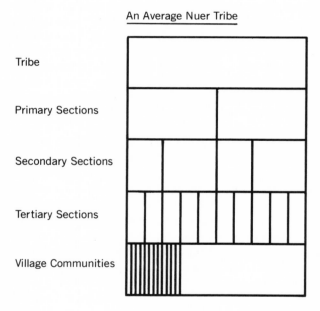

Tribe

Primary Sections

Secondary Sections

Tertiary Sections

Village Communities

FIG. 4. The Segmentary Organization of Territorial Groups in Nuer and Dinka Tribal Organization

tion, but also in the generally larger size of Nuer minimal segments. The latter difference is due to the fact that Nuer minimal segments include a greater number of local groups than their Dinka counterparts. While a Dinka subtribe (or section) is composed of the members of "several" local communities (Lienhardt, 1958:132), a large Nuer tertiary section may include a dozen such groups. This is substantiated by Bacon's (1917) census of the Gun primary section of the Lou Nuer (the tribe that represents the high end of the Nuer range in tertiary segment size). The Gun primary section, which includes a total of five tertiary sections, encompasses 59 communities or an average of 11.8 per tertiary section.[8] Evans-Pritchard (1940a:116) describes tertiary sections as containing "a number" of local groups and scattered sources suggest that four to eight are typical (see Upper Nile Province Handbook).

The size of minimal segments is a product of the number of local groups they incorporate, rather than the population of the latter. Hence Lou Nuer tertiary sections are larger than those of the Lak, Thiang, and Gaawar (as noted above), although the average size of Lou communities (250 persons) is actually smaller than the average size of Lak, Thiang, and Gaawar communities (292 persons). (These figures are derived from Bacon, 1917, and the Upper Nile Province Handbook, Zeraf Valley Section, respectively.) Similarly, Nuer minimal segments are considerably larger than those of the Dinka, although Dinka wet season agricultural settlements are characterized by a higher human density than those of the Nuer (as established in the preceding chapter). In other words, Dinka local groups contain a larger population than their Nuer counterparts, but Dinka minimal segments contain fewer such groups than those of the Nuer. This points up the fact that the Nuer advantage is organizational, and cannot be reduced to simple demographic or environmental factors.

The fact that Nuer minimal segments contain more local groups than those of the Dinka is a direct result of radical differences between these two cultural groups in the conceptualization of minimal segments, and in the principles that govern the inclusion of local groups within them. Among the Dinka, a minimal segment is conceived as a group of agricultural settlements that jointly herd their cattle in common wet season pasture areas (in which each settlement holds grazing rights). The size of a minimal segment, and the number of local groups it includes, is thus environmentally limited by the extent and distribution of available high ground. Among the Nuer, a minimal segment is conceptualized in terms of the lineage system and includes those local groups which contain local lines that are putatively related to a proximate common ancestor. This conceptualization is not tied to the co-use of commonly held wet season pasture, and the environmental distribution of such areas consequently places no upper limit on the size of minimal segments. These differences in the relative importance of lineage and territory in Nuer and Dinka social organization will be more fully explored in due course.

Thus far we have seen that Nuer territorial expansion was the end product of systematic cattle raiding, and that the Nuer advantage in conducting such raids hinged on their capacity to mobilize much larger raiding parties (and defensive forces) than the Dinka. The numerical superiority of the Nuer is directly attributable to the fact that Nuer tribes are more than three times as large as their Dinka counterparts (while tribes by definition represent the maximal groups that regularly combine for offensive and defensive purposes). This disparity in tribal size is a product of organizational differences. Nuer segmentary organization is more inclusive than that of the Dinka at both the bottom and the top. Nuer minimal segments incorporate more local groups and the resultant size advantage at this level carries over into each progressively more inclusive level of segmentary organization. Moreover, a Nuer tribe contains at least one more such level than a Dinka tribe.

These differences between the Nuer and Dinka in the inclusiveness of their respective segmentary organizations are explicable in terms of fission processes and the maintenance of post-fission relationships in each case. In brief, a Dinka tribe of ten thousand members tends to split into two entities which become fully autonomous tribes that no longer support each other in warfare, while a Nuer tribe of the same size will contain two discrete primary sections that nevertheless continue to operate as a single unit in conflicts with external enemies. The additional segmentary level that confers a decisive numerical advantage on the Nuer is thus a product of the propensity of higher-order Dinka segments to become fully independent political entities through fission, rather than maintaining a unit-to-unit relationship as the components of a more inclusive grouping, as do their Nuer counterparts. This difference between the Nuer and Dinka in the capacity to maintain post-fission relations between higher order segments is a product of corresponding differences in the conceptualization of tribal entities, and in the principles which govern the inclusion of constituent units within an encompassing segmentary framework. Hence it is to these dissimilarities in the conceptual foundations of segmentary inclusiveness that we now turn.

The Bases of Segmentary Inclusiveness

The Nuer and Dinka segmentary systems differ in the cultural conception and internal organization of their constituent segments, and likewise in the manner in which these segments are conceived to be interrelated within the tribal structure. In the Nuer system a single dominant clan is conventionally regarded as the ''owner'' of each tribal territory, although the territory itself is inhabited by a relatively fluid population which includes members of many nonowner descent groups that significantly outnumber members of the owning clan. The relationships between local groups, and between the higher-order segments of the tribe into which they are combined, are governed by the relations between the component lineages of the dominant (or owning) clan (Evans-Pritchard, 1940a:203–12).[9] Thus each community is associated with a specific minimal lineage of the dominant clan from which the community derives both its name and its position in the tribal segmentary system. The communities that jointly comprise a tertiary section each contain related minimal lineages of the dominant clan whose respective ancestors are siblings, putative sons of the same father.[10] These minimal lineages together comprise a minor lineage which serves as the organizational basis for a tertiary section. Minor lineages are subunits of major lineages that are grouped into maximal lineages that in turn constitute a dominant clan, and these progressively more inclusive descent groups provide the organizational basis for secondary sections, primary sections, and the tribe, respectively (see fig. 5).

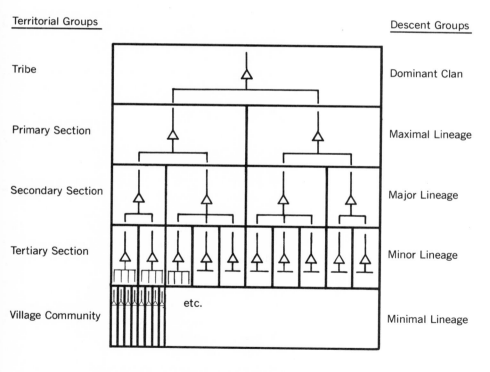

FIG. 5. The Relationship between Descent Groups and Territorial Groups in Nuer Segmentary Organization

The Dinka segmentary system differs from that of the Nuer in that the interrelationships of territorial units within a tribal entity is not consistently organized in terms of relations between segments of a dominant clan. Some subtribes of the same tribe contain members of a common descent group while others do not. As a result, a Dinka tribe as a whole is an association of

> agnatically unrelated lineages, and their interrelationship is consequently less systematic and stable than if they were identified simply with the single system of agnatic lineages of one dominant descent group. Two subtribes united in relation to the main lineages of one nuclear subclan are divided by the presence in them of associated nuclear groups from different clans. One of these other nuclear groups, however, may relate one of these subtribes to a third subtribe, in which there is no important lineage of the subclan which relates the first two. (Lienhardt, 1958:130)

Although Dinka tribesmen hold membership in exogamous clans, the component subgroups of these clans are widely dispersed and do not form the basis of an inclusive segmentary hierarchy of territorial groups as among the Nuer. In other words, Dinka clans do not function as dominant clans whose component lineages are represented within each local community of a tribe and exclusively govern their political interrelationship.

While territorial units are conceptually interrelated through the lineage system in the Nuer case, the cattle camp (*wut*)—and the shared grazing resources it represents—is the central metaphor of unit definition and interrelationship among the Dinka. A subtribe is composed of those communities that jointly herd their cattle at common wet season pastures and a tribe includes a number of subtribes that share (and mutually defend) common dry season pastures. Both are termed *wut* (Lienhardt, 1958:110, 116). Although the various descent groups of a Dinka tribe are partially interrelated by agnatic and matrilateral connections, these relationships are ineffective as a basis for continued association between groups that no longer share dry season pastures. In other words, the significance of these relationships in Dinka segmentary organization is contingent on a context of joint herding at common pastures. (The pattern of interrelationships between descent groups is discussed more fully in subsequent pages.)

Among the Nuer, in contrast, the local groups that comprise a tertiary section do not jointly herd their cattle at common wet season pastures and their relationship is not predicated on such association, but is grounded in the lineage system. Similarly, the primary sections of a Nuer tribe do not necessarily share common dry season pastures. Since the relationships between the territorial units of a Nuer tribe are based on corresponding relations between the local lineages of a dominant clan and are not contingent on joint herding, the fission of a Nuer territorial unit (and concomitant changes in pasture utilization) do not obviate the grounds for continued association between the two resultant groups. A Nuer tribe can thus increase in size through the growth and fission of its component segments, inasmuch as the products of fission continue to be interrelated through the lineage system. However, a Dinka tribe cannot increase beyond the limits of the population that can be accommodated by the extent of its dry season pastures, because the movement of a portion of the tribe to new pastures automatically defines the latter group as a separate tribe. A Dinka tribe thus lacks the Nuer capacity to grow through fission, and this largely accounts for the fact that Dinka tribes are characteristically much smaller than those of the Nuer. The numerical superiority of the Nuer is thus grounded in the distinctive features of Nuer segmentary organization vis-à-vis that of the Dinka. This contrast constitutes a précis of the general differences between the Nuer and Dinka in unit definition and interrelationship, and in the maintenance of post-fission relationships. However, it remains to be fleshed out in more detail.

The Organization of Minimal Segments, Fission, and Post-fission Relationships

In developmental terms, the differences between the Nuer and Dinka in segmentary organization are attributable to corresponding differences in the way in which fission proceeds at the level of minimal segments. The line of cleavage differs in each case, and it is the line of cleavage in fission that dictates both the nature of the emergent groups and the nature of the relationship between them. To understand these differences it is necessary to examine the internal organization of Nuer and Dinka minimal segments, and the axis along which they fission into separate entities in each instance.

A Dinka cattle camp of the rains includes the members of a number of different patrilineal descent groups. The agnatic descendants of ancestral figures credited with first establishing a wet season cattle camp at a particular elevated site have customary rights to the best-drained central area of the camp. Members of one or two (and occasionally three) subclans may hold these rights. (These descent groups are subsequently referred to as "founder lines" in this account.) Members of other subclans, lacking ancestral priority, occupy less favorable locations at the periphery of the site. (These descent groups are hereafter referred to as "latecomer lines.") The central group, of one or more founder lines, constitutes the focal point of interrelationships within the cattle camp and is regarded as the "maternal uncles of the camp" (Lienhardt, 1958:111). A cattle camp is thus conceptualized as being composed of founder and latecomer lines that are related as mother's brother to sister's son.

It should be noted that the descent group segments that form subunits of a

Dinka cattle camp correspond to the groups that play a role in bridewealth
accumulation and redistribution discussed in the previous chapter, and that the
relationships emphasized in Dinka bridewealth transactions are those that are
central to the organization of the cattle camp. Lienhardt (1958:112) points out
that

> the tests of genealogical distance and proximity of the formal segments of a
> Dinka descent group are two. Genealogical segments which consider themselves
> to take a common interest in the marriage cattle of the members of any one of
> them are what are here called sublineages. Genealogical segments which have
> formally divided for purposes of sharing marriage cattle, but which remain close
> enough to each other to prosecute the feud together, and to have, in theory,
> claims on each other for help in the payment of compensation for homicide are
> main lineages.

A number of main lineages constitute a subclan, which is the most inclusive
descent group represented in a tribe. (Subclans of the same clan are dispersed
among many different tribes and have no organizationally significant relationship to each other.) Sublineages, of two or three generations in depth
(ibid.), thus correspond to the *koc cuol tok* described by Stubbs (1962:455–
58) in his analysis of Dinka bridewealth. The bride's (or groom's) father's
patrikin (*koc cuol tok*) is coextensive with her (or his) father's sublineage in
Lienhardt's terminology. Similarly the bride's (or groom's) matrikin corresponds to her (or his) mother's sublineage.

A wet season cattle camp is composed of a number of spatially separated
shelters for herdsmen, each surrounded by pegs at which the group's cattle are
tethered. A large subtribal camp includes ten to twelve such herding groups
(Lienhardt, 1958:110). Each of these shelters is owned by several sublineages
of a particular subclan and occupied by them (and coresident kinsmen of other
groups). The constituent subgroupings of a wet season cattle camp—which
also represents a subtribe—are thus social groups that are defined by their
joint participation in bridewealth (sublineages) and homicide compensation
(main lineages).

The relationships that are emphasized in Dinka bridewealth transactions
are also the same relationships that are central to the organization of a subtribal cattle camp. The focal descent group (or groups) that founded the camp
and occupy the central sites are ''mother's brothers'' to the descent groups
that subsequently took up occupation of the periphery, their ''sister's sons.''
Analogously, the bulk of the Dinka bridewealth payment is allocated to the
bride's matrikin (i.e., the sublineage of her mother's brothers) and the mother's brother–sister's child relationship is central to the flow of bridewealth in
Dinka transactions. Similarly, the distinctive *ariek* payment of the Dinka

passes between men who have the same wife's father in common, and whose children will have the same mother's brother. *Ariek* thus entails recognition of a coaffinal relationship to the same line, and parallels the relationship among the various "sister's sons" lines of a subtribal cattle camp that have the same "mother's brothers of the camp" in common.

Dinka bridewealth transactions not only express, affirm, and reflect the principal lines of relationship in Dinka local organization, but also entail a dramatic enactment of these central relationships that makes them palpable to social actors. The bridewealth cattle are drawn from, and transferred to, sublineage herds that constitute both the symbol and essence of these social collectivities (sublineage herding groups). In both the bridewealth payment and the reciprocal *aruweth* payment, animals contributed by a person's own sublineage and (to a lesser extent) by mother's brother's sublineage are merged into a common pool, and these two groups likewise share (although unequally) in the distribution of the payment received. The importance of the mother's brother–sister's child relationship, and the links of mother's brother's sublineage to one's own sublineage, are inescapable. However, it is also important to note that just as the "mother's brothers of the camp" occupy the most favorable central locations, so do the mother's brothers of the bride receive the bulk of the bridewealth cattle. This focal relationship is thus an asymmetrical one.

Although the mother's brother–sister's child relationship is grounded in kinship amity and ideologically formulated as a bond characterized by special affection (Lienhardt, 1958:119), it is also a relationship that encodes and legitimates unequal access to cattle standings and bridewealth cattle (i.e., critical productive resources). This accounts for the previously established fact that cattle are quite unequally distributed among Dinka households, and makes it clear that these distributional characteristics are structurally determined. Stubbs (1962:451, 468) also notes that Dinka bridewealth customs serve to perpetuate and exacerbate unequal cattle holdings.[11]

The matrilateral relationship that is central to Dinka bridewealth transactions and to the organization of subtribal cattle camps is also central to a Dinka model of the larger tribal polity described by Lienhardt (1958:104–5, 118–19). The Dinka distinguish between two types of clans: priestly or spearmaster clans (*bany*) on the one hand and commoner or warrior clans (*kic*) on the other. Priests (whose symbol of office is the sacred fishing spear) are derived from the former and war leaders from the latter. The Dinka ideal tribal polity should contain subclans of both these types of clans and leaders drawn, respectively, from each. The relationship between priestly and warrior leaders, and between their respective descent groups, should be one of matrilateral kinship at both the subtribal and tribal level.

Each subtribe should have its own master of the fishing spear, whom all its members acknowledge as the first among several masters of the fishing spear who may live in its territory. One of these subtribal masters of the fishing spear should be acknowledged as pre-eminent throughout the whole tribe, and in times of tribal difficulty all the others, led by him, should provide spiritual guidance for the warriors of the tribe as a whole. Further, each subtribe should have an outstanding warrior, the *Keic,* to lead its warriors, and in times of crisis for the whole tribe, one of these subtribal war-leaders should emerge as the war-leader of the whole tribe.

In Dinka thought, if such dual leadership, either of the tribe or subtribe, is to be harmoniously maintained, the master of the fishing spear and the war leader should be maternal kin, and in any subtribe or tribe, those descent groups which traditionally have provided the master of the fishing spear and the war leader should have a classificatory kin-relationship through a woman. (Lienhardt, 1958:118–19)

It is in keeping with this organizational conception that the founder lines of wet season cattle camps are regarded as "maternal uncles of the camp" in relation to other resident groups. These founder lines may be of either spear-master or warrior subclans, although the former are numerically predominant (Lienhardt, 1958:120). Lienhardt (ibid.) also suggests that it is more appropri-ate for a spearmaster subclan to hold the position of "maternal uncles of the camp," since the mother's brother's role is culturally conceived as one of "peacemaker" between his own and his sister's son's descent groups and this role is more compatible with the status of master of the fishing spear than with that of war leader.[12] However, it is intrinsic to the fission process that those who are latecomers and "sister's sons" in the parent community will become founders and "mother's brothers" in the offshoot community, and the respec-tive positions of warrior and spearmaster subclans are thus also reversed.

Lienhardt (1958:115) relates the indigenous Dinka model of the fission process as follows: the founder/latecomer distinction is seen by the Dinka as characteristically forming the line of cleavage when a cattle camp splits into two groups. As the community grows in size, latecomers located on the less well drained periphery of the site lack sufficient space to tether their cattle on dry footings and consequently depart to form a new cattle camp. Original and offshoot communities are thus related to each other as mother's brother to sister's son since founders and latecomers are so related. A newly formed cattle camp constitutes a tribal section in the Dinka segmentary system. Ac-cording to Dinka political theory it will in time grow into a subtribe. This transition is marked by the creation of its own age sets, distinct from those of the parent community (Lienhardt, 1958:114). (Among the Dinka age sets are internal to subtribes, rather than encompassing the entire tribe as they do among the Nuer.)

When a Dinka subtribe fissions, the line of cleavage cuts through the mother's brother–sister's son relationship that constitutes the basis of its internal organization. This fracture of the central structural relation of internal cohesion is a characteristic feature of the fission process in segmentary systems, and generally reproduces the same relationship between the two resultant groups that previously formed the basis of their internal organization (Kelly, 1977:71). In the classic case (which is applicable to the Nuer), a patrilineal descent group fissions into two groups composed of the respective descendants of a pair of brothers who are the sons of the apical ancestor of the original unit. The emergent descent groups are: (1) structurally identical to the unit from which they developed, by fission, and consequently identical to each other; and (2) related to each other, as separate groups, in the same way that they were formerly related as the components of the parent unit. In the Dinka case, however, fission does not engender units that fulfill these two conditions. This is due to the fact that the central structural relation that constitutes the line of cleavage in fission is an asymmetrical relationship between complements, rather than a symmetrical relation between equivalents. An example will illustrate that such asymmetrical relationships are reversed in the course of fission, and that the resultant groups are inversions of each other with respect to this aspect of form.

Suppose that a Dinka subtribal cattle camp which undergoes fission is composed of a founder line of spearmaster subclan A that is related as maternal uncle to several latecomer lines of warrior subclans X and Y. The members of the warrior line of subclan X depart to found a new cattle camp at another location, where they are subsequently joined by individuals of spearmaster subclan B (see fig. 6). (The addition of the latter group fulfills the Dinka condition that a subtribe contain members of both categories of subclans and is consistent with the fact that there are several spearmaster subclans in every tribe [Lienhardt, 1958:131].) After fission, the parent community remains the same in form, containing a founding spearmaster line that is "mother's brother" to a warrior line. However, these relations are inverted in the offshoot community where a warrior line is founder and "mother's brother" to a spearmaster group. The two resultant units therefore are not structurally identical, nor is their original relationship to each other maintained entirely unchanged through the fission process. Although the warrior line of subclan X continues to be "sister's sons" to the spearmaster line of subclan A, this relationship is recontextualized within a broader set of relations that contains the inverse form, i.e., the "mother's brother" relation of the warrior line of subclan X to the spearmaster line of subclan B. This recontextualization modifies the asymmetrical quality of the original relationship. The latter is also transformed in other ways specific to the Dinka case, as is explained below. However, the point I seek to make here is a more general one concern-

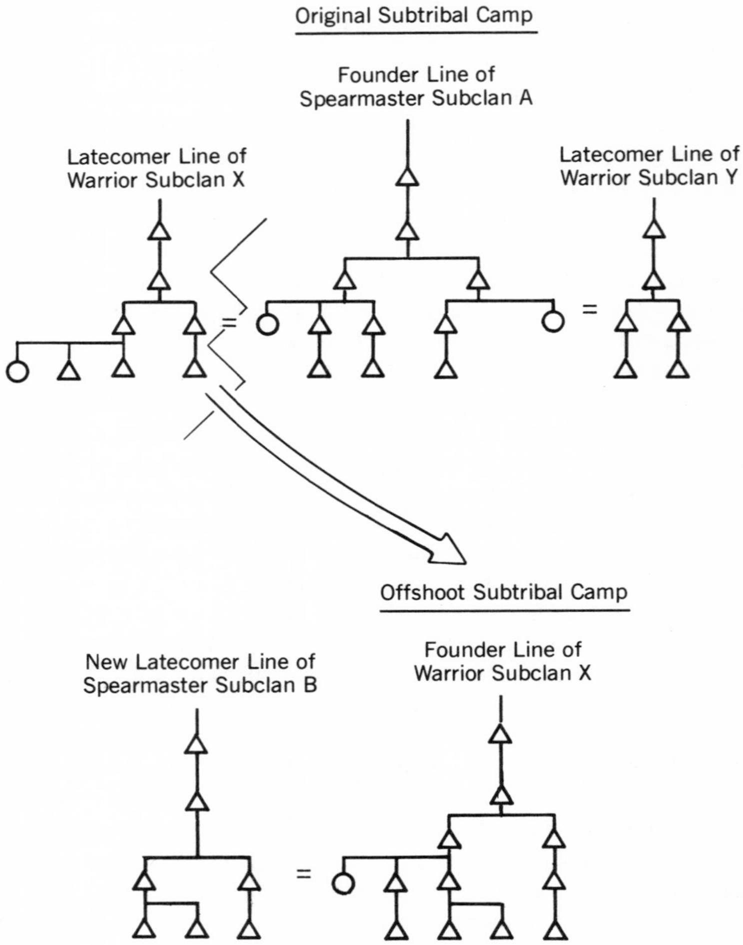

FIG. 6. A Model of the Fission of a Dinka Subtribal Camp

ing the formal properties of fission in instances in which the line of cleavage is an asymmetrical relationship between complements. In such cases, the asymmetrical relation present in the parent community (e.g., spearmaster/warrior) is inverted in the offshoot group (e.g., warrior/spearmaster).

The quality of reversal that is intrinsic to the formal properties of fission in the Dinka case is expressed in the nature of the event itself. Fission is instigated not only by a shortage of space but by resentment of the asymmetrical character of the founder/latecomer relationship that entails unequal access to it.

> The Dinka point out that when a group of late-comers to such a camp becomes rich and large, its members no longer have enough space to tether their cattle on dry standings, and resent the superior position of the first-comers. It then happens that, among such late-comers, an ambitious man . . . gathers to himself a group of his own kin and perhaps others whose places in the camp do not satisfy them, and sets off to form his own camp. (Lienhardt, 1958:115)

The offshoot group establishes itself as a founding line (or group of such lines) at a new location and is therefore no longer in an inferior position (as "latecomers") with respect to the founders of the community it left. Moreover, the offshoot group occupies the superior position at its new locale, so that its former asymmetrical relationship is not only dissolved but replaced by a symmetrical one between lineages that are each founders of their respective cattle camps. This equality of status within the tribe is accentuated when the offshoot group opens its own age sets and attains the position of a fully autonomous coordinate subtribe. The founding line of the parent community also ceases to be "mother's brothers of the camp" to the members of the newly established cattle camp, and this matrilateral relationship loses much of its original significance when recontextualized by fission, movement to a new location, as the dissolution of the parallel founder/latecomer relationship. In all, the relationship between the two groups that were formerly components of a single subtribe is transformed in such a way that it lacks nearly all the qualities that it previously possessed. Only a distant and attenuated matrilateral connection remains (in addition to the unity grounded in the continuation of joint herding at common dry season pastures).

The degree of cohesion between subtribes that is generated by this fission process is consequently limited by the nature of the process itself, and by the transformation and attenuation of former relationships that are intrinsic to it. The central structural relation that forms the basis of integration within subtribes, and the line of cleavage in fission, is an asymmetrical relation that is incompatible with the post-fission status of the emergent groups as coordinate units in a segmentary system. The attainment of coordinate status thus entails a marked diminution of the original relationship, which is not merely externalized but also stripped of several important connective dimensions.[13] Fission thus engenders subtribes whose autonomy is not fully counterbalanced by their integration as components of a more inclusive tribal entity. The unity of the tribe is principally grounded in joint herding at common dry season pastures rather than the attenuated matrilateral connections between the spearmaster and warrior founding lines of constituent subtribes. Hence, when a subtribe or group of subtribes moves to new dry season pastures, its relationship to coordinate segments that remain at the pastures they formerly shared is too weak to serve as a basis for continued association within a single tribal polity. The tribe therefore fissions into two tribes rather than generating a more inclusive level of segmentary organization. We will return to this question of fission at the tribal level after the full range of relationships between the subtribes of a tribe has been elucidated.

While some of the subtribes of a Dinka tribe are related to each other as mother's brother to sister's son, others are agnatically interrelated. The Dinka conceptualization of the fission process at the subtribal level readily accounts for the former type of relationship; the latter variety remains to be explained. The preceding discussion suggests how agnatic relations between subtribes might arise. Suppose that some members of a founder line of spearmaster subclan A marry women of another subtribe with a founder line of warrior subclan Y, and the sons of the union subsequently join their mother's brothers at the latter's cattle camp, becoming latecomers there. Several generations later this cattle camp fissions and the descendants of the sister's son of spearmaster subclan A depart to found a new cattle camp. The founding line of this new cattle camp will then be agnatically related to the founding line of the subtribal camp from which its ancestors emigrated several generations earlier.

Lienhardt (1958:115–16) offers an alternative model, entailing several different lines of cleavage, in order to account for agnatic relations between some subtribes and matrilateral relations between others.

> It may happen that the leader of such a splinter group is a member of a sublineage of one of the nuclear [founding] descent groups of the camp, and also of one of the subclans which are thought of as first settlers in the tribe as a whole. In such a case, the new segment will have as its agnatic nucleus [founding line] a genealogical segment of one of the central descent groups of the original subtribe and the tribe. It may also happen, however, that such a leader is a member of a subclan of no such subtribal or tribal importance, and in this case, the new subtribe which he has formed will be weakly linked genealogically, if at all, to these other nuclear groups only by such members of those groups as have been prepared to follow him, or by his relationships through women. (Lienhardt, 1958:115–16)

This account of the development of matrilateral relations between subtribes (i.e., "relationships through women") is consistent with the indigenous Dinka model of fission in which the line of cleavage is the matrilateral relation between founder and latecomer lines. However, the explanation of the emergence of agnatic relationships between segments is not consistent with this Dinka model, insofar as it locates the line of cleavage within the founder line itself. However, the alternative explanation presented earlier is fully consistent with the native viewpoint and can be recommended on these grounds. Although fission entailing an axis of division located within a founder line may occur, the significant point to note is that this represents a type of fission different from the one that the Dinka themselves regard as typical or characteristic.

A Dinka tribe is thus composed of a number of subtribes that jointly herd their cattle at common dry season pastures, but are not comprehensively and systematically interrelated in terms of descent. A Dinka tribe not only lacks a dominant clan that is represented in every territorial group and governs their interrelationships, it also lacks a single agnatic core to which all other groups are matrilaterally related. This is due to the fact that "every tribe contains members of several different subclans of spearmasters" (Lienhardt, 1958:131), and the warrior subclans represented within a tribe are likewise derived from different clans (in nearly all cases). Matrilateral relationships between subtribal founding lines of spearmaster and warrior subclans—envisioned in the Dinka ideal tribal polity—therefore lack any central node. Described in terms of the founding lines of subtribal cattle camps, a tribe will thus contain spearmaster subclan A that is matrilaterally related to warrior subclan X, and spearmaster subclan B that is matrilaterally related to warrior subclan Y (see fig. 7).

The Dinka ideal does not provide for structurally significant matrilateral relations between two spearmaster subclans, and these form competing nodes of interrelationship within the tribe. The competition produces political realignments, such that

> no matter which descent group of spearmasters may be traditionally associated with a particular political segment, it can, in time, be supplanted by another which has proved itself more effective. (Lienhardt, 1958:130)

In short, the several spearmaster subclans of a tribe each attempt to draw warrior subclans into their orbit and this engenders a major fissure in overall tribal organization located between these two competing nodes of interrelationship. Although a Dinka tribe is composed of spearmaster subclans that are matrilaterally related to warrior subclans, the former are related to each other only as members of the same category of clans (and the same applies to the latter). Such inclusion within a common category does not itself enjoin any significant relationship. Spearmaster subclans of different tribes are also members of a common category (as are warrior subclans of different tribes). The absence of either agnatic or structurally significant matrilateral relationships between the several spearmaster clans of a tribe thus constitutes a major disjunction in the interconnections between the constituent segments of a tribe. (This is illustrated by a general model of the relationship between descent groups and territorial groups in Dinka segmentary organization presented in fig. 7.)

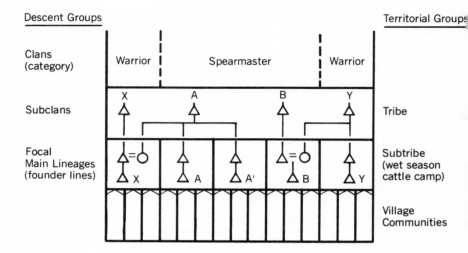

Fɪɢ. 7. The Relationship between Descent Groups and Territorial Groups in Dinka Segmentary Organization

When fission takes place at the tribal level, the split occurs at one of several points of disjunction in the interrelationship between the subtribes of a Dinka tribe. A subtribe with a founding line of a warrior subclan (e.g., X in fig. 7) may form a close association with a spearmaster subclan of another tribe to which they are matrilaterally related, subsequently join them in their dry season pastures, and hence hive off from one tribe to become part of another (see Lienhardt, 1958:124). In this case fission represents a political realignment analogous to that which takes place within tribes (described earlier). The potential for such realignments follows from the attenuated nature of the matrilateral connections between two subtribes that represent the products of fission at the subtribal level. If X originally split from A (as in the example presented earlier), the original matrilateral relationship between them is radically attenuated in the process of fission. Thus it is not surprising that it may be supplanted by a current matrilateral connection to another spearmaster subclan either within or outside the tribe.

Alternatively, a tribe may split along the axis that divides its separate spearmaster subclans, e.g., A may split from B, with warrior subclans X and Y dividing according to their current matrilateral relationships to these two groups. In both this case and the one described above there is no effective basis for the maintenance of a political relationship, as coordinate units of a larger entity, between the resultant groups. In the first instance this is precluded by the offshoot subtribe's incorporation within another tribal entity. In the second case it is due to the fact that fission at the tribal level does not entail division along the lines of a central structural relationship that can subsequently be reconstituted as a more distant, but still effective, bond between the two emergent groups. On the contrary, the division of a Dinka tribe along the axis that divides its several spearmaster subclans is the realization of an established discontinuity in the interconnections between the components of a tribe. There *is no extant relationship* that can be reformulated as a continuing bond. The inclusion of such unrelated units within a common tribal polity is predicated solely on joint herding in common dry season pastures, and the movement of an offshoot group to different pastures (or the division of shared pasture) thus terminates the only basis of interrelationship. Nothing remains.

This failure to maintain post-fission relationships between high-order segments accounts for the truncated nature of Dinka segmentary organization and the comparatively small size of Dinka tribes. A large tribe splits into two smaller ones rather than generating a more inclusive level of segmentary organization because there is no effective basis for continued association between the products of fission at this level. Although the size of a Dinka tribe is constrained by the extent of its dry season pastures, this limitation is itself a consequence of the absence of structurally effective relations that comprehensively interconnect all the subtribes of a tribe. Such relations make it possible to transcend joint herding as the criterion of inclusiveness within tribal entities, and hence to transcend the environmental limitations that pasture distribution imposes on tribal size.

The distinctive characteristics of Nuer segmentary organization can most readily be elucidated by consideration of the fission process at the level of the local groups that constitute the minimal units of the system. As in the Dinka case, the line of cleavage in fission dictates both the organizational features of the resultant groups and the nature of the relationship between them. However, it is necessary to briefly describe the salient characteristics of these local groups before examining the manner in which they split.

It should be recalled that Nuer rainy season settlement patterns differ from those of the Western and other Dinka and that the local groups forming the basic units of the segmentary system likewise differ. Among the Dinka agriculture and herding are spatially segregated. Villages (*bai*) are characterized by thick clusters of huts interspersed among closely spaced cultivations. The cattle herds of several such villages are aggregated at subtribal cattle camps (*wut*) further afield, and it is the latter that constitute the basic units of the segmentary system. Among the Nuer, agriculture and herding are intermixed in wet season settlements. Homesteads are scattered rather than clustered, with the dwellings and cattle shelters of a household (or several related households) separated from those of their neighbors by pasture areas as well as cultivations, at spaced intervals of several hundred yards (see

Lienhardt, 1958:99; Gleichen, 1905:140; Evans-Pritchard, 1951a:2–3).[14] A
Nuer wet season settlement consists of a substantial number of these scattered
homesteads (and their associated family herds) situated on an elevated site (or
a section thereof) that rises a few meters above the inundated flood plain.
These local groups constitute the basic units of the segmentary system. Each
community is associated with a specific minimal lineage of the tribe's dominant clan that determines its position in the segmentary system of the tribe as a
whole. A tertiary section is thus composed of a number of local groups whose
focal minimal lineages are descended from the sons of a common ancestor.

Nuer wet season settlements are similar to Dinka subtribal cattle camps
in that they are internally organized in terms of a focal descent group to which
members of other lines are matrilaterally (and affinally) related. However, the
Nuer do not conceive of the ideal tribal polity in terms of structurally central
matrilateral relations between two categories of clans, but rather in terms of
agnatic relations between the lineages of a dominant clan that is represented in
every community. The matrilateral connections that are evident at the community level do not form part of, or correspond to, ideologically significant
relationships in a larger system. They consequently receive little emphasis,
and the focal minimal lineage of a Nuer community is not regarded as the
"mother's brothers of the camp." In other words, Nuer and the Dinka local
groups are similar in that they both evidence a genealogical pattern of matrilateral relations to focal lines. However, they differ in the ideological and
structural significance of these relationships. It should also be noted that the
bulk of the matrilaterally attached lines in the Nuer system are of Dinka origin
and the character of their relationship to lineages of Nuer dominant clans is
fundamentally different from founder-latecomer relationships between Dinka
descent groups in the Dinka system. (The latter point is elaborated in the
following chapter.)

The marked difference between the Nuer and Dinka in the structural
centrality of matrilateral relationships is also evident in their respective bridewealth systems. This is manifested not only in the different proportions of the
bridewealth cattle allocated to the matrikin in each case, but also, and more
importantly, in the strong emphasis on the continuity and enduring significance of matrilateral relations that is an integral feature of the Dinka reciprocal payment. These interconnections between the bridewealth system
and the system of descent group relationships, within Nuer and Dinka tribes
(respectively), will be explored after the differences in tribal organization
have been fully established through a comparative analysis of the fission
process at the level of local groups.

When a Nuer wet season settlement fissions, the community divides
along an axis of differentiation located within the focal minimal lineage of the
tribe's dominant clan, with the members of other descent groups adhering to

the lineage segment to which they are most closely related through women. The process is described by Evans-Pritchard as follows:

> When brothers of an influential family live in different parts of a village and gather around them a cluster of relations and dependents, these hamlet-groups are named after them and they become the point at which the lineage is likely to bifurcate. . . . if later the grandchildren of one of them move to a different village site the lineage will split into two branches. (1940a:247)

The two communities resulting from this type of fission continue to be related to each other through the common patrilineal ancestry of their respective focal lineages of the dominant clan. Although what was formerly a single focal minimal lineage has now become two such units, at separate locations, the agnatic relationship between the members of these groups remains unchanged. They continue to be descendants of the same ancestor through which they were related prior to fission, although also recognizing their subdivision into the respective descendants of his two sons. They thus constitute minimal lineages of a more inclusive minor lineage. The agnatic relationship between these emergent minimal lineages is neither transformed nor radically attenuated in the process of fission and serves as a solid basis for continued association. The two new communities organized around these emergent minimal lineages thus form coordinate units of a tertiary section in the tribal segmentary system (see fig. 5).

The fission of Nuer local groups along a line of cleavage located within the focal lineage thus corresponds to the classic model of fission noted earlier. The resultant descent groups are (1) structurally identical to each other and to the unit from which they developed, and (2) related to each other, as separate groups, in the same way that they were formerly related as constituents of the parent unit. The transition from subgroups of one group to coordinate units of a higher-order entity thus entails only a change in the level at which the connective relationship is located. The relationship itself is not transformed in the process of being elevated to a higher level of organization (as it is among the Dinka). This same relationship (as the descendants of sons of a common ancestor) can consequently be transported, without alteration, to progressively higher levels of segmentary organization, when fission occurs within coordinate segments that previously emerged as such through fission.

In the Dinka case, relationships between the products of fission are transformed in the process of being elevated to a higher level of organization. The asymmetrical relationship between complements that is the basis of internal organization within subtribes is transformed into a symmetrical relationship between coordinate groups in the fission process, and the attenuation of the former relationship is intrinsic to the development of the latter (as explained earlier). The resultant higher-order groups are consequently weakly linked. When these comparatively tenuous relationships are pushed to a still higher level of segmentary organization by the subsequent internal subdivision of their constituent units, their fragility creates a predisposition to fission of the tribe into several autonomous political entities. This predisposition is realized when a portion of the tribe moves to new dry season pastures.[15]

As was pointed out earlier, the larger size of Nuer tribes conferred a definite numerical advantage in conducting large-scale raids that laid the groundwork for subsequent territorial expansion. Moreover, this difference between the Nuer and Dinka in tribal size is a product of organizational differences. Nuer segmentary organization is more inclusive at both the bottom and the top. Nuer minimal segments incorporate a larger number of local groups than their Dinka counterparts and the resultant size advantage at this level carries over into each progressively more inclusive level of segmentary organization. In addition, a Nuer tribe contains at least one more level of superordinate organization than a Dinka tribe.

The more inclusive nature of Nuer segmentary organization, compared to that of the Dinka, is directly attributable to differences between these two cultural groups in their respective capacities to maintain post-fission relationships between both lower- and higher-order segments. Moreover, these differential capacities are traceable to corresponding differences in the nature of the relationships that link coordinate segments in each case, differences that are themselves a product of distinctive lines of cleavage in fission that are initially established at the level of minimal segments and subsequently transported to upper levels of segmentary organization when growth occurs through internal subdivision. In the Nuer case, prior agnatic relationships between coordinate segments that represent the products of fission are maintained relatively unchanged through the fission process. In contrast, the prior matrilateral relationships that connect the products of fission in the Dinka case are transformed and radically attenuated in the course of the fission process itself. Among the Dinka these attenuated bonds are insufficient, in and of themselves, to serve as a basis for continued association between groups that do not jointly herd their cattle at common pastures. Joint herding, rather than prior matrilateral relationships, constitutes the conceptual basis of segmentary inclusiveness at both the subtribal and tribal level. The scale of these units is consequently limited by the environmental distribution of pasture areas in the wet and dry season, respectively. Among the Nuer the conceptual basis of segmentary inclusiveness is grounded in the lineage system and based on unchanging relations of patrilineal descent from a common ancestor that link the products of fission. A Nuer minimal segment (tertiary section) thus includes those local groups which contain focal lines that are putatively related to a proximate common ancestor. Being unlimited by the environmental distribution of high ground, Nuer minimal segments have the capacity to encompass many more local groups than their Dinka counterparts. Similarly, higher-order Nuer segments may fission and yet maintain a continuing relationship as coordinate units of the same tribal entity, irrespective of whether or not they continue to jointly herd their cattle at common dry season pastures. Nuer segmentary organization thus transcends ecological delineation while that of the Dinka does not. This same transcendence of ecologically defined aggregations provides the basis for the mobilization of large Nuer raiding parties at the beginning and end of the rains, when the Nuer population is widely dispersed among isolated wet season settlements.

The organizational basis of the decisive Nuer advantage in warfare is thus clearly established and we are now in a position to consider the development of the organizational differences between the Nuer and Dinka that conferred this advantage. However, before turning directly to this question it will be useful to point out some interconnections between the bridewealth system and lineage system of each of these cultural groups. This will draw together some of the central features of the general argument that have been developed through the analysis of data presented in separate chapters, and thus lay the groundwork for proceeding to the question of organizational differentiation.

One of the main points to be noted here is that the Nuer-Dinka divergence with respect to the reciprocal bridewealth payment had multiple effects, at a number of different levels, on the social and economic organization of these two cultural groups. This divergence not only produced differences in the scale of seasonal aggregations that eventuated in a disparity in tribal size, but also entailed a shift in conceptualizations of the structural significance of matrilateral relations, relations that are central to the organizational differences between the Nuer and the Dinka.

We have seen that the substantial reciprocal payment that characterizes Dinka bridewealth transactions—in contrast to those of the Nuer—accounts for the differences between the Nuer and Dinka in the magnitude of ideal bridewealth payments, in social requirements for cattle, and ultimately in more general features of economic organization. These differences in economic organization are grounded in distinctive herd management strategies at the household level that are reflected in herd structure, cattle per capita holdings, cattle density, grazing requirements, and the scale of wet and dry season aggregations. In the context of a Dinka (and proto-Nuer) meaning system in which those who jointly herd cattle in the dry season constitute a tribe, this divergence in the scale of dry season aggregations would be directly translated into differences in tribal size (and hence in military capabilities). This point, which will be developed in the following chapter, provides an explanation for the initial emergence of the proto-Nuer as a large and powerful tribe, capable of expanding at the expense of neighboring groups. However, this proto-Nuer tribe would not differ from its Dinka counterparts in the conceptual basis of segmentary inclusiveness, and would thus lack the capacity to transcend the environmental limitations on tribal size imposed by pasture distribution. The development of the organizational differences specified in this chapter thus requires further explication, and changes in the bridewealth system are relevant to this development as well.

The divergence of the Nuer and Dinka bridewealth systems with regard to the reciprocal payment engendered differences not only in the magnitude of bridewealth payments, but also in their distribution among the kinsmen encompassed by the transaction. Given the fact that the number of cattle allocated to the bride's matrikin is relatively fixed (and that the Nuer and Dinka do not differ significantly in this respect), changes in the magnitude of ideal bridewealth payments also entailed changes in distribution. These distributional changes, in turn, altered the degree of interdependence between matrilateral kin and the extent to which they were linked by shared interests in cattle. This is particularly evident when we consider the relative position of Nuer and Dinka fathers seeking to accumulate cattle for a son's marriage. A Dinka father relies on the cattle accrued from his sister's daughter's marriage to provide the bulk of his son's bridewealth. Moreover, the patrikin's contribution to this bridewealth payment is drawn from the herds of father's brothers (of the son and groom) that are likewise augmented by the marriage of the same sister's daughter (or sisters' daughters). The son's matrikin (and father's wife's brothers) also make a substantial contribution, although most of this is recouped in the redistribution of the subsequent reciprocal payment. In all, matrilateral (and affinal) relations are crucial to the acquisition of bridewealth cattle. In contrast, a Nuer father counts on the cattle generated by his own daughter's marriage to provide the bulk of the cattle necessary to secure a wife for his son, while cattle derived from a sister's daughter's marriage provide comparatively small additions to the family herd (and to the herds of father's brothers from which the patrikin's contribution is derived). The son's mother's brother (and father's wife's brother) is not obligated to contribute to the bridewealth, although he may do so as a token of affection for his nephew. Thus there is a high degree of interdependence between matrilateral kin among the Dinka, while this is comparatively attenuated among the Nuer.

This difference between the Nuer and Dinka in the significance of matrilateral relations is not only practical but also conceptual. Indeed it is the reciprocal payment itself that gives prominent and dramatic expression to the enduring importance of matrilateral relationships in the ceremony marking the union. The cultural evaluations of these relations conveyed by Nuer and Dinka bridewealth transactions are therefore quite different. Among the Nuer, the matrikin's portion of the bridewealth is conceived as a final payment standing over from the bride's mother's marriage. After this payment is made, the mother's brothers of the bride—and more importantly, of the bride's brothers—no longer hold a substantial interest in the herd from which the latter will later marry and draw their sustenance. Moreover, receipt of this final payment does not create any obligation to contribute to a sister's son's bridewealth (Evans-Pritchard, 1951a:163). Thus the relationship of sister's sons to mother's brothers is not only marked by this final payment but also transformed by the effective termination of formal obligations pertaining to the accumulation and redistribution of bridewealth cattle. Shared interests in cattle are correspondingly attenuated thereafter. However, at the same time, the bride's brothers acquire a lien on the bridewealth that will eventually be derived from the daughters born to their newly married sister. In other words, a shift from one set of matrilateral relations to another is effected in the course of a Nuer bridewealth transaction. The continuity of matrilateral relations is not emphasized and each mother's brother–sister's son relation is seen to wax and wane in accordance with the developmental cycle of domestic groups.

In contrast, the Dinka reciprocal payment expresses the continuing importance of existing matrilateral relations at the same time that the associated marriage initiates a new phase in the developmental cycle that will eventually produce another set of such relations. The distribution of a portion of the bridewealth (indeed, the largest portion) to the bride's matrikin is followed by the matrikin's subsequent contribution to the *aruweth* payment, and this reciprocal movement expressly negates the finality that characterizes the Nuer transaction. Likewise, the groom's matrikin not only contribute to bridewealth but also receive the largest portion in the redistribution of the reciprocal payment. Enduring relations of mutual support between mother's brothers and sister's sons are thus strongly marked on both the bride's and groom's sides of the transaction. Moreover, the matrikin receive the largest portion of both bridewealth and *aruweth* and the prominence of matrilateral connections is thereby emphasized at the same time that their continuity is stressed. In sum, this comparison of Nuer and Dinka bridewealth reveals that their divergence with respect to the reciprocal payment encompasses a corresponding divergence in conceptions of the durability and significance of matrilateral relations. This point will be amplified through a more detailed analysis in the following chapter.

We have seen that the mother's brother–sister's son relation between founder and latecomer lines constitutes the central structural relation of internal organization in a Dinka subtribal camp of the rains, and that such matrilateral relations are likewise envisioned as the principal connection between spearmaster and warrior subclans within the Dinka tribal polity as a whole. It has also been noted that these matrilateral relationships not only form the line of cleavage in the fission of subtribes but are also radically attenuated in the process and thus only weakly link the resultant groups. The matrilateral bonds between the spearmaster and warrior subclans of the tribe are equally tenuous over the long term, and a warrior subclan may hive off to become part of another tribe to which it is also matrilaterally related. In short, while matrilateral relations are central to the Dinka structural system, the durability of such relations is also a problematic feature of that system. In light of this, it is evident that *aruweth* contains an ideological assertion of the enduring significance of relationships between mother's brothers and sister's sons within the structural system as a whole. The continuity of these relations that is enacted and experienced in the context of a particular transaction also transcends that context and is analogically applicable to the central structural relations of the larger segmentary order.

It is important to note that this differential emphasis on the enduring importance of matrilateral relations expressed in the respective bridewealth transactions of the Nuer and Dinka is powerfully experienced by participating social actors. Both Evans-Pritchard (1940*a*:19) and Lienhardt (1961:20–24) emphasize that cattle are seen as the links in social relations between individuals and groups and that such relations are defined by shared interests in cattle and realized through transactions in cattle. The Nuer-Dinka divergence with respect to the reciprocal payment therefore did not simply "reflect" a change in the relative significance of matrilateral relations but indeed constituted such a change in and of itself. In short, cultural valuations of the relative importance of matrilateral and patrilateral relations in the fabric of social life were transformed by changes in the bridewealth system, since the bridewealth system represents a primary context in which kinship valuations are both encoded and experienced.[16]

It should be recalled that the Nuer-Dinka divergence with respect to the reciprocal payment can be dated to the period before the Atwot separated from the main body of the Nuer, an event that took place no later than 1600. This early divergence in bridewealth customs was of considerable importance in the subsequent organizational differentiation of these two cultural groups. It not only engendered economic changes that produced a disparity in tribal size but also altered both the degree of interdependence between matrilateral kin and cultural conceptions of the durability and significance of matrilateral relations that are central to the Dinka structural system, but not that of the Nuer. While joint herding at dry season pastures would continue to delineate the constituents of a tribe among both the Dinka and the proto-Nuer prior to the emergence of the latter as a distinct cultural group, these initial differences concerning the reciprocal payment provided both a proto-Nuer advantage in tribal size that enabled them to expand and a basis for reconceptualizing relationships between the newly formed local groups spawned by that expansion. This constitutes the general framework of the argument to be developed in the following chapter.

CHAPTER 5

The Development of Organizational Differentiation

The Nuer and Dinka of 1800 were the products of a mutual divergence from a single cultural group that shared the same language and customs in earlier times. Given this common derivation and the many similarities between the Nuer and Dinka that persist, it is important to attempt to understand the process of cultural divergence that resulted in the marked military superiority of the Nuer and enabled them to vastly expand their territory at Dinka expense. In developmental terms, Nuer ascendancy does not merely represent the marked dominance of one distinct cultural group over another, but rather the emergent hegemony of one sector of a common cultural system over the remainder of that system. The eventual Nuer conquest of the central Dinka is, in that respect, all the more intriguing.

It has already been established (in chap. 3) that the Nuer and Dinka each possess a distinctive economic organization of systematically interrelated features. These economic variants of transhumance are the product of divergent social requirements for cattle that are embedded in the respective bridewealth payments of these two cultural groups. While chapter 3 focused on the manner in which the distinctive features of Nuer and Dinka economic organization are shaped by the size and composition of bridewealth payments in each case, this chapter will be largely concerned with the relationship between these distinctive features of economic organization and the respective characteristics of the Nuer and Dinka segmentary systems identified in chapter 4. The establishment of this component of the general argument will lay the groundwork for elucidating the coevolution of the Nuer and Dinka (or proto-Nuer and proto-Dinka) as a sequence of interrelated developments. (The terms *proto-Nuer* and *proto-Dinka* will be employed in developmental contexts pertaining to the period from the fifteenth century to 1800, when these cultural groups did not fully manifest the characteristics that distinguish them in the ethnographic present. The unmodified terms are employed in comparative contexts that entail reference to the ethnographic data.)

The organization of the argument in this chapter follows the contours of the interrelationships denoted above. We thus begin by summarizing the critical differences between the Nuer and Dinka in bridewealth customs and economic organization identified in chapter 3. We then turn to consideration of the effects of these economic differences on features of proto-Nuer and proto-Dinka political organization related to tribal size. In other words, the political ramifications of economic divergence are elucidated, and two distinctive political economies are thus delineated. The organizational differentiation of the proto-Nuer and proto-Dinka is then explained in terms of the interactive coevolution of their respective political economies. Two phases of organizational development are distinguished, with the second being marked by proto-Nuer expansion within the homeland region west of the Bahr el Jebel. Nuer, Dinka, and Atwot oral traditions discussed in chapter 1 provide evidence for such expansion during the period from the sixteenth century to 1800. The second phase of coevolutionary divergence encompasses this period, although it may have begun earlier. Dating the inception of proto-Nuer expansion within the homeland region is not essential to the argument. However, it should be noted that this commenced before the end of the sixteenth century and thus predated proto-Dinka expansion beyond the margins of the ecological zone defined by the flood region of the Upper Nile Basin (see map 2). The developmental model presented here thus entails the differentiation of the proto-Nuer and proto-Dinka during a period when they jointly occupied a common ecological zone and were confronted with quite similar environmental conditions.

BRIDEWEALTH AND ECONOMIC ORGANIZATION: A SUMMARY OF NUER AND DINKA VARIANTS

During the rainy season, the Nuer and Dinka who occupy the flood region are confined to restricted areas of high ground surrounded by the inundated Nile flood plain. Each wet season site offers only a limited area that must accommodate both agriculture and grazing. Increased grazing utilization thus decreases the quantity of land available for agriculture and vice versa. The allocation of land between these competing utilizations is determined by the cattle per capita holdings of the local population. As the ratio of the cattle population to human population increases, grazing land requirements increase relative to agricultural land requirements. Since the bulk of the diet is derived from agricultural products, an increase in cattle per capita likewise reduces the human population that can be supported on a given site. The food derived from an increased cattle population does not fully replace that lost by decreased acreage in agricultural production, because cattle are comparatively inefficient food producers. A single cow requires a grazing area of 4.15 acres over the course of the wet season while the average household cultivates only 2.1 to 3.1 acres during the same period.[1] Thus, a large cattle population restricts the human population that can be supported on a given wet season site.

Although nutritional requirements dictate the minimum ratio of cattle per capita necessary for survival, social requirements necessitate the accumulation of additional livestock that can be deployed in social transactions without reducing family herds to a level below the subsistence minimum. Social requirements for cattle shape herd management practices and the latter determine the composition and growth rate of family herds. Both the ratio of cattle per capita and the herd structure of the cattle population are thus a product of culturally defined social requirements for cattle. Cultural conceptions of the ideal and minimum bridewealth payments are the most significant social requirements that affect cattle per capita holdings and herd structure because bridewealth payments require a larger number of cattle than any other social transaction (except homicide compensation) and because the accumulation of cattle for contributions to bridewealth is a constant and expectable requirement of social life. Family herds must be managed with a view to having sufficient cattle to meet kinsmen's requests for bridewealth contributions and to provide for both the marriage of sons and the ghost unions of brothers who died without producing a male heir.

The Nuer and Dinka differ markedly in their cultural definitions of both the magnitude and composition of ideal and minimum bridewealth payments. The Nuer ideal requires roughly twice as many cattle as that of the Dinka (and the Dinka custom of reciprocal payments largely accounts for the differences in net outlay). The Nuer also require a minimum payment of approximately eighteen cattle to bring about a union while the Dinka lack an inflexible minimum that must be met for a marriage to take place. Nuer social requirements for cattle are thus at least twice as large as those of the Dinka and this is necessarily reflected in higher cattle per capita holdings among the Nuer.

Nuer bridewealth payments also include a lower proportion of breeding and milk-producing stock than do those of the Dinka. This difference in the composition of the bridewealth herd is reflected in the herd structure of the Nuer and Dinka cattle populations, respectively. These differences in herd structure provide clear evidence of the direct effect that variations in social requirements for cattle have on herd management practices, and hence the characteristics of the cattle population. The comparatively small proportion of adult male animals in Dinka herds is a direct result of the systematic culling of male animals for meat consumption. This affects grazing requirements in several ways. First, the higher level of regular and dependable meat consumption reduces Dinka dependence on milk as a daily source of protein and allows the Dinka to satisfy nutritional requirements with fewer (living) cattle per capita. Second, a Dinka herd, with fewer male animals, produces more milk per head of cattle than a Nuer herd so that fewer cattle per capita are needed to sustain the same level of milk production. Both these factors are responsible for a lower ratio of cattle per capita among the Dinka, and hence reduced grazing requirements. Dinka grazing requirements are further reduced by the fact that female animals require less pasture area to maintain their smaller body weight. Available data indicate that the Lou and Western Nuer require 16.3 percent more cattle per capita and 27 percent more grazing area than the Aliab Dinka to achieve comparable levels of milk and meat production. (See note 12 of chap. 3 for the derivation of these figures and further explication of the points noted here.) This represents the degree of difference in these two variables that is attributable to dissimilarities in herd structure alone. The higher caloric intake of the Nuer (reflected in their comparatively greater average body weight) and the higher proportion of total caloric intake derived from cattle products (indicated by less intensive cultivation of a smaller quantity of land, on average, than the Dinka) necessarily entail higher (rather than comparable) levels of milk and meat production for the Nuer. This is derived from additional cattle and the latter further magnify the differences between the Nuer and Dinka in cattle per capita and grazing requirements noted above. In all, these data bear witness to the broad-ranging impact of the Nuer and Dinka bridewealth systems on their respective modes of economic organization.

The differences between the Nuer and Dinka in cattle per capita holdings and in grazing requirements engender corresponding differences in the human population density of wet season settlements.[2] A given unit of grazing land capable of supporting a fixed number of cattle will support fewer Nuer than Dinka, and Nuer local population density is consequently lower. This lower density per wet season settlement is reflected in the fact that the overall population density of the Nuer is 36.5 to 45 percent lower than that of the Dinka when adjacent districts are compared.

Nuer and Dinka wet season settlements thus differ significantly in several respects. Nuer settlements are characterized by a larger cattle population, with substantially greater grazing requirements, and 36.5 to 45 percent fewer households, each cultivating somewhat less land per season than their Dinka counterparts. This markedly reduced quantity of land devoted to agriculture increases that available for grazing and enables the Nuer to carry a larger cattle population through the wet season. Nuer grazing requirements are therefore substantially greater than those of the Dinka during the dry season as well, and this has a direct bearing on patterns of dry season aggregation.

These differences between the Nuer and Dinka in cattle density and grazing requirements are further magnified by dissimilar systems of fallow rotation. Available data suggest that the Nuer economic variant of transhumance facilitates the occupation of a comparatively larger proportion of elevated wet season sites at any given time, enabling the Nuer to support a much larger cattle population than the Dinka during the wet season. Thus, the Nuer possess a twofold advantage in this respect, with both a larger cattle population per site and a larger percentage of wet season sites under simultaneous occupation. This stems directly from differences between the Nuer and Dinka in the quantity of land allocated to agriculture, and the effects of this on the duration of both the cultivation and fallow periods. Both Evans-Pritchard (1937:44) and Howell (1954*b*:328) report that declining yields prompt the abandonment of one wet season settlement and relocation at another. A particular site may be cultivated for as long as ten years (Evans-Pritchard, 1937:44) and the fallow period is reported to be long enough for the natural vegetation to be fully reestablished (Howell, 1954*b*:328). The smaller human population of a Nuer wet season settlement, cultivating only half as much land as its Dinka counterpart, could clearly utilize a given site for a longer period before experiencing declining yields. Less intensive use and the rotation of cultivations within an elevated site would also shorten the fallow period necessary for the regeneration of natural vegetation. Both a longer use period and a shorter fallow period would enable the Nuer to occupy a larger portion of suitable wet season sites than the Dinka in any given environmental zone.[3]

It is evident here that the Nuer-Dinka divergence in bridewealth systems produced a corresponding divergence in economic organization. Bridewealth requirements determine both cattle per capita holdings and herd structure and these, in turn, delineate grazing requirements and the allocation of land between agricultural and herding components of the economy, with the latter having direct repercussions on the system of fallow rotation, which determines the effective limits of wet season pasturage, etc. The systemic interconnections between these tightly articulated facets of economic organization are readily apparent: a change in the value of one variable produces a change in another that cycles through the system. However, there is clear historical evidence that ideal bridewealth payments are unresponsive to changes in the variables to which they are directly or indirectly linked, and that they thus have a determinative effect on critical features of economic organization but are not determined by it (see chap. 3). The constitutive nature of this relationship will be discussed further in another context. The main point to be noted here is that a Nuer-Dinka divergence in bridewealth systems prior to 1600 engendered two distinctive economic variants of transhumance. While both are characterized by identical systems of interconnected variables, the values of those variables differ in each case (as a consequence of differences in bridewealth requirements). One axis of dissimilarity is of particular importance with respect to political organization, viz., the size of the cattle population that can be supported through the wet season. This dictates dry season grazing requirements and has important effects on the scale of dry season aggregations. We have seen that the overall density of the Nuer cattle population is much greater than that of the Dinka, and that differences in herd structure further magnify the disparity in dry season grazing requirements that follow from these differences in cattle density. As a result, the Nuer cattle population approaches and periodically exceeds the limits of dry season grazing while the Dinka cattle population is maintained at a level well below these limits. Thus the Nuer frequently encroach upon Dinka pastures at the height of the dry season (Evans-Pritchard, 1940a:62), while Dinka trespass on Nuer domains is unreported.

The high density of the Nuer cattle population and the maximum utilization of dry season grazing resources this entails requires the aggregation of a large number of local groups along major watercourses at the height of the dry season. In contrast, the Dinka cattle population, which is maintained at a lower density, can find sufficient dry season grazing at inland lakes and along the tributaries of major watercourses. Each of these scattered locations supports a comparatively smaller number of local groups. Although Dinka wet season settlements are larger than those of the Nuer, the Dinka population is thus more widely dispersed than that of the Nuer during the dry season.[4] This had a direct bearing on the maintenance of post-fission relationships (and thus on tribal size) during the period when the proto-Nuer and proto-Dinka were undergoing organizational differentiation. The distinctive features of the Nuer and Dinka economic systems summarized in the preceding pages thus provide the basis for understanding this process of organizational differentiation.

The proposed developmental sequence of organizational differentiation begins with initial differences between the proto-Nuer and proto-Dinka in economic organization corresponding to the differences outlined above. These two economic variants of transhumance are ultimately attributable to different social requirements for cattle embedded in the respective bridewealth requirements of these two cultural groups. It is important to recall that there are significant differences among Nuer tribes in ideal bridewealth payments and that such differences are expectable among the component tribes of a single cultural group. At the time period with which we are concerned (circa fifteenth century), the proto-Nuer and proto-Dinka were already linguistically distinct and much greater differences in ideal bridewealth than those found within a single cultural group would thus be expectable, together with the differences in economic organization associated with them. These economic differences had important effects on the political organization of the proto-Nuer and proto-Dinka that can be documented in terms of data derived from the ethnographic present. It is to consideration of these data that we now turn.[5]

DIFFERENCES IN TRIBAL SIZE: THE POLITICAL CORRELATE OF ECONOMIC DIVERGENCE

The continued association of original and offshoot communities at dry season cattle camps is an important factor in the maintenance of post-fission relationships as coordinate units of a larger segmentary entity among both the Nuer and Dinka. Evans-Pritchard (1940a:117–18) emphasizes such association as a significant element in accounting for differences in the size of the various Nuer tribes.[6] Lienhardt (1958:116, 133) defines a Dinka tribe as a unit that shares rights in and jointly defends a specific area of dry season pasture and argues that joint herding at common dry season pastures is the sine qua non of inclusion within a tribal polity. The size of a Dinka tribe is thus a direct product of the extent of its dry season pasture. Newcomer (1972) and Glickman (1972) have expanded on these arguments in an attempt to account for differences between the Nuer and Dinka in segmentary organization and superiority in cattle raiding, respectively. However, in considering the factors conducive to extensive dry season aggregations, all these authors have emphasized the relative size and spatial distribution of wet and dry season pasture areas, while failing to consider the determinative effects of the size and density of the cattle population. As was pointed out in chapter 2, Newcomer's and Glickman's environmental explanations run aground on the intractable fact that the Central Dinka formerly occupied the environmental area deemed most conducive to large-scale aggregations during the dry season, but were subsequently expelled by Nuer tribes that expanded from the environmental area least favorable to the development of large tribal entities. These environmental explanations are also grounded in the untenable assumption that the Nuer and Dinka economic systems are identical and do not differ with respect to grazing requirements.

The extent to which wet season communities aggregate at large dry season camps is determined not only by fixed environmental features, but also by the size of community herds in relation to grazing areas. At the close of the rainy season, the cattle move out from elevated village sites onto the surrounding plain. As the dry season progresses they are grazed near pools and smaller streams. When the water, pasture, and fishing resources at one location are exhausted the cattle are moved to another. There is a gradual progression of movement from small streams and pools to lakes and intermediate tributaries of major rivers and finally to these major watercourses themselves. It is primarily at the latter locations that particularly large numbers of wet season communities are brought into association. However, these maximal aggregations may not occur at all if grazing resources are sufficient at the intermediate locations adjacent to numerous lakes and tributary streams. Thus Evans-Pritchard (1940a:62) points out,

> the Lou stay inland as long as they can and in a wet year may remain inland throughout the dry season, falling back on the deeper pools, some large enough to be called lakes, e.g., [eight named locations listed]. If forced to leave them the Gun primary section moves north to the Sobat and southwest to the flooded plains of the Bahr el Zeraf in the county of the Twic Dinka, and the Mor primary section

moves northeast to the Nyanding river and east to the Geni and Pilbor. In the old days fighting frequently occurred if the Lou moved to these camping sites, because the banks of the Sobat were in the hands of the Balak Dinka while their occupation of the Geni and Pilbor was disputed by the Anuak and Bier and their move to the southwest was trespass on Dinka grazing grounds.

Whether grazing resources were sufficient at these dispersed inland lakes (or deep pools) was contingent on the size of Nuer herds as well as year-to-year variations in precipitation. With somewhat fewer cattle these areas would be adequate in most, if not all, years.

As noted earlier, the Nuer and Dinka economic systems differ with respect to the overall size and density of the cattle population and hence in the scale of dry season aggregations. Although Nuer wet season settlements have a much smaller human population than their Dinka counterparts, scores of such groups are regularly brought into association at large dry season camps along major rivers, while comparatively few Dinka wet season communities congregate at inland pools and tributaries for joint dry season herding. The association of original and offshoot communities at dry season pastures is conducive to the maintenance of post-fission relationships, and the larger dry season aggregations of the Nuer thus contribute to the development of a more inclusive segmentary organization. We have seen that the more inclusive nature of Nuer segmentary organization at both the bottom and the top accounts for the marked Nuer advantage in tribal size. Moreover, the specific characteristics of Nuer and Dinka segmentary organization are fully consistent with the differences in economic organization outlined here. In the Dinka case, several large agricultural communities (*bai*) comprise a minimal segment (subtribe or section) with a population typically in the range of eight hundred to thirteen hundred persons. Among the Nuer, a minimal segment (tertiary section) characteristically includes four to eight smaller wet season settlements with an aggregate population that frequently exceeds two thousand persons. In brief, Nuer segmentary organization encompasses a comparatively large number of small local groups, while the Dinka segmentary system displays the inverse characteristics (i.e., encompasses a small number of comparatively large local groups). These differences in segmentary organization correspond precisely to the scale of wet and dry season aggregations in each case, and we have seen that the latter are an integral feature of the distinctive Nuer and Dinka economic variants of transhumance delineated in the preceding pages.

The general argument advanced here contains a strikingly counterintuitive proposition: The Nuer, with a human population density 36.5 to 45 percent lower than that of neighboring Dinka groups, nevertheless displaced the latter (and continued to expand as their population density declined through territorial acquisition). The basis of the Nuer capacity to expand under these demographic conditions should now be evident. The Nuer held a marked advantage in tribal size despite their disadvantage in density, inasmuch as Nuer tribes encompassed local groups over a broader region than their Dinka counterparts. Demography is not destiny.

The development of the argument thus far may be summed up as follows: It is clear that differences between the Nuer and Dinka in social requirements for cattle would necessarily entail a divergence in economic organization and that the resultant economic variants are conducive to the development of organizational differentiation. Moreover, an extensive array of economic, political, and social organizational differences between the Nuer and Dinka can be accounted for as systematic transformations of a common set of interrelated variables. Before proceeding it will be useful to provide further documentation of this by demonstrating the relationship between bridewealth and tribal size.

The preceding explanation of the development of a Nuer advantage in tribal size presupposes a correlation between two variables that have no obvious or intrinsic interconnection; i.e., the magnitude of ideal bridewealth payments on one hand and tribal size on the other. The central argument entails a causal sequence in which A determines B, B produces C, C engenders D, and so forth. The magnitude of bridewealth payments and tribal size represent the initial and final variables in this causal sequence, and differences in the latter should consequently co-vary with differences in the former. Such a correlation would provide substantial confirmation of the central argument. More specifically, the causal sequence to be tested may be summarized as follows. If the magnitude of ideal bridewealth payments dictates social requirements for cattle by influencing herd management practices, and if social requirements for cattle and associated herd management practices have an important effect on economic organization with respect to herd structure, cattle per capita holdings, land use at wet season settlements, cattle density, and hence dry season grazing requirements, and if dry season grazing requirements dictate the scale of dry season aggregations, and if the latter has an important effect on the maintenance of post-fission relationships, and if the maintenance of such relationships is directly expressed in the degree of segmentary inclusiveness, and if tribal size is a function of segmentary inclusiveness, *then* tribes manifesting comparatively high ideal bridewealth payments should also be comparatively large in terms of tribal size. Although other data have been introduced in earlier chapters to independently support these causal relationships, a correlation between the magnitude of bridewealth payments and tribal size provides a test of the causal sequence as a whole.

The Nuer and Dinka clearly conform to this expectation, with a two to one difference in ideal bridewealth corresponding to an even larger difference

TABLE 4

The Distribution of Nuer Tribes in Relation
to Ideal Bridewealth and Tribal Size

Tribal Size (in persons)	Ideal Bridewealth (in head of cattle)	
	32–35	*38–40*
5,000–12,000	5	1
17,000–42,000	1	4

in tribal size. Moreover, the expected correlation is well supported by an internal comparison of the eleven Nuer tribes for which ideal bridewealth data are available (table 4). Five of the six Nuer tribes with a bridewealth of thirty-two to thirty-five head of cattle fall in the size range of five thousand to twelve thousand persons per tribe, while four of the five tribes with a bridewealth of thirty-eight to forty head of cattle fall in the range of seventeen thousand to forty-two thousand members.[7] This comparison clearly supports the central argument outlined above, and the significance accorded to bridewealth payments within the framework of that argument. Having demonstrated that the general interpretation and the line of reasoning on which it is based are well supported by available ethnographic data, we may now directly address the question of the progressive organizational differentiation of the proto-Nuer and proto-Dinka. The correlation presented above only constitutes a preliminary step in the development of this explanation.

Thus far, we have been concerned to specify fundamental differences between the proto-Nuer and proto-Dinka in economic organization, in tribal size, and in the nature of their respective socioecological systems. Although these differences are clearly the product of an earlier evolutionary divergence, they are taken to represent initial differences, or differences present at "time one" in the developmental model that follows (see note 5). This model focuses on the interactive coevolution of these two systems (which encompass two distinctive transformations of a common set of social, political, economic, and ecological interrelationships). A number of basic features of present-day Nuer and Dinka political organization that have yet to be addressed can be accounted for in terms of the direct interaction of these two respective systems. In particular, these features include Nuer transcendence of joint herding at common dry season pastures as the sole basis for segmentary inclusiveness, the development of the distinctive Nuer segmentary lineage organization, and the accentuation of points of disjunction in the more truncated Dinka segmentary organization.

It is evident from Evans-Pritchard's description of dry season aggregations among the Lou Nuer (cited earlier) that the entire Lou tribe does not forgather at one location but is rather divided among four separate areas of concentration. The inclusion of these four large dry season herding groups within a single tribal polity is thus based on relations grounded in the lineage system of the dominant clan rather than shared dry season pastures.[8] This represents a later (i.e., post-"time one") development that will be addressed in the following pages. Initially, the proto-Nuer would more closely resemble the Dinka from whom they diverged and consequently tribal size would correspond directly to the scale of dry season aggregations, as it does among the Dinka. However, within the terms of this common delineation of tribal inclusiveness, proto-Nuer tribes would nevertheless be larger than their proto-Dinka neighbors and thus possess an initial advantage that itself played a significant role in further organizational differentiation.

THE FIRST PHASE OF COEVOLUTIONARY DIVERGENCE

The initial development of a proto-Nuer tribe that was somewhat larger than the tribal units of its Dinka neighbors, and possessed the economic and distributional characteristics outlined earlier, would set in motion a process of progressive differentiation that would accentuate these original differences. The seasonal migration of the proto-Nuer to major watercourses not only increased contact between the constituent local groups of the tribe, but also assembled these large aggregations of local groups along tribal boundaries where they were brought into conflict with neighboring groups over limited dry season pastures. (The prevalence of border conflicts at the height of the dry season is evident in Evans-Pritchard's account of Lou Nuer seasonal migrations cited earlier.) These conflicts pitted the larger dry season herding groups of the proto-Nuer against one or two of the smaller, more widely dispersed dry season cattle camps of the Dinka. The proto-Nuer would thus possess a decisive advantage in these encounters that would enable them to appropriate the additional dry season grazing they required in lean years and hence permit them to maintain their cattle population at high densities. At the same time, recurrent conflict would be expected to reinforce the Dinka pattern of utilizing scattered inland locations, since these afforded a measure of security due to their distance from the riverine borders that have historically demarcated tribal territories.

The divergent economic variants of the proto-Nuer and proto-Dinka thus constituted a mutually interactive coevolutionary system in which the distinctive features of each type of economic organization were further accentuated by the presence of the other type along its borders. In order to accommodate their larger herds, the proto-Nuer regularly utilized riverine grazing areas that their Dinka counterparts held in reserve as a margin of security against particularly unfavorable years. The massing of the Nuer at these border points also enabled them to appropriate Dinka grazing lands when shortages occurred. The environment to which the proto-Nuer adapted was thus one in which dry season grazing resources were expandable and did not impose a rigid limit on the growth of the cattle population. Conversely, the environment to which the neighboring proto-Dinka adapted was characterized by a shortage of reliable dry season grazing in lean years that restricted the size of the cattle population (and cattle per capita holdings). The smaller cattle population reinforced the pattern of utilizing scattered inland pools throughout the dry season and further inhibited the Dinka capacity to defend their reserves of dry season grazing along major rivers, thus rendering these areas more readily available to the Nuer.

The restricted dry season grazing resources available to the proto-Dinka in poor years would require an adjustment in herd management practices. When inland grazing was insufficient and shortages occurred, it would be necessary to cull some animals from the family herd and reduce their numbers in order to maintain the condition and milk production of the remainder. The logical recourse under these circumstances would be to conserve potential breeding and milk-producing stock by reducing the number of male animals in the herd and utilizing the latter for meat consumption. Moreover, increased meat consumption would reduce the quantity of milk needed by the human population at a time when milk production was restricted by grazing shortage, and thus reduce mortality among calves that depend upon the same source of supply for their survival. Pre-existing proto-Dinka herd management practices and the distinctive herd structure of the proto-Dinka cattle population were thus accentuated by adaptation to an environmental context shaped by the presence of the proto-Nuer. The Nuer, on the other hand, were not subjected to comparable constraints and could afford to maintain a larger proportion of male animals (that served as a reserve against crop failures) and to pursue a herd management strategy geared to the growth of the cattle population. This further divergence in herd management practices accentuated corresponding differences in the herd structure of the proto-Nuer and proto-Dinka cattle populations and thus also accentuated original differences between these two cultural groups in cattle per capita holding and grazing requirements. In addition, the reduced herds of the proto-Dinka would increase the quantity of agricultural land available at wet season settlements and allow them to compensate for their increased vulnerability to crop failures by increasing the quantity of land in production and staggering the planting dates of different parcels. (Crop failures are generally a result of untimely drought or heavy rains that wilt or wash out seedlings [see Howell 1954*b*:323–24].)

The higher ratio of cattle per capita among the proto-Nuer would entail a smaller human population per wet season community than that of their proto-Dinka counterparts. In a context of small-scale raiding carried out by one community against another, these less populous proto-Nuer communities with extensive herds would be appealing targets for cattle raids by the larger Dinka communities of neighboring tribes. The proto-Nuer would be at a numerical disadvantage in both defending their settlements and in raiding those of the proto-Dinka during the rainy season. The vulnerability of small proto-Nuer wet season settlements to systematic proto-Dinka predation thus represented an important dimension of the social environment with which they were confronted. However, this vulnerability could readily be obviated by cooperation between wet season settlements in counterattacking Dinka raiding parties, and in conducting large-scale raids against the Dinka that would serve to pin them down in defense of home territory. Moreover, the proto-Nuer were preadapted to the development of such patterns of cooperation as a consequence of annual multicommunity aggregations at large dry season camps. The communities that jointly herded their cattle during the dry season also shared in the defense of those pastures and joined forces in appropriating proto-Dinka grazing areas in lean years. Although cooperation in situations of conflict was governed by the same principles among the proto-Dinka, the smaller dry season aggregation of the latter limited the scale of mobilization for rainy season raids to a level below that of the proto-Nuer. The proto-Nuer advantage during the dry season thus served as the basis for the development of a comparable advantage during the wet season as well. In contrast, the initial proto-Dinka advantage in carrying out small-scale, single community raids during the rainy season contained no comparable basis for uniting during the dry season and was intrinsically self-limiting. Moreover, the progressive development of the Nuer system operated to inhibit an effective adaptive response on the part of the Dinka by limiting the size of Dinka dry season aggregations and hence tribal size.

It should be noted that the above argument suggests that the development of a proto-Nuer advantage in conducting rainy season cattle raids was both defensive and conservative in the first instance, being prompted by proto-Nuer vulnerability to proto-Dinka predation. However, the development of this raiding capacity also entailed as yet unrealized potential for both stimulating and facilitating territorial expansion.

THE SECOND PHASE OF COEVOLUTIONARY DIVERGENCE

The development of a proto-Nuer capacity to mobilize raiding parties that outnumbered proto-Dinka defensive forces ushered in a new phase in the divergence of these two socioecological systems. Annual large-scale cattle raids carried out by the Nuer resulted in the capture of substantial numbers of cattle that significantly increased the Nuer cattle population while decreasing that of neighboring Dinka tribes. The progressive differentiation of these two systems thus became much more closely interlocked, since an increase in proto-Nuer cattle per capita holdings entailed a simultaneous and corresponding decrease in proto-Dinka cattle per capita holdings. This served to further accentuate all the initial differences between these two cultural groups that stemmed from a disparity in the ratio of cattle population to human population (i.e., the differences in herd management practices, herd structure, patterns of dry season aggregation, etc.). Moreover, the proto-Nuer were now able to recoup stock losses (caused by endemic cattle diseases) at proto-Dinka expense. Natural restraints on the growth of the Nuer cattle population were thus superseded. This insured a continuous rate of increase in the proto-Nuer cattle population such that the latter would regularly exceed current dry season grazing resources. A built-in impetus to territorial expansion thus became embedded in the Nuer socioecological system. The capacity to effectively carry out large-scale raids in which more than a thousand cattle were taken not only generated this intrinsic impetus to expansion but also constituted the mechanism by which territorial appropriation was accomplished. The Dinka were regularly expelled from their wet season communities in the course of these raids and the Nuer occupied the deserted sites.

It was during this second phase that the proto-Nuer began to expand within the area that subsequently came to be regarded as the Nuer homeland and to grow from one or two proto-Nuer tribes to the twelve tribes that occupied this region by 1800. The growth of the Nuer population was brought about by the capture of young women and female children in the course of the same raids through which territorial expansion was accomplished. As was explained in chapter 1, the annual capture of a relatively small number of reproductive females would subsequently result in a significant increase in the Nuer population as a whole, with the full effect of this increase being realized several generations after initial capture. This insured that the Nuer population would increase as the Nuer territorial domain was expanded, since the intensive raiding associated with expansion also added reproductive females to the population.[9] In short, the demographic characteristics of the Nuer were largely governed by the intensity of their raids on the Dinka, and these characteristics were thus partially divorced from demographic trends that characterized the region as a whole. Both the Nuer cattle population and human population were governed by the internal dynamics of a system of relations that possessed the capacity to override natural constraints.

The existence of a significant bridewealth differential between the proto-Nuer and proto-Dinka could potentially have produced a net inflow of reproductive females into the proto-Nuer population, contributing to population growth. Although available data suggests that this did not, in fact, occur, it is important to explain why as the explanation elucidates a central feature of Dinka bridewealth customs. A potential loss of reproductive females among the proto-Dinka and a corresponding gain among the proto-Nuer would result from the inability or unwillingness of the proto-Dinka to provide the larger bridewealth necessary to obtain a wife from the proto-Nuer. The latter, on the other hand, would have no difficulty meeting proto-Dinka bridewealth re-quirements. The fact that a bridewealth differential can lead to a net loss (and gain) of reproductive females in this way is documented by the cases of the Shilluk and Mandari. Both these cultural groups are reported to have exported women to neighboring higher bridewealth areas under such circumstances (Howell, 1954*b*:205, 241). (The Dinka were the principal beneficiaries in both cases.) The conditions conducive to a net outflow of women are com-plex, but appear to hinge on the existence of a rigid minimum payment. Under these circumstances, the export of daughters brings in bridewealth cattle that will unblock a number of prospective internal unions. In the absence of such a minimum, temporary shortages of cattle do not preclude or delay marriages within the cultural group and external unions need not be sought.

The Dinka lack a rigid minimum bridewealth payment and it is thus unlikely that a significant frequency of female outmarriage to Nuer husbands occurred. The bridewealth differential between the proto-Nuer and proto-Dinka thus appears not to have been a major factor in augmenting the number of reproductive females in the proto-Nuer population and thus contributing to Nuer population increase. (The capture of reproductive females in raids, on the other hand, was of considerable significance in this respect.) While the potential role of a bridewealth differential in Nuer population growth is thus a null hypothesis, consideration of it puts the absence of a Dinka minimum payment in a new light. The latter can be seen as an adaptation to the higher bridewealth of the neighboring Nuer that served to prevent the continual loss of reproductive females. However, such an adaptation would have signifi-cantly reduced social requirements for cattle among the Dinka, contributing to the general economic and political divergence between the proto-Nuer and proto-Dinka elucidated here. Such a reduction in the Dinka minimum pay-ment would have taken place very early in the period when the ''initial differences'' between these two cultural groups were established, and thus contributed to successive coevolutionary divergence.

As noted earlier, the development of a proto-Nuer capacity to carry out large-scale raids produced both the impetus to Nuer expansion and the means by which it was effected. This initiated an expansion process that continued until 1890. Periodic shortages of dry season pasture prompted successive rounds of proto-Nuer expansion while systematic large-scale raids devastated Dinka border communities and created a weakly held periphery that was easily appropriated. Each territorial gain reduced the density of the proto-

Nuer human and cattle populations, while at the same time providing a base for future growth. The food-limited cattle population, with much shorter generations separating reproductive females, would increase much more rapidly than the human population once its food supply was expanded. Nuer herd management practices and effective raiding would also insure rapid growth. The disease-limited human population would grow through the addition of captured reproductive females rather than significant changes in the food supply. However, the delayed effect of such additions, and the longer generational span of humans, would produce a slower rate of growth. These differential rates of increase would insure the maintenance of a high ratio of cattle per capita and hence the maintenance of the economic characteristics associated with it. When the cattle population once again exceeded dry season grazing resources, another round of territorial expansion would ensue. However, this would take place at human densities well below those that could be attained, as was the case throughout the successive phases of the later Nuer expansion of the nineteenth century.

The gradual expansion of the proto-Nuer from one or two tribes to a dozen such units occupying an extensive territorial domain west of the Nile had important effects on the development of Nuer political organization. The occupation of newly conquered territory necessarily entailed the fission of existing wet season settlements and the formation of new communities. However, the conditions under which these new communities were settled would itself generate a transformation in their internal organization and the development of a Nuer type of organization from one that originally resembled that of the Dinka. Recall that a Dinka local group characteristically splits along a matrilateral (mother's brother–sister's son) axis of differentiation between resident descent groups. The offshoot group, formerly related as sister's sons and latecomers to the parent community, becomes a founding line of a new local group. The fission process thus entails agnatic purification, i.e., the reduction of the resultant communities to agnatic founder lines without matrilaterally attached lines coresiding. The latter pattern is eventually regenerated in the Dinka case when sister's sons subsequently join the respective offshoot and parent communities as "latecomers." However, under conditions of territorial expansion, there would be little impetus for any descent group segment to join an existing settlement in the comparatively unfavorable status of "latecomers" rather than founding their own community at one of the numerous sites made available by the expulsion of the Dinka. Parent communities would thus be stripped of sister's son lines that departed to become founders elsewhere, and the resultant offshoot communities would likewise experience difficulty in recruiting occupants to this disfavored position in local organization. In short, fission under conditions of territorial expansion inhibited the reproduction of matrilateral founder-latecomer relationships as the central axis of internal organization among the proto-Nuer.[10]

The new communities formed in the course of territorial expansion would thus contain the members of a single agnatic line as the predominant segment of the local population. Matrilaterally related accretions would be limited to individual kinsmen rather than descent group segments. As these communities grew over a period of generations, they would thus tend to develop internal segments differentiated by their agnatic descent from the respective sons of the ancestor of the original founders. When fission then took place in conjunction with a new round of territorial appropriation, these communities would split along an established agnatic line of cleavage producing like relations between the products of fission. The two resultant wet season settlements would thus be linked by descent from a common ancestor as well as continued association at dry season pastures. Moreover, the characteristic features of the Nuer fission process would be established at the level of local groups, subsequently to be transported to higher levels of segmentary organization as growth occurred through internal subdivision. The maintenance of post-fission relations would thus superimpose lineage organization on territorial organization. The emergence of a single dominant clan within each Nuer tribe, with minimal lineages of the clan represented in every wet season settlement, can thus be seen as the logical end point of the process of agnatic purification operating within a context of continuing growth through territorial expansion (cf. Gough, 1971:89–90).

This process of agnatic purification at the tribal level is attested in Nuer oral traditions concerning the origin of present-day tribes and the genealogical relationships between the founders of their dominant clans. One group of tribes is represented as the descendants of the sons and daughters of Gee, the first leopard-skin priest (Evans-Pritchard, 1940a:238–39; 1956:114). The dominant clan of the Jikany tribes traces its descent to Kir, who married several of Gee's daughters.[11] The dominant clans of the Leek and Lak are descended from Ril, who married another of Gee's daughters (Evans-Pritchard, 1940a:232, 239). The Thiang, Lou, and Jagei tribes are descended from three of Gee's sons. The original Gee tribe would thus have been organized in accordance with the familiar Dinka pattern, containing three distinct patrilineal descent groups, two of which were matrilaterally related to the third. These matrilaterally related segments subsequently became separate tribes through fission. Each of the three emergent tribes thus contained a single dominant clan, rather than the two (or more) matrilaterally related descent groups characteristic of Dinka tribal organization.

The progressive development and elaboration of a segmentary system based on relationships between the lineages of a dominant clan enabled the

Nuer to transcend joint herding at common dry season pastures as the sole basis of tribal inclusiveness. Primary segments that aggregated at different dry season pastures continued to be included within a single tribal polity on the basis of agnatic relationships between their respective focal lines. The original proto-Nuer advantage, grounded in comparatively larger dry season aggregations, was greatly magnified by this transformation of Nuer political organization. The later quadrupling of the Nuer territorial domain between 1800 and 1890 was thus made possible by a decisive Nuer advantage in tribal size that represented the culmination of the developmental processes outlined above, operating over an extended period of time. While the initial proto-Nuer expansion within the homeland region extended over several centuries, it ultimately engendered Nuer tribes that were substantially more than twice as large as their Dinka counterparts. This laid the groundwork for the exceptionally rapid Nuer conquest of the Central Dinka region in the nineteenth century.

Although agnatic purification resulting from fission under conditions of territorial expansion contributed to the development of a segmentary system based on patrilineal relationships between the lineages of a dominant clan, the assimilation of Dinka tribesmen resulting from that same expansion process was conducive to the reproduction of matrilaterally attached Dinka lineages within local groups. Although this latter process ran counter to the former, and regenerated local communities characterized by internal matrilateral relationships, it did not regenerate the original structure. Matrilateral relationships between several proto-Nuer lineages were replaced by like relations between a founding Nuer line and one or more Dinka descent groups.

The matrilateral relationship between a focal line of a Nuer dominant clan and a Dinka lineage linked to it through a woman is similar in form, but fundamentally different in character, from the matrilateral relation between founders and latecomers in the Dinka social system. In the latter instance, latecomer lines have an independent agnatic identity. When they depart to found new communities they consequently retain a matrilateral relationship to the founding line of the community from which they have separated. In contrast, Dinka lineages within the Nuer social system lack an independent agnatic identity as subunits of a descent group other than the Nuer focal line to which they are matrilaterally linked (as the descendants of a female agnate). In the course of several generations, such matrilateral connections are thus rephrased in agnatic terms and erstwhile Dinka lineage members "come to be regarded as true agnates of the dominant core" locally and full members of the aristocratic clan of which it constitutes a subunit (Gough, 1971:83–84; see also Evans-Pritchard, 1945:65). In the event of fisson, the line of cleavage is thus agnatic rather than matrilateral and the resultant groups are so linked. Alternatively, should the members of a Dinka lineage move to another community before several generations have passed, their matrilateral relation to the Nuer focal line with whom they formerly resided would necessarily be recontextualized as a kin relation, indistinguishable from that between any two lineages that had previously intermarried. The relation could not be construed as one of descent. The formerly coresident lines would not constitute coordinate segments of a higher-order entity but merely coresidents that had parted company. In other words, the matrilateral attachment of a Dinka lineage to a Nuer focal line (of the dominant clan) is a transitional relationship that cannot constitute a line of cleavage in fission and hence cannot link the products of fission. Such matrilateral relations are thus largely confined within Nuer local groups and do not, in most instances, permanently link one such group to another within the larger segmentary system.[12] (In the ethnographic present, the exceptions primarily pertain to large, territorially discrete Dinka enclaves produced by the irregular pattern of nineteenth-century expansion; see Evans-Pritchard, 1940*a*:228–29. This pattern would not have characterized earlier proto-Nuer territorial appropriation.) Proto-Nuer expansion within the homeland region thus transformed the segmentary system through agnatic purification while at the same time recreating a local organization that was superficially similar to previous patterns of relationship. This represents an instance in which reproduction at one level entailed structural transformation at another (cf. Sahlins, 1981:67–68). Both persistence and change are evident in this developmental process, which is more fully explained in the next section of the chapter.

Proto-Nuer expansion within the homeland region affected the organization of proto-Dinka tribes and local groups as well as those of the Nuer. Dinka tribesmen expelled from their wet season settlements by proto-Nuer raids were forced to seek refuge among kinsmen residing at other locations. Both the founder and latecomer lines of a disbanded community thus found it necessary to join existing local groups as latecomers. This increased both the proportional representation of latecomer lines in Dinka wet season communities and the total number of coresident descent groups represented. Proto-Nuer expansion thus had opposite effects on proto-Nuer and proto-Dinka local organization, inhibiting the reproduction of matrilateral founder-latecomer relationships as the central axis of internal organization among the former and accentuating these same relationships among the latter. While fission reduced and simplified proto-Nuer local organization, the accretion of a multiplicity of agnatically unrelated descent groups rendered that of the Dinka more complex and less well integrated. Dinka wet season cattle camps would come to include refugee lines related by kinship to existing latecomer lines but not to community founders, or a variety of latecomer lines respectively linked to the founding lines but unrelated to each other. Similarly, when a displaced Dinka cattle camp relocated among kinsmen of another tribe, the latter would then encompass several agnatically unrelated spearmaster descent groups and several equally unrelated warrior descent groups. As noted earlier, this pattern entails disjunctions in tribal integration that are conducive to the dissolution of post-fission relationships and hence a truncated segmentary organization. The accentuation of these features of Dinka organization thus becomes intelligible as a product of dislocations and accretions generated by Nuer territorial expansion. Howell (1951:250–51) makes a similar point with respect to the effects of nineteenth-century Nuer expansion on Ngok (Ngork) Dinka segmentary organization and Southall (1976) has recently generalized and expanded upon this interpretation.

STRUCTURAL CHANGE: THE DEVELOPMENT OF THE NUER
SEGMENTARY LINEAGE SYSTEM

Thus far, we have been concerned to show that differences between the proto-Nuer and proto-Dinka in the magnitude of bridewealth payments produced a divergence in economic organization that engendered differences in the scale of dry season aggregations. Given a concept of tribal inclusiveness based on joint cattle herding during the dry season, this translated directly into differences in tribal size. An initial proto-Nuer advantage in this respect enabled them to expand within the homeland region and the fission of local groups under conditions of territorial expansion both produced communities with an agnatic core and engendered agnatic relationships between them. While agnatic relationships between segments were a regular feature of the original tribal organization shared by both the proto-Nuer and proto-Dinka, such relationships only linked the main lineages of a spearmaster or a warrior subclan. Matrilateral relationships between these subclans (and between founder and latecomer lines) were the central structural relations in this form of tribal organization. The development of the Nuer segmentary lineage system (as we know it) thus entailed fundamental changes in structure, and in the conceptual basis of the segmentary order intrinsic to it. These developments have not as yet been fully explained.

Although we can point out that proto-Nuer segmentary organization provided a conceptual basis for the recognition of agnatic relationships—and that proto-Nuer expansion produced de facto changes in the agnatic composition of local groups and the provenience of agnatic relationships between them—this is insufficient to account for the basic structural and conceptual changes that took place. We know from the work of both Evans-Pritchard (1940a; 1951a:28) and Sahlins (1965) that the empirical composition of local groups and the actual state of genealogical relations between descent groups does not require a strictly comparable conceptualization of the social order. It follows that de facto changes in these do not require a reconceptualization.

But then what does? This difficult question, central to an understanding of structural change, remains to be answered. The explanation we seek to develop here is that the same divergence in bridewealth systems that set in motion the processes leading to proto-Nuer expansion, and eventuating in the de facto changes noted above, also provided a basis for reconceptualization of the segmentary system. As was pointed out at the end of the last chapter, the early divergence with respect to the reciprocal payment entailed changes in the cultural valuation and representation of structurally central matrilateral relations (as well as changes in the magnitude of bridewealth payments that impinged on economic organization). Having established the nature of the de facto changes that resulted from proto-Nuer expansion, we are now in a position to consider the interplay between the bridewealth system and the segmentary system in the context of that transformation. However, it is first necessary to more fully delineate the proto-Nuer and proto-Dinka bridewealth systems. As a means to this end we begin by showing that the basic differences between these two cultural groups in the magnitude of bridewealth payments (instrumental to their original economic divergence) were not susceptible to changes resulting from that divergence, or from the process of territorial expansion stemming from it.

Although many aspects of proto-Nuer and proto-Dinka social and economic organization were transformed or markedly accentuated by the interactive coevolution of these two systems, long-standing differences between them in the magnitude of ideal and acceptable bridewealth payments were not altered. As was pointed out in chapter 3, the acceptable to ideal range of payments represents a mechanism for accommodating wide fluctuations in cattle per capita holdings without modification of these cultural conceptions themselves. An increase in the ratio of cattle population to human population among the proto-Nuer, and a corresponding decrease in this same ratio among the proto-Dinka, thus had a direct effect on the number of cattle transferred in actual transactions but only a muted effect on the conceptions governing these transactions, and hence on social requirements for cattle that are a product of the latter. However, changes in the magnitude of actual transactions had significant effects on other aspects of the proto-Nuer and proto-Dinka social systems.

Although the proto-Nuer cattle population increased manyfold as a consequence of successful raiding and unimpaired growth (facilitated by continuous expansion of grazing resources), the proto-Nuer human population also increased dramatically through the addition of reproductive females captured in raids. While the comparatively slower rate of growth of the human population insured an increase in the ratio of cattle population to human population, the growth of the human population nevertheless limited the expansion of cattle per capita holdings over the long term. Proto-Nuer territorial expansion within the homeland region thus produced a significant, but nevertheless limited increase in cattle per capita holdings that were comparatively high at the outset. This enabled the proto-Nuer to regularly exceed minimum bridewealth payments and to more frequently fulfill the conditions of the ideal payment in actual transactions.

This shift toward larger bridewealth payments entailed changes in the distribution of bridewealth among the kinsmen encompassed by the transaction. As explained in chapter 3, distribution is a function of the magnitude of bridewealth payments. Nuer minimal payments, which are approximately the same size as Dinka ideal payments, also most closely resemble the latter in their distributional characteristics. However, as the size of a Nuer payment increases within the minimal to ideal range, the proportion allocated to the bride's immediate family and patrikin also increases, while that allocated to the bride's matrikin declines. When the ideal payment is made, about three-fourths of the cattle accrue to the bride's patrilineage (her father, brothers, and patrikin) and the transaction has a decidedly patrilineal emphasis. It is predominantly a transaction between two agnatic groups (the groom's and bride's) in which the participation of maternal kinsmen is comparatively attenuated, and it is quite different from Dinka transactions in this respect. This change in the relative weighting of agnatic and matrilateral relationships in actual transactions reinforced and accentuated preexisting features of proto-Nuer bridewealth pertaining to the degree of interdependence between matrilateral and patrilateral kin. The significance of this will be explored later in this section.

Among the proto-Dinka, cattle per capita holdings decreased more markedly than they increased in the Nuer case. Although the combination of the loss of both cattle and reproductive females to proto-Nuer raids produced partially counterbalancing decreases in both the proto-Dinka human and cattle populations that tended to limit the decline in cattle per capita holdings, additional factors modified this outcome. A proto-Dinka population characterized by a comparatively high human density and a comparatively low cattle density was expelled by proto-Nuer territorial expansion within the homeland region and replaced by a proto-Nuer population with the inverse characteristic (i.e., lower human density and higher cattle density). In other words, the proto-Nuer did not appropriate proto-Dinka reproductive potential to the same extent that they appropriated proto-Dinka cattle and territory. The proto-Dinka human population therefore did not decrease in proportion to their losses of cattle and land. As neighboring proto-Dinka tribes were compressed into a portion of their former territorial domains, population density thus increased while cattle per capita holdings declined. Since population decline due to loss of reproductive females was only fully realized in subsequent generations, these effects were further exaggerated in the interim.

Displaced proto-Dinka tribesmen fled from communities overrun by proto-Nuer raids with the few cattle they were able to salvage. They consequently constituted a cattle-poor segment of the population in the communities where they sought refuge, increasing local human densities while adding little to the cattle population. The accommodation of a larger human population that derived a reduced proportion of its total nutritional requirements from cattle products necessitated increased reliance on agriculture and required an intensification of the agricultural component of the transhumant economy. This was effected by increasing both the quantity of land in production and the labor devoted to weeding and the protection of standing crops. Planting schedules were also elaborated. However, increased utilization of land for agricultural purposes necessarily restricted the quantity available for grazing. This precluded the recovery of the family herds of the refugee population to former levels and hence perpetuated a general decrease in cattle per capita holdings, while at the same time altering the relative importance of agriculture and animal husbandry within the proto-Dinka economic system.

As latecomers, refugees were allocated land on the margins of existing settlements, in an area subject to partial inundation in wet years. This marginal zone periodically lacked dry footings for their cattle and adequate wet season pasturage, further inhibiting growth in the size of family herds among this segment of the population. Unequal access to the resources essential to effective animal husbandry thus perpetuated an unequal distribution of cattle between refugee households and those of prior occupants of the settlement. Thus, while proto-Nuer raids and territorial expansion produced a reduction in the total cattle per capita holdings of neighboring proto-Dinka tribes, existing patterns of resource allocation among the proto-Dinka served to maintain and reproduce the differential impact of this reduction on different segments of the population.

Proto-Dinka conceptions of ideal bridewealth payments were unaffected by these changes, since there was in fact no change in the capacity of favored segments of the population to fulfill the conditions of the ideal transaction. Similarly, the absence of a rigidly defined minimum payment readily facilitated marriage among the cattle-poor portion of the population. As pointed out in chapter 3, the broad minimum to ideal range of Dinka bridewealth payments is consistent with, and accommodates, ingrained inequalities in the distribution of cattle among households. Such inequalities are themselves a product of differential access to the resources essential to animal husbandry that are embedded in the spatial component of the founder-latecomer organization of local groups. This form of organization and the broad range of Dinka bridewealth payments are mutually consistent and interlocking features of the Dinka social system. The Dinka (and proto-Dinka) bridewealth system was thus geared to marked disparities in cattle per capita holdings among households and need not have changed in order to accommodate those resulting from Nuer predation. Nuer cattle raids and Nuer territorial expansion did not create a class of cattle-poor Dinka that had not previously existed, but only augmented the membership of that class.[13] It should also be recalled that an explanation of the absence among the Dinka of an inflexible minimum bride-wealth payment (characteristic of neighboring Nilotic tribes) has already been proposed. This Dinka characteristic is intelligible as an adaptation to a differ-ential in the bridewealth payments of the proto-Nuer and proto-Dinka that would prevent the continual loss of reproductive females through outmar-riage. It is also noteworthy that Atwot oral traditions represent the historical differences between themselves and their Dinka neighbors concerning the reciprocal payment as having constituted a bar to intermarriage. Both of the distinctive features of the proto-Dinka (and Dinka) bridewealth system thus had the effect of curtailing intermarriage with neighboring proto-Nuer tribes that would have produced a net loss of proto-Dinka women.

Although the bridewealth system has a determinate effect on critical features of economic organization, it is capable of accommodating wide fluc-tuations in economic conditions and is thus largely unresponsive to economic change. As a result, the economic differentiation of the proto-Nuer and proto-Dinka resulting from initial differences in the magnitude of ideal bridewealth payments did not produce a modification of these two bridewealth systems. Initial differences were thus maintained.

As noted earlier, these initial differences in the magnitude of ideal bride-wealth payments are largely attributable to an early divergence with respect to the reciprocal payment, and this altered other features of bridewealth transac-tions as well. Proto-Nuer bridewealth differed from that of the proto-Dinka in displaying a reduction in the degree of interdependence between matrilateral kin and in the emphasis placed on the continuity of matrilateral relationships. These differences are significant inasmuch as they directly pertain to the matrilateral relations that are structurally central to the political system ini-tially shared by both the proto-Nuer and proto-Dinka, and also to the de facto changes that took place in the course of proto-Nuer expansion. Matrilateral relationships between founder and latecomer lines were not maintained in the generations following the departure of the latter to form new communities and this is consistent with the representation of these relationships in the proto-Nuer bridewealth system. In the following pages we seek to show that the bridewealth system historically shaped perceptions of the political system, that it played a significant role in the failure to reproduce structurally central matrilateral relationships during proto-Nuer expansion, and that it provided a basis for reconceptualizing the relationships between the newly formed local groups spawned by that expansion. This constitutes the general outlines of the argument to be developed.[14]

As noted in chapter 4, Dinka sublineages are conceptually defined by their members' common interest in bridewealth cattle. The parties to a Dinka bridewealth transaction are thus the minimal descent groups that constitute the building blocks of the Dinka social system. The transaction itself is characterized by the joint participation of matrilaterally related sublineages in the accumulation and redistribution of both the bridewealth and the reciprocal payment. Moreover, the reciprocal movement of cattle between these descent groups emphasizes both the significance and continuity of matrilateral relations—the same relations that are central to the organization of a Dinka subtribal camp and to the articulation of spearmaster and warrior subclans within the tribal polity as a whole. It is this resonance between the matrilateral relationships emphasized in bridewealth transactions and analogous relations within the larger segmentary system that is critical here. Bridewealth transactions do not constitute the larger system but rather provide a representation of it that is repeatedly enacted and experienced by social actors in the secular ritual of marriage that occurs regularly within every community. This is significant because the de facto transformation of relationships within and between proto-Nuer communities would effectively recontextualize those aspects of bridewealth transactions that drew their primary meaning from a broader context. The meaning of bridewealth transactions would thus change, providing a vehicle for the reconceptualization of central structural relationships. However, before developing this point we must first consider the initial differences between the proto-Nuer and proto-Dinka in their bridewealth systems.

Although the present Nuer and Dinka bridewealth systems differ, there are a number of points at which they more closely approximate each other. Discussion of these will clarify the nature of the initial divergence connected with changes in the reciprocal payment. While Dinka ideal bridewealth uniformly requires a reciprocal payment (*aruweth*) the latter is omitted in small payments of five cattle or less and limited to two cattle on a bridewealth of ten head. A few Nuer tribes also make a reciprocal payment (*thiuk*) of two animals, to which the bride's matrikin and patrikin each contribute equally. However, this constitutes a dowry assigned to the newly formed domestic group and is not shared among the maternal and paternal kinsmen on the groom's side of the transaction (as are Dinka reciprocal payments). The joint participation of matrilaterally related groups is thus manifested in a small way at one point in the proceedings, but is not a feature throughout. Similarly, among the Nuer, the mother's brother of the groom is not formally obligated to contribute to his nephew's bridewealth, although he may do so as a token of affection. The contribution thus betokens a personal kin relationship, in contrast to the formal obligation between matrilaterally related sublineages that dictates the matrikin's contribution in Dinka bridewealth accumulation. As noted earlier, the accumulation and redistribution of the Dinka reciprocal payment emphasizes the continuing significance of matrilateral relationships. Apart from the partial exception mentioned above, Nuer bridewealth lacks the reciprocal payment that provides this emphasis. However, the ideal bride-wealth payments of some Western Nuer tribes include a token recognition of prior generation's matrilateral relationships in the allocation of one calf apiece to the bride's father's mother's brother and mother's mother's brother. The continuing significance of matrilateral relationships is thus accorded some recognition, although this is slight in comparison with Dinka transactions. In both Nuer and Dinka transactions the bride's matrikin receive a significant portion of the bridewealth—25 percent or more—but again this is invariably smaller among the Nuer. While the Nuer minimal payment most closely approximates the Dinka ideal payment in terms of both size and distribution among participating kinsmen, it is noteworthy that the composition of the Nuer bridewealth herd is identical in minimal and ideal payments and is invariably quite different from that of the Dinka.

The main point that emerges from this comparison is that Nuer and Dinka bridewealth differ principally in degree. In general, Nuer bridewealth is larger, includes a higher proportion of male animals, displays a reduction in the degree of interdependence between matrilaterally related kin, and accords less emphasis to matrilateral relations between individuals and descent groups. These last two characteristics are of particular concern here. For virtually every feature of Dinka bridewealth transactions that involves ma-trilateral relationships, one can identify a corresponding feature among one or another of the Homeland Nuer tribes. However, in each case the Nuer version is a pale reflection of its Dinka counterpart. These differences are primarily connected to the Dinka-type reciprocal payment (*aruweth*) and, given the early divergence between the Nuer and Dinka with respect to this payment, they are thus attributable to the proto-Nuer and proto-Dinka as well.

Proto-Nuer segmentary organization originally resembled that of the Dinka and the initial divergence between these cultural (or subcultural) groups centered on changes in their respective bridewealth systems. These changes entailed differences of degree within a context of persisting similarities. In both cases the parties to a bridewealth transaction were minimal descent groups that constituted the basic units of the social system. In both cases the transaction entailed the joint participation of matrilaterally related kin or descent groups and accorded recognition to the importance and continuity of mother's brother–sister's son relationships—the same matrilateral relations central to the larger structural system. But within the context of these broader similarities, the proto-Nuer diverged in the direction of a diminished and restricted emphasis on the collaboration of matrilaterally related kin. The changes in proto-Nuer bridewealth can be seen to be interrelated, and they become intelligible as a series of sequential developments following from an initial divergence concerning the reciprocal payment.

The reciprocal payment characteristic of Dinka (and proto-Dinka) bridewealth provides for the prominent participation of matrikin in all phases of the proceedings. This participation also conveys a strong sense of mutuality as matrikin are seen to contribute substantially to both bridewealth and *aruweth*, as well as receiving the major portion of both payments (on the opposite sides of each respective transaction). However, this mutuality is one of appearance rather than substance. When one computes the net gains and losses from these complex transfers, it emerges that a man's matrikin actually contribute only one animal to his bridewealth payment while receiving thirteen of the twenty cattle accruing from his sister's marriage (based on Malwal Dinka data presented earlier).

Proto-Nuer bridewealth did not diverge from that of the proto-Dinka with respect to the token nature of the matrilateral contribution (which took the form of the mother's brother's bequest), or in the substantial portion of the bridewealth payment allocated to the matrikin. It continued to be the case that the latter received a great deal more than they gave. However, the proto-Nuer lacked the reciprocal payment (or type of reciprocal payment) that provided for the prominent *participation* of the groom's matrikin despite their minimal assistance in real terms. Proto-Nuer bridewealth thus lacked the concomitant display of mutuality and foregrounded the underlying reality—the fact that the matrikin receive many cattle and contribute few. This represented a change in the appearance, rather than substance, of matrilateral relations. However, the net effect was to render the patrilineal descent group much more visibly prominent in bridewealth accumulation and to forthrightly display what proto-Dinka bridewealth customs are designed to mute—the asymmetrical nature of the mother's brother–sister's son relationship.

It is important to note that the bridewealth systems of the proto-Nuer and proto-Dinka are both equally consonant with a social system in which asymmetrical matrilateral relations between founder and latecomer lines are central to the organization of local groups. They differ principally in the way in which the social system is represented to social actors, and in the latter's perception of social reality. However, these differences are quite significant and can be seen to have paved the way for further changes in proto-Nuer bridewealth.

As noted in chapter 3, both the Nuer and Dinka allocate about the same *number* of cattle to the bride's matrikin. This represents another area in which proto-Nuer and proto-Dinka bridewealth remained the same. However, the divergence with respect to the reciprocal payment significantly increased the magnitude of proto-Nuer bridewealth payments and thus changed their distributional characteristics. While the number of cattle accorded to the matrikin

remained unchanged, their proportion of the total payment declined and that
of the members of the bride's patrilineal descent group increased. Again, this
shift was one of degree. Nevertheless, it altered the flow of bridewealth cattle
such that animals derived from daughters' and brothers' daughters' marriages
exceeded those derived from sisters' daughters' marriages in providing incre-
ments to the family herd that would subsequently serve to fund a son's
marriage. The enhanced prominence of the groom's patrilineal descent group
in bridewealth accumulation (noted above) was thus reinforced by their correspondingly increased significance in practical terms.

Without the somewhat contrived mutuality provided by *aruweth*, the
matrikin's share of a bridewealth payment appears starkly disproportionate to
their contribution. Given kinship amity, and the ideology of a special affection of mother's brother toward sister's son, this requires some explicit ra-
tionale. The conception of the matrikin's share of bridewealth as a final
payment standing over from the bride's mother's marriage clearly provides
this. It is logical, in terms of this conception, that a man's matrikin would
receive a large portion of his sister's bridewealth but contribute little to his
own (with the latter contribution being a token of mother's brother's affection, and thus a tribute to the ideology noted above). However, at the same
time the concept of a "final payment" would tend to limit the matrikin's
claim to a relatively fixed amount. As a result of this the proportion allocated
to the matrikin would then vary, constituting a large portion of a smaller
payment and a small portion of a larger payment. The concept of a final
payment thus created the preconditions for the changes in distribution noted
above.

The reconceptualization of the matrikin's portion of bridewealth as a
final payment—rather than one phase in a reciprocal movement of cattle
between matrilaterally related groups—engendered further changes in the
meaning of the transaction. A "final payment" inescapably connotes finality,
the fulfillment of an outstanding obligation and the transformation of the
relationship between the parties formerly linked by it. In this respect, proto-
Nuer bridewealth lacked an emphasis on the continuity of matrilateral relationships manifested in the proto-Dinka counterpart. However, this was offset
to some extent by the allocation of one calf apiece to father's mother's brother
and mother's mother's brother. This provided recognition of the past generation's matrilateral relations and hence of the durability and continuing significance of matrilateral relations generally. The interpretation that this allocation
is an analogue of the reciprocal payment is supported by their complementary
distribution. The Dinka, who uniformly make reciprocal payments, also uniformly exclude the bride's parents' respective mothers' brothers in their ideal
bridewealth distribution, despite their generally greater emphasis on matrilateral relationships. The Aak and Jagei Nuer, who make a small reciprocal

payment of two animals, also lack this feature. The Lak, Thiang, Western Jikany, Leek, and Bul Nuer include father's mother's brother and mother's mother's brother in bridewealth distribution, but lack the reciprocal payment of the Aak and Jagei. Only the Dok Nuer appear to manifest both features. However, Howell (1954a:108) reports that the Dok were generally inconsistent in stating their ideal and this inconsistency may be indicative of a transitional state.

These data suggest that the proto-Nuer added the claims of father's mother's brother and mother's mother's brother to their ideal bridewealth distribution in order to maintain an emphasis on the continuity of matrilateral relations, an emphasis that was lost with the discontinuance of reciprocal payments and the resultant reconceptualization of the matrikin's portion as a final payment. This added feature appears among all Homeland and Western Nuer tribes that lack the small reciprocal payment (*thiuk*) except the Dok, and the latter appear to be in a state of transition between these two variants. The recognition of the mutuality and continuing significance of matrilateral relations expressed in the small reciprocal payment, and in the inclusion of the bride's parent's matrikin (respectively), are intelligible in the context of a proto-Nuer social system based on matrilateral relations between founder and latecomer lines.

As noted in chapter 3, the Western Jikany manifest an attenuated version of the father's mother's brother-mother's mother's brother allocation that alternates between these kinsmen on the marriage of successive daughters. The Eastern Jikany, derived from the latter, omit both claims and include father's father's brother's son in their place, as do the Lou. On Evans-Pritchard's report, the Lou and Eastern Jikany employ the same term to designate the father's father's brother's son's claim (*kethar*) that the Western Nuer use to designate the father's mother's brother's and mother's mother's brother's claim (see Howell, 1954a:104–5). The sequential nature and directionality of these changes in Nuer bridewealth is thus readily apparent, with the sequence proceeding from the small reciprocal payment to the *kethar* claims, which are then progressively modified and redefined, culminating in the Eastern Nuer version. The progressive shift in emphasis from matrilateral to patrilateral relationships parallels the transformation of the Nuer social system. This both raises the question of the precise nature of the relationship between these two sets of parallel transformations and lays the groundwork for answering it.

Initially, at ''time one,'' proto-Nuer ideal bridewealth differed from its proto-Dinka counterpart in that the former required only the small, dowry-type reciprocal payment (*thiuk*) while the latter required the extensive reciprocal payment (*aruweth*) entailing a return of one-third to one-half of the bridewealth cattle. As a result, proto-Nuer bridewealth transactions differed not only with respect to the concomitant sociological features identified in

preceding discussion, but also in the magnitude of ideal bridewealth payments. It has previously been established that the large Dinka-type reciprocal
payment accounts for differences between these two cultural groups in the
magnitude of ideal bridewealth payments and that the composition of the
bridewealth herd co-varies directly with the latter. The economically significant differences in bridewealth that engendered both the means and impetus to
proto-Nuer territorial expansion were thus established by the same divergence
in reciprocal payments that produced differences in sociological features. The
latter were thus in place at the time proto-Nuer expansion began, and were
consequently in a position to have played a role in the structural changes
wrought by it.

Despite these initial differences between the proto-Nuer and proto-Dinka
bridewealth systems, many features remained unchanged and many points of
similarity persisted. These are readily intelligible in terms of the relationship
between the proto-Nuer bridewealth system and social system, since the latter
continued to closely resemble that of the proto-Dinka. The changes that had
taken place entailed differences of degree, subtle shifts in the proportion of
the bridewealth payment allocated to matrikin, and a revision of the appearance rather than the substance of matrilateral relations. However, the
degree of interdependence between matrilateral kin declined while that between members of the patrilineal descent group increased. The latter also
emerged as much more visibly prominent in bridewealth accumulation. These
differences, which would not have appeared remarkable to an observer at the
time (circa 1600), acquired considerable significance in light of the subsequent changes in the proto-Nuer social system that accompanied their initial
expansion within the homeland region.

As the proto-Nuer expanded their territorial domain, latecomer lines split
off from existing communities to become the founders of new settlements in
the areas from which the proto-Dinka had been expelled. Under conditions of
territorial expansion, wet season settlement sites were widely available and
former latecomer descent groups could readily become founders. By the same
token, these new founder lines were unable to recruit matrilaterally related
descent groups to the comparatively unfavorable status of latecomer lines, and
thus failed to reproduce the original structure of interrelationships within (and
between) local groups. It may be argued that the proto-Nuer bridewealth
system—lacking the type of reciprocal payment that emphasized the mutuality of matrilateral relations and muted their asymmetrical characteristics—
played a role in social actors' perceptions of the unfavorable nature of
latecomer (and sister's son) status. It is important to recollect that the bridewealth system is a primary context in which the nature of particular kin
relations is encoded and that these evaluations are directly experienced by
social actors in bridewealth transactions. Moreover, the patrilineal descent

groups and matrilateral relations that play a role in bridewealth transactions paralleled the main structural features of the segmentary system.

The critical role of the bridewealth system in shaping conceptualizations of the larger social system can be further elucidated by a closer examination of the structurally pivotal mother's brother–sister's son relationship and the differential representation of it in the proto-Nuer and proto-Dinka bridewealth systems. This key relationship encompasses contradictory characteristics that are subject to quite different treatment in each case. The contradiction is readily apparent. On one hand, the mother's brother is considered to have a special affection for his sister's son (Lienhardt, 1958:119) and in this respect manifests the characteristics of the "male mother" specified by Radcliffe-Brown in his classic article on matrilateral relations in patrilineal systems (Radcliffe-Brown, 1952:15–31). On the other hand, founder lines are "mother's brothers of the camp," entitled to the most favorable central locations and occupying a position of nominal political authority over less favorably situated latecomer lines related as their sister's sons. Similarly, the master of the fishing spear occupies a position of spiritual authority over the leader of the warrior subclan, ideally related as his sister's son, and this encapsulates the relation between the spearmaster and warrior subclans that constitute the tribe as a whole.

The contradictory characteristics of these two kinds of mother's brothers pertain to different contexts or domains. It is the personal kin relationship between mother's brother and sister's son that the Dinka think of as "closer" than agnatic relationships and marked by a special affection, courtesy, and amity (Lienhardt, 1958:119). In contrast, the "maternal uncles of the camp" occupy a position of political authority within the community and the preeminent master of the fishing spear occupies a position of spiritual authority within the tribe. Here the matrilateral relation is located within the political domain and links descent groups (founder and latecomer lines in one instance, spearmaster and warrior subclans in the other).[15] This contextual distinction compartmentalizes the two types of matrilateral relations but offers no resolution of their contradictory characteristics. However, the bridewealth system provides a third context in which the contradiction can potentially be ameliorated, since matrilateral relationships between individuals and between groups both enter into bridewealth transactions, but without an intrinsic contextual segregation by time, space, or domain of activity. Indeed ego's senior mother's brother is both a personal kinsman and the representative of a matrilaterally related descent group in these transactions.

Among the proto-Dinka, matrilaterally related sublineages collaborate in the accumulation and redistribution of bridewealth payments, with the identity of these minimal descent groups being realized through their members' collective interest in the transaction. Moreover, the bride's (and her brother's) senior mother's brother serves as the representative of his descent group, responsible for the internal distribution of their share of the bridewealth payment. The groom's senior mother's brother is likewise the representative of his descent group, responsible for the internal distribution of their share of *aruweth*. But in each case, this individual is also the close kinsman who is seen as having a special affection for ego. The contextual distinction between two types of mother's brothers that each pertain, respectively, to individual and group relationships can thus be dissolved. The same person embodies both within the unitary framework of a secular ritual experienced as a whole.

The main thrust of the proto-Dinka bridewealth system is to capitalize on this dissolution by rendering the contradictory characteristics of the two kinds of mother's brothers as merely the two poles of reciprocity, give and take. Matrilateral contributions to both bridewealth and *aruweth* provide for a display of indulgent generosity that counterbalances, at least in spirit, a distribution that accords the largest portion of both payments to mother's brother and his descent group (consistent with their superordinate status). Both aspects of the mother's brother–sister's son relationship, derived from these different domains, are thus merged through their recontextualization as juxtaposed components of a fundamental reciprocity. The essential mutuality of these relationships is thus conveyed to participating social actors, and this representation provides the dominant ideology that governs perceptions of structurally central matrilateral relations within the political domain.[16]

In contrast, the proto-Nuer bridewealth system emphasizes the distinction between domains and thus maintains the compartmentalization of the contradiction rather than achieving a resolution of it. Both types of mother's brothers are represented, but on opposite sides of the transaction. The "male mother" contributes to the groom's bridewealth, as a token of affection, but does not otherwise play a role in the proceedings. Only the personal kin relation is invoked, and it is fundamentally asymmetrical in that the mother's brother gives but does not receive. On the other side of the transaction the superordinate mother's brother, together with other members of his descent group, receive a substantial share of the bridewealth payment. Inasmuch as this is seen to satisfy an outstanding debt, no reciprocity is required. Asymmetry is evident here as well. However, this is partially modified by the donation of a single cow to the bride's dowry (*thiuk*). Although available data do not specify the source of this animal, it is likely that it is provided by the senior mother's brother himself. This would serve to mark off the personal kin relation of mother's brother to sister's child from the matrilateral relation between descent groups in a manner consistent with other features of the transaction. Both are fundamentally asymmetrical, but are inversions of each other. The "male mother" gives out of affection, while the mother's brother's descent group receives by virtue of a superordinate relation. The distinctiveness of each type of matrilateral relationship is thus accentuated. The only unitary feature they share is their common asymmetry, which is realized in a different way in each case.

It is evident here that the bridewealth system addresses a fundamental contradiction concerning matrilateral relations, relations that are central to the political domain. The bridewealth system provides a representation of these relationships that is repeatedly enacted and experienced by social actors in the secular ritual of marriage that occurs regularly in every community. This recurrent experience governs actors' interpretations of these relationships and thus effectively shapes their perception of the larger political system. In light of this, it is necessary to modify the earlier statement that the proto-Nuer and proto-Dinka initially shared a common political system. While both systems were the same in terms of formal structural properties of group definition and interrelationship, they differed in terms of the ideology of matrilateral interrelationships between groups. The initial divergence in bridewealth systems changed the meaning of the central structural relation of the political domain while leaving its centrality unaltered.

These differences in the ideology of matrilateral relations had a direct bearing on the capacity of newly established founder lines to recruit descent groups related as sister's sons to the communities settled by the former. Given the proto-Nuer perception of matrilateral relations as fundamentally asymmetrical, the subordinate status of sister's sons (and latecomers) held little attraction. But by the same token, the subsequent development of client lineages of Dinka descent, related as sister's sons to community founders (and members of the dominant clan), was entirely consistent with Nuer ideology. Moreover, this pattern of relations reinforced the prevailing ideology since the subordinate status of sister's sons coincided with the analogous status associated with Dinka origin. (Ideological differences between the proto-Nuer and proto-Dinka also account for the maintenance of the Dinka political system under comparable conditions of territorial expansion. The proto-Dinka moved westward into the savannah-forest at the same time that proto-Nuer expansion was taking place within the homeland region. Although proto-Dinka expansion also entailed the fission of local groups, the prevailing ideology of mutual and reciprocal relations between founder and latecomer lines ensured the recruitment of the latter and thus the regeneration of prior patterns of community organization.)

The widespread fission of proto-Nuer settlements that took place in the course of territorial expansion within the homeland region repeatedly activated another contradiction intrinsic to the proto-Nuer political system (as well as that of the proto-Dinka), i.e., the mutual incompatibility of pre- and post-fission relationships. The matrilateral relationship between founder and latecomer lines that constitutes the basis of integration within wet season settlements, and the line of cleavage in fission, is an asymmetrical relation that is incompatible with the post-fission status of the emergent groups as coordinate units in a segmentary system. It is clear that the representation of matrilateral relations encoded in the proto-Dinka bridewealth system ameliorates this contradiction to some extent by emphasizing the mutuality of the mother's brother–sister's son relation in the political domain and muting the asymmetrical characteristics of it. However, the proto-Nuer bridewealth system foregrounds the asymmetrical characteristics of matrilateral relations in the political domain and thus accentuates the contradiction. This alteration was one of the important consequences of the divergence in bridewealth systems. It had the effect of attenuating former matrilateral relations between the segments of a proto-Nuer tribe at the same time that new patrilineal relationships, grounded in co-membership in a dominant clan, were being generated by the fission of wet season settlements along an agnatic line of cleavage. It is important to recall that agnatic relationships between segments were a regular feature of proto-Nuer (and proto-Dinka) tribes, but that such relationships linked only a limited number of segments. There was consequently a pre-existing basis for the recognition of such relationships in the political domain, and the initial change merely altered the provenience of agnatic (and matrilateral) relationships between segments. Tribal unity, which was largely grounded in joint herding at dry season pastures, therefore remained undiminished through the transitional period.

It is important to recall that the bridewealth transactions that are a recurrent feature of community life do not constitute the political system but rather provide a representation, in miniature, of the component groups and interrelationships that are central to it. This representation is empowered with the capacity to shape actors' perceptions of the political system by the resonance between the relationships emphasized in bridewealth transactions and analogous relations within the larger segmentary system. But at the same time, this analogy is selective. The nature of matrilateral relationships between descent groups, enacted in the accumulation and redistribution of the bridewealth payment, corresponds only to selective features of a more diffuse political reality subject to varying ideological conceptions (as the foregoing comparison reveals). Bridewealth transactions, as a representation of the political system, are thus effective in shaping actors' perceptions because they foreground selective aspects of the political realities with which they resonate.

This is significant because the de facto transformation of relationships within and between proto-Nuer communities recontextualized bridewealth transactions and thus altered the points of resonance in which their representational power was grounded. This altered the meaning of bridewealth, which, in turn, redefined the political system. The conceptualization of the matrikin's portion of bridewealth as a final payment was particularly important in this respect. In the context of the original proto-Nuer political system, this conceptualization had justified the disproportion between the token contribution of mother's brother and the substantial portion of bridewealth accorded the members of his descent group. It encoded an obligation to the latter that was both substantial and invariant, in acknowledgment of their superordinate status. However, this same conceptualization also contained a latent meaning. It implied the fulfillment of an outstanding obligation that effectively terminated the relationship between the groups linked by it. In a context in which former matrilateral relationships between founder and latecomer lines were consistently dissolved by fission and emigration, this meaning emerged forcefully and overshadowed the others. Transformed by a shifting point of resonance, the allocation of a substantial portion of bridewealth to the members of mother's brother's descent group thus became a model for the dissolution of matrilateral relations rather than a ratification of their structural centrality.

Other features of the proto-Nuer bridewealth system were similarly recontextualized. As explained earlier, the distribution of proto-Nuer bridewealth shifted in favor of the bride's patrilineal descent group as a consequence of the reduction in the reciprocal payment. This distributional characteristic was further accentuated as the proto-Nuer wealth in cattle increased in conjunction with territorial expansion, thereby increasing their capacity to regularly fulfill the conditions of the ideal payment in the actual transactions germane to actors' experience. This altered the flow of bridewealth cattle and thereby increased the degree of interdependence among patrilateral kin while at the same time rendering patrilineal descent groups much more visibly prominent in bridewealth accumulation and redistribution. These features of bridewealth transactions resonated with the characteristics of newly formed wet season settlements, largely composed of the members of a single agnatic group that constituted the dominant force in community affairs. Drawing representational significance from that resonance, bridewealth transactions thus reshaped conceptions of community organization.

The enhanced significance of agnation in proto-Nuer bridewealth likewise resonated with, and foregrounded, preexisting agnatic relationships between descent groups within the proto-Nuer segmentary system (i.e., the relationships between the main lineages of a subclan). These relationships constituted the basis of integration within the component subclans of a tribe. Moreover, they differed from the structurally central matrilateral relationships between founder and latecomer lines in that they had never been grounded in local organization, but rather linked localized lineage segments scattered among a number of wet season settlements. Their conceptual basis was consequently unimpaired by the processes of fission and emigration that progressively undercut matrilateral relationships. As fission at the tribal level transformed subclans into the dominant clans of the emergent tribes, the conceptual basis of integration within these major segments was promoted to the conceptual basis of segmentary inclusiveness within the tribe as a whole.[17] The critical role of the bridewealth system in this process is that it provided a model for the termination of matrilateral relations that effectively inhibited their regeneration at the apex of the segmentary order. Structurally central matrilateral relations had formerly constituted a line of cleavage in fission and single subclan tribes had previously been generated in the manner described above. However, such tribes had always reproduced their original prefission structure by drawing in new segments of spearmaster (or warrior) subclans to which they were matrilaterally related through recent marriages.

The role of the bridewealth system in reshaping actors' perceptions of the structural significance of matrilateral and patrilateral relationships within the larger segmentary order thus accounts for critical aspects of a structural transformation that cannot be explained as a mechanical product of de facto changes alone. But at the same time, these changes in the composition of local groups and the character of their external relations were instrumental in recontextualizing bridewealth transactions and thereby altering their meaning, such that they had the capacity to reshape perceptions. However, it is important to recall that these de facto changes resulted from a proto-Nuer territorial expansion that was itself a product of the effects of the bridewealth system on economic organization, and hence tribal size. At a more general level, we can thus see that an initial divergence in the bridewealth systems of the proto-Nuer and proto-Dinka had profound effects on a number of different aspects of the proto-Nuer sociocultural system and that there was a secondary process of mutual interaction among these that produced further changes. This initial divergence in bridewealth systems thus engendered not only the means and impetus to proto-Nuer territorial expansion but also the subsequent structural transformation of the segmentary system.

By 1800, the proto-Nuer had developed the distinctive characteristics of the Nuer, including the segmentary lineage system that has figured so prominently in the anthropological literature. Like the Dinka subclans from which it was derived, this lineage system was based on agnatic relationships between segments that were dispersed among wet season settlements. These relationships were not grounded in local organization or conceptually based on seasonal aggregation. A tribal organization based on such agnatic relationships thus had the capacity to transcend the limits that pasture distribution formerly imposed on tribal size. The Nuer advantage in tribal size was thus significantly increased, setting the stage for the rapid and massive territorial expansion that took place between 1800 and 1890.

In a brief survey of Nuer history, Howell (1954a:7) remarks that given the many cultural similarities between the Nuer and Dinka, and their derivation from a common stock, it remains a mystery why the Nuer should have emerged as a separate people with comparative suddenness about the beginning of the nineteenth century, driven the Dinka out of much of their country, seized so many of their women and cattle, and absorbed whole sections of Dinka into their own society.

While the Nuer conquest of more than twenty-six thousand square miles of Central Dinka and Anuak territory within the short span of seventy years continues to represent one of the most dramatic instances of tribal imperialism in the ethnographic record, it no longer remains an incomprehensible mystery. The impetus to Nuer expansion and the means through which it was effected have been elucidated, and the cultural divergence from a common stock that eventuated in the polarity of Nuer ascendancy and Dinka vulnerability is intelligible in terms of the same explanatory framework. What. remains is to draw some general conclusions concerning the structural characteristics of expansionist socieconomic systems.

CHAPTER 6

The Formal Causes
of Nuer Expansion

Although the proximate and efficient causes of Nuer territorial expansion have been elucidated, the formal causes pertaining to this phenomenon have not been fully explored. The development of this level of explanation constitutes the main focus of this concluding chapter. The principal objective here is to identify the structural characteristics of the Nuer sociocultural system that engendered a predisposition to unremitting territorial appropriation, i.e., the structural characteristics of an intrinsically expansionist system. In this context structure does not refer to social morphology, but to the relationships between relationships within the analytically identifiable ensemble of interconnections characteristic of the Nuer sociocultural system. The relations between the variables that constitute a homeostatic self-regulating system constitute a structure in this sense. However, the constitution of the analogous Nuer system of relations differs from the latter in important respects, and the elucidation of these differences will contribute to an understanding of its expansionist character. The general applicability of a prominent theoretical framework grounded in the concept of self-regulating systems is also at issue here. Rappaport's (1979) comprehensive formulation of this concept is thus assessed in relation to the Nuer case. Consideration of the theoretical issues this raises also furthers one of the more general objectives of this study, viz., to delineate the character and formal properties of the system of relations in which material causality is embedded.

A comparison of Nuer and Dinka economic organization also contributes to a specification of properties germane to Nuer expansionism. Of particular importance here are differences that pertain to the effects of exchange-based objectives (grounded in the bridewealth system) upon the organization of production. There are also noteworthy differences between the Nuer and Dinka in redistributive aspects of economic organization and particularly in the redistributive features of their respective bridewealth systems. These differences are considered in a later section of the chapter with a view to delineating the characteristics that are instrumental to Nuer expansionism, and to the constitution of intrinsically expansionist systems more generally. However, it is first necessary to show that expansionism was inherent to the constitution of the Nuer sociocultural system.

The insatiable character of Nuer territorial expansion is its most striking characteristic. We have seen that the Nuer increased their territorial domain fourfold within the short span of seventy years (1820–90). In the 1870s, after the bulk of these gains had already been secured, the Nuer launched a major invasion of Anuak country that penetrated 140 miles to the extreme southwest border of the latter. Nuer settlement of this vast area was precluded only by the depletion of their herds (due to trypanosomiasis). Nuer expansion was thus checked in this instance by extrinsic environmental limitations. The cessation of Nuer expansion in the early 1890s was likewise externally induced. The introduction of rinderpest drastically reduced the Nuer cattle population and obviated the recurrent dry season grazing shortages that provided the immediate impetus to round after round of territorial appropriation. Although Nuer expansion was thus capable of being halted by external forces, the operation of the Nuer sociocultural system over time provides no indication of internal limits or constraints.

This apparent absence of internal limits and constraints frames the central questions we seek to answer concerning the formal causes of Nuer territorial expansion. Was the Nuer sociocultural system constituted so as to provide an unending, internally generated impetus to territorial appropriation? Does the system entirely lack countervailing internal mechanisms that would come into play at some point? Is there a point at which expansion would cease due to the fulfillment of Nuer conceptions of ideal conditions? If these conditions were not fulfilled during the course of the nineteenth-century territorial expansion are they in some way unattainable? The larger issue to which these questions pertain is whether the Nuer sociocultural system was internally regulated or merely externally constrained.

A review of the operation of the Nuer socioeconomic system through several successive rounds of territorial expansion will lay the groundwork for answering the questions posed above. This will show that continuing expansion entails progressive changes in human density and cattle per capita holdings. These changes tend toward the fulfillment of Nuer ideals, which can also be specified. This will provide a framework for assessing the potential for their attainment.

The Nuer cattle population is food-limited and consequently tends to increase until it reaches the limits imposed by available dry season grazing. The shortages that occur at this point lead to Nuer encroachment on Dinka dry season pastures, engendering conflict along Nuer borders. The raids carried out by the Nuer during the rainy season tend to be directed against the wet season settlements of the Dinka groups with whom they have come into conflict over pastures, and these raids eventually precipitated the abandon-

ment of these settlements and the contested dry season pastures associated
with them. The resultant enlargement of Nuer grazing resources temporarily
alleviated dry season shortages, but at the same time set the stage for the rapid
growth of the food-limited cattle population. The capacity of the latter to
increase at 3.5 percent per annum under these conditions insured that the
sequence of events outlined above would soon recur. Cattle acquired in the
course of the raids through which pasture was expanded likewise contributed
to the rapid reestablishment of shortages.

While a new round of expansion would take place when the cattle population had once again bred up to the limits of dry season pasture (and attained
maximum density), other variables would not have returned to the same states
that obtained at the inception of the previous enlargement of Nuer territory.
More specifically, human density would be lower and cattle per capita holdings higher. Although the population of Nuerland was augmented by the
assimilation of captured and displaced Dinka, these additions were limited to
about half of the original Dinka population of the appropriated territory.
Moreover, the internal growth rate of the disease-limited human population
was negligible in comparison to that of the food-limited cattle population.
Each successive round of territorial appropriation thus took place at progressively lower human population densities. Cattle per capita holdings progressively increased, since more cattle than Dinka were incorporated into the
Nuer system and the former population grew much more rapidly than the
latter. The resultant augmentation of family herds was entirely consistent with
Nuer objectives. This raises the possibility that the Nuer might have
eventually acquired sufficient cattle to satisfy their culturally defined requirements. This question will be addressed shortly.

Although Nuer expansion entailed a progressive decline in human density and a progressive increase in cattle per capita, the extent of these progressive changes was ultimately limited by the Nuer practice of assimilating
captured and displaced Dinka on a massive scale. If the Nuer regularly incorporated nearly half of the former Dinka population of the territory they appropriated (as was the case historically), Nuer density could never fall below a
certain point. Gains in cattle per capita holdings would likewise be limited.
This can be illustrated by considering the estimated changes in Nuer population density and cattle per capita holdings that took place historically, and by
evaluating the potential effects of further territorial gains (accompanied by the
characteristic rate of assimilation).

In chapter 2 it was estimated that the Nuer population increased from
about 127,000 to 200,000 persons between 1818 and 1890 while the Nuer
territorial domain was expanded from 8,700 to 35,000 square miles. Nuer
population density thus declined from 14.6 to 5.7 persons per square mile
during this period. If the cattle population were at maximum levels at both of

these dates, this decline in human density would entail a 156 percent increase in cattle per capita holdings (or 256 percent of initial holdings). However, the Nuer cattle population would not have had an opportunity to increase to the capacity of recently acquired territory in 1890, so the gain in cattle per capita holdings would be somewhat less. As the cattle population increased, the human population would also increase due to the delayed effects of the prior incorporation of substantial numbers of reproductive females during the course of territorial expansion. For the purposes of discussion, it will thus be assumed that the Nuer population would increase by 10 percent (to 220,000) by the time the cattle population reached maximum density. At that point Nuer density would be 6.29 persons per square mile and cattle per capita holdings would be 132 percent greater than they had been in 1818.

The consequences of further territorial gains can be illustrated in relation to these figures. Suppose the Nuer appropriated the remainder of Southern Dinka territory (the Bor District) and assimilated 47 percent of the resident population. This would add about 4,000 square miles to the Nuer domain and 20,000 persons to their population.[1] Nuer density would then decline from 6.29 to 6.15 persons per square mile. Cattle per capita holdings would advance from a 132 to a 137 percent increment above 1818 levels. The gains in cattle per capita holdings are quite small, both in relation to previous gains and relative to the amount of territory added. Given a constant 47 percent rate of assimilation, changes in cattle per capita holdings and human density necessarily become progressively smaller as Nuer density approaches a figure equivalent to half the density of the Dinka territory appropriated. In other words, increases in cattle per capita holdings would conform to the pattern of an S-shaped growth curve. If the density of Dinka territory appropriated were 10 persons per square mile, Nuer cattle per capita holdings would stabilize at about 160 percent above 1818 levels.[2]

It is important to note that Nuer assimilation of very large numbers of captured and displaced Dinka also had the effect of insuring the continuation of Nuer expansion by preventing Nuer population density from falling to a point where they would be unable to dislodge their more densely settled Dinka neighbors or hold the territory they had seized. Massive assimilation thus perpetuated Nuer expansion by precluding the development of conditions incompatible with its continuation. In other words, the process of territorial expansion, as a whole, entailed the systematic reproduction of conditions conducive to further expansion. This included the reproduction of dry season grazing shortages and the maintenance of sufficient personnel to implement the Nuer organizational advantage in raiding.

The question of Nuer culturally defined requirements for cattle and the potential for their fulfillment remains to be addressed. Nuer cattle provide essential components of the diet, constitute the primary medium of exchange in social transactions, and play a central role in ritual. The number of cattle that the Nuer would require for these three purposes—under ideal conditions—can be roughly assessed. It can then be shown that Nuer cultural requirements are in excess of the upper limit of cattle per capita holdings attainable through raiding and territorial expansion.

Although the Nuer rely heavily on grain, they express a disdain for agricultural pursuits and regard the latter "as toil forced upon them by poverty of stock" (Evans-Pritchard, 1940*a*:1). The Nuer consequently seek to increase family herds in order to reduce the size of their cultivations. The ideal state to which they aspired was one in which agriculture was largely unnecessary (ibid.). Inasmuch as grain provided about two-thirds of caloric intake and milk and meat about 23 percent, the attainment of this ideal would necessitate 290 percent more cattle per capita than the Nuer possessed in the 1950s (from which these nutritional data are derived). However, we have seen that the Nuer capacity to increase cattle per capita holdings through territorial appropriation was limited by assimilation of the Dinka and by the necessity of maintaining sufficient population density to hold conquered territory. These limits were well below the levels necessary for an entirely pastoral existence. It is unlikely that the Nuer could have reduced their dependence on grain to less than one-third of total caloric intake.[3] Nuer pastoral aspirations thus constituted an unattainable goal, but one toward which the Nuer might continue to strive. The possibility of reducing the area under cultivation (and thus agricultural labor) would continue to appeal to individual actors.

While pastoralism represented an ultimate Nuer objective, the accumulation of bridewealth cattle was of much more immediate concern. Bridewealth requirements dictated the growth objectives and composition of family herds and thus constituted the primary factor affecting herd management practices. The acquisition of cattle for bridewealth was also one of the principal motives for participating in raids against Dinka wet season settlements.

Although a marriage could be contracted for as little as eighteen head of cattle, the ideal bridewealth payment required thirty-two to forty head (varying from tribe to tribe as explained in earlier chapters). Only this ideal payment fully satisfied the claims of the "people of rights" and this was what every individual hoped to achieve. Evans-Pritchard (1940*a*:20) reports that this was in fact achieved in the later stages of Nuer expansion.[4]

> All Nuer agree that in the last generation their herds were more considerable and that the payment of bride-wealth and blood-wealth were forty, and sometimes fifty to sixty, head of cattle, whereas today the kinsmen of the bride do not expect to receive more than twenty to thirty.

It is evident that ideal bridewealth requirements did not effectively limit or constrain the magnitude of bridewealth payments, since amounts far in excess of the ideal are reported here. Although fulfillment of the terms of the ideal transaction represented the attainment of one important social goal entailing satisfaction of the recognized claims of the ''people of rights,'' there was an additional goal to be achieved by still larger payments. This is explicitly specified in the wedding ceremony itself. The master of ceremonies (who is a member of a lineage collateral to that of the bride and represents higher-order agnatic groups) delivers a long address, during the course of which he invokes the spear-name of the clan and

> calls on the ghosts of the bride's ancestors to witness that she is married openly with fifty cattle (it is conventional to say this number) and not with shame and by stealth. (Evans-Pritchard, 1951a:66; see also 1956:287–88)

This discourse has no relevance to bridewealth negotiations, which have already been settled. The fifty cattle mentioned also bears no relationship to the size of the actual bridewealth agreed upon, which was characteristically half this amount during the period the text was recorded. The master of ceremonies thus employs poetic license, saying in effect that the bridewealth was a princely sum and not a pittance (or ''a steal''). However, it is noteworthy that the hyperbole does not denote the ideal bridewealth payment but an amount well above this. Moreover, the latter is contrasted with shameful circumstances.

The objective of exceeding the ideal is thus explicitly endorsed. Payments of this magnitude honored both the parties to the transaction, and conveyed the elevated social standing of the groom's family vis-à-vis their peers in one of the few ways that was acceptable within the context of a generally egalitarian ethos. Bridewealth payments were thus evaluated in terms of a comparative social metric that was intrinsically unbounded. The sum that the Nuer aspired to transfer would always be in excess of both the ideal and the prevailing rate, and would rise as the latter increased. The accumulation of sufficient cattle per capita to meet ideal bridewealth requirements on a regular basis therefore did not diminish the Nuer's desire to add to their herds, and to the territory necessary to maintain them. The invasion of Anuak country at a time when cattle per capita holdings were probably already sufficient to fund bridewealth payments of forty cattle supports this conclusion. In sum, culturally defined requirements for bridewealth cattle were effectively unlimited.

The payment of bridewealth in excess of the ideal indicates that social objectives took precedence over more narrowly defined economic goals. The herds of the groom's family and kin were substantially reduced by the transfer of bridewealth cattle and this necessitated a corresponding increase in household agricultural production in order to satisfy nutritional requirements. A bridewealth payment of fifty to sixty head of cattle (rather than thirty-two or

forty) further augmented this increased dependence on agricultural production, although the latter condition was directly contrary to the Nuer's pastoral
aspirations. The groom's family and kin were required to do no more than
meet the stipulated ideal, and the successful arrangement of a union was not
contingent upon satisfying requests for additional cattle. The provision of
such cattle would thus be inexplicable, from the actor's point of view, unless
the social objectives fulfilled by this took precedence over the desire to reduce
agricultural production (thereby reducing agricultural labor and moving toward satisfaction of dietary preferences).

This substantiates the point that bridewealth-related concerns were central to herd management practices. Economic and social goals were partially
consistent with respect to the accumulation of cattle, but diverged at the point
when cattle were deployed in bridewealth or other social transactions. In other
words, the same cows designated for eventual inclusion in a son's bridewealth
payment also facilitated reduced agricultural production in the interim. However, the accumulation of bullocks and oxen for bridewealth purposes did not
contribute to the Nuer objective of reducing their reliance on grain, since male
animals held in reserve for future exchange provided neither milk nor meat. It
is evident that bridewealth effectively organizes economic production and that
objectives inconsistent with bridewealth requirements are of secondary importance. We will see that this point is equally applicable to ritual sacrifice.

Ritual requirements for cattle remain to be considered. The central role
that cattle play in Nuer ritual is concisely summarized by Evans-Pritchard
(1940*a*:18):

> A man establishes contact with the ghosts and spirits through his cattle. If one is
> able to obtain a history of each cow in a kraal, one obtains at the same time not
> only an account of all the kinship links and affinities of the owners but also of all
> their mystical connexions. Cows are dedicated to the spirits of the lineage of the
> owner and of his wife and to any personal spirit that has at some time possessed
> either of them. Other beasts are dedicated to ghosts of the dead. By rubbing ashes
> along the back of a cow or ox one may get in touch with the spirit or ghost
> associated with it and ask it for assistance. Another way of communicating with
> the dead and with spirits is by sacrifice, and no Nuer ceremony is complete
> without the sacrifice of a ram, he-goat, or ox.

The cows that are dedicated to ghosts and spirits are retained by their
owners although they may ultimately be sacrificed (and one of their future
male calves is marked for sacrifice) (Evans-Pritchard, 1956:261). These cows
are consequently withheld from deployment in social transactions and are
secure from the claims of a bride's family and kin during bridewealth negotiations. However, the milk production of these same animals supports the
household, and cows that provide basic subsistence would be reserved in any

event. This form of ritual designation consequently appears to add little to Nuer cultural requirements for cattle. A more precise assessment would require additional data (that are unavailable) concerning the number of cows actually dedicated to ghosts and spirits by a sample of Nuer households.

The sacrifice of an ox fulfills ritual purposes while at the same time reducing the family herd. Sacrificial requirements therefore run counter to the tendency toward the accumulation of cattle that is embedded in Nuer bridewealth custom and in their pastoral aspirations. Comparison with the Dinka indicates that more frequent sacrifice would have the potential to reduce Nuer grazing requirements by 27 percent, thereby ameliorating the grazing shortages that provided a recurrent impetus to territorial appropriation. The Nuer's failure to realize this potential is clearly attributable to the fact that substantial numbers of oxen and bullocks are required for inclusion in Nuer bridewealth payments (but not in those of the Dinka). Moreover, many of the ritual occasions that entail the sacrifice of an ox are not urgent and may readily be deferred for extended periods of time (Evans-Pritchard, 1940a:26). There is typically an extensive backlog of unfulfilled ritual commitments. Although an ox should ideally be sacrificed on most occasions, an infertile cow, ewe, wether, nanny goat, or castrated billy goat may be substituted (Evans-Pritchard, 1956:202). Thus while ideal cultural requirements for the sacrifice of oxen are high, effective requirements are relatively slight due to deferrals and substitutions. This accommodates the accumulation of oxen and bullocks for bridewealth purposes.

Although the discussion has focused on the instrumental value of cattle in subsistence, exchange, and ritual, it is important to note that cattle also played a central symbolic role in the Nuer cultural system. This is equally true of the Dinka, and Ortner (1973:1340) points out that Lienhardt's delineation of the place of cattle in Dinka thought is one of the best exemplifications of the concept of key symbols. Dinka perceptions of color are based on the color configurations of cattle (Lienhardt, 1961:23, cited in Ortner, 1973:1340). The morphology of a sacrificial bull or ox metaphorically encodes relationships of kinship, descent, and coresidence that are realized in the distribution of its component parts in accordance with these relationships (ibid.). In the distribution of bridewealth cattle—as in the distribution of the portions of a sacrificial animal—cattle are vehicles for the conceptualization of relationships of kinship and descent that are central to the organization of the local group and the wider tribal polity. Although there are important differences between the Nuer and Dinka in bridewealth custom, bridewealth is a key symbol in both cultural systems (in addition to cattle themselves). This is equally true of sacrifice. However, among the Nuer the flesh of the sacrifice is distributed among the same kinsmen who receive bridewealth cattle and apportioned on the pattern of bridewealth distribution (Evans-Pritchard, 1951a:62, 66–67;

1956:214, 287–89). Bridewealth and collective sacrifice not only resonate, but also constitute alternative means of presenting a common symbolic representation of the social order.[5] In terms of distinctions drawn by Ortner (1973), bridewealth and sacrifice are key symbols of the elaborating type in which cattle are vehicles for the conceptualization of relationships. Cattle per se are also key symbols of the summarizing type by virtue of the wide variety of contexts in which they serve as vehicles for the conveyance of meaning. (These contexts are extensive; for example the Nuer designate the leading figure in the local group as the "bull of the camp" and many other cattle-based metaphors could be adduced.) The main point here is that cattle have a symbolic value that transcends their instrumental role in subsistence, exchange, and ritual. This value is contingent upon, but greater than, the sum of these analytic parts.

Although the value of cattle cannot be reduced to any one of the dimensions discussed in this section, a clear set of priorities is nevertheless evident in the manner in which cattle are utilized. In other words, instrumental values can be ranked. We have seen that the accumulation of oxen and bullocks did not contribute to the Nuer objective of reducing agricultural production. The more frequent sacrifice of male animals would have not only increased meat consumption, enabling the Nuer to reduce their agricultural efforts accordingly, but would also have contributed to the satisfaction of an extensive backlog of ritual commitments. However, the achievement of these two cultural objectives was clearly less compelling than the accumulation of oxen and bullocks for eventual deployment in social transactions. The payment of bridewealth in excess of the ideal further substantiates this point. Such payments included cattle that could have been withheld for sacrifice or for furtherance of economic objectives. These transactions also indicate that the accumulation of cattle was not a primary goal (else cattle in excess of the ideal would have been retained). Cattle on hand that represented an analogue of "discretionary income" were deployed in bridewealth transactions and this utilization clearly emerges as the highest priority.

The channeling of available cattle into bridewealth transactions—and the resultant tendency of prevailing bridewealth payments to increase as cattle per capita holdings increased—are explicable in terms of the significance of bridewealth as a key symbol. Bridewealth inflation followed from the desire of social actors to contribute a meaningful number of cattle, in relation to their current holdings, given the social and symbolic significance of the event. It would be as inappropriate for a father to contribute a pittance to his son's bridewealth (relative to the number of cattle he possessed) as it would be for the bride's father to agree to accept it. The same logic applied to other kin relations encompassed by the transaction.

Although bridewealth inflation was a product of the impact of symbolic significance on practice, such inflation also effectively maintained the relative value of a system of relations that provided a model for the social order vis-à-vis the more diffuse and evolving social practices that were ordered and rendered meaningful by it. In other words, bridewealth inflation prevented the devaluation of a key symbol and its displacement from a key position in the symbolic system. This precluded a direct revaluation, through practice, of the relations between kin relations that bridewealth encoded while at the same time facilitating a more gradual evolution of this key symbol through reconceptualization (cf. Sahlins, 1981:70–72).[6] However, the maintenance of key position was itself a consequence of the impact of symbolic significance on practice (as noted above). The latter generated the bridewealth inflation that insured the former.

The set of priorities delineated above was instrumental to the maintenance of a continuing impetus to Nuer expansion. If the Nuer had slaughtered a larger proportion of their male animals in a manner consistent with their ritual commitments and pastoral aspirations, their grazing requirements would have been substantially reduced. The grazing shortages that prompted expansion would have occurred far less frequently and the Nuer territorial domain would have been much less extensive in 1890.

It is evident from the preceding discussion that Nuer territorial expansion would not cease at some definable point due to the fulfillment of culturally defined requirements for cattle. This was largely due to the fact that Nuer goals pertaining to cattle were not directed to the maintenance or reproduction of existing conditions but to substantial quantitative changes in those conditions. The Nuer did not seek to maintain a traditional relationship between the agricultural and herding components of their economy but espoused a desire to radically alter the relationship between them. The Nuer conception of their subsistence requirements consequently entailed cattle per capita holdings that were both well above traditional levels and, in practical terms, unattainable. Similarly, the Nuer did not seek to match the prevailing bridewealth payments of the preceding generation, or merely to fulfill the terms of the ideal transactions, but to exceed both by a socially impressive margin. Nuer objectives with respect to the magnitude of bridewealth payments were governed by their aspiration to make reality conform to the hyperbolic description of it contained in the wedding address. These objectives were thus perpetually subject to upward revaluation and were, by their very nature, unattainable. The social and symbolic significance of bridewealth transactions was thereby maintained, but in a manner that precluded the fulfillment of cultural requirements for bridewealth cattle while at the same time encouraging continual striving toward this objective.

Limits intrinsic to the expansion process also rendered Nuer goals unattainable, and this outcome was thus doubly determined. The massive assimilation of captured and displaced Dinka that took place in conjunction with territorial expansion insured that increases in cattle per capita holdings would become progressively smaller with each new territorial gain and ultimately cease entirely. The maximal level of cattle per capita holdings that could be achieved was not sufficient to satisfy Nuer pastoral aspirations.

The high rate of assimilation that was the source of this upper limit was also instrumental to the perpetuation of Nuer expansion insofar as it precluded the development of conditions incompatible with its continuation. Moreover, the historical evidence indicates that the rate of assimilation increased as Nuer density declined (being greatest in the eastern region, during the final phases of expansion). There is consequently no identifiable trend toward reduced assimilation that would enable one to forecast the eventual development of conditions under which Nuer expansion might cease. There is, in short, no evidence that the analytically identifiable ensemble of interrelationships characteristic of the Nuer sociocultural system manifests internal regulatory properties conducive to the cessation of territorial expansion.

THE PROPERTIES OF AN EXPANSIONIST SYSTEM

The Nuer case thus raises an important issue concerning the general applicability of analytic models based on the concept of a self-regulating system. The theoretical prominence of this framework is largely attributable to Rappaport's (1967) well-known study of the Maring which employs such a model to show that ritual regulates the density of both a human population and a domestic animal population (pigs), as well as the frequency of armed conflict. The variables subject to regulation thus parallel those important in Nuer territorial expansion and the contrasts between the two cases are also of interest in this respect. While Rappaport does not expect that this constellation of variables will typically be ritually regulated, he does propose that the more general concept of self-regulation is intrinsic to adaptation and therefore applicable, in principle, to every ethnographic case (Rappaport, 1979:147). This suggests that the variables denoted above should be encompassed within a self-regulating system of some sort. The nature of this system, and the extent to which it displays self-regulating properties, is the central issue.

The importance of the Nuer case should be noted here. Given their evolutionary success (and the presumed relation between adaptiveness and the latter), the Nuer potentially constitute a significant exception rather than the inevitable ringer that haunts virtually every anthropological generalization. The main goal of the present inquiry is not simply to adduce an exception but rather to elucidate the distinctive features of a continuously expanding system that is of considerable relevance to evolutionary and adaptive theory. It should not be surprising that such a system would manifest characteristics foreign to the model of a self-regulating system principally designed to illuminate homeostasis. The point is to specify the nature of these differences. For these purposes, I will employ the general model of self-regulation developed by Rappaport (1979) as a standard for comparison. This model represents the most sophisticated and comprehensive formulation of concepts that are broadly applied within the field of ecological anthropology.[7]

An adaptive self-regulating system maintains the states of crucial variables within a range of viability consistent with the persistence of the system (Rappaport, 1979:147). The range of viability (or goal range) is typically defined in relation to biological or ecological limits, such as the point at which environmental degradation occurs. Causal factors that contribute to the development of nonviable states are termed *stressors* and characteristically take the form of environmental perturbations external to the system (ibid.:161). Mechanisms internal to the system reverse the effects of stress. The most significant of these are variable-dependent negative feedback mechanisms.

A change in the value of a variable itself initiates a process that either limits further changes or returns the value to its former level. (Ibid.:72)

Equilibration frequently takes place with respect to culturally defined "reference values" rather than the goal ranges pertaining to the limits of viability (ibid.:67). A thermostatically controlled heating system thus regulates the temperature of a confined space with respect to reference values far above the point at which the pipes begin to freeze or the survival of the occupants is threatened. However, Rappaport (1979:70) points out that the reference values to which negative feedback mechanisms are linked may also exceed the upper or lower limits of the goal range. The relation between reference value and goal range is taken to be an empirical question. A system in which the former is inconsistent with the latter is considered maladaptive (ibid.:70, 145–71).

The operation of the Nuer system conforms to the aspects of Rappaport's formulation concerned with reference value equilibration. An increase in cattle density to the point where grazing shortages occur stimulates territorial appropriation, which in turn reduces cattle density to a level where grazing is adequate (temporarily). Territorial expansion may thus be construed as a negative feedback mechanism and maximum cattle density as the reference value that initiates compensatory adjustment.

However, the regulatory sequence outlined above was unrelated to the maintenance of crucial variables within biologically or ecologically defined ranges of viability essential to the persistence of the system as constituted. Although the enlargement of grazing resources reduced cattle density to a level compatible with the maintenance of the existing cattle population, this merely accommodated an accumulation of cattle that was not vital to biological survival, or to the conservation of an institutional status quo, but to the attainment of cultural objectives that transcended present conditions. If the Nuer had not added to their territory, grazing shortages would have curtailed the growth of the food-limited cattle population, maintaining cattle density at a level compatible with available resources.[8] The resultant size of Nuer herds would have been ample to insure both biological and institutional persistence. Although cattle density was temporarily reduced by territorial enlargement, this compensatory adjustment was neither necessary (since cattle density would have declined in any event) nor vital to the persistence of the system.

At issue here is the nature of the relationship between a culturally defined reference value and a biologically or ecologically defined goal range. Equilibration with respect to the former appears unrelated to the latter. The upper limits of the goal range are difficult to specify because they were never approached. There is no evidence that environmental degradation constituted a potential problem. Overgrazing of critical dry season pastures was precluded by high water levels that rendered them inaccessible during the years when shortages occurred. On the clay soils characteristic of the Nuer homeland, *Striga hermonthica* infestation prompted abandonment of an agricultural plot to fallow long before soil fertility declined, thereby precluding destructive overutilization (see note 13, chap. 3). The environment was thus protected by its intrinsic characteristics and invulnerable to degradation at the hands of the Nuer (given their available technology). The disease-limited status of the Nuer human population (before 1920) also maintained human density at levels far below ecological limits. In other words, the ecosystem was independently secure from degradation. Environmental relations pertinent to the latter were neither ordered, nor capable of being disordered, by human agency.[9] Equilibration with respect to culturally defined reference values therefore did not maintain the states of crucial ecological variables within a range of viability or cause that range to be exceeded.

Although the Nuer system is not self-regulating in terms of criteria fundamental to Rappaport's formulation, consideration of the applicability of the latter reveals essential properties of the system connected with reference value equilibration. We have seen that territorial appropriation operated as a variable-dependent negative feedback mechanism that reduced cattle density to a viable level compatible with the maintenance of the existing cattle population. The system may thus be described as self-regulating with respect to this variable. However, territorial appropriation also insured the growth of the food-limited cattle population to the former density at which grazing shortages had occurred. In this respect, the system may be described as self-destabilizing. This combination of self-regulating and self-destabilizing attributes is the essential feature of the Nuer system and largely accounts for its constitutional predisposition to unremitting territorial expansion.

Nuer herd management practices, governed principally by bridewealth requirements, insured the growth of the Nuer cattle population to the point at which dry season grazing shortages occurred. These were temporarily alleviated by territorial acquisition that also regenerated shortages, both in itself and by the accumulation of cattle in the course of the raids through which it was effected. The consequences of territorial appropriations were thus self-contradictory.

Human density was likewise reduced by expansion, only to be increased both by the incorporation of substantial numbers of reproductive females taken in raids, and by the extensive assimilation of displaced Dinka. The same raids that facilitated expansion also generated a desperate population of Dinka refugees seeking to join the Nuer. The more Nuer density declined, through territorial appropriation, the more the rate of assimilation increased. The consequences of expansion were thus self-contradictory with respect to human density as well as cattle density.

These self-contradictory effects of Nuer territorial expansion were responsible for the fact that self-regulation entailed self-destabilization. The operational sequence may be more precisely described as follows: an increase in the value of the variable "cattle density" to a reference point (dry season grazing shortages) initiated a process of territorial expansion that reduced cattle density temporarily, but at the same time sowed the seeds of future increases, insuring a repetition of the sequence. Territorial expansion thus manifests the properties of both a negative feedback mechanism and a stressor (i.e., a causal factor contributing to the development of a nonviable state of a key variable). The destabilizing effects of expansion do not appear to fit the principal characteristic of a positive feedback mechanism since deviations from reference values are introduced (after a time lag) rather than amplified.[10]

The Nuer system would be somewhat analogous to a temperature control system in which the thermostat turned on the furnace at 65°, shut it off at 68°, and at the same time turned on an air conditioner, insuring a decrease in temperature to 65°, at which point the air conditioner is shut off and the furnace activated. Such a system regulates the temperature of a confined space, but without any reference to environmental conditions grounded in nature.

In the Nuer case equilibration also takes place with respect to the state of a variable that is effectively determined by the operation of the system itself, and insulated from environmental inputs. Paradoxically, the internally generated stress to which the system responds is partially a product of highly successful regulatory responses to environmental perturbations. It may be recalled that natural sources of mortality that might otherwise have restricted the growth of the cattle population were effectively countered by the Nuer practice of raiding the Dinka to replace stock lost to disease. The insulation of the cattle population from environmental inputs, through successful compen-

satory adjustments, facilitated a system-based (cultural) determination of cattle density. The density of the cattle population was a product of the frequency
of sacrifice, rather than the incidence of disease. This enabled the Nuer to
entirely control the value of the variable that was the focus of equilibration. In
other words, both the reference value (analogous to the setting on a thermostat) and the state of the variable involved (analogous to room temperature)
were culturally determined.

The replenishment of stock lost through disease effectively regulated a
decline in cattle density (through negative feedback) but at the same time
deregulated increases in cattle density. In other words, the same mechanism
that prevented density from dropping below one reference value point enabled
it to be pushed above another (triggering the compensatory adjustment
achieved through territorial appropriation). This represents another instance in
which self-regulation entails self-destabilization, requiring further regulation.

Self-regulatory processes are clearly in evidence here, indeed abundantly
so. Although some of these operate in response to the environmental perturbations that are the foci or ultimate referent of self-regulation in Rappaport's
formulation, others are responses to the consequences of regulation itself. The
operation of the system in relation to internally generated states, the self-
contradictory nature of responses to the latter, the consequent properties of
self-destabilization, and the disconnection between reference value equilibration and the states of variables pertaining to ecologically defined goal ranges
are the distinctive characteristics of the system. This constitutes a systemic
configuration not envisioned by Rappaport's concept of self-regulation or his
specification of adaptive structure as a structured set of regulatory processes
that produce an ordered sequence of responses to *external* perturbations (Rappaport, 1979:151).[11]

Although the Nuer system displays certain self-regulatory properties, it
differs in significant respects from the principal extant model of a self-regulating system. The Nuer case thus suggests the important conclusion that
continuously expanding systems possess quite distinctive characteristics. Intrinsically unattainable cultural objectives insure self-destabilization, i.e., the
internal generation of crisis conditions (or nonviable states) that are resolved
externally, through territorial appropriation, at the expense of neighboring
groups. The systemic response to self-induced stress is characteristically self-
contradictory, entailing short-term compensatory adjustments that at the same
time regenerate the conditions requiring a corrective response (after a relatively brief time lag).

There is perhaps a more general point that can be made here. The Nuer
case suggests that models of adaptive structure and regulatory process drawn
from cybernetics and evolutionary biology may fail to fully bring out the
distinctive pattern of relationships between relationships that obtains within

sociocultural systems. No man-made regulatory system (e.g., a thermostat) that possessed self-destabilizing properties would be likely to be constructed. A biological system that transcends natural constraints is a contradiction in terms. Analogies drawn from machines and biological systems do illuminate some aspects of the complex interconnections found in sociocultural systems, but the distinctive features of the latter necessarily elude such an approach. Further theoretical advance in the understanding of adaptive structure thus requires the detailed study of key cases. This may also provide a basis for reformulating a cybernetically derived conceptual apparatus that appears to be less than fully adequate for analyzing features that are both self-regulating and self-destabilizing.

The distinctive characteristics of the Nuer system also contrast markedly with those implied by the population pressure argument that is typically invoked to explain territorial expansion, both in the Nuer case and in many other cases as well. More specifically, the population pressure argument contains a number of unstated assumptions concerning both the nature of expansionist systems and the character of evolutionary success that are entirely at variance with the Nuer case. It is important that these differences be specified.

As noted in chapter 2, the population pressure argument implicitly assumes that the expanding population is food-limited. The latter breeds up to the environmental limits of its territorial domain, in accordance with Malthusian principles, and overflows its borders appropriating the land resources necessary to preclude starvation. The actors in this drama are thus represented as unfortunate victims of their own reproductive biology who are motivated by readily understandable biological needs for sustenance. Expansion is thus made to appear justifiable. It is generally assumed that the high-density population experiencing shortages displaces lower-density neighbors. This both adjusts man/land ratios on a regional basis and at the same time entails a redistribution in which land is apportioned to each population in accordance with its biological needs. Expansion also constitutes a negative feedback mechanism that maintains population density within an ecologically viable range. The system is thus self-regulating and the changes that take place in territorial disposition reestablish homeostasis. However, evolutionary change is also in evidence as a more densely settled population spreads at the expense of lower-density neighbors. In this process, evolutionary success is a direct product of reproductive success.

In contrast, the Nuer case reveals that expansion is grounded in cultural rather than biological imperatives. The expanding population is not food-limited and the shortages that stimulate expansion are thus unrelated to biological needs. They are systematically generated by the constitution of the sociocultural system. The motives of actors are intelligible in terms of this system, but a process of expansion grounded in cultural rather than biological needs is not so readily justifiable. Moreover, man/land ratios are not adjusted on a regional basis, but are rather progressively skewed as a low-density population displaces a higher-density population and compresses the latter into a diminishing domain. While resources are indeed redistributed, this does not take place in accordance with biological needs. It is the displaced rather than the expanding population that is confronted with starvation. Finally, evolutionary success (measured in cultural terms) is evident, but is not a direct consequence of reproductive success. The Nuer sociocultural system spread over areas formerly occupied by the Dinka, although the Nuer were initially much less numerous than the latter.

It is important to note that the proximate cause of Nuer territorial expansion was a material cause, i.e., dry season grazing shortages. However, these shortages were not an index of human population pressure due to the nature of the relationship between the human population and the cattle population, a relationship mediated by cultural as well as nutritional requirements for cattle. In other words, the principal difficulty with the population pressure argument does not reside in its reliance on material causality, but in the implicit assumptions it entails concerning the nature of the system of relations in which material causality operates. The more general objectives of this case study are to contribute to a better understanding of the latter at two levels. The first concerns the prior sociocultural determination of the material forces that come into play in Nuer territorial expansion. The second concerns the delineation of the formal properties of the system of relations that governs the process of expansion over time.

To show that material forces are socially and culturally constituted is scarcely novel (although the prevalence of population pressure arguments indicates that this wisdom has not been received in all quarters). However, the present study entails an effort to do more than simply arrive at this important point by way of conclusion. The extended analysis presented here is intended to elucidate the transformative effects of socioculturally constituted material forces upon the sociocultural system. The analysis thus encompasses and interrelates both the constituted and consequential aspects of material forces. More often than not, these have been represented as two sides of a polemical argument rather than two integral aspects of developmental (or historical) process.

THE ECONOMIC ORGANIZATION OF NUER EXPANSIONISM

Thus far, I have principally been concerned to examine the regulatory properties of the Nuer sociocultural system and to establish certain aspects of its intrinsically expansionist character that pertain to systemic interrelationships.

Other aspects of this expansionist character can be elucidated by consideration of Nuer economic organization and by comparative analysis of the interconnections between social and economic spheres in the Nuer and Dinka cases. This comparison elaborates upon differences between the Nuer and Dinka that were initially noted in chapter 3.

The Nuer and Dinka differ in the extent to which changes in economic variables pertaining to cattle engender corresponding changes in social variables pertaining to cattle and vice versa. Among the Nuer, a general increase in cattle per capita holdings produces a commensurate increase in bridewealth requirements and in the magnitude of bridewealth payments. This follows from the stipulation that ideal payments must be met to the extent that the groom's family and kin possess sufficient cattle to do so. The expansion of family herds leads directly to a corresponding increase in bridewealth payments because livestock in excess of subsistence requirements are subject to the demands of the bride's kin. When cattle per capita holdings are more than sufficient to fulfill the terms of the ideal transaction, the prestige value associated with making a payment greater than the ideal is conducive to the same outcome. Bridewealth requirements are thus maintained at a level that continuously restricts the frequency of sacrificial slaughter and this, in turn, precludes herd reductions sufficient to bring an expanding cattle population into balance with existing resources. Among the Dinka, a general increase in the cattle population also produces an increase in the magnitude of bridewealth payments. However, social requirements for cattle do not increase proportionately since expanded bridewealth payments (including those greater than the ideal) are accompanied by progressively larger return payments, restricting the increase in net outlay. Increases in social requirements for cattle do not keep pace with increases in the cattle population and consequently do not constitute an impediment to the herd reductions necessary to restrict growth.

A decline in the cattle population also has quite different social consequences in these two cases. Dinka bridewealth can be adjusted downward in accordance with decreased availability of cattle so that marriages are not delayed by poverty of stock. In contrast, Nuer bridewealth is impervious to reduction below a fixed minimum payment and poverty of stock does preclude marriage. A general decline in the cattle population thus increases the percentage of households that find it necessary to defer the marriage of eligible sons. This, in turn, stimulates an intensification of cattle raids against the Dinka to repair stock losses and acquire sufficient cattle to meet minimum payments.

It is evident here that the economic and social spheres are more tightly interconnected in the Nuer case than in that of the Dinka. Fluctuations in the cattle population have significant social repercussions for the Nuer that are either absent or attenuated in the Dinka instance. Moreover, the Nuer bridewealth system imposes social requirements for cattle that constrain the frequency of sacrificial slaughter and thus impede the herd reductions necessary to obviate grazing shortages. In other words, the social sphere has a significant impact on economic variables as well as the reverse. The Dinka differ in this respect as well. The Dinka bridewealth system does not impinge on herd management practices in the manner described above because progressively larger reciprocal payments limit the expansion of social requirements for cattle. Due to the absence of a minimum payment, cattle per capita holdings effectively determine the magnitude of bridewealth payments rather than the reverse. The lack of a minimum payment makes it unnecessary to maintain the cattle population above a certain level in order to facilitate marriage arrangements. The net effect of these features is to partially insulate herd management practices from bridewealth requirements. At the same time, this renders Dinka herd management more responsive to pasture availability. The cattle population can thus be brought into balance with existing grazing resources in the event that shortages arise.

Many of the differences between the Nuer and Dinka socioeconomic systems outlined above are essentially differences in the interrelation between aspects of production (i.e., herd management) and exchange (i.e., bridewealth transactions). It is the partial insulation of production from exchange requirements that buffers the interconnections between the economic and social spheres in the Dinka case. This renders herd management more responsive to resource availability and facilitates accommodation to a finite territorial domain. In the Nuer case, production is largely governed by exchange-based considerations and this engenders a greater density of socioeconomic interconnections. Moreover, the intrinsically expansionist character of the Nuer sociocultural system is attributable, in part, to the extent to which the productive process is dominated by priorities that are grounded in exchange (i.e., bridewealth) and thus inherently dissociated from resource availability. These preliminary observations concerning the relationship between production and exchange can be elaborated by a more detailed examination of accumulation, distribution, and consumption in the Nuer economic system.

Among the Nuer, the flesh of a sacrificial ox is distributed among the same kinsmen who share in the distribution of bridewealth cattle and is divided in accordance with the same pattern that governs the allocation of bridewealth cattle (as noted earlier in this chapter). Both the social relations of distribution and the symbolic representation of relations between kin relations are thus essentially the same in each instance. Both distributions are also encompassed within a framework of reciprocal exchange, i.e., those who distribute on one occasion receive on another.[12] In other words, economic resources are socially utilized in an equivalent manner in both forms of distribution. However, the effects on the cattle population and the adequacy of available pasture are not at all the same. In other words, it is not simply the articulation of the social and economic spheres that is relevant to Nuer expansionism but the specific character of the transactions through which they are interconnected. Of particular importance here are the differential consequences of production for consumption and production for exchange, each of which culminates in a different form of distribution.

One of the principal features of the Nuer bridewealth system is that it entails protracted periods of accumulation during which cattle are stockpiled by a prospective groom's family. The bulk of the family herd is effectively withheld from redistribution during this accumulative phase and this withholding is both necessitated and legitimated by bridewealth requirements. This is particularly notable with respect to male animals. Oxen that are potentially subject to sacrificial slaughter and subsequent distribution to kinsmen are instead accumulated. (Eleven such animals are included in the ideal bridewealth payment.) Some cattle are of course contributed to the bridewealth payments of others during the accumulative phase. However, the range of kinsmen to whom such contributions are in order is actually quite narrow. From the standpoint of a head of household with a son of marriageable age it includes only brothers and brother's sons. An animal may be contributed to sister's son's bridewealth as a token of affection but this is not obligatory. In the main, the Nuer bridewealth system is thus conducive to lengthy periods of accumulation at the household level. The ultimate release of this accumulated surplus in the form of bridewealth payment reduces the family herd to a bare subsistence minimum and, at the same time, initiates another accumulative phase. Efforts are made to rebuild the family herd with a view to an envisioned bridewealth payment for a second wife, ghost wife, etc. The Nuer do not enter into exchange for the purposes of accumulation, but rather engage in accumulation as a prerequisite to exchange that culminates in redistribution. However, Nuer households are nevertheless almost continuously involved in the accumulation of surplus cattle (i.e., cattle in excess of subsistence requirements). Production, in the form of herd management, is thus continuously governed by exchange-based considerations pertaining to bridewealth.

The accumulation of cattle is counterbalanced by the widespread sharing of cattle products and other foods.

> Although each household owns its own food, does its own cooking, and provides independently for the needs of its members, men, and much less, women and children, eat in one another's homes to such an extent that, looked at from outside, the whole community is seen to be partaking of a joint supply. Rules of hospitality and conventions about the division of meat and fish lead to a far wider sharing of food than a bare statement of the principles of ownership would suggest. Young men eat at all byres in the vicinity; every household gives beer parties which their neighbors and kinsmen attend; the same people are given food

and beer at co-operative work parties that assist in any difficult or laborious task; in camps it is considered correct for men to visit the windscreens of their friends to drink milk, and a special gourd of sour milk is kept for guests; when an ox is sacrificed or a wild animal is killed the meat is always, in one way or another, widely distributed [through secondary distribution by initial recipients]; people are expected to give part of their catch of fish to those who ask for it; people assist one another when there is a shortage of milk or grain; and so forth. (Evans-Pritchard, 1940a:84–85)

While food is thus defined as a community resource to be widely shared and given upon request, live animals are in an entirely different category. Although an individual is obligated to share a surplus of any "good thing" with kinsmen and neighbors,

> no Nuer is expected to part with his cattle or household property and, except in special circumstances, these would not be asked for. (Evans-Pritchard, 1940a:183)

Cattle on the hoof are thus clearly marked as items of exchange that are subject to accumulation at the household level for the purposes of future exchange.[13] As such, cattle can legitimately be withheld from the general redistributive claims of the local community that are applicable to food, tools, and indeed to surpluses of any other "good thing." Although culturally defined as exchange items, cattle are scarcely trinkets or counters. They are, in fact, productive resources and a major component of the means of production for subsistence (i.e., the means of producing milk and meat). The Nuer bridewealth system thus governs the distribution of the means of production as well as governing the productive process.

While the Nuer bridewealth system legitimates the accumulation of a major productive resource it also insures periodic redistribution that is essentially egalitarian in character. Of particular importance in this respect is the provision that all cattle in excess of subsistence requirements are subject to the claims of the bride's family and kin in meeting the terms of a very substantial ideal payment. Cattle that represent surplus productive capacity are thus subject to redistribution. Moreover, cattle beyond the requirements of the ideal payment are regularly given when they are available. Nearly all surplus is thus redistributed. Even the most wealthy households are consequently destined to be reduced to a near subsistence level by the payment of bridewealth (see Evans-Pritchard, 1940a:20).

Access to this redistribution of surplus productive resources is open to anyone who has a daughter. In other words, access is linked to a characteristic unrelated to the existing distribution of resources. The redistributive process thus favors no particular segment of the population other than those families who possess more daughters than sons. (Polygyny does not contribute to the attainment of this condition.) Moreover, the magnitude of the bridewealth payment is determined by the resources of the groom's family and kin and is entirely unrelated to those of the bride's family. The daughter of a family with few animals is entitled to the same ideal payment applicable to a girl from a family with greater means. A girl's father may hope she will marry someone with sufficient cattle to meet the ideal, as opposed to the minimum payment, but does not attempt to block her choice (Evans-Pritchard, 1951a:56). Moreover, there is no comparable concern on the part of a young man's father pertaining to the cattle holdings of the bride's family (see Evans-Pritchard, 1951a:53–58). This is readily understandable since a man has no significant claim on the cattle of his wife's father or brother, nor do his children have any obligatory claims on the cattle of their mother's brother. The main thrust of the Nuer bridewealth system is thus toward an egalitarian redistribution of surplus productive resources. Cattle are given in bridewealth by each family in accordance with their means and are received by each family in accordance with the number of their daughters of marriageable age. (See Goody and Tambiah, 1973:13, concerning the "leveling function" of bridewealth.)

The preceding discussion provides a basis for elucidating the relationship between Nuer economic organization and Nuer expansionism. A summary of the main points will make the connection apparent. Live cattle are culturally defined as items of exchange that may legitimately be accumulated and held in reserve for anticipated bridewealth payments. Polygyny, ghost marriage, and the provision of wives for one's sons insure that such payments are almost invariably envisioned. Nuer households are thus regularly engaged in the accumulation of cattle for exchange purposes. This has several important consequences. First, the productive process is largely governed by exchange-based considerations and production for exchange predominates over production for consumption. Second, exchange requirements push production to a level well beyond that required for subsistence purposes and engender the accumulation of surplus productive capacity. Third, surplus cattle held in reserve for future payments must of course be fed and grazing requirements are thus significantly expanded. This creates a propensity to the development of grazing shortages that cannot satisfactorily be resolved by herd reductions, since the latter are antithetical to the accumulative goals of production for exchange. Territorial expansion thus represents the only solution that is consistent with the exchange-based organization of production.[14]

One of the principal objectives of this chapter is to open an anthropological discussion concerning the distinctive features of expansionist systems. While one swallow does not make a summer, it may nevertheless be useful to formulate general propositions that can be evaluated and refined through further study. The Nuer case suggests that an exchange-dominated organization of production is instrumental to the constitution of intrinsically expansionist sociocultural systems in providing a continuous impetus to territorial acquisition. Exchange requirements are directly linked to the nonhomeostatic properties of the Nuer system noted earlier. The system is characterized by unattainable cultural objectives of which those pertaining to bridewealth are of primary and overriding importance. Bridewealth requirements also insured that the growth of the cattle population would be unimpaired following the acquisition of additional territory, that grazing shortages would be regenerated, and that territorial expansion would thus possess self-destabilizing as well as self-regulating attributes. These nonhomeostatic properties are unlikely to be associated with a sociocultural system that is primarily oriented toward production for consumption. Although a system of this type may occasionally expand its territorial base to alleviate shortages, the acquisition of additional productive resources should extinguish the impetus to expansion. Of greater importance is the fact that subsistence-based shortages are potentially self-correcting. They may well produce increased mortality, obviating the demographic pressure that prompts expansion. This inherent homeostatic characteristic is not intrinsic to shortages that are linked to exchange requirements. For this and other reasons noted above, an exchange-dominated organization of production would appear to be necessary (but not sufficient) for the development of a continuous impetus to territorial appropriation. This suggests that expansionist systems within the respective categories of tribal and state societies may be comparable rather than contrastive, and that expansionism is rooted in aspects of economic organization that can be found in both egalitarian and socially stratified societies.

It has been noted that the Nuer bridewealth system has important effects on the distribution of the means of production as well as the organization of production. However, the relation between the distributive aspects of the bridewealth system and Nuer expansionism remains to be explored. These are, in fact, quite closely interconnected. The same features that are conducive to an egalitarian redistribution of cattle as a productive resource are also directly linked to the expansionist character of the Nuer sociocultural system. A comparatively large ideal bridewealth payment to which all available cattle beyond subsistence requirements must be committed has the effect of rendering all (or nearly all) the surplus productive resources of the groom's household subject to redistribution. This strongly mitigates against the development of any permanent concentration of wealth in cattle. However, these features of the Nuer bridewealth system also insure that the magnitude of bridewealth payments will increase as cattle per capita holdings increase, precluding the herd reductions necessary to bring an expanding cattle population into balance with existing grazing resources. In other words, the cattle that are *not* slaughtered are precisely those cattle that are subject to redistribution by virtue of their inclusion in bridewealth payments. (Although these include a number of oxen and bullocks, twenty-five or twenty-six of the animals in an ideal payment are current or potential breeding and milk-producing stock that represent surplus productive capacity.) The expansionist character of the Nuer sociocultural system is thus linked to an exchange-based organization of production in which the critical exchanges culminate in an egalitarian redistribution of essential productive resources.

It is important to recollect that the substantial numbers of cattle taken in raids on the Dinka are also subject to redistribution (Evans-Pritchard, (1940*a*:128). Both of the principal mechanisms conducive to equalizing differences in cattle holdings are thus connected, directly or indirectly, to Nuer expansionism.

The Dinka lack both of these redistributive features. Cattle taken in raids are not subsequently reallocated and the Dinka bridewealth system accommodates and maintains an unequal distribution of cattle among households. As was noted in earlier chapters, the absence of a Dinka minimum payment facilitates intermarriage among families with scant resources. Wealthy families also intermarry and unusually large bridewealth payments characterize these unions. Inasmuch as marriage tends to occur between families at the same economic level, bridewealth does not have significant redistributive consequences. Indeed, Stubbs (1962:45) suggests that the Dinka bridewealth system favors the rich. Of particular importance in this respect are bridewealth payments in excess of the ideal. In the Dinka case these are dictated by, and vary in accordance with, the social and political standing of the bride's family (Deng, 1971:257). Among the Nuer, bridewealth payments greater than the ideal are unrelated to the status of the bride's family but confer prestige upon that of the groom (as an expression of both wealth in cattle and generosity). The Dinka arrangement of the relationship between bridewealth and social standing insures that particularly large bridewealth payments will circulate among wealthy and powerful families that are entitled to receive them and capable of making them. This precludes redistribution. In the Nuer case, the relationship between bridewealth and prestige turns on a willingness to give more than is formally required. This promotes redistribution. However, it also entails unbounded requirements for bridewealth cattle.[15]

In historical terms, Nuer ascendancy represents the emergent hegemony of one variant of a common cultural system and its expansion at the expense of the other. It is evident here that it was the more economically egalitarian variant that prevailed. The bridewealth system that effectively shaped the proto-Nuer version of a shared transhumant system of production and provided a continuing impetus to expansion also encompassed redistributive features conducive to an equalization of cattle holdings. In the course of Nuer expansion, productive resources in the form of land and cattle were not only appropriated from a more stratified Dinka sociocultural system but also internally redistributed among the Nuer.

The process of expansion also entailed the dissolution of asymmetrical relations between founder and latecomer lines in which the former stood as mother's brothers of the camp to the latter, their sister's sons. The assimilation of displaced Dinka regenerated an analogous asymmetrical relation between local lineage segments of dominant (or aristocratic) Nuer clans and matrilaterally attached Dinka lines. However, this form of social differentiation was not accompanied by mechanisms capable of maintaining a congruent economic differentiation over time. Impoverished Dinka families that joined the Nuer could not readily intermarry among themselves because they lacked sufficient cattle to meet the minimum bridewealth payment. Intermarriage among those poor in cattle was not a possibility given the strictures of the Nuer bridewealth system, and this precluded the maintenance of an economically disadvantaged Dinka sector within Nuer society.

The daughters of émigré Dinka families were thus married by Nuer men capable of making the required bridewealth payment.[16] This insured assimilation and at the same time insured the transference of cattle from amply supplied Nuer to impoverished Dinka. Moreover, the number of cattle transferred was determined by the resources of the Nuer groom's family rather than the social standing of the Dinka bride's family. Fulfillment of the ideal payment was likely given the wealth in cattle that the Nuer acquired in the course of their territorial expansion. When the son of such a Dinka family sought to marry, utilizing the bridewealth received on the occasion of his sister's marriage, the egalitarian features of the Nuer bridewealth system again came into play. The family could legitimately retain cattle needed for subsistence and consequently obtain a wife for less than the ideal payment. Following the marriage of a daughter and son, the Dinka family of this example would find itself in precisely the same position as a Nuer counterpart, and with the same prospects for rebuilding a subsistence-level family herd. Access to grazing was not contingent upon lineage membership but was rather "a common right of all members of the community" (Evans-Pritchard, 1940a:65).

Social differentiation was implicit in the matrilateral attachments by which Dinka refugees were incorporated into the Nuer social system. An initial economic differentiation was likewise intrinsic to a situation in which cattle-less (or cattle-poor) Dinka families joined the cattle-rich Nuer. However, a redistributive bridewealth system, the redistribution of cattle taken in raids, and equal access to grazing were conducive to a progressive erosion of this initial economic differentiation over time.[17] The Nuer sociocultural system differed from that of the Dinka in this respect. These differences may well have played a role in the readiness of vast numbers of Dinka tribesmen to join the Nuer.

The preceding discussion elucidates the interconnections between Nuer expansionism and the economically egalitarian features of the Nuer sociocultural system. The key point is that the Nuer bridewealth system is central to both. The bridewealth system entailed an exchange-based organization of production that provided a continuing impetus to Nuer territorial expansion. However, these same exchanges culminated in a redistribution of cattle that was conducive to an equalization of cattle holdings among households. I have proposed that an exchange-based organization of production is instrumental to the constitution of intrinsically expansionist sociocultural systems. Although the relevant exchange transactions are ultimately redistributive in the Nuer case, there are no logical grounds for postulating the generality of this particular feature. Nuer expansionism was principally grounded in the accumulative rather than redistributive aspects of exchange, and in the impact of the former upon the organization of production. There is consequently no reason to suppose that expansionist tribal social systems will necessarily manifest forms of exchange that entail a redistribution of productive resources among households. (The degree of association between expansionism and redistributive exchange thus becomes an empirical question that can only be elucidated by further comparative study of the ethnographic record.) This conclusion is consistent with the more general point noted earlier, viz., that expansionism is rooted in an exchange-dominated organization of production that can be articulated with both egalitarian and socially stratified organizational forms.

It is particularly noteworthy that Nuer territorial expansion represents the spread of a comparatively egalitarian sociocultural system at the expense of a more socially and economically differentiated counterpart derived from a common stock. Such an event runs counter to the general expectations that flow from a cultural evolutionary theory largely oriented toward elucidation of the development of social stratification (and the origin of the state). There is, in other words, a tendency to associate socioeconomic differentiation with evolutionary success. The Nuer case points up the fact that this association is not invariant. It thus raises interesting questions concerning the conditions under which incipient hierarchy secured a foothold in a relatively egalitarian tribal world. It may be recalled that Dinka political units have only a limited capacity to grow in size through the maintenance of post-fission relationships, and that this is partly attributable to the fact that an asymmetrical relation forms the line of cleavage in fission. Socioeconomic differentiation, along the same axis, also contributed to Dinka defections. The Dinka disadvantage, vis-à-vis the Nuer, can thus be directly related to hierarchical features of the Dinka social system.

This chapter is principally concerned with delineating the specific features of the Nuer sociocultural system that are instrumental to its intrinsically expansionist character. The broader objective is to open an anthropological discussion of the general features of expansionist systems. In pursuing this second objective I have necessarily raised questions that a comparative analysis of two related sociocultural systems cannot satisfactorily resolve. I hope these questions are of sufficient interest to attract further scholarly attention.

A *Chronology of Nineteenth-Century Nuer Expansion*

It should be made clear at the outset that the main events and phases of Nuer territorial expansion cannot be precisely dated to specific years. However, it is possible to establish a time span of ten years or so during which a given event is likely to have taken place. This type of chronology will considerably facilitate the presentation of the main sequence of events in chapter 1. It is also sufficient for the purposes of this book since the general interpretation advanced does not depend upon an exact dating of events. The principal objective of this appendix is thus to establish a general chronological framework that will serve to organize the presentation of Nuer history, and to confine the somewhat tedious discussion this entails to a separate context. A secondary objective is to provide a brief contact history of the Nuer and Dinka. This is conveniently included here, since many of the dates employed in establishing the chronology are based on the reports of traders, explorers, and missionaries. In other words, a history of contact emerges from the chronological discussion and can be economically summarized at its conclusion.

There are a number of sources that can be employed to establish the approximate dates of key events pertaining to Nuer territorial expansion. The most important of these sources are the reports of traders and missionaries who were in the region between 1839 and 1875. The firsthand observations of these individuals provide very reliable dating concerning the location of the Nuer at various points in time. Although these reports do not tell us when major Nuer incursions began, they do indicate that they had already occurred by certain dates. This provides a general chronological framework that can be fleshed out and extended through dating derived from second-order sources (that are not based on direct observation). These include published dates based on an estimate of an informant's age (and thus the elapsed time since an event that occurred earlier in his lifetime) and dates that can be estimated by employing Nuer age sets and the Shilluk king list. Although these second-order sources are all subject to some margin of error, the approximate magnitude and direction of error can be determined in each case and incorporated into the results in the form of a range. The discussion will thus proceed along an axis of reliability, from known dates to those that can be estimated within a specified margin of error. It consequently will not adhere to a simple chronological order. The resultant chronology will be presented at the conclusion of the discussion.

In 1820, what is now the Sudan was invaded by Muhammed 'Ali, the viceroy of Egypt (which was then a province of the Ottoman Empire) (Gray, 1961:2–3). In one of the campaigns of the following year the viceroy's army engaged the Dinka at Renk (see map 1) and again on the upper reaches of the Khor Rau (Gleichen, 1905:129). We thus know that the White Nile Dinka extended as far north as Renk in 1821.

In 1839, an Egyptian flotilla succeeded in penetrating the vegetation-choked channels of the Upper Nile and gaining access to the Bahr el Jebel, which was explored as far south as Bor and Aliab Dinka territory (Gray, 1961:3, 17–18). The reports of this voyage (and of another the following year) indicate that the Nuer already occupied both banks of the Bahr el Jebel by 1839 (Johnson, 1980:664). (These reports include letters and published accounts by several Europeans who accompanied the Egyptians. See Gray, 1961:20, Johnson, ibid., and Johnson, 1981:509 for a discussion of these sources.) We thus know that Nuer eastward expansion across the Bahr el Jebel began sometime *before* 1839 (and preceded any external influences derived from Egyptian and subsequent European penetration).

These same sources report that the Nuer had occupied the area along the Sobat, near the point where it joins the Nile, sometime prior to the voyages of 1839–41, and that they were pushed southeast by the Shilluk "some years earlier" (Johnson, 1980:100). This indicates that the Jikany migration also took place sometime *before* 1839.

The Egyptians carried out annual voyages to trade for ivory in the decade following the initial exploration of the Upper Nile and European missionaries and traders entered the area in progressively increasing numbers after 1851 (Gray, 1961:20–69). Although contact with the Nuer and Dinka was largely confined to the riverbanks and to suitable landing spots at Shambe and Bor (see map 1) until the late 1850s, there are a number of reports that provide information concerning the extent of Nuer territory during this period. Beltrame (1975[1861]:132) notes that the Nuer inhabited the banks of Bahr el Zeraf as far south as 8° N latitude in 1859. This indicates that the Nuer had expanded eastward across the Bahr el Zeraf *before* 1859, and that they held the elevated ground adjacent to the east bank of the Zeraf as far south as their present zone of wet season occupation (see Howell, 1954e: map E8). It appears that they did not as yet control the adjacent dry season pastures further south that they currently utilize, although the accuracy of this inference is uncertain.

Beltrame (ibid.:130) also states that his Dinka interpreter told him the White Nile Dinka withdrew northward from the Sobat under the pressure of constant Nuer attacks "about thirty years ago." This report is not based on the writer's firsthand observation and thus does not have the same status as the other material presented in this section. The basis of the dating is also unspecified. However, the interpreter who provided this information was a "Dunghoil" (Dunjol) Dinka (ibid.:138) and thus a native of the area directly north of the Sobat to which he refers. Since he is described as "old" (ibid.:130) it would appear that his report is based on events that took place earlier in his own lifetime. It is likely that the date of "about thirty years ago" is based on a deduction concerning the informant's age, and it would thus be prudent to allow for a margin of error. Available data indicates that casual age estimates of the Nuer and Dinka tend to be too low by as much as ten years (Johnson, 1980:657). Incorporating an error of this magnitude and direction suggests that the Dinka were pushed northward by the Nuer between 1819 and 1829.

Although the dating is not precise, Beltrame's report is nevertheless of considerable interest. The Dunjol lived south of the Sobat with the Padang prior to 1800 (Johnson, 1980:72). According to Johnson (ibid.), the Dunjol separated from the Padang and moved north of the Sobat "sometime in the first half of the nineteenth century." The statement of Beltrame's Dunjol informant indicates that the Dunjol had already settled north of the Sobat between 1819 and 1829, and that they were pushed still farther north by the Nuer sometime during that period. This also indicates that the Nuer were in the vicinity of the Sobat, in force, between 1819 and 1829. This is consistent with reports that the Nuer were dislodged from the mouth of the Sobat by the Shilluk "some years before" 1839.

In the late 1850s and 1860s traders expanded their operations into previously unexplored river systems and also moved into the interior of the Upper Nile Basin at several points. Their published accounts, which have been thoroughly surveyed by Johnson (1980), provide additional information on the extent of Nuer territory at this time. In 1859, members of the Lou tribe were reported to be settled south of the Sobat, and to be utilizing the elevated wet season sites to the southwest that they currently cultivate (Johnson, 1980:101). In other words, the Lou were already well established on the critical high ground in the north central portion of their present territory by 1859. Further east, the Jikany are reported to have begun raiding the Anuak on the Bonjak (Oboth) River by 1855, and on the Baro by 1860 (Johnson, 1980:100). The Eastern Jikany thus also appear to have been well established in the general area of their present territory by 1860. However, substantial pockets of Dinka and Anuak settlement persisted along the Sobat for many years after this date (and in some instances well into the present century). Many of these settlements gradually disappeared through assimilation (rather than expulsion) and this process played an important role in the consolidation of Jikany territorial gains.

In 1863–65 the main channel of the Bahr el Jebel was blocked by vegetation and the Bahr el Zeraf became the main route through the Upper Nile Basin. Two companies engaged in the slave and ivory trade established camps near the Zeraf, and inland at Ayod, in about 1865 (Johnson, 1980:184–85). The Gaawar were already in control of the area around Luang Deng at this time, but had not progressed as far as the Duk ridge (which runs from about forty kilometers north of Ayod due south through the latter to Duk Fadiat and Duk Faiwil). Oral traditions indicate that elements of the Gaawar occupied the northern tip of the Duk ridge in about 1874 (Johnson, 1980:212).

In 1874, an effort was made to terminate the slave trade by gaining control of the main rivers along which the slaves were transported north (Gray, 1961:105–19). The merchant camps along the Zeraf were disbanded at this time, and government stations were established at Nasir, at the mouth of the Sobat, and somewhat later at Bor (ibid.; Johnson, 1980:305). These posts had the desired effect and greatly curtailed merchant activity in the area with which we are concerned. However, Egyptian government presence in this area was confined to the vicinity of the Nasir and Bor posts and did not extend to the interior. From the beginning of the Madhia (1881–98), the attention of the Anglo-Egyptian government was directed to more pressing concerns in the north and troops were withdrawn from the southern region as a whole. The result of the withdrawal of the merchants and their replacement by a very attenuated government presence is a dearth of information, based on firsthand observation, concerning Nuer expansion during the period from 1874 to the reentry of the British into the southern Sudan in 1898–1900. The Nuer territorial domain had already reached its maximum extent by the latter date. However, sources of information other than firsthand observation indicate that the Nuer were already entrenched throughout their present territory by 1874. This material will be discussed shortly.

No significant expansion of the Nuer territorial domain took place during the period from 1900 to 1910. Nuer raids continued, but with very minor exceptions the Nuer did not occupy any territory they had not previously held. The early colonial administration was sufficiently well established to have known about any major Nuer appropriations, although not yet in a position to have done more than observe them. We can thus conclude that Nuer expansion was completed *before* 1900, and that the colonial administration did not bring about its cessation.

The material presented thus far constitutes the most reliable information available and thus provides the basic framework for establishing a chronology of Nuer expansion. We know that both the Nuer invasion of Zeraf Island and the Jikany migration to the vicinity of the Sobat River had already taken place by 1839. We also know that the Nuer had completed the occupation of Zeraf Island and were already well established in what is presently Gaawar, Lou, and Eastern Jikany territory by 1860. The Nuer were thus entrenched in all the areas they later controlled by this date. Finally, we know that the Nuer had not expelled the Dinka from the Duk ridge by 1874 (although they may have occupied the northern tip of it) and that territorial gains in this area took place between 1874 and 1900.

This general chronological framework can be fleshed out through dating derived from second-order sources (described earlier). These can be employed to provide estimated dates for three events that are significant with respect to the present study: (1) the inception of Nuer territorial expansion, (2) the introduction of epidemic cattle diseases into the Upper Nile Basin, and (3) the occupation of the last areas appropriated by the Nuer. These will be considered in reverse order, beginning with the more recent (and more easily dated) events.

What we know of Nuer movements between 1875 and 1900 is largely based on the statements of informants recorded by early colonial administrators and by Evans-Pritchard, supplemented by oral traditions collected more recently. The events related by these informants occurred during their own lifetimes and are collaborated by the testimony of Nuer and Dinka alike. We thus have no reason to doubt their accuracy. However, the dating of these events, which is based on age estimates and genealogical information, may be subject to a margin of error of about ten years.

Fergusson (1921:154) reports that the Nuong Nuer drove the Chich (Shish) Dinka south from 7°52' N latitude to 7°40' in "about 1845" and that the Nuong moved further south to approximately their present boundary at 7°23' "about 45 years ago," i.e., in 1876. The southward expansion of the Nuer west of the Nile thus appears to have been completed by 1876. The basis of Fergusson's dating is not indicated, and the potential magnitude and direction of error therefore cannot be assessed.

The Duk ridge was occupied by the Gaawar (in the north) and the Lou Nuer (in the south) between 1875 and 1895. Wyld's (1930) statements in the Upper Nile Province Handbook are the source of these dates, which have been widely employed by other authors (cf. Johnson, 1980:682–84). The basis of the 1895 date is clear in the following quotation from Wyld's (1930) account:

> In the first half of the 19th century, the country East of the Bahr el Jebel, from the R. Sobat Southwards to Bor, was all Dinka. The Lau [Lou] Nuer are reported to have crossed the Rivers Jebel and Zeraf and established a footing in this Dinka country about 1850. By about 1875, the Nuer had overrun tribal areas of the Root [Rut], Luac, Fadung, and Thoi Dinka.

About 1895 the annexation of the Niarreweng, Ghol and Dwar countries had
been completed. This last date is fairly accurate, as men who are now about 35
years of age were born in their own country and taken as infants by their refugee
parents to Bor or Twi country, where they were brought up.

Johnson (1980:657) points out that age estimates made by colonial administrators generally tend to be too low. He cites several examples, including one in which a prophet was taken to be only twenty-five at a time when he
was very probably over thirty-five. If Wyld's age estimates are incorrect, they
are thus likely to err on the low side. The men he considered to be "about 35"
may consequently have been as old as forty-five. In this case, the occupation
of the Duk ridge would have been completed in 1885 rather than 1895. The
appropriation of the southern end of the Duk ridge may thus be dated to the
time range 1885–95, which incorporates the probable range and direction of
error in Wyld's estimate. (It should be noted that Wyld's other dates are also
too late. We know that the area east of the Bahr el Jebel was not "all Dinka"
before 1850, since the Nuer already occupied the east bank in 1839.)

As noted earlier, the Duk ridge is known to have been in the hands of the
Dinka when the Zeraf trading stations were disbanded in 1874. Oral traditions
indicate that the Gaawar leader Nuar Mer and his followers occupied the
northern tip of the ridge at about this time (Johnson, 1980:212). Nuar Mer had
been allied with the traders and his following included a disparate group of
Nuer and Dinka tribesmen in which the Gaawar element (of the Radh primary
section) was probably a minority. This will be discussed more fully in a later
section. The point to be noted here is that Nuar Mer's largely Dinka following
was decisively defeated by the Lou Nuer in the battle of Pading in 1875 and
routed in 1878 by the Bar primary section of the Gaawar with whom Nuar
Mer had been in conflict for the previous decade (Johnson, 1980:201–2, 213,
223). The Gaawar were rapidly reunited after the death of Nuar Mer in the
battle of 1878 and made substantial gains in the occupation of the Duk ridge
between 1878 and 1883 (Johnson, 1980:678). As noted above, the complete
expulsion of the Dinka was accomplished sometime between 1885 and 1895.

The final phase of Nuer southward expansion began at about the same
time on both sides of the Bahr el Jebel. Nuong Nuer movement from 7°40' to
7°23' was reportedly accomplished relatively rapidly in about 1876. Although
Gaawar (and Lou) appropriation of the Duk ridge stretched over at least a
decade, it began at about the same time. Nuar Mer's occupation of the
northern tip of the Duk ridge dates to about 1874 and the reunited Gaawar
made substantial gains in the appropriation of the ridge after 1878. (The role
of external influences in the timing of the last phase of Nuong and Gaawar
expansion is discussed in a later section.)

The final phase of Nuer expansion in the east also occurred during the

1870s. Evans-Pritchard (1940c:10) reports that the Nuer carried out a large-scale invasion of Anuak country that proceeded along the Akobo through the entire length of Anuak territory "sixty or seventy years ago," i.e., between 1870 and 1880. The Nuer withdrew shortly thereafter (largely as a result of loss of cattle from trypanosomiasis endemic to the area) and subsequently made "no attempt to settle in the main Anuak country" (ibid.). In Evans-Pritchard's account, the occupation of new territory thus came to a close between 1870 and 1880.

In a footnote to this passage Evans-Pritchard (ibid.) notes that this invasion can be dated by the age of elderly Anuak nobles who were small children at the time, by succession to emblems of nobility, by Nuer traditions, and by reports of early explorers on the Sobat and Pibor. Johnson (1980:597) suggests, on the basis of his recalculations of Nuer age set initiation periods, that this invasion may have occurred somewhat earlier. However, this argument is not compelling inasmuch as Nuer age sets did not serve as the basis of Evans-Pritchard's dating, and Johnson (1980:653–59, 675) himself points out that they do not provide an entirely reliable means of dating events. I am persuaded that Evans-Pritchard was able to estimate the age of elderly Anuak nobles within the ten-year margin of error incorporated in his date of 1870 to 1880 and thus will employ this dating.

Between 1899 and 1904 the British colonial administration surveyed the Sobat and its tributaries and found the Nuer occupying an area that corresponds quite closely to their present territory (Gleichen, 1905:132–41). However, isolated pockets of Anuak settlement persisted along the Sobat between Abwong and Shawei (map 1) and also along the Pibor (ibid.:132, 136). A similar settlement was located near the Nasir post in 1876, but by the early 1900s had been largely assimilated by the Nuer population that predominated in the area (Johnson, 1980:100; Gleichen, 1905). Such assimilation was a common phenomenon throughout Nuer expansion, and particularly in the later phases of it. However, this is to be distinguished from Nuer occupation of large blocks of territory from which the Dinka and Anuak had previously been expelled by intensive raiding. It is the latter type of territorial appropriation that came to a close in the eastern region by about 1880.

In summary, available data indicate that the final thrusts of Nuer territorial expansion commenced between 1870 and 1880 throughout Nuerland. In the west, territorial acquisition was completed by about 1876. In the east, the Nuer made no attempts to occupy present-day Anuak country after the invasion that took place sometime between 1870 and 1880. In the central region, expulsion of the Dinka from the Duk ridge began in about 1874 but was not finally completed until sometime between 1885 and 1895. However, significant gains were probably achieved by 1883.

In the main body of the book I sometimes refer to "the Nuer expansion of 1800 to 1880.'' In this shorthand expression, I employ an end date of 1880 because available evidence, surveyed here, indicates that Nuer territorial acquisition was 90 to 95 percent complete by that time. With the exception of a portion of the Duk ridge, Nuer appropriations after 1880 largely entailed the assimilation of pockets of Dinka and Anuak settlement within regions already dominated by an entrenched Nuer population.

It will be argued elsewhere that the introduction of epidemic cattle diseases into the southern Sudan was responsible for the marked tapering off of Nuer territorial expansion after 1880. It is thus important to establish the date at which these diseases first entered the Upper Nile Basin. However, before taking up this question, it is necessary to specify precisely what we seek to date, namely, a change in the mortality rate of the cattle population attributable to a number of introduced diseases. Howell (1954b:209) notes that the Nuer themselves attribute the depletion of their herds to the introduction of rinderpest, foot and mouth disease, contagious bovine pleuropneumonia, haemorrhagic septicaemia, trypanosomiasis, and still other diseases. Although contagious bovine pleuropneumonia and trypanosomiasis are not thought to be recent introductions, the Nuer are nevertheless correct in their general assessment because it has been demonstrated that the reduction of both the cattle and wild herbivore population by rinderpest (and other diseases) engendered ecological changes resulting in an extension of the range of the tsetse flies that transmit trypanosomiasis (Grunnet, 1962:5–20). What we seek to date, then, is a change in patterns of disease that increased the mortality rate of the cattle population. While rinderpest was the single most important factor in this alteration, it was not the only disease involved. Moreover, the beginning of this period of increased cattle mortality is not linked to the introduction of rinderpest per se, but may be attributable to the earlier introduction of other diseases such as haemorrhagic septicaemia.

Nuer age sets are often named for an event or incident that occurred during the opening years of the initiation period, and the Boilac age set is named in relation to an unusual cattle plague that swept through Nuerland (Evans-Pritchard, 1936:251). This marks the first epidemic cattle disease recollected in Nuer oral traditions. Evans-Pritchard (ibid.:247) assigns an opening date of 1883 to this age set, which suggests that this epidemic occurred between 1883 and 1885.

Elsewhere, in an unfortunately worded passage, Evans-Pritchard (1940a:68) notes that

> Rinderpest entered the Sudan not more than fifty years ago and Nuer refer to the period before it came, along with Arab invaders, at the time the Boiloc age set was being initiated, as ''life of the cattle.''

As Johnson (1980:670–71) points out, this seems to imply a date of 1890 (rather than 1883) for the initiation of the Boilac age set. It also appears to link the introduction of rinderpest, the coming of the Arabs, and this initiation period as events that occurred at about the same time, although this is clearly not the case. As Evans-Pritchard himself was well aware, the Arabs (employed by merchants involved in the slave and ivory trade) had been in the region as early as the 1850s, but had largely withdrawn by 1874, well before the date of "fifty years ago." One must conclude that Evans-Pritchard could not have intended to link these three events in time. What he was evidently trying to convey is that the Nuer recall a "golden age" prior to all three events. On this reading, the date of 1890 refers only to the introduction of rinderpest.

Johnson (1980) concurs in the view that rinderpest could not have entered the Sudan before 1890. He also points out that early government documents

> suggested that the reason the rinderpest epidemic of 1900 in the Sudan was much milder than in other parts of Africa was due to an earlier introduction of the disease to the Sudan than to the rest of Africa. (Johnson, 1980:610)

This points toward a date of 1890, or at least the early 1890s, for the introduction of rinderpest per se.

As noted earlier, the Nuer's initial experience with epidemic cattle diseases coincided with the early years of the Boilac age set's initiation period. The latter is dated to 1883 by Evans-Pritchard. Johnson (1980:665) dates the beginning of the Boilac initiation period to 1874, with an alternate date of 1869. The epidemic thus could have occurred during any of the following periods: 1869–71, 1874–76, or 1883–85. In any case, it is clear that the disease responsible was not rinderpest, which was introduced no earlier than 1890. However, it could have been any one of a number of other cattle diseases not previously present in the region. The significant conclusion here is that patterns of cattle mortality began to change sometime prior to 1890, and were drastically altered thereafter.

There are a host of problems associated with the use of age sets in establishing fixed dates, and many of these are reviewed by Johnson (1980:653–59). Relatively slight differences in the assumptions employed produce a fairly wide range of potential dates, as is illustrated by the three possible opening dates for the Boilac age set (i.e., 1869, 1874, or 1883). Moreover, as one goes farther back in time, the effects of these slight differences are compounded and the range of potential dates expands further. Given this intrinsic limitation, the most that one can reasonably expect to achieve is the delineation of a time range, rather than a specific date. Nevertheless, the plausible time range for the Boilac age set can be confined to a somewhat narrower range than that provided by the preceding estimates.

The main features of the Nuer age set system are described by Evans-Pritchard (1936, 1940*a*) and Howell (1948). Those features relevant to dating age sets may be briefly noted here. The approximate age of initiation was sixteen to eighteen traditionally, but had decreased to fourteen to sixteen years of age by the time of Evans-Pritchard's fieldwork (Evans-Pritchard, 1940*a:*249). Traditionally, there was a four-year interval between the closure of one age set and the commencement of the next. At the time of Evans-Pritchard's fieldwork, initiation was conducted annually, without closed periods, and age sets were divided by pronouncement of the Man of the Cattle, who had formerly opened and closed each successive set (Evans-Pritchard, 1940*a:*254). In either case, the members of a particular named age set are those individuals initiated during a specific time period. Evans-Pritchard (1937:247) estimates that there is a ten-year interval between age sets, on average, while recognizing that the interval may vary somewhat from set to set. Johnson (1980:656) employs the same average interval in his calculations.

Members of the Thut age set, which preceded Boilac, were alive at the time of Evans-Pritchard's fieldwork. An estimate of the age of these surviving members of Thut thus provides a basis for dating the set. Johnson (1980:671–72) relies on Huffman's ([1931]1970) estimate that these individuals were born in 1849–54. (The youngest would then have been seventy-seven years of age in 1931 and the eldest eighty-two.) The eldest individuals would, of course, be those initiated closer to the opening of the set, and the youngest would be those initiated at its close. The latter are most important for our purposes. A man born in 1854 would first be eligible for initiation, at the traditional age of sixteen, in 1870. If a man born in 1854 were initiated at the younger age of fourteen, in order to be included in a set about to be closed, this would have occurred in 1868. Given Huffman's age estimates, 1868 is the *earliest* date one can arrive at for the closure of the Thut age set. The traditional four-year interval between initiation periods would thus provide a date of 1872 for the opening of Boilac. Men born in 1855, one year after the youngest members of Thut, would be seventeen in 1872 and would be the first to be initiated when Boilac was opened. Huffman's age estimates, which are employed by Johnson (1980), thus do not support his "alternate" date of 1869 for the opening of Boilac (although they are consistent with his 1874 dating).

An earlier estimate for the opening of Boilac would depend on higher age estimates for the surviving members of Thut, the oldest members of Nuer society in the early 1930s. However, such estimates would not be consistent with what we know of mortality during this period. In another context, Evans-Pritchard (1940a:82) observes that the older age sets were expected to be "wiped out" by the co-occurrence of rinderpest epidemics and crop failure. Data presented in chapter 2 document the prevalence of chronic crop failures, and rinderpest substantially reduced Nuer herds in the decade preceding Evans-Pritchard's fieldwork (ibid.; Jackson, 1923). Under these circumstances, it is improbable that the surviving members of Thut were older than seventy-seven to eighty-two years of age when observed by Huffman and Evans-Pritchard in 1931. Indeed it is likely that they were somewhat younger. An age estimate of sixty-seven to seventy-two (i.e., ten years younger) would yield an opening date of 1882 for Boilac, quite close to Evans-Pritchard's estimate of 1883. In my view, the time range 1872 to 1882 represents the most plausible span of possible opening dates for Boilac. The cattle plague for which this set is named could thus have occurred as early as 1872–74 or as late as 1882–84.

The earliest incidence of epidemic cattle disease recalled in Nuer oral traditions may thus be dated to sometime between 1872 and 1884. The increased mortality resulting from this undoubtedly reduced the growth rate of the cattle population. The latter went into a serious decline after the introduction of rinderpest, which probably first affected Nuer cattle in the early 1890s. This period during which Nuer herds first ceased to grow as rapidly as they are capable of growing (i.e., 3.5 percent per annum), and then began to decline, corresponds quite closely to the period during which Nuer territorial expansion slowed dramatically. As noted in the preceding section, the appropriation of new territory was largely completed by the late 1870s, and the occupation of the Duk ridge was completed no later than 1895. The correspondence between these changes in the cattle population and the pace of Nuer expansion are discussed more fully in the main body of the book.

The remaining dates to be considered here are those pertaining to the two initial thrusts of nineteenth-century Nuer expansion, namely, the invasion of Zeraf Island by the Lou and Gaawar and the establishment of the Jikany enclave on the Sobat. We know, on the basis of firsthand observation, that both events occurred before 1839. Other sources of information provide a basis for estimating the probable time range at which each movement commenced.

Jikany oral traditions uniformly state that the Jikany passed through Shilluk territory in the course of their eastward migration. Shilluk oral traditions confirm this, and link Jikany movements to the early years of Awin's reign as *reth* (Jackson, 1923:78; Stigand, 1919:226; Bacon, 1922:116; Riad, 1959:161; Johnson, 1980:686). The date of Awin's succession thus provides a date for the beginning of the Jikany migration. There are, however, two possible dates for Awin's reign and this method thus yields a general time range rather than a specific date.

Nyidok was *reth* of the Shilluk at the time of the initial Egyptian voyage of 1839 and held the position until his death in 1859. He was preceded by Akoc, who is believed to have reigned for five years. Akoc was preceded by Awin, whose reign is thought to have been somewhat less than five years (see Johnson, 1980:687). The period of Awin's reign can thus be established by working backward from the time of Nyidok's succession to the office of *reth*. We know that this occurred sometime before 1839. The memoirs of a Shilluk soldier in the Egyptian Army, published in 1896, maintain that Nyidok "was *reth* in 1836, and that he ruled for forty years" (Johnson, 1980:686). Johnson (ibid.) regards the date of 1836 as more likely to be reliable than the reported forty-year reign and employs it in estimating the time of Awin's succession as 1828. In other words, Johnson suggests that Awin was *reth* from about 1828 to 1830, Akoc held the position from about 1831 to 1835, and Nyidok reigned from 1836 to 1859. This is a conservative appraisal, since it assumes that Nyidok had only just succeeded to the position of *reth* in 1836 while the report states he held the position at that time. The date of 1828 for Awin's installation thus provides the latest plausible date for the Jikany migration linked to the beginning of his reign.

Alternatively, the report that Nyidok ruled for forty years—which is drawn from the same source—yields a date of 1812 for Awin's succession. More specifically, the successive reigns would be: Awin 1812 to 1814, Akoc 1815 to 1819, Nyidok 1820 to 1859. Taken together, these alternate dates provide a broad but highly plausible time range for the Jikany migration. It is unlikely that this event took place prior to 1812 or later than 1828.

As was noted earlier, Beltrame's (1975 [1861]:130) report suggests that the Nuer were established on the upper Sobat between 1819 and 1829. This overlaps the time range based on the Shilluk king list, and is consistent with Nuer oral traditions. The latter hold that the Jikany passed through Shilluk territory near Melut. After crossing the Nile, they fought the Dinka, captured a large number of their cattle, and moved southward to settle on the upper Sobat (between the mouth of the latter and Abwong) (Stigand, 1919:226; Bacon, 1922:115; Jackson, 1923:78; Johnson, 1980:97–98). Nuer settlement in this area, and their subsequent expansion along the Sobat (to the southeast) was responsible for the northward withdrawal of the Dinka reported by Beltrame's Dunjol informant. A Jikany migration that passed through Shilluk territory sometime between 1812 and 1828 would thus be consistent with a Dinka withdrawal from the Sobat sometime between 1819 and 1829. However, available evidence indicates that the Nuer proceeded directly from Melut to the Sobat. The dating derived from Beltrame's report therefore suggests that the Jikany migration probably did not begin before about 1817. In other words, the most plausible time range can be narrowed somewhat, to the period 1817 to 1828. While a migration beginning between 1812 and 1816 cannot be ruled out, this dating is somewhat less plausible than the following ten-year period.

The Egyptian Army invaded White Nile Dinka territory in 1821 and again in 1827. While the initial invasion turned back at Khor Rau, the second penetrated all the way to the Sobat River and resulted in the capture of many slaves (Johnson, 1980:82). Although the Nuer occupied the lower Sobat sometime between 1817 and 1828, neither historical sources nor Nuer oral traditions report any conflict between the Nuer and the Egyptian Army. This suggests that the Nuer had already moved upstream *before* 1827. The most plausible time range for the Jikany migration can thus be further narrowed, to the period from 1817 to 1826.

There is little information that can be employed to date the initial movement of the Lou and Gaawar across the Bahr el Jebel into Zeraf Island. However, this is widely regarded as having been roughly contemporary with the Jikany migration. Howell (1954*b*:212) maintains that the Jikany "were, in fact, the first [Nuer group] to move eastward." The basis of this conclusion is not provided, but it presumably rests on the statements of Nuer informants and we have no reason to doubt it. Given this sequence, the time range for the Lou and Gaawar crossing would then be slightly later than the 1817 to 1826 time range for the Jikany migration.

Johnson (1980:664) employs age sets to arrive at an approximate date of circa 1820 for the Gaawar crossing. However, he notes that informants do not agree concerning the number of age sets that have been marked since this event and that this uncertainty detracts from the reliability of the estimate. He points out that Howell (1954*b*:207) also suggests a tentative date of "circa 1820?" for the Gaawar incursion and goes on to conclude

> since estimates of the date of the Eastern Jikany migrations also point to the decade of the 1820's, we can assume for the time being that this date is very nearly correct. (Johnson, 1980:664)

My own assessment is much the same. On the basis of the limited information available, it is plausible to assume that the Lou and Gaawar invasion of Zeraf Island took place between 1818 and 1829. We know that the Nuer were already established on Zeraf Island in 1839. There are no indications in the early historical sources that the initial movement into this area had just taken place, and the occupation would have taken some time to accomplish. It is thus unlikely that it commenced later than 1829. If the eastward migration of the Jikany preceded that of the Lou and Gaawar, then the latter is unlikely to have begun before 1818.

The chronological conclusions drawn from the present inquiry are listed below. They may be very briefly summarized as follows: The Jikany migration that marks the first main thrust of nineteenth-century Nuer expansion probably began between 1817 and 1826, and the Lou and Gaawar invasion of Zeraf Island followed shortly thereafter. By 1859, Zeraf Island was in the hands of the Lak, Thiang, and Gaawar, and the Lou and Eastern Jikany were well established in the vicinity of their present territories. The last major thrust of Nuer expansion commenced between 1870 and 1880 throughout Nuerland. With the exception of Lou and Gaawar occupation of portions of the Duk ridge, the final appropriation of large blocks of Dinka and Anuak territory were also completed during this decade. The most active phase of Nuer territorial expansion is thus confined to the relatively brief period from about 1820 to 1880.

The tapering off of Nuer expansion between 1880 and 1895 coincides with the period during which the Nuer cattle population was increasingly subject to introduced diseases that initially reduced, and ultimately reversed, a high intrinsic growth rate. The first epidemic occurred sometime between 1872 and 1884, either during or shortly after the final wave of expansion. The cattle population began to decline after the introduction of rinderpest in the early 1890s, and no significant territorial expansion took place thereafter, with the possible exception of the final occupation of the Duk ridge which was completed between 1885 and 1895. The period from 1880 to 1917 was characterized by intensive cattle raiding, through which the Nuer attempted to recoup their stock losses at Dinka expense. Earlier territorial gains were consolidated by the assimilation of pockets of Dinka and Anuak settlement within areas of Nuer occupation (and this process continued well into the twentieth century). However, there was relatively little change in the boundaries between the Nuer, Dinka, and Anuak during the period from 1880 to 1910. The colonial administration began its efforts to fix the boundaries between these cultural groups in 1910, and restored the southern portion of the Duk ridge to the Dinka at that time. Present boundaries thus approximate those that obtained in about 1880.

Key Dates in Nineteenth-Century Nuer Territorial Expansion

Beginning of the Jikany Nuer migration	1817–26
Beginning of the Gaawar and Lou Nuer invasion of Zeraf Island	1818–29
Nuong Nuer southward expansion from 7°52′ to 7°40′	1845
Eastern Jikany entrenched in the general area of their present territory	by 1855–60
Gaawar established on the west bank of the Zeraf (to 8° south)	by 1859
Lou established on the high ground in the north central portion of their present territory	by 1859
Last Eastern Jikany invasion of upland Anuak territory	1870–80

Initial Gaawar occupation of the Duk ridge	1874
Nuong Nuer southward expansion to 7°23'	1876
Initial introduction of epidemic cattle diseases	between 1872 and 1884
Lou and Gaawar complete the occupation of the Duk ridge	1885–95
Introduction of rinderpest and marked decline in Nuer and Dinka cattle population	early 1890s

CONTACT HISTORY

Establishing the foregoing chronology of Nuer expansion has necessarily entailed consideration of the history of Nuer and Dinka contact with the outside world, since many of the dates are derived from the reports of traders, explorers, and missionaries. Many of the principal events of Nuer and Dinka contact history have thus already been mentioned, and the main outlines of this history may be usefully summarized here. This will provide a basis for assessing the role of external factors in Nuer territorial expansion and addressing Sacks's (1979:437–47) recent argument in which these factors are accorded causal primacy. Although it may be noted in advance that the historical data do not support this interpretation, it is nevertheless important to establish the internally generated nature of Nuer expansion.

During the period from about 1600 to 1820, the Funj kingdom of Sennar was the principal external force that impinged on the Dinka (and, indirectly, the Nuer) inhabitants of the Upper Nile Basin. The Funj took slaves from an extensive peripheral region to the south of Sennar that encompassed the area north of the Sobat and east of the Nile. This probably constituted a deterrent to Dinka settlement of this area during a period when the Dinka population was expanding toward the periphery of the ecological zone defined by the flood plain of the Upper Nile Basin. The northward expansion of the Dinka into this area in the latter half of the eighteenth century largely coincides with the decline of the Funj kingdom that began in 1758 and culminated in political dissipation in 1786.

In the north central region, the Shilluk served to buffer the Nuer and Dinka from any direct contact with cultural or political influences emanating from the north. In the west the Dinka initially bordered the mound-building Lwel (discussed in chap. 1) whom they eventually displaced. Dinka expansion to the west and northwest between 1600 and 1800 ultimately brought them into contact with the Baggara Arabs of the Messiria Homr who were themselves expanding southward toward the Bahr el Arab during the eighteenth century. The first contact between these two cultural groups is believed to have occurred in about 1745 (Howell, 1951:241; Henderson, 1939:57, 76).

In general, one may conclude that the Upper Nile Basin remained quite isolated from external forces until the 1800s. The most significant interactions were those between and among the Nuer, Dinka, Shilluk, and Anuak (and between the Dinka and their western neighbors). Indeed, it was the expansion of the Dinka to the boundaries of the Upper Nile Basin and beyond in the latter half of the eighteenth century that brought them into contact with Arab populations in the north. In other words, it was not the outside world that began to impinge on the Dinka but rather the Dinka that began to impinge on the outside world.

Muhammed 'Ali's conquest of the northern Sudan in 1820–21 marked the beginning of the end of this period of relative isolation. The White Nile Dinka came into conflict with the Egyptian Army in 1821 and again in 1827. The objective of the 1827 campaign was to procure slaves and similar raids (although on a smaller scale) occurred frequently during the next forty years (Johnson, 1980:82). However, it is important to note that the Dinka prevailed in some of these conflicts and, most significantly, that they did not withdraw southward under the pressure of these periodic raids (Gleichen, 1905:129). They continued to hold the east bank of the Nile as far north as Renk and carried out counterraids that penetrated as much as 110 miles farther north (ibid.; Johnson, 1980:83).

The most important factor in opening the southern Sudan to external influences was the first successful navigation through the vegetation-choked channels of the Upper Nile in 1839 (Gray, 1961:1). This paved the way for commercial activity in the region during the latter half of the nineteenth century. However, the initial effects were slight. Between 1839 and 1851 the Egyptians carried out small annual expeditions to trade for ivory. Contact between the Egyptians and the Nuer and Dinka was limited to the riverbanks and to the relatively few points at which high banks and an absence of peripheral swamp made it possible for the boats to draw close to the land (Gray, 1961:34). The principal docking points were at the present site of Malakal in Shilluk territory, at Shambe and Bor in Dinka territory, and at Gondokoro among the Bari. There were few landings at other points, and in these instances the Egyptians did not venture far from the river. As a result, the Nuer and Dinka could readily avoid any contact with the Egyptians simply by vacating the area around a suitable landing spot for several days. The key point here is that the Nuer and Dinka held the initiative in making contact with Egyptian trading expeditions rather than the converse (see Gray, 1961:36–37). Although there were some hostile interactions that were important in shaping Nuer and Dinka reactions to later commercial traders (and vice versa), the period of Egyptian voyages had very little material effect on the Nuer and Dinka and no effect whatsoever on the process of Nuer expansion.

After 1851, European traders entered the area in increasing numbers. Initially, this did not alter the terms of interaction in which the Nuer and Dinka held the initiative in establishing contact. However, the establishment of permanent trading stations staffed by large numbers of armed Arab servants radically altered this situation after 1857 (Gray, 1961:46–69). Between 1857 and 1874 it was common practice for the traders' private armies to ally themselves with one of the groups engaged in a local conflict and to participate in raids in which large numbers of cattle and captives were taken. The cattle supported the operation of the stations and served as the currency in both obtaining ivory and arranging for it to be carried to the river for shipment. The captives supplied remuneration to the Arab mercenaries who sold them into slavery in the north. The details of these practices are well described by Gray (ibid.). The main point, for our purposes, is that the establishment of permanent trading stations altered the indigenous distribution of power between the parties involved in local feud or tribal warfare.

The establishment of permanent trading stations, and their intervention in local conflict, raises the question of the potential role these external influences may have played in Nuer territorial expansion. An evaluation of available data indicates that this role was negligible. Three main points are conducive to this conclusion. First, Nuer expansion began no later than 1826 and the Nuer were firmly entrenched throughout the area of their present territory by the late 1850s. In other words, the major gains of Nuer territorial appropriation were completed before the traders were in a position to influence the outcome of Nuer-Dinka conflicts. Second, trading stations were generally absent from the borders along which Nuer expansion was taking place during the period from 1857 to 1874. The bulk of these stations were located in Western Dinka territory on the edge of the ironstone plateau (in the vicinity of the present towns of Yirol, Rumbek, Tonj, and Wau shown on map 1) (Gray, 1961:61). The only stations located in relevant areas were at Shambe, in Chich Dinka territory, and along the Zeraf in Gaawar Nuer territory. There were no trading stations in the eastern area where the Jikany and Lou Nuer were consolidating and extending earlier territorial gains during this period (Johnson, 1980:184). Third, the timing of the final stages of Nuer expansion in the west and central areas suggests that the presence of trading stations inhibited rather than facilitated Nuer territorial acquisition between 1857 and 1874.

This point is supported by the dates of Nuong Nuer expansion against the Chich Dinka. It may be recalled that the Nuong pushed south from 7°52' to 7°40' in 1845. This was eleven years before the first trading station was established at Shambe about thirty miles to the south (see Gray, 1961:47). The final thrust of Nuong expansion (to 7°23') took place in 1876, after the activities of the traders had been curtailed by the closing of the Nile to the transportation of slaves to markets in the north. A small government force of ten or twenty soldiers had also been established at Shambe by this date (Gray, 1961:115). In short, Nuong Nuer southward expansion resumed after the Chich were no longer in a position to enlist the support of the traders' private armies located at Shambe.

More detailed data are available concerning the effects of the traders' presence on Gaawar (and Lou) expansion against the Southern Dinka, and these data are conducive to the same conclusion. It may be recalled that several trading stations were established along the Zeraf, and inland at Ayod on the Duk ridge, in about 1865. An aspiring Gaawar leader, Nuar Mer, allied himself with the traders in accordance with the pattern prevalent throughout the southern Sudan during this period. Nuar Mer was a Thoi Dinka who had been adopted in his youth by the leading land priest among the Gaawar (Mer Teng) (Johnson, 1980:208). After his father's death, Nuar Mer sought to succeed to this position against substantial (and violent) opposition. Johnson (1980:210) suggests that this opposition led Nuar Mer to ally himself closely with the traders and to enlist their armed assistance in conflicts with the Gaawar aligned against him. The full extent of his activities is well described by Johnson (ibid.).

> Nuar Mer raided for both cattle and people, and he traded the people to the merchants for tobacco, sugar, and other minor items. His raids took him to the Lak, Thiang and Lou Nuer as well as some Gaawar, the Nyarraweng, Twij and other Dinka. Though many Gaawar now view his activities as senseless rapaciousness, acts committed out of extreme pride (*gueth*) there was an element of political terror in his attacks. Individuals who came into conflict with Nuar often had their children captured, or were sold as slaves themselves. Nuar got the aid of the slavers to herd the men of the Nyadikuony section into an enclosure where they were burned to death in revenge for the murder of another man they had killed. In this way Nuar came into increased conflict with other Gaawar, especially the dominant Jamok lineage of the Bar, as well as members of other segments of his own Radh primary section.

Nuar Mer's following among the Gaawar was progressively eroded by the internal conflicts he generated. However, at the same time a number of Dinka from the Thoi, Luac, Rut, Ngok, and Dwor tribes attached themselves to him. By 1874, his following appears to have consisted predominantly of Dinka tribesmen, members of his own Gaawar lineage, and some Lak and Thiang Nuer (Johnson, 1980:211–12). In other words, Nuar Mer not only perpetuated a sustained conflict between sections of the Gaawar, but also recruited members of other Nuer and Dinka tribes to fight against his own people. This unprecedented pattern of alliance was only possible as a consequence of the armed support provided by the traders, and the indigenous segmentary structure regenerated traditional alignments after their departure.

When the Zeraf trading stations were disbanded by Gordon in 1874, Nuar Mer was left without the external support that buttressed his position. He was attacked by Gaawar of the Bar primary section and withdrew inland, to the northern tip of the Duk ridge, with his mixed following. From this base he launched raids against the Nyarraweng and Twij Dinka and the Lou Nuer.

However, his followers were defeated by the Twij and routed with heavy losses by the Lou in the battle of Pading in 1875 (Johnson, 1980:202–3, 213). Finally, in 1878, a Gaawar prophet (Deng Lakka) succeeded in uniting Nuar Mer's many enemies among the Gaawar and led an attack on Nuar Mer's settlements in which the latter was killed and his followers scattered with substantial casualties (ibid.:223).

This ended the protracted conflict among the Gaawar and the formerly opposed sections joined in raids that successfully displaced the Dinka from the northern half of the Duk ridge in the following decade. Traditional lines of military alliance based on the segmentary system were thus rapidly re-established after the eviction of the traders. Nuer territorial expansion, which had been in abeyance for the duration of the Zeraf trading stations' period of operation, was likewise resumed.

The detailed data provided by Johnson (and summarized here) support the conclusion that the intervention of the traders in the Zeraf area inhibited, rather than facilitated, Nuer territorial expansion. There is no question that the Dinka were severely affected by the raids carried out by the traders (directly) and by Nuar Mer. Their capacity to resist Nuer incursions was probably impaired. However, the Nuer were at least equally, and probably more heavily, affected. The disruption and devastation wrought by the traders thus conferred no relative advantage upon the Nuer, and cannot be taken to account for the Nuer appropriation of Dinka territory that resumed after their departure. The military success of the Nuer, both at this time and in prior periods of expansion, is attributable to organizational differences discussed more fully in the main chapters.

This resolves the issues raised by Sacks's (1979:444) suggestion that "Nuer expansion eastward, while it may have been precipitated by the *Zeriba* [trading station] raids and Dinka refugees west of the Nile, was fueled by the Zeraf trade." As noted earlier, Nuer eastward expansion began at least thirty years before the trading stations were established and thus cannot have been "precipitated" by their raiding activities, or by the displacement of Dinka refugees. There is no evidence that Dinka refugees west of the Nile (or Bahr el Jebel) played any role in Nuer eastward expansion. Although Dinka were displaced by the activity of the traders, this predominantly took place in the southwest corner of Dinkaland, in a region far removed from the area where Nuer expansion was taking place. Finally, the Zeraf trading stations did not "fuel" Nuer expansion, but rather inhibited it by sustaining a protracted conflict among the Gaawar that lasted more than a decade, deflected their attention from the Dinka, and produced levels of casualties far in excess of those normally experienced in intratribal feud.

Notes

INTRODUCTION

1. Unfortunately these government reports are not readily accessible. They can be consulted in the science library of the British Museum in London. (It may be noted here that I have followed the Garsse bibliography in the listing of these government reports.)

2. Whether or not this relational cluster includes ecological or environmental features that co-vary with structural differences is an empirical question. In the Nuer/Dinka case, there are no apparent co-variants of this type. The Nuer and Dinka populations are predominantly located within a common ecological zone delineated by the flood plain of the Upper Nile Basin, and were confined within this zone prior to the sixteenth century. Although this ecological zone is not uniform with respect to micro-ecological factors such as soil type, vegetation, plant parasites, the proportional representation of ecotypes, and the like, differences in the distribution of these factors do not co-vary with the historical loci of Nuer and Dinka occupation. The same constellation of microecological factors that characterizes the area occupied by the Nuer in earlier times is equally characteristic of adjacent territory to the south (and, to some extent, the east) that was formerly occupied by the Dinka. In other words, the strip of land on the west side of the Nile (or Bahr el Jebel) is microecologically homogeneous. The central point here is that I have been unable to discover any microecological differences that co-vary with the initial spatial distribution of the Nuer and Dinka. Although the Nuer and Dinka differ with respect to their relative reliance on cattle herding and agriculture, these dissimilar economic variants of a common transhumant system of economic production are unrelated to ecological variations. Moreover, the Nuer economic variant was maintained as Nuer tribes expanded eastward into areas characterized by a significantly different microecology. It is particularly noteworthy that the Lou Nuer cultivate the same acreage per household as the Western Jikany, Jagei, Dok, and Nuong (west of the Nile) despite the fact that the incidence of crop failure (attributable to microecological differences) is two and one-half times greater. In summary, available data—which are quite extensive—indicate that there are no known ecological phenomena that are exclusively confined to the area originally inhabited by the Nuer, and which might consequently be employed to account for the distinctive features of Nuer economic organization. Second, these distinctive features were maintained by Nuer tribes that later occupied microecologically dissimilar areas characterized by significant differences in the reliability of agricultural production. The relational cluster that provided the dynamic of the Nuer structural transformation

thus excludes ecological co-variants. This is one of the aspects of the case that makes it particularly intriguing.

3. Many of the reinterpretations of the Nuer data entail an effort to interrelate what Evans-Pritchard has analytically disjoined. This is particularly true of Gough's insightful discussion of Nuer kinship. It should be noted that Gough (1971:88) suggests that a number of features of the Nuer sociocultural system are explicable with respect to Nuer expansion. She also suggests (ibid.:116) that a controlled comparison of the Nuer and Dinka, together with consideration of the history of the nineteenth-century Nuer expansion, would prove fruitful. The present study follows these suggestions. It is also indebted in a more general way to one of the underlying points of Gough's analysis. She implicitly challenges the distinction between the domestic and the politico-jural domains. However, it would be misleading if I did not also note that my analysis differs from that proposed by Gough with respect to aspects of economic differentiation upon which she placed considerable emphasis.

4. It is noteworthy that the challenge to received analytic wisdom represented by alliance theory was primarily engendered by two comparative works, Lévi-Strauss's *Elementary Structures of Kinship* (1949) and Leach's *Political Systems of Highland Burma* (1954). The latter is a controlled comparison in which the relational cluster that encompasses structural variation includes distinctive marriage systems but excludes descent. Leach makes this point quite explicitly in a number of publications (e.g., Leach, 1966:116).

5. The basis of this contention is developed progressively throughout the book. The reader who prefers to have this firmly established at the onset is referred to note 5 of the final chapter. The applicability of the concept of key symbol is also discussed in the passage to which this note refers.

CHAPTER 1

1. See Greenberg (1966) concerning the classification of Nilotic languages.

2. If the Nuer and Dinka languages differentiated from each other after the common language from which they are both derived began to diverge from other Nilotic languages, then one would expect Nuer and Dinka (respectively) to display similar percentages of shared cognates with these other Nilotic languages. However, this is not the case. McLaughlin's figures (see text) indicate that the Nuer share a higher percentage of cognates with the Anuak than do the Dinka, and Johnson's figures both confirm this and show that the Nuer also share a higher percentage of cognates with the Shilluk than do the Dinka. This pattern could simply be the result of a spatial distribution in which the population from which proto-Nuer later developed represented that portion of proto-Nuer/Dinka speakers that abutted proto-Shilluk/Anuak speakers at the time of the original divergence. The neighboring population (which eventually became the Nuer) might then be expected to diverge less rapidly from proto-Shilluk/Anuak than the nonneighboring population (which eventually became the Dinka). Johnson (1980:86–87) proposes, alternatively, that the Nuer were originally a Luo-speaking group, or were closely allied with Luo speakers (i.e., the language group that includes the Anuak and Shilluk). Although this would account for the fact that the Nuer manifest higher shared cognate percentages with Anuak and Shilluk than do the Dinka,

it is inconsistent with the even higher percentage of shared cognates between Nuer and Dinka. Johnson thus finds it necessary to attribute the latter to subsequent contact between these two linguistic groups. The logical difficulty with this interpretation is that it assumes the Nuer were linguistically influenced by the Dinka more than the Dinka were influenced by the Nuer. If this were not the case, the words the Nuer share with the Anuak and Shilluk would have more readily been adopted by the Dinka. Thus Johnson (1980:87) invokes "a fundamental 'Dinkaization' of the Nuer" that took place at the time of the Dinka's westward migration into the Bahr el Ghazal. The conventional view presented in the text does not require this improbable concept of one-sided influence, and it continues to be the simplest and most plausible interpretation of available lexico-statistical data.

3. The branch of the Ruweng that currently inhabits the area between the Thoi and Shilluk (see map 1) reportedly moved there from the vicinity of Lake No in about 1890, during the Madhia (Howell, 1945:321). If I am correct in deducing that this was the former homeland of the Ruweng, this would constitute a return to it.

4. It is of interest that there are no reports of Dinka expansion to the southern edge and southeast corner of this ecological zone. These areas are occupied by the Mandari and Murle.

5. These segmentary processes are described by Evans-Pritchard (1940*a*:143–44); their role in Nuer expansion has been emphasized by Sahlins (1961). They will be fully examined in a later chapter.

6. Jackson's account of the Jikany migration (1923:78) differs somewhat from those of Stigand (1919) and Bacon (1922) in that it includes a second party of Jikany that traveled along the White Nile. The latter are said to have joined forces with the migrants who took the northern route at Kodak.

7. In a footnote to this passage, Evans-Pritchard references the writings of D'Antonio, Vannutelli, Citerni, Michel, and Bacon.

8. Early censuses of the Lou indicate that the Gun primary section outnumbered the Mor by better than two to one (Bacon, 1917; Alban, 1930). This suggests that the Jinaca component of the Jikany migration was relatively small and that most of the Lou are derived from the second wave of eastward expansion.

9. The Lou are derived from the Rengyan component of the four small Jagei tribes, and lineages of the Jinaca clan are dominant in both the Lou and Rengyan tribes (Evans-Pritchard, 1940*a*:212).

10. In this eastern half of what was then Nyarraweng territory, the high ground suitable for wet season occupation is almost exclusively concentrated in the vicinity of 8° N latitude, 32° E longitude, with the area to the south and east of this serving only as dry season pasture (see Howell, 1954*e*: map E11). The appropriation of a relatively small area of high ground thus conferred control over this extensive pasture area.

11. The Nuong, Lak, Thiang, Gaawar, Lou, and Eastern Jikany Nuer occupy an area of about 22,560 square miles (Howell, 1954*a*:239) that was inhabited by the Dinka and Anuak prior to nineteenth-century Nuer expansion. In circa 1930 censuses, these Nuer tribes had a combined population of 186,000 (Evans-Pritchard, 1940*a*:117). However, in an early 1950s census these Nuer tribes numbered over 293,000. The former Dinka and Anuak population of this area is estimated to have been at least as large as the Nuer population of 1930. However, inasmuch as the Nuer

were thinly settled as a result of their recent conquest, it is likely that the former Dinka and Anuak population was considerably larger.

12. See Johnson (1980, 1982) for an examination of administrative policy and the role this played in Nuer-Dinka relations. These sources also include a more detailed chronicle of events during this period.

13. A survey of fourteen Gaawar settlements was carried out at the height of this 1908 epidemic and the corpses of dead cattle were estimated to represent 30 to 40 percent of the total herd (*SIR* 165, 1908:3).

14. The Nuer did not occupy Faijing nor are they reported to have shifted their settlements southward into the no-man's-land separating the Nuer and Dinka along this border (*SIR* 177, 1909:16). This is consistent with the Nuer's general lack of interest in territorial acquisition after 1890.

15. Although a critique of British administration is outside the scope of this work, it is clear that this settlement heavily favored the Dinka while offering the Nuer nothing they valued. In the Nuer view, the government simply presented itself as an ally of their ancient enemy, the Dinka. A comprehensive review of British policy and administrative practice may be found in Collins (1971), Digerness (1978), and Johnson (1980, 1982).

16. It is worth pointing out that these government reports only specify precise figures when there is some sound basis for doing so. The reports represent military intelligence, and casual estimates of the strength and effectiveness of the "opposition" could prove disastrous to the relatively small patrols dispatched to deal with them. Since the return of stolen cattle was a major concern, determination of the exact number taken was the object of investigation. Compensation for deaths likewise necessitated a precise accounting of casualties.

17. Anuak raids on the Jikany during this period are not well reported. In February, 1912, "serious fighting" between the Anuak and Nuer was reported to be taking place in the neighborhood of the Adura and Pibor Rivers, in Jikany and Lou territory, respectively (*SIR* 211, 1912:4). Brief reference to an unsuccessful Anuak raid on the Jikany is also made in the March, 1912, report (*SIR* 212, 1912:3). The general discussion seems to indicate that this was the most recent of a number of engagements.

18. The last Nuer raid on the Anuak, in April, 1914, was explained to government officers as a preemptive strike intended to forestall an anticipated Anuak offensive (*SIR* 237, 1914:5).

19. Jikany raids on the Burun are described in the following *Sudan Intelligence Reports:* 253, 254, 294, 297, 299, 300, 302, 303, 304, 311, 312, 313, and 314.

20. Government taxes, or tribute, were generally assessed at 1 or 2 percent of estimated Nuer (and Dinka) herds annually. Only the Machar section of the Gaawar is reported to have refused to pay their assessment and the amount due is not specified. Judging from scattered reports on tribute collection it is unlikely that it exceeded two hundred head.

21. *Sudan Intelligence Reports* for 1916 and most of 1917 are unavailable at the Public Record Office in Kew, England. However, lengthy extracts of the sections of those reports dealing with Nuer-Dinka conflict are reproduced in Johnston (1934), but without page references to the originals.

22. *Sudan Intelligence Reports* covering the period November, 1925, to August,

1927, are unavailable at the Public Records Office. Reports for November, 1927, to August, 1928, are available, after which the file is, at present, closed to inspection.

23. The account provided by Coriat (who had administrative responsibility for the Lou Nuer at this time) makes it clear that arrest was not actually contemplated.

The tribesmen were warned that after the expiration of a time limit all men found outside the settlements were liable to arrest. It was hoped by such means to induce Gwek and his followers either to submit [to settlement requirements] or to fight. (Coriat, 1939:235).

No effort was made to arrest Gwek, although various stratagems were employed to induce him to lead a frontal assault into the waiting Maxim guns.

24. See *Sudan Intelligence Reports (SIR)*, Nos. 245, 250, 253, 299, 304, 326, 333, 336, and 338.

25. The Nuer suffered heavy casualties on two occasions when government forces (accompanied by Dinka tribesmen) attacked Nuer raiding parties, losing 290 men in one case and 100 in another (*SIR* 298, 1919:4; *SIR* 236, 1922:6).

26. These raids are not mentioned in *Sudan Intelligence Reports* from January, 1923, to November, 1925, and evidently took place between the latter date and the end of 1926, a period for which reports are unavailable at the Public Records Office.

27. Johnson (1981, 1982) is critical of Evans-Pritchard's (1940*a*) account of Nuer-Dinka relations on the grounds that Evans-Pritchard overlooked "how intermarriage between Nuer and Dinka had a pacifying effect on inter-tribal warfare" (Johnson, 1981:510). Although Johnson's research adds a dimension to our understanding of Nuer-Dinka interrelations, he fails to note that intermarriage had the broader effect of undercutting the unity of Dinka tribal units.

28. The sample includes the Nuer raids on the Southern and Southwestern Dinka discussed in the previous section. With one exception, these raids took place during the years 1908 to 1922. The rainy season extends from May through October and the dry season from November through April.

29. The Southern Dinka area inhabited by the Ric, Ghol, Nyarraweng, Twij, and Bor is most similar environmentally to the Central Dinka region conquered by the Nuer. Indeed the northern third of this southern area *was* appropriated by the Nuer, and subsequently restored to the Dinka by the colonial administration. The economy of the Southern Dinka therefore can be taken to closely resemble that of the former Dinka inhabitants of the territory conquered by the Nuer.

30. These differences will be taken up in a later chapter. See Howell (1954*b*:244–48) for a discussion of the main factors responsible.

31. This separate June planting is omitted by the Nuer, who also tend to plant the main crop somewhat later (see Evans-Pritchard, 1940*a*:97). In other respects, the Nuer conform to the same agricultural calendar as the neighboring Ghol and Nyarraweng. The Bor and Twi Dinka further south interplant early and late varieties in April–May and September–October (Howell, 1954*b*:366).

32. Evans-Pritchard (1940*a*:129) notes that the corpses of fallen Dinka were "thrown on the flaming byres and huts," indicating that burning of villages formed part of the standard Nuer repertoire. Burning is specifically reported for a number of twentieth-century raids (described earlier). It is not clear that this failed to occur when it is not mentioned, since government reports rarely provide detailed accounts of Nuer

raids and focus on casualties, captives, and stolen cattle that were subject to compensation or return. However, the loss of food supplies was not entirely contingent upon burning, since untended crops were subject to the unrestricted depredations of birds, antelope, and other wildlife. Tornay's (1979:104) account of the effects of raiding in another East African society indicates that an entire crop could be lost in a matter of days.

33. This figure is based on 1950s rates of 1.62 cattle per capita for the Bor District inhabited by the Southern Dinka (Howell, 1954b:230).

34. Detailed data concerning community size are available for the Nuer but not the Dinka. The average size of the seventy-six Lou Nuer villages enumerated by Bacon (1917:1–8) is 250 persons. The comparable figure for the Homeland Nuer west of the Bahr el Jebel is 194 persons (Kerreri, 1931:265–67) and that for the Lak, Thiang, and Gaawar is 292 persons (Upper Nile Province Handbook, Zeraf Valley section, 1930:2A). Since community size varies according to environmental conditions and the Southern Dinka region is most similar to that of the Gaawar, the latter figure provides the most suitable basis for estimating Southern Dinka community size. During the conquest of Zeraf Island, the Nuer would have been attacking communities located precisely in this area where latter-day Nuer settlements average 292 persons. Hence the estimate of 300 persons per Dinka community will serve for considering both Nuer expansion and subsequent twentieth-century raids on the Southern Dinka. This is a conservative estimate in that Dinka population density is higher than that of the Nuer, and Dinka settlements are said to be more concentrated. These features will be explored in a later chapter.

Recent studies indicate that males aged fifteen to forty-five constitute 24.8 percent of the Southern Dinka population (Payne and El Amin, 1977:10). Thus the fighting men of a Dinka community are taken as one-quarter of the total population.

35. This account follows Titherington's description in attributing the ambush to elements of the same Nuer column involved in the initial engagement. However, it is more likely that Nuer strategy entailed the withdrawal of one contingent to a point where a second was in position to reinforce them.

36. As noted earlier, government forces accompanied by Dinka warriors twice defeated *small* Nuer raiding parties, inflicting heavy casualties (see note 26).

37. These twenty-nine raids include twenty-five described in available *Sudan Intelligence Reports,* and four additional engagements discussed by Titherington (1927:198–99) and Digerness (1978:81).

38. Nuer losses appear to have been only a small fraction of those they inflicted on the Dinka. Excluding engagements with government forces, the only Nuer losses reported are eight warriors killed in one raid on the Dinka and three in another (*SIR* 245, 1914:4; *SIR* 239, 1914:3).

39. Eight men, eight women, and two girls were killed in this same raid, reportedly carried out by only twenty-five men. Captives taken thus outnumber casualties by thirty-four to eighteen. The suggestion that this pattern is largely a product of the Dinka response to raids is confirmed by the small size of the raiding party in this case. Sustained resistance to this attack by Dinka warriors would surely have engaged the attention of the raiders long enough to allow more of the women and children to escape.

40. This estimate is based on an average village population of three hundred persons (established earlier), multiplied by the 1950s ratio of 1.62 cattle per capita reported by Howell (1954*b*:230) for the Bor District.

41. The Nuer are said to have taken the same route, along a ridge of relatively high ground on which Dinka communities are clustered, in 1914 and 1916 as well as 1928. Consequently the figure of thirty villages attacked in 1928 can reasonably be applied to the raids of 1914 and 1916, which penetrated the same distance into Dinkaland along the same route. The source of the figures utilized for average Dinka village size and cattle per capita holdings are explained in note 40. These figures are employed here to illustrate the approximate dimensions of the population directly affected by Nuer raids, and the order of magnitude of herd reductions resulting from them. However, it should be kept in mind that rinderpest epidemics periodically reduced the cattle population by as much as 30 percent after 1890 and that cattle per capita fluctuated widely as a result. The Dinka probably possessed fewer cattle during the period from 1914 to 1928 than they did in the early 1950s when veterinary programs to control rinderpest and other cattle diseases had been in effect for some time. On the other hand, the 1950s cattle per capita figures more accurately reflect conditions during the period of Nuer expansion, prior to the introduction of rinderpest.

42. In 1930, the total Nuer population of former Dinka and Anuak territory on both sides of the Bahr el Jebel was 186,000 persons. For present purposes, it will be useful to exclude Nuong Nuer territory and population (9,000) and focus on the region east of the Bahr el Jebel. In this region the Dinka tribes that migrated to adjacent areas under the pressure of Nuer raids are at least partly distinguishable from the prior inhabitants of these areas.

43. The period from 1818 to 1905 extends from the inception of Nuer expansion to the date at which the Anglo-Egyptian colonial government began to constitute an impediment to Nuer raids. It is important to recall that the Nuer continued to raid the Dinka in order to recoup their stock losses (due to rinderpest and other introduced diseases) long after territorial expansion had tapered off in the early 1880s. Captives continued to be taken in these raids, as they were well into the twentieth century.

44. The administrative census of the early 1950s is employed here because it lists the population of the Nuer and Dinka by tribal units, while the more accurate official government census of 1955–56 lists population by census units. Although the number of Nuer and Dinka enumerated in the official census is somewhat larger than the figures given here, this would not materially change the relationship between the size of the two populations being compared. It should be noted that the population of the Western Ngok is not supplied in the principal source (Howell, 1955:77–80), but is derived from Howell (1951:241).

45. Population growth during the period from 1930 to the early 1950s was largely a consequence of the introduction of inoculation programs and a modicum of medical care into a population formerly characterized by both high birth rates and high mortality rates. This is discussed more fully in the next chapter. The more rapid growth of the displaced Dinka tribes (compared to the Nuer) was probably a consequence of migration. Some Dinka groups that took refuge among the Nuer may have rejoined their natal tribes after the cessation of Nuer raids (e.g., the Nyarraweng).

46. The figure of thirty-one thousand represents a minimum estimate because any

captive or immigrant who does not marry (or participate in a legal union) and have two surviving offspring contributes only one non-Nuer to the population rather than three. Immigrant Dinka tribesmen were often the consorts of Nuer widows and women involved in ghost marriage. The children of these consort relationships were counted as children of their Nuer pater (i.e., the widow's deceased husband or the ghost husband, see Evans-Pritchard, 1940*a*:224; 1951:109–14). Such children are Nuer rather than "Dinka-Nuer." The greater the number of captives and immigrants without "Dinka-Nuer" offspring, the greater the total number of captives and immigrants required in order to produce the specified social composition. It may be noted that Nuer customs concerning the social classification of the offspring of widows and women involved in ghost unions served to incorporate the children of male immigrants into the Nuer lineage system. Male captives were adopted (Evans-Pritchard, 1940*a*:221). The children of female captives belonged to their Nuer father's lineage. In all, the social system readily facilitated a massive assimilation of Dinka and Anuak.

47. Evans-Pritchard (1933:53) estimates that 75 percent of the Lou Nuer are of recent Dinka extraction and this proportion would also be applicable to the Eastern Jikany. A recalculation of the rate of assimilation necessary to produce a social composition of 75 percent Dinka-Nuer for these two tribes, and 50 percent for the Gaawar, Lak, Thiang, and Nuong, yields a figure of 82,666 rather than 62,000.

48. The higher estimate is based on the assimilation of eighty-two thousand captives and immigrants (see note 47) and thirty thousand members of Dinka lineages. The lower estimate includes eighty thousand of the former and twenty thousand of the latter.

CHAPTER 2

1. This would be true in any case, since the Bor District occupied by the Southern Dinka is within the true savannah and is very similar, environmentally, to the area occupied by the Nuer. The complete conquest of a specified ecological niche would therefore include the conquest of this area, irrespective of the specific features employed in the definition of niche boundaries. However, the main thrust of the latter phase of Nuer expansion was precisely in this area, and Sahlins is correct in pointing out that the Nuer generally sought to appropriate the environmental areas most similar to those they already inhabited.

2. The average Nuer density reported here (12.5 persons per square mile) is somewhat lower than the average based on 1955–56 census figures presented earlier (i.e., 14.7 persons per square mile). This is partly due to the fact that Nuer population increased between the administrative census of the early 1950s, on which the former figure is based, and the national census of 1955–56. It is probably also due to a degree of underenumeration in the administrative census. In addition, the area employed in the calculation is not the same in each case. The size of the Nuer "districts" in the administrative census is somewhat larger than the size of Nuer territory reported by Howell (1954*a*:239) used in the earlier calculation. (Howell's figure was used in that context because it was equally applicable to the 1930 census material reported by Evans-Pritchard.)

It is important to note that the figures employed in the present comparison of Nuer and Dinka densities are strictly comparable, being based on census material collected by the same agency at the same time. Although these figures may reflect a degree of underenumeration, this would be equally applicable to both the Nuer and Dinka. Precise scientific measures of Nuer and Dinka density are not available. However, the data that are available consistently indicate that the population density of Dinka administrative districts and/or census units is higher than the density of comparable Nuer units. Although data which would permit a precise determination of density in relation to economic resources are not available, they would undoubtedly support the same conclusion. Nuer territory is all savannah while Dinka territory includes extensive tracts of forest that represent marginal grazing resources. This suggests that effective Dinka density exceeds that of the Nuer by a greater margin than indicated by the rough measures presented in the text.

3. Sahlins's designation of the Nuer as "invaders" apparently applies to the true savannah ecological niche bounded on the west by the savannah forest region presently occupied by the Western Dinka. However, the previously discussed ambiguity concerning Sahlins's delineation of niche boundaries clouds his intended meaning on this point.

4. Newcomer's hypothesis is based on Lienhardt's (1958) observations concerning differences between the Nuer and Dinka in seasonal patterns of aggregation. Lienhardt (ibid.:132–33) also suggests that these differences have some bearing on tribal size. Lienhardt's suggestions draw on Evans-Pritchard's (1940a:117–18) explanation of differences in the size of Nuer tribes discussed more fully in the next section.

5. Differences between the Nuer and Dinka in segmentary organization are discussed at length in chapter 4.

6. Southall feels it is preferable to designate the Nuer as Naath and the Dinka as Jieng, these being the names each group applies to itself. This is also consistent with his view that these labels refer to ethnic identifications. He criticizes Newcomer and Glickman for speaking of the Nuer and Dinka as "unambiguously distinct groups, each one capable of distinctive characterization and concerted action" (Southall, 1976:466). On my reading, neither author is guilty of this charge. Moreover, it is important to note that several Nuer tribes did, on occasion, participate in concerted action against the Dinka, joining forces in large-scale raids. In addition, the expansion of one Nuer tribe was frequently facilitated by the territorial gains and raids of another. For example, raids launched from the Eastern Jikany enclave certainly contributed to the ease and rapidity with which the Lou Nuer were able to expand in that direction. Although Lou and Eastern Jikany expansion were not mutually contrived, they were mutually supportive. It is, in this sense, quite reasonable to speak of Nuer territorial expansion as a coherent phenomenon. It did not consist of totally independent and unrelated events.

7. Southall (1976:467) suggests that Naath (Nuer) expansion and incorporation of the Jieng (Dinka) began more than three hundred years ago. The organizational differentiations of these two cultural groups thus took place throughout this period.

8. I hasten to concede that I have not done justice to Evans-Pritchard in this respect. His remarks concerning Nuer-Dinka interrelations are contextualized within an elegant theory of political structure that is too lengthy and complex to be summarized in this book.

9. These figures are based on comparable administrative censuses conducted in 1930 and 1931. An earlier (1916) census of seventy-six Lou Nuer villages yields an average of 250 persons per community (Bacon, 1917:1–8). Since the Nuer population is known to have increased between 1917 and 1930, it is probable that Lou Nuer settlements would be about the same size as those of the Zeraf Valley in 1930.

10. Although available evidence suggests that the expanding Nuer tribes assimilated larger numbers of Dinka than the Homeland Nuer tribes, this does not constitute a sufficient explanation of their larger size. Differences in tribal size can only be satisfactorily explained by differences in the level at which fission takes place. The larger tribal polities of the eastern region are not only a product of growth but also, and more importantly, a product of factors conducive to the maintenance of relations between primary segments that forestall fission (see Evans-Pritchard, 1940a:117–18).

11. The average height of the Shilluk is the same as that of the Nuer, while the Dinka are one centimeter shorter (Howell, 1954b:249).

12. Both the Western and Eastern Nuer are considerably better off than the Central Nuer in terms of reliable grain production. Howell (1954b:197–98, 369) reports that the Western Nuer District includes some tribal territories that experience regular shortages (e.g., Leik) and others (especially Bul) that characteristically produce an annual surplus. As a whole, the district "is just self-supporting, though imports are required in some years" (ibid.:197). The Eastern Nuer District produces a surplus of three hundred metric tons of grain in most years. This is precisely equivalent to the average shortfall in the Central Nuer District (Howell, 1955:179), which is discussed more fully in the text.

13. Crop failures tend to occur within limited areas for two reasons. First, rainfall varies between localities in any given year and second, soils are sufficiently variable from place to place so that conditions that pose difficulty in one area may be ideal in another. For example, heavy rains may impair yields on poorly drained soils while increasing yields on sandy soils. In a year characterized by periods of drought the results would be reversed (Howell, 1954b:210).

14. Although the Nuer possess large numbers of sheep and goats, their contribution to the diet is slight in comparison with that of the cattle population. There are a number of reasons for this. First, the milk production of sheep and goats is negligible, with ewes producing barely enough to supply their lambs and nannies yielding only a few ounces of milk a day (Tothill, 1948:641, 644; see also Evans-Pritchard, 1937:222; Payne and El Amin, 1977:86–90). Milk is a much more important component of the diet than meat (see fig. 1) and nearly all of it is derived from cattle. Second, the body weight of mature sheep and goats is only 12 to 25 kilograms (Payne and El Amin, 1977; Tothill, 1948), while mature cows weigh 200 to 220 kilograms and mature oxen 300 to 340 kilograms (Payne and El Amin, 1977:111). Although sheep and goats are utilized as meat animals, each provides only 7.8 percent as much meat as an ox which serves the same purpose. Since the Nuer cattle population is about two and one-half times larger than the combined sheep and goat population (Howell, 1955:77–79), the latter provide only about 3 percent of meat consumption. Their contribution to combined milk and meat supplies would be less than 1 percent.

15. It is clear that land was plentiful in the 1920s and 1930s, since the Nuer population at that time was only about half as large as the 1955 population. Despite the

fact that the quantity of land in production had doubled by 1955, further expansion was still possible. The situation is described by Howell (1954*b*:232, 328) as follows. Within the flood region inhabited by the Nuer and adjacent Dinka, high land that is secure from flooding is extremely scarce. Agriculture is predominantly carried out on slightly elevated sites that represent marginal land due to the risks of flood and drought discussed in the text. In the context of a discussion of fallow rotation, Howell (1954*b*:328) describes these land resources as "almost unlimited," and notes that the fallow period is characteristically long enough "for the natural vegetation to reach its ecological climax." This clearly indicates that the limits of agricultural utilization had not been reached at this time. However, it is also important to note that much of this potentially available agricultural land is currently devoted to grazing. On any given wet season site under current occupation, agriculture and grazing represent competing utilizations of the limited elevated ground available. The complexities of this situation will be more fully explained in due course. The point to be noted here is that the agricultural component of the economy could readily be expanded, thereby reducing Nuer dependence on cattle products (and also reducing grazing requirements).

16. At the height of the rains, the savannah grasses are tall, dense, and stemmy with high bulk and low nutritional content. Mud and water impede the cattle's movement and effective grazing is precluded. In late September and October the seed heads of some of these grasses appear and provide both more nutritional and more accessible feed. At the same time, the receding floodwaters ease the difficulty of movement, although the vegetation is still dense.

17. Payne and El Amin (1977:48–63) provide an extensive list of prevalent cattle diseases.

18. It is important to note that heavy and protracted flooding during the wet season results in favorable grazing conditions during the following dry season. The savannah retains sufficient moisture to provide adequate grazing at inland locations throughout the dry season, and movement to major watercourses is consequently unnecessary. The fact that the latter may provide poor grazing due to high water therefore poses no difficulties. It should also be noted that the level of the Nile at the height of the dry season is primarily determined by the amount of rainfall in the interlacustrine region far to the south of Nuer territory. Heavy flooding of Nuerland in the wet season therefore does not necessarily produce high water levels in the dry season as well, although these co-occurred in 1917–18.

19. Although some Central Nuer groups are reported to have lost "many" cattle (*SIR* 283, 1918:3), no more specific information is available. However, it should be noted that substantial herd reductions would not be expected during this period due to the fact that Nuer herds had already been severely depleted by rinderpest. Although wet season grazing was constricted in 1917–18, it may nevertheless have been nearly adequate to support the comparatively small cattle population of that period.

20. Payne and El Amin's data indicate that this potential rate of increase was not realized in the Southern Dinka area during the period from 1954 to 1976. Informants reported that the cattle population had not increased at all in the past twenty-five years. This would be expected if the cattle population had reached ecological limits in the 1950s, after recovering from the impact of introduced diseases.

21. The diseases mentioned in the literature as playing a role in morbidity or

mortality include: malaria, tuberculosis, yaws, cerebrospinal meningitis, try-panosomiasis, kala-azar, schistosomiasis, onchocerciasis, dysentery, gastroenteritis, anthrax, smallpox, measles, typhoid fever, yellow fever, relapsing fever, and influenza (Jackson, 1923:71, 186; Titherington, 1927:207–8; Howell, 1954*b*:251–52; Lolik, 1976:103–4; Payne and El Amin, 1977:48). An outbreak of smallpox is reported to have occurred in Sennar during the reign of Ansu, 1635–71, indicating the presence of this disease at an early date (Gleichen, 1905:229).

22. The provision of medical services was adopted as a central element of the colonial government's policy of "peaceful penetration" in the 1920s and substantial resources were allocated to this program in the years that followed (Digerness, 1978; Butt, 1952:20–21). A hospital ship was commissioned in 1921 and general inoculation programs were initiated the same year (Jackson, 1923:163, 186). By 1935, each province had a central hospital, a network of local dispensaries for treatment of less severe cases, and a group of trained native "dressers" working out of each of the latter (Butt, 1952). This medical organization was also mobilized to combat the outbreak of particular diseases.

23. The derivation of these estimates is discussed in the last section of chapter 1.

24. As explained in note 2, the national census of 1955–56 indicates a larger population (and higher density) than the administrative census of the early 1950s. The density of the homeland area in 1955–56 is 15.9 persons per square mile while the density of the Western Nuer District with which it largely corresponds was reported as 13.9 persons per square mile based on administrative census figures from the early 1950s. The 1955–56 figures are most relevant to a consideration of Nuer population growth, while the administrative census figures are most useful for a comparison of Nuer and Dinka densities (see note 2). It should also be noted that the Homeland Nuer territory of eight thousand seven hundred square miles in 1800 includes all of the Western Nuer District except the territory of the Nuong Nuer, which was acquired in the course of the Nuer expansion of 1800 to 1880.

25. The Homeland Nuer tribes include the Bul, Leik, two Western Jikany tribes, four Jagei tribes, and the Dok. The tribes that participated in Nuer expansion include the Nuong, Lak, Thiang, Gaawar, Lou, Gaajak, Gaagwang, and Gaajok. The 1930 population figures for these tribes were presented earlier in the chapter. In 1800, the Nuer homeland was occupied by the Gaajok, Gaagwang, and Gaajak (from which the Eastern Jikany subsequently split), the four Jagei tribes, the Bul, Leik, Dok, Nuong, Lak, Thiang, Gaawar, and Lou. This yields a total of fifteen tribes. However, the four Jagei tribes typically operated as a single military unit in conflicts with the Dinka, and counting these as equivalent to a single tribe reduces the number of such units to twelve. Based on the median estimated population of the homeland (127,000), the average size of these twelve tribal (or military) units would be 10,583 at the inception of Nuer expansion in the early 1800s.

26. This is confirmed by the fact that Nuer expansion took place in areas where there was dry season conflict with neighboring Dinka tribes and did not proceed in areas where such conflict was precluded by the location of dry season grazing areas. For example, the Bul Nuer utilize dry season pastures adjacent to a large marsh to the southeast of their wet season settlements (see map 1) and consequently move away from their border with the Western Dinka (Howell, 1954*e:* map E7). Bul Nuer ter-

ritorial expansion is not reported for the nineteenth century. Similarly, the Lak Nuer primarily repair to dry season grazing located along the Bahr el Jebel, in the opposite direction from their border with the Rut Dinka (see Evans-Pritchard, 1940*a:*60 and Howell, 1954*e:* map E6. The latter map differs from the former in showing no eastward movement at all.) The Rut Dinka move to the Khor Atar and thus also move away from their Zeraf River border with the Lak Nuer (Howell, 1954*e:* map E10). The general eastward expansion of the Nuer curved south at precisely this point, bypassing the Rut. The Gaawar likewise seek dry season pastures to the south and west, in the opposite direction from the Rut, Thoi, and Eastern Luaich Dinka, but bringing them into conflict with the Ghol (see Evans-Pritchard, 1940*a:*60; Howell, 1954*e:* map E6; again the latter map shows this most clearly while the former omits the Gaawar's southern grazing grounds). The Gaawar expanded southward in the nineteenth century and rainy season raids against the Southern Dinka continued during the early colonial period. The Eastern Ngok find dry season grazing along the Khor Fullus to the west and the Khor Wol to the northeast (Howell, 1954*e*), while the dry season pastures of their Lou Nuer neighbors are located to the east and south (Evans-Pritchard, 1940*a:*56). The Lou and Ngok are thus out of contact in the dry season. Evans-Pritchard (1940*a:*127) points out that the Ngok were "left in peace," but attributes this to their poverty of stock and their mythological connection to Kir, the putative ancestor of the Jikany tribes. However, the absence of Nuer wet season raids on the Ngok also fits the larger pattern detailed here. The generally southward movement of the Lou in the dry season brought them into conflict with the Southern Dinka (Evans-Pritchard, 1940*a:*62), and Lou rainy season raids were directed against these same groups in the early 1900s. Finally, Nuong Nuer raids (and territorial expansion) also took place in precisely the areas where dry season conflict occurred. The overall pattern of Nuer expansion thus emerges quite clearly. The Nuer regularly experienced dry season grazing shortages which brought them into conflict with certain neighboring Dinka tribes. These same tribes were subject to annual rainy season raids that eventually led to their withdrawal from the area, and the Nuer moved into the unoccupied territory in due course.

CHAPTER 3

1. When a man dies without male issue, his brother (and other close kinsmen) have an obligation to marry a woman to his spirit. These "ghost marriages" are contracted to carry on a man's name and to insure the perpetuation of his lineage. The brother or other kinsman initiating the union fulfills the duties of husband to the ghost's wife and the obligations of fatherhood to her children, while the dead man is the legal father from whom descent is traced (see Howell, 1954*a:*74–79; Evans-Pritchard, 1951*a:*109–12).

2. In the ideal bridewealth payment, cattle are allotted specifically to father's full and half siblings, the former being further distinguished as to elder and younger. In the acceptable payment, cattle are designated for undifferentiated paternal uncles (and likewise for maternal uncles). However, additional claims (absent from the ideal list) are phrased in terms of the rights of paternal and maternal grandparents. The latter claims are recognized only if the particular grandparents were alive when the bride was

born and are therefore contingent rather than fixed. In the event that none of the four grandparental claims meet this requirement, the acceptable bridewealth would decrease to eighteen cattle. If the grandparent was alive at the time of the bride's birth but died before she married, these claims are inherited in a specified manner by the sons of the grandparents (excluding the bride's father). Father's father's claim passes to father's paternal half brother, father's mother's to father's full brother, mother's father's to mother's paternal half-brother, and mother's mother's to mother's full brother (see Evans-Pritchard, 1951a:77). In the comparison of ideal and acceptable bridewealth distributions presented in the text, grandparental claims are represented as those of the bride's uncles that inherit them.

3. The Nuer conceptualize bridewealth transactions in terms of a "paternal side" and a "maternal side" corresponding to the two sibling sets within which bridewealth is distributed. The bride's father and full brothers are seen as part of the paternal side by all Nuer tribes. The bride's mother and uterine half brothers are seen as part of the maternal side by the Lou Nuer but as part of the paternal side by the Zeraf and Western Nuer tribes (see Howell, 1954a:103). The difference concerns the conceptualization of the proportional allotments to each side. The Lou Nuer view the bridewealth cattle as shared equally between the two sides, while the Zeraf and Western Nuer see the proportion as two to one, favoring the paternal side. Since the cattle allocated to the mother and uterine half brothers of the bride do in fact join the bride's father's herd everywhere, the Lou conceptualization appears somewhat disingenuous. Actually, Lou ideal bridewealth favors the bride's father and patrikin by a ratio of three to one.

4. Evans-Pritchard (1951a:85–86) does not include this claim among those which define the Lou ideal bridewealth payment (described earlier), but regards it as on the borderline between the latter and a category of "small gifts" that kinsmen of the bride may request as part of the total payment. However, the distinction Evans-Pritchard makes is analytical rather than cultural, since the claim is phrased in the same way as those of the "people of rights" and the animal equally subject to return in the event of divorce. It should also be mentioned that Howell (1954a:105) points out that Evans-Pritchard confuses this Lou Nuer claim of the bride's father's father's brother's son with the Western Nuer claim of the bride's father's mother's brother. The confusion seems to be due to the fact that the Lou themselves see these claims as alternative variants. In other words, they see their recognition of this distant patrilateral claim as an analogue of the distant matrilateral claim recognized by the Homeland Nuer. Both are uniformly designated as the *kethar* claims, despite the fact that the recipients differ.

5. In assembling these figures for comparative purposes I have included the cattle allotted to the bride's father's mother's brother and mother's mother's brother as part of the portion of the patrikin and matrikin, respectively, in the case of those tribes which include these kinsmen. The reciprocal payment made by the Dok includes two cows, one derived from the paternal side and one from the maternal side (that are given to the bridegroom's family). I have thus deducted one animal each from the cattle received by the matrikin and the bride's immediate family (conceptualized as part of the paternal side). However, it is not entirely clear in Howell's (1954a:113) account whether the return-gift cow from the paternal side is contributed by the bride's immediate family or by father's siblings (i.e., the bride's patrikin).

6. Jackson (1923:154) reports that Nuer bridewealth declined from the early 1900s

to 1920 as a consequence of "cattle plague." Bridewealth payments of forty cattle were not unusual at the earlier date, while marriages were frequently contracted for as little as thirteen to fifteen animals at the time of his writing. Coriat (cited in Evans-Pritchard, 1946:254) likewise reports that Gaawar Nuer bridewealth declined from fifty head of cattle to fifteen or thirty by about the same date. These are the lowest figures for Nuer bridewealth transactions reported in the literature. However, these figures evidently refer only to the animals transferred at the time the bride joins her husband and do not take deferred payments into account. Howell (1954a:115) reports an actual case from 1948 in which only twelve cattle were paid at the time of the marriage and five more promised when the groom's sister married, bringing the total to within one animal of the established minimum of eighteen head. It is probable that the transfers of thirteen to fifteen cattle observed by Jackson and Coriat were the initial installment of comparable payments.

7. Howell (1951:281) provides the most detailed data concerning the sequence of cattle transfers associated with Dinka marriage. A few cattle may be handed over at each of the first three phases of the proceedings, i.e., at betrothal (*amac*), at a ceremony attended by close relatives on both sides (*kweth athiek*), and at a more widely attended celebration of the forthcoming union (*kwen athiek*). The outstanding (and largest) portion of the bridewealth is presented at the final ceremony (*thok de thiek*).

> The bride herself is [then] handed to her husband and after he has made a suitable sacrifice, (*mior de thiek*), returns with him to his home. Either then or very shortly afterwards the bride's family will hand over the *arweth* cattle to the bridegroom. (Howell, 1951:281–82)

Neither Stubbs (1962:457–58) nor Deng (1971:262) mention a time lapse between the transfer of bridewealth and the presentation of the reciprocal payment. (The latter is termed *aruweth* by the Malwal Dinka and *arweth* by the Ngok.) However, Titherington (1927:206) reports that the latter follows "about a year later, if all goes well." There may consequently be differences among Dinka tribes concerning the timing of their respective reciprocal payments. Alternatively, Titherington's account may reflect his familiarity with problem cases brought to his attention as an administrative official.

8. *Ariek* payments are also made by the Ngok Dinka and the custom is reportedly widespread among the Western Dinka (Howell, 1951:286–87). However, it is not entirely clear whether the ideal bridewealth payment is increased by the additional cattle required, or the allocation among the bride's kin is internally adjusted to accommodate this additional claim that arises on the marriage of younger daughters. Stubbs's (1962:458) choice of words appears to indicate the latter and Howell's (ibid.) the former. If *ariek* does represent an increment to the cattle required to fulfill an ideal bridewealth payment, it would apply to only about one-quarter of all marriages (since sibling cohorts composed of two or more daughters would comprise only one-fourth of all such cohorts in a stable population). Given this, *ariek* will be omitted from the figures employed in subsequent comparison of the size of Nuer and Dinka bridewealth.

9. Deng (1971:259–61) also describes the kinship-based claims that delineate a Dinka ideal bridewealth payment and provides a list comparable to that presented by Howell (1951). However, Deng does not designate the specific tribe or subcultural

group for whom this ideal is applicable. He maintains, in the introduction to his book, that his study "applies to the Dinka as a whole, but with the focus on the Ngok" (Deng, 1971:xxv). Irrespective of whether Deng's data are to be interpreted as representing a composite picture or a variant of the Ngok ideal, the distribution of bridewealth conforms to the general Dinka pattern identified earlier. The total bridewealth payment is twenty-nine cattle and the reciprocal payment is denoted as about one-third (Deng, 1971:260 citing Howell, 1951:287), giving a net outlay of nineteen or twenty head of cattle. Disregarding contributions to *arweth,* for which no data are available, the cattle are distributed among the bride's kin as follows: bride's immediate family 27.6 percent, patrikin 27.6 percent, matrikin 44.8 percent. Again, we see that the matrikin are favored. The matrikin also contribute little to a bridewealth accumulation, providing only four of the twenty-nine animals required (Deng, 1971:257).

10. The "paternal side" (including the bride's immediate family and patrikin) predominates in Nuer bridewealth distributions while the "maternal side" is much more prominent in those of the Dinka. This corresponds to, and expresses, differences in local organization. Dinka communities include members of several different descent groups whose relationship to each other is conceptualized as one of matrilateral kinship (Lienhardt, 1958:111). Nuer communities are conceived of as containing several hamlet-groups founded by the descendants of a pair of brothers, with each of these sets of patrilineal descendants forming the nexus of a bilateral network of kinsmen, including matrikin (Evans-Pritchard, 1940a:247). This correspondence is more fully developed in a later chapter.

11. These reciprocal payments are reported to consist of two or three head of cattle (Howell, 1951:287). The total amount of Bor District and Ruweng Dinka bridewealth is not reported. However, if the general relationship noted earlier between the size of reciprocal payments and the size of bridewealth holds for these Dinka groups, the bridewealth payment would be approximately twenty head of cattle.

12. While an Aliab Dinka herd of 100 adult animals contains 91 cows, a Nuer herd with the same number of cows would include 118 adult animals. To achieve comparable milk production the Nuer would thus require 18 percent more grazing land. However, this figure is increased by the fact that the grazing requirements of bulls and oxen are 50 percent higher than those of cows. Payne and El Amin (1977:76) estimate that cows weigh 200 to 220 kilograms while bulls and oxen weigh 300 to 340 kilograms. Grazing requirements correspond to the amount of body weight maintained, and the 19 percent additional adult male animals in the Nuer herd (of 91 cows) thus require 27 percent more grazing area than the comparable Dinka herd. Nuer herd composition thus translates into substantially greater grazing requirements than that of the Dinka.

It should be noted that the larger herd maintained by the Nuer to achieve comparable milk production does not augment meat production. The Dinka cull male animals at twenty-seven months, or shortly thereafter, when they have already attained adult body weight (Payne and El Amin, 1977:73). There is consequently nothing to be gained, in terms of meat consumption, by maintaining these animals for the remainder of their life span of nine to fifteen years (Grunnet, 1962:11). There are no more male cattle born into a Nuer herd of 91 cows than into a Dinka herd that contains the same number, and only the timing of their consumption is at issue.

Dinka herd management practices are also more effective than those of the Nuer in terms of dietary inputs. Dinka practices entail the timely slaughter of male animals that effectively reduces daily dependence on milk by providing regular additions of meat to the diet. In contrast, a higher proportion of Nuer male animals are consumed when they die of natural causes. These dietary inputs are greatest when the herd is affected by contagious diseases (that have no necessary relation to the dietary needs of the human population). These irregular additions of meat to the Nuer diet cannot be anticipated and therefore do not reduce the number of milk cows that must be maintained to ensure a regular supply of protein. Moreover, while every slaughtered animal is consumed, a few of those that die of natural causes are not (Howell, 1955:107) and Nuer practices increase the risk of such wastage. Weight loss typically precedes death from natural causes and this also constitutes a form of wastage. The net effect of these factors is that the Nuer require a somewhat larger population of milk cows to compensate for a lower level of regular and dependable meat consumption derived from comparable herds. Since herd composition is constant, this would entail adding about one ox for each three additional cows. In all, these data indicate that the Nuer would require a herd of at least 122 adult animals (containing 94 cows and 28 bulls and oxen) to derive the same nutritional values that the Dinka obtain from a herd of 100 adult animals (containing 91 cows and 9 bulls and oxen).

Nuer herd composition clearly requires both more cattle per capita and more grazing area than that of the Dinka. However, it is important to note that Nuer grazing requirements are much greater than the differences in cattle per capita alone would indicate due to the greater food intake of the excess bulls and oxen. If we add one calf for every two cows (as reported by Howell [1954b:309] for both Aliab and Western Nuer herds), the Nuer herd described above would contain 47 calves and the Dinka herd 45.5 (say 46). If each of these nutritionally equivalent herds supported 91 people, this works out to 1.6 cattle per capita for the Dinka (with 146 animals) and 1.86 for the Nuer (with 169). While the Nuer possess only 16.3 percent more cattle per capita, this nevertheless translates into 27 percent greater grazing requirements. The latter figure is based on wet season grazing requirements of 6.2 acres for bulls and oxen, 4.15 acres for cows, and 1.24 acres for calves (derived from Payne and El Amin, 1977). The Dinka herd in our example requires a total of 490 acres over the course of the wet season while the Nuer herd requires 622 acres.

It is important to note that the preceding example illustrates the differences between the Nuer and Dinka in cattle per capita holdings and grazing requirements that are attributable to differences in herd structure alone. The figures presented do not take into account the higher caloric consumption of the Nuer, reflected in their greater average body weight, nor available data indicating that the Nuer derive a larger proportion of their total caloric intake from cattle products than do the Dinka, who rely more heavily on grain (see note 14). Both these factors would substantially increase the differences in cattle per capita and grazing requirements outlined above.

13. On sandy soils, soil nutrient exhaustion is the main cause of declining yields that prompt shifting cultivation. On clay soils, *Striga hermonthica* infestation is more important in producing declining yields. This semiparasitic plant attaches itself to the roots of sorghum, bullrush millet, and finger millet and may reduce yields to almost nothing. It is difficult to control because no aerial parts appear for the first four to six

weeks, by which time the main damage to the host has already occurred. (See Howell, 1954b:328, 354.)

14. Dinka requirements for agricultural land are greater than those of the Nuer because of the larger human population per wet season community. However, this difference in agricultural acreage would be further expanded if the Dinka cultivated more land per capita than the Nuer. There is evidence that this is the case. Howell (1954b:368–69) reports that the Nuong, Dok, Jagei, Western Jikany, Gaawar, Thiang, and Lou Nuer cultivate no more than about two feddans (2.074 acres) per household. Only the Lak Nuer cultivate more, about two to three feddans per household. The Bor, Twij, and Nyarraweng Dinka cultivate about two feddans per household (Howell, 1954b:367). However, the Ruweng (Kwil, Awet, and Alor) Dinka, the Luaich, and the Chich Dinka cultivate two to three feddans and the Ruweng (Paweng) and Thoi Dinka about three to four feddans (Howell, 1954b:365, 369). Overall, the Dinka average of 2.6 feddans per household is higher than the Nuer average of 2.1 feddans, by about 24 percent. However, the Southern Dinka (Bor District) who occupy the environmental area most similar to that of the Nuer also cultivate the same acreage per household. On the other hand, the Southern Dinka plant four grain crops per year while the Nuer plant only three (ibid.). These data suggest a heavier reliance on grain in the Dinka diet, and a correspondingly reduced reliance on cattle products. This would entail even fewer cattle per capita for the Dinka than the differences between the Nuer and Dinka in herd composition alone require. In sum, the Dinka either cultivate more acreage per capita than the Nuer or cultivate the same acreage more intensively. The higher grain consumption associated with this reduces reliance on cattle products and hence reduces the cattle per capita necessary for subsistence. With fewer cattle, more land is available for agricultural utilization.

15. As was noted earlier in the chapter, the Lou and Eastern Jikany ideal bride-wealth of forty cattle is larger, by two animals, than the maximum ideal bridewealth payment found among the Homeland Nuer (i.e., the thirty-eight-head ideal bride-wealth of the Bul Nuer). This suggests that the ideal bridewealth payments of these expanding Nuer tribes either increased by a small amount, as a consequence of the expansion process, or were originally slightly higher than the comparable payments of their Homeland Nuer counterparts.

CHAPTER 4

1. Evans-Pritchard (1940a:150) also reports that the Dinka rarely took the offensive.

2. Bacon's account of his reconnaissance of the Lou Nuer in 1916 provides a striking example of Nuer tribalwide mobilization for defensive purposes. As Bacon moved into Lou territory, runners spread the word from one Lou territorial section to another and "nearly the whole of the Lou tribe" assembled at Denkur within three days (Bacon, 1917:9).

3. Nuer and Dinka "tribes" are defined by Evans-Pritchard (1940a:122) and Lienhardt (1958:102–3) with respect to four principal criteria: that they represent the maximal group that acknowledges a moral obligation to unite in warfare, that internal feuds may be settled by the payment of homicide compensation, and that they possess

a common name and distinct territory. As noted earlier most Nuer raids were conducted by the members of a single tribe, and these are consequently the most relevant units for our purposes. Although the Lou and Gaawar Nuer (for example) occasionally participated in joint raids on the Dinka, they did not regularly combine in this way nor did they acknowledge a moral obligation to unite in warfare.

4. Both the Eastern and Western Jikany include the same three main groups, the Gaajok, Gaagwang, and Gaajak. Among the Western Jikany the Gaagwang form part of the Gaajok tribe, while all three groups are distinct tribal entities in the east (Evans-Pritchard, 1940a:140).

5. Data from the 1955 census indicate that the average size of completed families among the Nuer is 5.8 persons versus 5.52 persons among the Dinka. Similarly, women of childbearing age constitute 21.84 percent of the Nuer population and 20.81 percent of the Dinka population. This suggests only a slightly higher growth rate for the Nuer than for the Dinka in the past generation. Hence, the rate of increase of the Dinka population between 1930 and 1955 can be assumed to have been roughly comparable to that of the Nuer during the same period.

6. Lienhardt's (1958) terminology is here applied to Howell's description to simplify the discussion. However, it is clear that the units Howell tentatively labels as "sections" possess the characteristics that define a "tribe" in Lienhardt's terms, i.e., a common name and territory and an acknowledged moral obligation to unite in warfare. (See Howell, 1951:255, 261.) The Ngok as a whole lack any tradition of collective action (ibid.:251) and thus constitute a tribal grouping rather than a tribe.

7. The next smallest Nuer tribes are the two Western Jikany tribes with a combined population of 11,000. Evans-Pritchard (1940a:140) notes that these tribes possess the same primary sections and some of the same secondary sections as the Eastern Jikany tribes, indicating that they likewise manifest four orders of segmentation. Hence, Nuer tribes over about 5,500 members contain the full complement of segmentary levels.

8. Bacon's (1917) census data yield an average of 3,322 persons per tertiary section for the Gun primary section, a somewhat higher figure than that derived from Evans-Pritchard's (1940a) material for the Lou as a whole. However, the Mor primary section includes six to eight tertiary sections (as opposed to five for Gun) and the average size of these would thus be smaller, bringing the overall average within the range noted earlier.

9. Evans-Pritchard (1940a:194, 207, 214, 215) reports, but does not particularly emphasize, the fact that dominant clans are conventionally regarded as the "owners" of tribal territories. The point is given more emphasis here in order to bring out an authentic similarity between the Nuer and Dinka that is otherwise masked by the different terminologies employed by their respective ethnographers.

10. Although the ancestors of coordinate descent groups are invariably siblings, the nature of the sibling bond is itself variable. In addition to the full brother relationships represented in figure 5, the sibling relationships include those of patrilateral half brothers, brother and sister, and brothers by adoption (see Kelly, 1977:291). In those instances in which cross-sex sibling bonds link coordinate groups, and one lineage is therefore composed of the patrilineal descendants of a female ancestor, this arrangement is specifically addressed and justified in myth. In one such myth, reported by Evans-Pritchard (1940a:230), a man's brothers died before marrying and the be-

reaved individual was instructed by his father to treat his two sisters as if they were his deceased brothers. The myth thus emphasizes that female links in the generally agnatic clan genealogy are only justified by special circumstances and are not ideologically endorsed as such. At the same time, the myth makes it apparent that siblingship is the underlying basis of unit-to-unit relations within the segmentary system (see Kelly, 1977).

11. Although Stubbs does not specifically explain the mechanism by which this is effected, it can readily be deduced. Since the bulk of a Malwal Dinka ideal bridewealth payment accrues to the bride's mother's brothers, unequal cattle holdings would be accentuated if a wealthy and influential family that occupied the position of "mother's brother of the camp" received more cattle on the occasion of a sister's daughter's marriage than it provided to secure a wife for a son. Moreover, one would expect the sister's daughter of a founding lineage to command a more substantial bridewealth payment than other women as a consequence of the political significance of the matrilateral relationship that links founder and latecomer lines who are the joint recipients of the payment in these instances. It should be recalled that the mother's brother's portion represents a deferred payment standing over from the bride's mother's marriage, that the bride herself embodies the matrilateral relationship engendered by her parents' union, and that her marriage is the primary context in which that matrilateral relationship is accorded social recognition. In the case of a bride related as sister's daughter to a founding line, the bride's mother's marriage served as the vehicle for establishing a structurally central matrilateral relationship between founder and latecomer lines. The occasion on which this focal relationship is accorded social recognition should consequently be marked by the transfer of a substantial number of cattle, i.e., by a large bridewealth payment. It should also be recalled that Dinka bridewealth payments may include as many as one hundred cattle (with a reciprocal payment of forty), although the ideal payment does not exceed forty cattle (with a reciprocal payment of twenty). This spread provides ample scope for the "mother's brothers of the camp" to receive more cattle from a sister's daughter's marriage than they contribute to a son's bridewealth that fully meets the specifications of the ideal transaction. Thus one can readily envision the manner in which Dinka bridewealth customs would amplify inequalities in the distribution of cattle as Stubbs (1962) reports. In sum, while the mother's brother–sister's child relationship encodes and legitimates unequal access to cattle standings and bridewealth cattle, the bridewealth system itself provides one of the central mechanisms through which this unequal access is translated into an unequal distribution.

12. Lienhardt's point here seemingly rests heavily on the meaning of the Dinka term he translates as "peacemaker," and the consequent incongruity of a warrior leader fulfilling this role. However, the context suggests that "mediator" is potentially an alternative translation, and the incongruity is thereby attenuated.

13. The mutual incompatibility of the asymmetrical relation between the components of subtribes, on one hand, and the equivalent and symmetrical relation of coordinate subtribes, on the other, represents a structural contradiction that is inherent in the Dinka segmentary system.

14. Although the Western Dinka differ most markedly from the Nuer in settlement pattern, the same differences are evident when the Nuer are compared with other

Dinka groups. Gleichen (1905:139–40) reports a marked discontinuity in settlement pattern along the border between the Eastern Luaich Dinka and the Lou Nuer that corresponds precisely to that described above. While the savannah-forest zone inhabited by the Western Dinka does differ environmentally from the true savannah inhabited by the Nuer, there is no comparable environmental discontinuity along the Eastern Luaich–Lou border. These differences in settlement pattern, therefore, are not reducible to environmental terms, but relate to differences in economic organization discussed earlier. Moreover, they are long-standing differences, having been noted by early explorers (see Evans-Pritchard, 1951*a:*2). It should therefore be possible to archaeologically date the economic divergence of the proto-Nuer and proto-Dinka, and the spatial distribution of these economic variants in earlier times.

15. It is important to emphasize that the critical contrast developed here does not pertain to the relative strength of matrilateral and agnatic relationships as such. Rather the contrast concerns the degree to which central structural relationships that constitute the line of cleavage in fission are attenuated by the fission process itself.

16. Differences between the Nuer and Dinka in the composition of the bridewealth herd that are of considerable economic importance may also be symbolically significant. While the cattle involved in social transactions are seen as links between people, those links are primarily female cattle among the Dinka, while male cattle are much more prominent in Nuer transactions. This difference corresponds to the greater social significance of relationships through women in Dinka social organization.

CHAPTER 5

1. Payne and El Amin (1977:15) report wet season stocking rates of 1.9 to 3.9 hectares per 300-kilogram livestock unit, with a median of 2.5 hectares, or 6.2 acres. In other words, one bull or ox utilizes about 6.2 acres of grazing land during the course of the wet season (based on the median figure of 2.5 hectares per livestock unit). A 200-kilogram cow utilizes 4.15 acres. In contrast, the average household cultivates 2 to 3 feddans, or 2.074 to 3.111 acres during the wet season. Thus, at least two households can be supported on the quantity of land required by a single bull or ox. A small increase in cattle per capita holdings therefore necessitates a proportionally greater reduction in the human population that can be supported on a given site. Aggregation for defensive purposes promotes the full occupation of each wet season settlement so that grazing and agriculture represent competing land utilizations despite the fact that the overall population density of the Nuer is well below ecological limits.

2. For convenience in exposition in this comparative discussion, the term *wet season settlements* is employed to refer to both Nuer and Dinka groupings during the rainy season. The differences in settlement pattern between these two cultural groups are nevertheless understood. Thus while Dinka wet season agricultural settlements are proximate to, but spatially and conceptually distinct from, wet season cattle camps, the term *wet season settlement* will here serve as a shorthand reference to this combined entity, and to the Nuer counterpart in which these two components of the economy are spatially intermixed.

3. It should be pointed out that the Nuer occupation of a comparatively larger proportion of wet season sites at any given time affects other factors discussed earlier,

particularly the size of wet season settlements. The 36.5 to 45 percent lower density of the Nuer reported in the literature would require an even greater difference than this in the population of wet season settlements, since the Nuer occupy more such settlements than the Dinka. Thus Nuer settlements would not be comprised of 36.5 to 45 percent fewer households than their Dinka counterparts (as indicated in previous discussion), but something on the order of 50 percent or more fewer households. This, in turn, would further reduce land in cultivation per site and increase grazing resources, augmenting the number of cattle that could be supported at each site and contributing to further extension of the cultivation period. It should also be recalled that Dinka agricultural practices are more intensive than those of the Nuer, and that this would be reflected in a comparatively shorter use period and a longer period of fallow regeneration. In other words, the differences between the Nuer and Dinka in the intensity of cultivation are fully consistent with the general patterns identified here.

4. Lienhardt (1958:101) notes comparable differences between the Nuer and Dinka in the scale of wet and dry season aggregations, but attributes them solely to environmental factors. This would lead one to expect that these differences would not obtain when the proto-Nuer and proto-Dinka occupied a common ecological zone. In contrast, the differences in the scale of seasonal aggregations outlined here are the product of differences in the density of the cattle population that are an integral aspect of two distinctive economic systems. The proto-Nuer would thus evidence smaller wet season settlements and larger dry season aggregation than the proto-Dinka when both inhabited a common ecological zone.

5. The fact that the developmental sequence presented here begins with the divergence in bridewealth systems raises the question of what engendered the initial differentiation of the proto-Nuer and proto-Dinka in this respect. I consider this question to be essentially unanswerable due to the early date at which this divergence took place (i.e., prior to 1600) and to limitations pertaining to the distribution of available data. Well-documented material concerning tribal variations in ideal bridewealth payments among the Nuer provides a basis for analyzing developmental changes in the bridewealth system. (These are discussed later in the chapter.) However, we lack comparably detailed data concerning tribal (or subcultural) variations in other important aspects of the Nuer sociocultural system. It is particularly unfortunate that we do not know more about the Jagei tribes, inasmuch as they most closely resemble the Dinka in both the retention of a small reciprocal payment and in tribal size (and likewise differ most extensively from other Nuer tribes in these respects). If the Jagei also most closely resemble the Dinka in the degree of internal socioeconomic differentiation, in the prestige-related aspects of the bridewealth system, or in some other respect, such covariation might well provide a basis for elucidating the early divergence of the proto-Nuer and proto-Dinka with respect to the reciprocal payment. However, such data are unavailable and this undercuts the feasibility of providing an adequately supported explanation. The developmental sequence considered here thus begins with the divergence in bridewealth systems and traces out the consequences that can be shown to follow from well-documented differences in bridewealth custom that predate Nuer expansion. These differences represent a historically given point of departure in the same sense that the Reformation constitutes a historically given point of departure in Weber's analysis of the Protestant ethic. The principal objective of the present analysis

is to show that the economic systems of the Nuer and Dinka are shaped by sociocultural factors (pertaining to bridewealth) and that these economic systems also engendered changes in the sociocultural systems of these two cultural groups (pertaining to political organization). The analysis thus encompasses both the causes and consequences of two economic variants of a shared transhumant system of production.

6. Evans-Pritchard (1940a:118) also points out that "people of one section have to cross the territories of other sections to reach their camps, which may be situated near the villages of yet another section." Although this is true, these wet season villages and intermediate grazing territories would be largely or completely deserted at the height of the dry season when they are crossed. Hence, contact between members of different sections would not be materially increased by this factor.

7. The data on which this distributional analysis is based have been presented in earlier chapters. The size of Nuer tribes is derived from Evans-Pritchard's (1940a:117) summary of early 1930s census figures and the magnitude of ideal bridewealth is derived from Howell (1954a:97–123) and Evans-Pritchard (1951a:74–88). The five tribes with a bridewealth of thirty-two to thirty-five head of cattle are the Dok, Thiang, Leik, and the two Western Jikany tribes. The single large tribe with this same lower magnitude of bridewealth payments is the Lak. The four large tribes with a bridewealth of thirty-eight to forty head of cattle are the Bul, Lou, Gaajak, and Gaajok. The single small tribe with a comparably higher bridewealth payment is the Gaagwang, which had recently fissioned from the Gaajok.

8. See Evans-Pritchard (1940a:56) for a map of the distribution of Lou Nuer tribal sections during the dry season. It should also be noted that Evans-Pritchard clearly does not propose that a tribe corresponds to a dry season herding group (as it does among the Dinka). He only argues that larger dry season aggregations are, in a general way, conducive to the development of larger tribes.

9. It may be noted that Sahlins's (1961) formulation (discussed in chap. 2) provides no initial mechanism which would account for the growth of the proto-Nuer population such that fission and the maintenance of post-fission relationships would also convey numerical superiority. In the absence of population growth, fission would merely expand the number of units in the segmentary system without increasing the number of individuals that could be mobilized. The difficulty confronting Sahlins's argument is that the Nuer must expand, increase in population, fission, and maintain post-fission relationships in order to develop the segmentary organization deemed to be the source of their capacity for territorial expansion. The proposed interpretation resolves this problem in that the large-scale dry season aggregations of the proto-Nuer would convey an initial advantage conducive to expansion (without a fully developed segmentary lineage organization), while the capture of reproductive females in raids would produce the requisite population growth necessary for fission to have the effect of expanding the segmentary system.

10. It may be noted in passing that structurally central matrilateral relationships represent an organizational pattern that extends into the distant past. This is evident from Lienhardt's (1955:29–41) consideration of the role of such matrilateral relations in the oral traditions of the Shilluk and Anuak. This suggests that structurally central matrilateral relationships predate the cultural differentiation of the Dinka, Shilluk, and Anuak as well as that of the Dinka and Nuer.

11. In other versions, Kir is represented as having married the daughters of the founder of another clan. However, in either case the Jikany were formerly a matrilaterally related descent group within another tribe, and one that subsequently emerged as a separate tribe, through fission. In other words, agnatic purification is equally evident in each version of Jikany origins.

12. The analysis presented here places the famous Nuer paradox in a somewhat different light. The paradox turns on Evans-Pritchard's (1951*a:*28) statement that

> it would seem that it may be partly just because the agnatic principle is unchallenged in Nuer society that the tracing of descent through women is so prominent and matrilocality so prevalent. However much the actual configurations of kinship clusters may vary and change, the lineage structure is invariable and stable.

Inasmuch as "the vast majority" of people tracing descent from the dominant lineage through a female are Dinka (ibid.:25), the invariance of the lineage structure is attributable to the fact that the only possible outcomes of such attachments over the long run are agnatic relationships or no relationships whatsoever. In other words, the segmentary system is structurally insulated from matrilateral relations at the local level. The latter cannot be promoted to relationships between groups within the segmentary system when a Dinka lineage is involved, because the matrilateral attachment cannot constitute a line of cleavage in fission. This clarifies some aspects of Evans-Pritchard's original point, although there are other aspects of the paradox that are of interest from other perspectives (see Kelly, 1977:290–96; Gough, 1971:85, 88–90).

13. The distribution of cattle among the bride's kin in small Dinka bridewealth payments is not reported in the literature. It is consequently not possible to assess the effects of an increased frequency of such payments. However, all available data indicate that the claims of the bride's matrikin are least subject to reduction, and that the proportion of the total payment allocated to the matrikin increases as bridewealth payments decrease. It is consequently likely that matrilateral relationships were accentuated by an increased frequency of small payments. This would parallel the proliferation of matrilaterally related latecomer lines and the concomitant emphasis on such relationships in Dinka local organization.

14. The marriage system is not considered here, because it does not co-vary with either bridewealth or political organization in the Nuer/Dinka controlled comparison with which we are concerned. While the Nuer and Dinka differ in both of the above mentioned respects, they do not differ significantly with regard to the regulation of marriage. In other words, the marriage system falls outside the "relational cluster" isolated by controlled comparison. It cannot have played a role in the development of differences between the Nuer and Dinka and must also be loosely interconnected to bridewealth, local organization, and segmentary structure. While all these features changed in the course of Nuer/Dinka divergence, the marriage system remained unchanged. One must therefore conclude that the marriage system neither contributed to, nor was affected by, the transformation of other features of the Nuer and Dinka sociocultural systems.

It will be useful to document the similarity between the Nuer and Dinka marriage systems noted above. In both cases, marriages are widely dispersed by various prohibitions. The principal prohibitions enunciated by the Nuer and Dinka are essentially identical. In both cases a man may not marry: (1) a woman of the same clan; (2) any

Jean-Paul Dumont
Professor and Graduate Adviser
Department of Anthropology, DH-05

University of Washington
Seattle, Washington 98195
(206) 543-4793; 543-5240

Home: 3818 Eastern Ave. N.
Seattle, Washington 98103
(206) 547-3025

nealogically related through a common antecedent in oximate, generation; and (3) the daughter of an age-prohibit marriage with a brother's wife's close cogwife's sister). The only apparent differences between e quite minor and particularistic and may be attributar descriptive phraseology. Apparent differences iniage with the daughter of father's age-mate (unless ed) and a Dinka prohibition on taking a wife from e Evans-Pritchard, 1951*a*:30–36; Deng, 1971:150–?:154–57.

an analogous contradiction among the Shilluk and nteresting analysis of it in the argument presented nd proto-Dinka) social system.

h the parties to an asymmetrical relation have an y mutual and reciprocal. For those on the superor-..ugitimate an advantage. For those in the subordinate position, an emphasis on mutuality and reciprocity serves to moderate the implementation of that advantage, since those who hold it must fulfill the terms of its legitimation. Given this, the development of a dominant ideology of mutuality does not require its imposition by a dominant group.

17. The term *promotion* is derived from Flannery (1972), who employs it to cover a range of phenomena that are analogous to that described here. Flannery, in turn, draws on an earlier article by Rappaport (1969), who uses a somewhat different terminology for the same phenomena. Both identify this as a recurrent feature of cultural evolution.

CHAPTER 6

1. In chapter 1 it was estimated that the Nuer assimilated 100,000 to 112,000 of an estimated 225,000 Dinka and Anuak residing in the territory east of the Bahr el Jebel appropriated by the Nuer. The median figure of 106,000 persons assimilated would represent 47 percent of the indigenous population. The density of the latter would be 10.6 persons per square mile. A comparable figure is used for the Bor District in this illustration.

2. Changes in the internal distribution of cattle that took place during the course of Nuer expansion should also be noted here. Initially, the Nuer would possess many more cattle per capita than the Dinka they assimilated. However, incorporated Dinka girls commanded the same bridewealth as Nuer girls and intermarriage would thus tend to equalize cattle per capita holdings between these two segments of the population over time. The participation of assimilated Dinka (and their descendants) in raids had the same effect, since captured cattle were redistributed among those who took part. Internal redistribution is discussed at greater length later in the chapter.

3. It was estimated earlier that the Nuer human population would have increased to 220,000 persons by the time the cattle population reached maximum density, following the final territorial gains of the late nineteenth century. This figure represents 48 percent of the 1955–56 Nuer population of 460,000 persons to which the nutritional

data apply. At this point (circa 1900), the Nuer would then possess 109 percent more cattle per capita than they did in 1955–56 (assuming maximum cattle density at both dates). This would enable the Nuer to derive 48 percent of their nutritional requirements from cattle products (rather than the 23 percent characteristic of the 1950s), and thus reduce the contribution of grain from 67 percent of the total diet to 42 percent (fish and other minor foods supply the remaining 10 percent of caloric intake). However, it has been noted that the acquisition of additional territory (beyond 1890 levels) would have produced only slight and progressively diminishing gains in cattle per capita holdings. It follows that Nuer reliance on grain could not be reduced to much less than the 42 percent of total caloric intake noted above. It is doubtful that the Nuer could have progressed beyond a point where cattle products provided 57 percent of nutritional requirements and grain 33 percent. In other words, reliance on grain could at most be reduced from two-thirds to one-third of total caloric intake by substitution of cattle products.

4. This is consistent with the estimates of increases in cattle per capita holdings presented earlier. An increase in prevailing bridewealth payments from a minimum of eighteen head to an ideal of thirty-two or forty represents a 78 to 122 percent increment (respectively). It was estimated that cattle per capita holdings would be about 132 percent above 1818 levels when the cattle population had had an opportunity to breed up to recent pasture additions (circa 1900), and would be increasing at a relatively slow rate. The gains in cattle per capita attained by 1890 (before rinderpest was introduced) would thus be in the vicinity of 120 to 130 percent, sufficient to fund an increase in prevailing bridewealth payments from minimum to ideal levels (or more probably, an increase from somewhat above the minimum to more than the ideal).

5. This is not the case among the Dinka, where sacrificial distribution presents a more encompassing and therefore somewhat different representation of the social order than bridewealth distribution. This accords with both a greater emphasis on sacrifice, and a higher frequency of occurrence (reflected in Dinka herd structure).

It could readily be argued that marriage ceremonies provide the most encompassing representation of the social order among the Nuer. There is a betrothal ceremony, a wedding ceremony, and a third ceremony that takes place at the time the bride joins her husband. An ox is sacrificed on each of these occasions by the master of ceremonies, who is a member of a lineage collateral to that of the bride (or groom in the third instance), and who calls out the spear-name of the more encompassing agnatic group he represents. The sacrificial oxen are distributed in accordance with the pattern of bridewealth distribution (twice to the groom's kin and once to the bride's). Beer is likewise distributed to these matrilateral and patrilateral kin, each of whom shares his pot with members of his age set. There is consequently repeated emphasis on the relations between kin relations that bridewealth encodes. The reduplication serves to highlight the centrality of bridewealth distribution, which provides the same representation on a grand scale. The segmentary lineage system is represented through the master of ceremonies. The spear-names of the bride's and groom's respective clans are called out by their agnates and the ghosts of the ancestors are invoked. It is especially noteworthy that the latter are specifically invoked "to look upon the cattle of the bridewealth" (Evans-Pritchard, 1951a:61–62). This makes the ghosts partners to the union, but at the same time serves to focus the participants' attention on the bridewealth transaction itself. The third ceremony is primarily concerned with the conjugal relationship and the incorporation of the bride into the husband's group. Submission of the bride to her husband's authority is enacted through a mock beating and consummation of the union by force. In sum, Nuer marriage ceremonies encompass all aspects of Nuer social organization and, more importantly, specify the interrelationships among them. The distribution of bridewealth cattle receives repeated emphasis. (See Evans-Pritchard, 1951a:60–71 with respect to the material presented here.)

6. The evolution of the Nuer bridewealth system has been described and analyzed in some detail in earlier chapters and an account of the nature of the process has been presented. What I am concerned with in the present context is the maintenance of the ordering capacity of a key symbol, and its position in the symbolic system, rather than the maintenance of the precise nature of the ordering it provides. The evolution of the latter is contingent upon the maintenance of the former.

7. Friedman (1974, 1979) has questioned the applicability of the concept of self-regulation employed by Rappaport (1967) in his analysis of the Maring and Rappaport (1977, 1979:43–93) has responded to Friedman's criticism. This exchange is relevant to the present discussion at some points, but introduction of the Maring data to which it pertains would take us too far afield. It is the character of the Nuer system that is at issue and the discussion will focus on the latter.

8. Intrinsic biological constraints that would otherwise have regulated cattle density were thus supplanted by an alternative cultural solution, i.e., territorial appropriation. However, this cultural transcendence of biological constraint is not a distinctive feature of expansionist systems, but of all cultural systems. It constitutes the basic theme of the story of cultural evolution.

9. Rappaport (1979:23) depicts coral atoll ecosystems as possessing similar characteristics and the Nuer ecosystem is consequently not unique in these respects.

10. It is the characteristics of the system rather than the terminology employed to label them that are important here. Inasmuch as these characteristics are foreign to extant formulations, they do not fit readily into the existing terminological framework. Territorial expansion has some attributes in common with negative feedback mechanisms, positive feedback mechanisms, and stressors. The fact that these divergent attributes are not segregated among discrete phenomena may be indicative of conceptual (rather than merely terminological) difficulties connected with the application of a cybernetic model.

11. The Nuer also do not fit into the alternative category of systems with maladaptive characteristics. Rappaport defines maladaptation with reference to his general specification of adaptive structure (see Rappaport, 1979:145–60 for a full account of the latter).

If adaptive processes are those tending to maintain homeostasis in the face of perturbations, maladaptations are factors internal to systems interfering with their homeostatic responses. They reduce the likelihood of a system's persistence, not so much by subjecting the system to stress as by impeding its ability to respond to stress. Maladaptations are not to be confused with stressors or perturbing factors, although they themselves can, of course, produce stress. (Rappaport, 1979:161)

The Nuer system is characterized by the internally produced stress that Rappaport seeks to differentiate from maladaptations and also lacks the impediments to its ability to respond to stress that are central to the definition of the concept. The persistence of the Nuer system was not in question (although that of the Dinka was). The operation of the system did not produce environmental degradation, which is the material consequence of maladaptation (and diagnostic of it) (ibid.:161). In short, the Nuer system is not maladaptive in terms of Rappaport's formulation of the concept. It does, however, display one of the maladaptive features Rappaport discusses, namely hypercoherence (ibid.:162). I have employed this useful concept in earlier chapters.

12. These reciprocal exchanges are equivalent among patrikin while matrikin receive more than they give. On the occasion of a girl's marriage her mother's elder brother receives four head of cattle. When the daughter of this mother's brother marries, only one animal is given to father's sister (i.e., the first girl's parental household). In other words, a man transfers four animals to his wife's brother but receives only one (via his wife) as a consequence of the bridewealth distributions that follow from the marriage of both men's daughters. The distribution of sacrificial meat is analogous and thus also characterized by nonequivalent reciprocity along the same axis.

13. Cattle are sacrificial offerings as well as items of exchange. However, from a strictly economic standpoint sacrifice constitutes a process of conversion whereby live cattle are transformed from items of exchange, subject to household level accumulation, into food, subject to distribution among specified kin (and subsequently distributed by them to other members of the community). In other words, sacrifice is the mode of conversion between spheres of exchange. It is of interest that the claims of God (*kwoth*), to whom sacrifices are made, are congruent with the claims of the community upon the resources of its constituent households.

14. The intensification of production may potentially constitute an alternative solution. However, the intensification of animal husbandry through the provision of fodder requires substantial increases in land in production and thus may not alleviate an impetus to territorial acquisition.

15. The differences between the Nuer and Dinka in the relation between bridewealth and prestige that are noted here may have been significant in the differentiation of these two cultural groups insofar as they fall within the relational cluster of covarying differences discussed earlier. In other words, the Nuer and Dinka not only differ in their bridewealth systems and in economic and sociopolitical organization, but also in regard to their prestige systems. The latter differences may have played a role in differentiation of the proto-Nuer and proto-Dinka bridewealth systems that engendered a subsequent divergence in economic and sociopolitical organization, in accordance with the interpretation developed in chapter 5. However, the early date of the proto-Nuer/proto-Dinka divergence in bridewealth (concerning the reciprocal payment) and the absence of information concerning variation in prestige systems among Nuer and Dinka tribes (comparable to available data concerning variations in bridewealth) preclude the development of a cogent analysis along these lines.

16. Evans-Pritchard (1951*a*:20) reports a high degree of intermarriage between natal Nuer and incorporated Dinka and notes that a Dinka tribesman "readily attaches himself to his wife's people or to the people who have married his sister or daughter, as do his children to their maternal uncle's kin." Such marriages presuppose the bridewealth transactions described in this paragraph.

17. In examining the degree of inequality among the Nuer it is particularly important to make a distinction between disparities in social status on one hand and disparities in the distribution of cattle on the other. The former are much more marked than the latter. Gough (1971) argues quite convincingly that members of aristocratic lineages tended to occupy a privileged sociopolitical position in local groups vis-à-vis members of stranger lineages and incorporated Dinka. However, she is not able to show that cattle or access to grazing were unequally distributed between these two groups. Although members of aristocratic lineages did have ''superior land rights,'' as Gough (ibid.:118) notes, these did not apply to grazing. Evans-Pritchard (1940*a*:65) is quite explicit on this point. ''Grazing and the use of grass, trees, etc., is a common right of all members of the community.'' Gough's claim that members of dominant lineages ''tended to inherit more cattle than other men'' is not substantiated by reference to ethnographic data but rests on inference. Available data do not support this inference for several reasons. First, Evans-Pritchard (1940*a*:20) reports an absence of marked disparities in cattle holdings (other than those related to the developmental cycle of domestic groups). Second, there is no differential access to grazing resources that would contribute to the development of such disparities. Third, the bridewealth system is conducive to an egalitarian redistribution of cattle. Fourth, the substantial numbers of cattle taken in raids upon the Dinka are also redistributed within local groups. Inheritance is only capable of maintaining existing inequities in the distribution of cattle across generations; it does not in itself engender such inequities. All the points noted above indicate that there were no ingrained disparities in cattle ownership that might be preserved over the long term by inheritance. The redistributive features of the Nuer social system would clearly work against the maintenance of an unequal distribution of cattle between members of dominant lineages, on one hand, and both incorporated second-generation Dinka and members of stranger lineages on the other. If this were not the case then the Nuer who are of Dinka extraction—more than half the members of the expanding tribes—would have continued to be as impoverished as their cattle-less ancestors who joined the Nuer. However, no marked economic differentiation of this large segment of the Nuer population is reported. (See Schneider, 1979, for an interesting discussion of the basis of a general association between egalitarianism and substantial dependence on cattle.)

The Nuer sociocultural system thus lacks the ''tendency toward unequal accumulation, especially of cattle'' that Bonte (1979:210), drawing on Gough's analysis, attributes to it. There is consequently no inherent tendency toward ''increasing economic and social differentiation'' capable of forming the basis of contradictions that, in turn, promote territorial expansion (ibid.:211). However, Bonte's attention to the role of inequality in Nuer expansion contributes to an elucidation of the process of agnatic purification described in chapter 5.

Selected Bibliography

Garsse (1972) provides a comprehensive bibliography of published materials relating to the ethnology of the Southern Sudan; Collins (1971:339–49) and Johnson (1980:738–67) describe the unpublished and published sources relevant to the history of the area in considerable detail. The bibliography presented here includes literature and unpublished materials cited in the text, and a selection of the most useful sources consulted in the course of the research.

Alban, A. H.
  1930.   Abwong District Notes, Upper Nile Province Handbook, chap. 3. Durham: University of Durham, School of Oriental Studies, Sudan Archives 212/14/7.
Arkell, A. J.
  1966.   *The history of the Sudan: from the earliest times to 1821.* 2d ed., rev. London: University of London, Athlone Press.
Armstrong, C. L.
  1930.   Nasir District Notes, Upper Nile Province Handbook, chap. 3. Durham: University of Durham, School of Oriental Studies, Sudan Archives 212/14/3.
Bacon, C. R. K.
  1917.   *The Lau Nuers.* Durham: University of Durham. School of Oriental Studies, Sudan Archives.
  1922.   The Anuak. *Sudan Notes and Records* 5:113–29.
Barbour, Kenneth M.
  1961.   *The republic of the Sudan: a regional geography.* London: London University Press.
Balfour, Andrew, and Archibald, R. G.
  1908.   *Review of the recent advances in tropical medicine: supplement to the third report of the Wellcome Research Laboratories at the Gordon Memorial College, Khartoum.* London: Balliere, Tindall, and Cox.
Beavan, J.
  1931.   Renk District Notes, Upper Nile Province Handbook, chap. 3. Durham: University of Durham, School of Oriental Studies, Sudan Archives 212/14/1.
Bedri, Ibrahim.
  1948.   More notes on the Padang Dinka. *Sudan Notes and Records* 29:40–57.

Beidelman, T. O.
    1971. *The translation of culture: essays to E. E. Evans-Pritchard.* London: Tavistock.

Beltrame, Giovanni.
    1975[1861]. On the White Nile from Khartoum to Gondokoro, 1859–1860. In *The opening of the Nile Basin,* edited by E. Toniolo and R. Hill, 129–39. New York: Barnes and Noble.

Bloss, J. F. E.
    1955. Nutrition and society among the Nilotics. In *Food and society in the Sudan: being the proceedings of the 1953 annual conference of the Philosophical Society of the Sudan.* Khartoum: McCorquodale and Co.

Bonte, Pierre.
    1979. Pastoral production, territorial organization and kinship in segmentary lineage societies. In *Social and ecological systems,* edited by P. C. Burnham and R. F. Ellen, 203–34. London: Academic Press.

British Government.
    n.d.(1882). *Report on the Egyptian Provinces, the Sudan, Red Sea and Equator.* Compiled in the Intelligence Branch, Quartermaster-General's Department, Horse Guards, War Office. London: H. M. Stationary Office. Durham: University of Durham, School of Oriental Studies, Sudan Archives.

Bryan, Margaret A.
    1948. *Distribution of the Nilotic and Nilo-Hamitic languages of Africa.* London: Oxford University Press.

Burnham, P. C., and Ellen, R. F., eds.
    1979. *Social and ecological systems.* Association of Social Anthropologists Monograph no. 18. London: Academic Press.

Burton, John W.
    1978*a*. God's ants: a study of Atuot religion. Ph.D. dissertation, State University of New York at Stony Brook. Ann Arbor: University Microfilms International.
    1978*b*. Ghost marriage and the cattle trade among the Atuot of the southern Sudan. *Africa* 48:398–405.
    1980. Atuot age categories and marriage. *Africa* 50:146–60.
    1981. Ethnicity on the hoof: on the economics of Nuer identity. *Ethnology* 20:157–62.

Butt, Audrey.
    1952. *The Nilotes of the Anglo-Egyptian Sudan and Uganda.* In East Central Africa, part 4 of Ethnographic survey of Africa, edited by Daryll Forde. London: Oxford University Press.

Cohen, D. W.
    1968. The river-lake Nilotes from the fifteenth to the nineteenth century. In *Zamani: a survey of East African history,* edited by Bethwell A. Ogot and J. A. Kieran, 142–57. New York: Humanities Press.

Collins, Robert O.
    1971. *Land beyond the rivers: the southern Sudan, 1898–1918.* New Haven: Yale University Press.

Coriat, P.
  1939. Gwek the witch-doctor and the pyramid of Dengkur. *Sudan Notes and Records* 22:221–38.
Cummins, S. L.
  1904. Sub-tribes of the Bahr-el-Ghazal Dinkas. *Journal of the Anthropological Institute of Great Britain and Ireland* 34:149–66.
David, Nicholas, et al.
  1979. British Institute in Eastern Africa. *Nyame Akuma* 14:52–56.
Deng, Francis M.
  1971. *Tradition and modernization: a challenge for law among the Dinka of the Sudan.* New Haven: Yale University Press.
  1972. *The Dinka of the Sudan.* New York: Holt, Rinehart and Winston.
Digerness, Olav.
  1978. Appearance and reality in the Southern Sudan: a study in the British administration of the Nuer, 1900–1930. Major thesis in History for the Higher Degree, University of Bergen, Norway.
Eggan, Fred.
  1954. Social anthropology and the method of controlled comparison. *American Anthropologist* 56:743–63.
Elsammani, Mohamed Osman, and El Amin, Farouk Mohamed.
  1977. *The Impact of the Extension of Jonglei Canal on the Area from Kongor to Bor.* Report No. 3, Economic and Social Research Council, National Council for Research. Khartoum: Democratic Republic of the Sudan.
Evans-Pritchard, E. E.
  1933. The Nuer, tribe and clan. (secs. 1–4) *Sudan Notes and Records* 16:1–54.
  1934. The Nuer, tribe and clan. (secs. 4 cont.–7) *Sudan Notes and Records* 17:1–58.
  1935. The Nuer, tribe and clan. (secs. 7 cont.–9) *Sudan Notes and Records* 18:37–88.
  1936. The Nuer: age sets. *Sudan Notes and Records* 19:233–69.
  1937. Economic life of the Nuer, cattle. (pt. 1) *Sudan Notes and Records* 20:209–46.
  1938. Economic life of the Nuer, cattle. (pt. 2) *Sudan Notes and Records* 21:31–78.
  1940a. *The Nuer: a description of the modes of livelihood and political institutions of a Nilotic people.* Oxford: Oxford University Press.
  1940b. The Nuer of the southern Sudan. In *African political systems,* edited by Meyer Fortes and E. E. Evans-Pritchard, 272–96. London: Oxford University Press.
  1940c. *The political system of the Anuak of the Anglo-Egyptian Sudan.* Monographs on Social Anthropology, no. 4. London: Percy Lund Humphries and Co.
  1945. Some aspects of marriage and family among the Nuer. Rhodes-Livingston Institute Paper No. 11. Lusaka: Rhodes-Livingston Institute.
  1946. Nuer bridewealth. *Africa* 16:247–57.
  1947a. Further observations on the political system of the Anuak. *Sudan Notes and Records* 28:62–97.

1947*b*. A note on courtship among the Nuer. *Sudan Notes and Records* 28:115–26.

1947*c*. Bridewealth among the Nuer. *African Studies* 6:181–88.

1950*a*. Kinship and the local community among the Nuer. In *African systems of kinship and marriage,* edited by A. R. Radcliffe-Brown and Daryll Forde, 360–91. London: Oxford University Press.

1950*b*. The Nuer family. *Sudan Notes and Records* 31:21–42.

1951*a*. *Kinship and marriage among the Nuer.* Oxford: Oxford University Press.

1951*b*. *Social anthropology.* London: Cohen and West, Ltd.

1956. *Nuer religion.* Oxford: Oxford University Press.

Fergusson, V. H.

1921. The Nuong Nuer. *Sudan Notes and Records* 4:146–55.

Flannery, Kent V.

1972. The cultural evolution of civilizations. *Annual Review of Ecology and Systematics* 3:399–426.

Fortes, M., and Evans-Pritchard, E. E., eds.

1940. *African political systems.* London: Oxford University Press.

Friedman, Jonathan.

1974. Marxism, structuralism and vulgar materialism. *Man,* n.s., 9:444–69.

1979. Hegelian ecology: between Rousseau and the world spirit. In *Social and ecological systems,* edited by P. C. Burnham and R. F. Ellen, 253–70. London: Academic Press.

Fukui, Katsuyoshi, and Turton, David, eds.

1977. *Warfare among East African herders.* Papers presented at the First International Symposium. Osaka: National Museum of Ethnology.

Garsse, Yvan Van.

1972. Ethnological and anthropological literature on the three southern Sudan provinces: Upper Nile, Bahr el Ghazal, Equatoria. *Acta Ethnologica et Linguistica,* no. 29. Series Africana 7. Vienna.

Gessi, Romolo.

1968. *Seven years in the Soudan: being a record of explorations, adventure, and campaigns against the Arab slave hunters.* Edited by Felix Gessi, 1892. Reprint. Farnborough: Gregg International.

Gleichen, Count.

1905. *The Anglo-Egyptian Sudan: a compendium prepared by officers of the Sudan government.* Vol. 1. London: Harrison and Sons.

Glickman, Maurice.

1971. Kinship and credit among the Nuer. *Africa* 41:306–19.

1972. The Nuer and Dinka: a further note. *Man,* n.s., 7:587–94.

1974. The Dinka and the Nuer. *Man,* n.s., 9:141–42.

Goody, Jack, and Tambiah, S. J.

1973. *Bridewealth and dowry.* Cambridge Papers in Social Anthropology, no. 7. Cambridge: Cambridge University Press.

Gough, Kathleen.

1971. Nuer kinship: a re-examination. In *The translation of culture: essays to E. E. Evans-Pritchard,* edited by T. O. Beidelman, 79–122. London: Tavistock.

Gray, Richard.
    1961. *A history of the Southern Sudan 1839–1889*. London: Oxford University Press.
Greenberg, Joseph H.
    1966. *The languages of Africa*. Bloomington: Indiana University Press.
Greuel, Peter J.
    1971. The leopard-skin chief: an examination of political power among the Nuer. *American Anthropologist* 73:1115–20.
Grunnet, Niels.
    1962. An ethnographic-ecological survey of the relationship between the Dinka and their cattle. *Folk* 4:5–20.
Haaland, Randi.
    1978. The seasonal interconnection between Zakiab and Kadero: two Neolithic sites in the Central Sudan. *Nyame Akuma* 13:31–35.
Haight, Bruce.
    1972. A note on the leopard-skin chief. *American Anthropologist* 74:1313–18.
Henderson, K. D. D.
    1939. The migration of the Messiria into South West Kordofan. *Sudan Notes and Records* 22:49–77.
Howell, Paul P.
    1945. The Zeraf hills. *Sudan Notes and Records* 26:319–27.
    1948. The age-set system and the institution of Nak among the Nuer. *Sudan Notes and Records* 29:173–82.
    1951. Notes on the Ngork Dinka. *Sudan Notes and Records* 32:239–93.
    1954a. *A manual of Nuer law: being an account of customary law; its evolution and development in the courts established by the Sudan government*. London: Oxford University Press.
    1954b. *The equatorial Nile project and its effects in the Anglo-Egyptian Sudan, being the report of the Jonglei investigation team*. Vol. 1, A survey of the area affected. London: Printed for the Sudan Government by Waterlow and Sons.
    1954c. *The equatorial Nile project and its effects in the Anglo-Egyptian Sudan, being the report of the Jonglei investigation team*. Vol. 2, The equatorial Nile project: its effects and the remedies. London: Printed for the Sudan Government by Waterlow and Sons.
    1954d. *The equatorial Nile project and its effects in the Anglo-Egyptian Sudan, being the report of the Jonglei investigation team*. Vol. 3, Special investigations and experimental data. London: Printed for the Sudan Government by Waterlow and Sons.
    1954e. *The equatorial Nile project and its effects in the Anglo-Egyptian Sudan, being the report of the Jonglei investigation team*. Vol. 4, Maps and diagrams. London: Printed for the Sudan Government by Waterlow and Sons.
    1955. *Natural resources and development potential in the southern provinces of the Sudan: a preliminary report by the southern development investigation team*. London: Sudan Government Office.

1961. Appendix to chap. 2 of *Divinity and experience: the religion of the Dinka,* by Godfrey Lienhardt, 97–103. Oxford: Oxford University Press.

Huffman, Ray.
1970[1931]. *Nuer customs and folk-lore.* London: Frank Cass and Co.

Huntingford, G. W. B.
1963. The peopling of the interior of East Africa by its modern inhabitants. In *History of East Africa.* Vol. 1, edited by Roland Oliver and Gervase Mathew, 58–93. Oxford: Oxford University Press.

Jackson, H. C.
1923. The Nuer of the Upper Nile province. *Sudan Notes and Records* 6:59–189.

James, Wendy.
1977. The Funj mystique: approaches to a problem of Sudan history. In *Text and context: the social anthropology of tradition,* edited by R. Jain. Philadelphia: Institute for the Study of Human Issues.

Johnson, Douglas H.
1980. History and prophecy among the Nuer of the southern Sudan. Ph.D. dissertation, University of California, Los Angeles. Ann Arbor: University Microfilms International.
1981. The fighting Nuer: primary sources and the origins of a stereotype. *Africa* 51:508–27.
1982. Tribal boundaries and border wars: Nuer-Dinka relations in the Sobat and Zeraf valleys, c. 1860–1976. *Journal of African History* 23:183–203.

Johnston, R. T.
1934. Handing over report: Bor and Duk District, 13 April 1934. Durham: University of Durham, School of Oriental Studies, Sudan Archives G/S 586.

Jonglei Investigation Team.
1952. A short account of the equatorial Nile project and its effects in the Sudan. *Sudan Notes and Records* 33:3–41.

Junker, Wilheim.
1890. *Travels in Africa: during the years 1875–1878.* London: Chapman and Hall.
1891. *Travels in Africa: during the years 1879–1883.* Translated by A. H. Keane. London: Chapman and Hall.
1892. *Travels in Africa: during the years 1882–1886.* London: Chapman and Hall.

Kaplan, David.
1960. The law of cultural dominance. In *Evolution and culture,* edited by Marshall D. Sahlins and Elman R. Service, 69–92. Ann Arbor: University of Michigan Press.

Karp, Ivan, and Maynard, Kent.
1983. Reading *The Nuer. Current Anthropology* 24:481–503.

Kaufmann, Anton.
1975[1881]. The White Nile Valley and its inhabitants. In *The opening of the Nile Basin,* edited by E. Toniolo and R. Hill, 140–95. New York: Barnes and Noble.

Kelly, Raymond C.
    1977.   *Etoro social structure: a study in social contradiction.* Ann Arbor: University of Michigan Press.
    1983.   A note on Nuer segmentary organization. *American Anthropologist* 85(4):905–6.
Kerreri, S. G. S. (Office of the Western Nuer District Administration)
    1931.   Western Nuer District Notes, Upper Nile Province Handbook, chap. 3. Durham: University of Durham, School of Oriental Studies, Sudan Archives 212/14/9.
Kingdon, F. D.
    1945.   The Western Nuer patrol 1927–28. *Sudan Notes and Records* 26:171–78.
Klichowska, Melinda.
    1978.   Preliminary results of paleoethnobotanical studies of plant impressions on potsherds from the Neolithic settlement of Kadero. *Nyame Akuma* 12:42–44.
Krzyzaniak, L.
    1976.   The fifth season at Kadero. *Nyame Akuma* 9:41–43.
    1977.   Polish excavations at Kadero. *Nyame Akuma* 10:45–46.
Leach, Edmund.
    1954.   *Political systems of highland Burma.* Boston: Beacon Press.
    1966.   *Rethinking anthropology.* London: Athlone Press.
Lévi-Strauss, Claude.
    1969[1949].   *The elementary structures of kinship.* Boston: Beacon Press.
Lewis, B. A.
    1951.   Nuer spokesmen. *Sudan Notes and Records* 32:77–84.
Lienhardt, Godfrey.
    1955.   Nilotic kings and their mother's kin. *Africa* 25:29–42.
    1958.   The Western Dinka. In *Tribes without rulers: studies in African segmentary systems,* edited by John Middleton and David Tait, 97–135. London: Routledge and Kegan Paul.
    1961.   *Divinity and experience: the religion of the Dinka.* Oxford: Oxford University Press.
Lolik, P. L., et al.
    1976.   *Primary health care programme: southern region Sudan 1977–1984.* The Democratic Republic of the Sudan. Khartoum: Khartoum University Press.
Mac Dermont, B. H.
    1972.   The Nuer and not Dinka. *Man,* n.s., 7:480.
McLaughlin, John.
    1967.   Tentative time depths for Nuer, Dinka, and Anuak. *Journal of Ethiopian Studies* 5:13–27.
Middleton, John, and Tait, David, eds.
    1958.   *Tribes without rulers: studies in African segmentary systems.* London: Routledge and Kegan Paul.
Newcomer, Peter J.
    1972.   The Nuer are Dinka: an essay on origins and environmental determinism. *Man,* n.s., 7:5–11.
    1973.   The Nuer and the Dinka. *Man,* n.s., 8:307–8.

Ogot, Bethwell A.
  1967. *History of the Southern Luo*. Vol. 1, *Migration and Settlement 1500–1900*. Nairobi: East African Publishing House.
Ogot, Bethwell A., and Kieran, J. A., eds.
  1968. *Zamani: a survey of East African history*. New York: Humanities Press.
Oliver, Roland, and Mathew, Gervase, eds.
  1963. *History of East Africa*. Vol 1. Oxford: Oxford University Press.
Ortner, S. B.
  1973. On key symbols. *American Anthropologist* 75(5):1338–46.
O'Sullivan, Hugh.
  1910. Dinka laws and customs. *Journal of the Royal Anthropological Institute of Great Britain and Ireland* 40:171–91.
Payne, W. J. A., and El Amin, Farouk Mohamed.
  1977. *An interim report on the Dinka livestock industry in the Jonglei area*. Technical Report no. 5, United Nations Development Programme, Economic and Social Research Council. Khartoum: Democratic Republic of the Sudan.
Petherick, John.
  1869. *Egypt, the Soudan and Central Africa*. Edinburgh: William Blackwood and Sons.
Philosophical Society of the Sudan.
  1955. *Food and society in the Sudan: being the proceedings of the 1953 annual conference of the Philosophical Society of the Sudan*. Khartoum: McCorquodale and Co.
  1958. *The population of the Sudan: report of the sixth annual conference of the Philosophical Society of the Sudan*. Khartoum: McCorquodale and Co.
Radcliffe-Brown, A. R.
  1952. *Structure and function in primitive society*. New York: Free Press.
Rappaport, Roy A.
  1967. *Pigs for the ancestors*. New Haven: Yale University Press.
  1969. Sanctity and adaptation. *Io* 7:46–71.
  1977. Ecology, adaptation, and the ills of functionalism (being, among other things, a response to Jonathan Friedman). *Michigan Discussions in Anthropology* 2:138–90.
  1979. *Ecology, meaning and religion*. Richmond: North Atlantic Books.
Riad, Mohamed.
  1959. The divine kingship of the Shilluk and its origin. *Archiv Für Völkerkunde* 14:141–284.
Riches, David.
  1973. The Nuer and the Dinka. *Man*, n.s., 8:307–8.
Sacks, Karen.
  1979. Causality and chance on the Upper Nile. *American Ethnologist* 6:437–48.
Säfholm, Per.
  1973. *The river-lake Nilotes: politics of an African tribal group*. Acta Universitatis Upsalensis, Studia Sociologica Upsaliensia no. 8. Uppsala.

Sahlins, Marshall D.

1961. The segmentary lineage: an organization of predatory expansion. *American Anthropologist* 63:322–45.

1965. On the ideology and composition of descent groups. *Man* 65:104–7.

1976. *Culture and practical reason*. Chicago: University of Chicago Press.

1981. *Historical metaphors and mythical realities: structure in the early history of the Sandwich Islands kingdom*. Ann Arbor: University of Michigan Press.

Sahlins, Marshall D., and Service, Elman R., eds.

1960. *Evolution and culture*. Ann Arbor: University of Michigan Press.

Santandrea, P. Stefano.

1967. The Luo of the Bahr el Ghazal (Sudan): historical notes. *Annali Del Pont. Museo Miss. Etn.* 31:23–204.

Schneider, Harold K.

1970. *The Wahi Wanyatura: economics in an African society*. Viking Fund Publications in Anthropology, no. 48. Chicago: Aldine.

1979. *Livestock and equality in East Africa*. Bloomington: Indiana University Press.

Schweinfurth, Georg.

1969. *The heart of Africa: three years' travel and adventures in the unexplored regions of Central Africa, from 1868–1871*. 2 vols. 1873. Reprint. Farnborough: Gregg International.

Seligman, Charles G.

1911. Dinka. In *Encyclopaedia of religion and ethics,* edited by James Hastings, 4:704–13. Edinburgh: T. and T. Clark.

Seligman, Charles G., and Seligman, Brenda Z.

1932. *Pagan tribes of the Nilotic Sudan*. London: Routledge and Kegan Paul.

SIR No. 90–410.

1902–1928. *Sudan (Monthly) Intelligence Reports*. Cairo and Khartoum: Intelligence Office. Kew, England: Public Records Office. (See list of reports consulted following bibliographic entries.)

Smith, Robert Leo.

1966. *Ecology and field biology*. New York: Harper and Row.

Southall, Aidan.

1976. Nuer and Dinka are people: ecology, ethnicity and logical possibility. *Man,* n.s., 11:463–91.

Stack, Major General L. O. F., Acting Sirdar of the Egyptian Army.

1917. Operations in Lau-Nuer country. Report of Major General Stack to Governor-General Wingate, 14 November 1917. Kew, England: Public Records Office.

Stigand, C. H.

1918. Warrior classes of the Nuers. *Sudan Notes and Records* 1:116–18.

1919. The story of Kir and the white spear. *Sudan Notes and Records* 2:224–26.

Struve, Governor.

1926. Handing over notes: Governor Struve to C. A. Willis, 8 November

1926. Durham: University of Durham, School of Oriental Studies, Sudan Archives 212/7.

Stubbs, J. N.
1934. Beliefs and customs of Malwal Dinka. *Sudan Notes and Records* 17:243–54.
1962. Customary law of the Aweil District Dinkas. In *The Sudan Law Journal and Reports,* edited by Robert A. Cook, 450–69. Khartoum: The Judiciary.

Stubbs, J. N., and Morrison, C. G. T.
1938. Land and agriculture of the Western Dinka. *Sudan Notes and Records* 21:251–65.

Sudan Government.
1906. *Sudan Almanac.* Compiled by the Intelligence Department, Cairo. London: Printed for H. M. Stationary Office by Harrison and Sons. Durham: University of Durham, School of Oriental Studies, Sudan Archives.
1928. *Report of the Rejaf Language Conference.* London: Sudan Government Office. Durham: University of Durham, School of Oriental Studies, Sudan Archives.

Sudan Government Census of 1955–56.
1957–58. *First population census of Sudan: interim reports 1–8.* Khartoum: Republic of Sudan Ministry for Social Affairs, Population Census Office.

Sudan Government, Intelligence Department.
1911. *The Bahr el Ghazal Province.* Anglo-Egyptian Sudan Handbook Series. London: Harrison and Sons. Durham: University of Durham, School of Oriental Studies, Sudan Archives.

Sutton, J. E. G.
1968. The settlement of East Africa. In *Zamani: a survey of East African history,* edited by Bethwell A. Ogot and J. A. Kieran, 69–99. New York: Humanities Press.

Titherington, G. W.
1927. The Raik Dinka of Bahr el Ghazal province. *Sudan Notes and Records* 10:159–209.

Toniolo, Elias, and Hill, Richard, eds.
1975. *The opening of the Nile Basin: writings by members of the Catholic Mission to Central Africa on the geography and ethnography of the Sudan, 1842–1881.* New York: Barnes and Noble.

Tornay, Serge.
1979. Armed conflict in the lower Omo Valley, 1970–1976: an analysis from within Nyangatom society. In *Warfare among East African herders,* edited by Katsuyoshi Fukui and David Turton, 97–117. Osaka: National Museum of Ethnology.

Tothill, John D., ed.
1948. *Agriculture in the Sudan: being a handbook of agriculture as practised in the Anglo-Egyptian Sudan.* London: Oxford University Press.

Tucker, Archibald N., and Bryan, Margaret A.
　1956.　*The non-Bantu languages of north-eastern Africa.* Handbook of African languages, vol. 3. Oxford: Oxford University Press.
　1966.　*Linguistic analyses: The non-Bantu languages of north-eastern Africa.* Handbook of African languages, pt. 3, 2d ed., rev. Oxford: Oxford University Press.
Tunnicliffe, E. C.
　n.d.　Akobo District Notes, Upper Nile Province Handbook, chap. 3. Durham: University of Durham, School of Oriental Studies, Sudan Archives 212/14/4.
Upper Nile Province Handbook, Yirrol Section.
　1930.　Upper Nile Province Handbook, chap. 3. Durham: University of Durham, School of Oriental Studies, Sudan Archives 212/14/6.
Upper Nile Province Handbook, Zeraf Valley Section.
　1930.　Upper Nile Province Handbook, chap. 3. Durham: University of Durham, School of Oriental Studies, Sudan Archives 212/14/8.
Urrutia, Benjamin.
　1973.　The Dinka and the Nuer. *Man,* n.s., 8:479–80.
Verdon, Michel.
　1982.　Where have all their lineages gone? cattle and descent among the Nuer. *American Anthropologist* 84(3):566–79.
　1983.　Response to Kelly. *American Anthropologist* 85(4):906–7.
Werne, Ferdinand.
　1849.　*Expedition to discover the sources of the White Nile in the years 1840–1841.* Translated by Charles W. O'Reilly. 2 vols. London: Richard Bentley.
Willis, Governor C. A.
　1927.　Report to Civil Secretary, Khartoum, 6 August 1927. Durham: University of Durham, School of Oriental Studies, Sudan Archives 212/11.
　1928.　The cult of Deng. *Sudan Notes and Records* 11:195–208.
　n.d.(1930–31).　Upper Nile Province Handbook, chap. 2. Durham: University of Durham, School of Oriental Studies, Sudan Archives 212/13.
Wingate, Governor-General Reginald.
　1911.　Dispatch no. 114: Governor-General Wingate to Lord Kitchener, 7 December 1911. Durham: University of Durham, School of Oriental Studies, Sudan Archives 301/6/2.
Wyld, J. W. G.
　1930.　Bor District Notes, Upper Nile Province Handbook, chap. 3. Durham: University of Durham, School of Oriental Studies, Sudan Archives 212/14/5.

SUDAN (MONTHLY) INTELLIGENCE REPORTS (SIR) CONSULTED

Year	Report Numbers	Public Records Office Reference Number
1902	90,91	FO78/5239
1904	115, 118, 123, 124	FO78/5373
1905	130, 131	FO78/5437
1906	139, 144, 145	FO371/59
1907	151, 153, 154, 155, 157, 158	FO371/246
	160, Index to numbers 77–161	FO371/449
1908	164–73	FO371/449
1909	174–83	FO371/659
	184–85	FO371/890
1910	186–90; 192–95	FO371/890
	196–97	FO371/1111
1911	198–207	FO371/1111
1912	210–19	FO367/311
	220–21	FO367/353
1913	222–31	FO367/353
	232–33	FO371/1965
1914	234–43	FO371/1965
	244–45	FO371/2349
1915	246–55	FO371/2349
1917	279–81	FO371/3199
1918	282–89	FO371/3199
1919	294–305	WO33/997
1920	306–17	WO33/997
1921	318–29	WO33/997
	Appendix 1921	WO33/997
1922	330–41	WO33/997
	Annual Report 1922	WO33/997
1923	342–53	WO33/999
	Annual Report 1923	WO33/999
1924	354–65	WO33/999
	Annual Report 1924	WO33/999
1925	366–67, 369–73	WO33/999
1926	388	FO371/12378
1927	400, 401	FO371/13142
1928	402–7, 409	FO371/13142

Index

Adaptation, 73–79, 155–56, 236–42
Age sets, 174, 260–63
Agriculture (Dinka): acreage in production, 290; and animal husbandry, 153–55, 190; planting schedules, 47, 99; use of manure, 99
Agriculture (Nuer): acreage in production, 230, 232, 273, 290; and animal husbandry, 100, 153–55, 190, 232–35, 293; attitudes toward, 99–100, 230; fallow period, 154, 289; land availability, 99, 282–83; planting schedules, 99, 277; seasonal cycle, 83–84; variability of harvest, 97–98, 273, 282. *See also* Economic organization; Foods; Nutrition
Animal husbandry, 282. *See also* Cattle; Herd management practices
Anuak: Nuer displacement of, 27–28, 32. *See also* Conflict

Bacon, C. R. K., 167, 275, 278, 290–91
Beltrame, G., 254–55, 264
Bloss, J. F. E., 96, 106
Bonte, P., 301
Bridewealth payments (Dinka), 133–56; and cattle availability, 133–34, 139, 141, 146–49; composition, 137, 148–51; and herd management, 140–56; "ideal," 134, 136, 287–88; and kin relations, 134–38, 144, 173, 186–88, 212–24, 287–88; magnitude, 133, 137–39, 142, 145, 152; reciprocal payment, 134–35, 137–38, 142–43, 186–88, 213–18, 287–88; relation between size and dis-

tribution, 144–45; and social standing, 139–40, 173, 249, 292, 300; sources of, 186; tribal variants, 134–38. *See also* Bridewealth system; Cattle
Bridewealth payments (Nuer), 119–33, 140–56; and cattle availability, 119–20, 123, 146–47, 209, 286–87; and cattle distribution, 113–14; compared to Dinka, 134–48; composition, 148–51; and herd management, 112–14, 125, 140, 148–56; "ideal" and acceptable, 119–22, 127, 147, 285–86; as key symbol, 6, 188, 233–35, 299; and kin relations, 119, 126–28, 130–33, 144, 212–24, 285–86; magnitude, 123, 133, 145, 152, 230–32, 235, 243, 286–87; reciprocal payments, 130, 145–46, 216–17, 286; and redistribution of cattle, 113, 246–51, 297, 301; relation between size and distribution, 126–28, 133, 144–45; and social standing, 121–22, 231, 243, 249, 300; sources of, 186–87; and tribal size, 197–99; tribal variants, 119, 128–33. *See also* Bridewealth system; Cattle
Bridewealth system (Dinka): compared to Nuer system, 140–56, 191–92, 213–24, 300; and economic organization, 148–56, 190–94, 212, 242–51; and herd management practices, 141, 148–56, 191; and prestige system, 249, 300; and segmentary organization, 172–73, 209, 212–24, 295; sociological features, 133–40. *See also* Bridewealth payments

315